Principles of
Data Processing
SECOND EDITION

Principles of Data Processing

SECOND EDITION

Robert A. Stern

Nancy B. Stern

John Wiley & Sons

New York   Chichester   Brisbane   Toronto

Library of Congress Cataloging in Publication Data

Stern, Robert A.
  Principles of data processing.

  1. Electronic data processing. 2. Electronic
digital computers. I. Stern, Nancy B., joint author.
II. Title
QA76.S745 1979   001.6'4   78-16178
ISBN 0-471-01696-9

Printed in the United States

10 9 8 7 6 5 4

To Melanie and Lori

About the Authors

Robert A. Stern is an attorney, and a Professor of Mathematics and Computer Processing at Nassau Community College. He holds a B.S. in Industrial Engineering and a B.S. in Business Administration, both from Lehigh University, an M.S. in Operations Research from New York University, and a J.D. from St. John's University School of Law. He is the co-author of several other texts including *COBOL Programming, Business Data Processing Systems,* and *IBM 370/360 Assembler Language Programming.* Mr. Stern has had diverse business experience as a systems analyst, an industrial engineer, and an attorney.

Nancy B. Stern is an Educational Consultant and an Assistant Professor of Administrative Computer Systems at Hofstra University. She holds an A.B. degree from Barnard College and an M.S. degree from New York University, both in mathematics, and a Ph.D. from the State University of New York at Stony Brook. She is the author of *Flowcharting: A Self-Teaching Guide* and the co-author of several other texts, including *COBOL Programming, Business Data Processing Systems,* and *IBM 370/360 Assembler Language Programming.* She has also written several articles for professional journals, including the *Social Studies of Science.* Dr. Stern is Assistant Editor-in-Chief of the *Annals of the History of Computing,* an AFIPS publication, and is a member of several ACM committees.

Preface

Second editions of data processing texts are frequently nothing more than edited and updated versions of first editions, with references to recent advances merely appended to the text. Such an approach is acceptable only in fields that undergo change at a conservative rate. It is, however, inappropriate in a subject such as data processing where the rate of change is exceedingly rapid.

This revised edition of *Principles of Data Processing* is an entirely new text, one which maintains and improves on the pedagogic features of the first and which also provides the student with a firm understanding of the current state of the art.

Objectives

The primary purpose of this book is to provide the student with an understanding of the fundamentals of data processing from a business perspective.

The emphasis throughout will be on the interaction between the businessman and the computer specialist. We have attempted to provide two perspectives in this text:

1. The data processing operation from the businessman's point of view.
2. The data processing operation from the computer specialist's point of view.

The objective of this approach is to enhance the ability of future businessmen and computer specialists to communicate with one another. By focussing on the problems that arise between these professionals we hope to bridge the communication gap which commonly exists and which in recent years seems to be widening.

The text, then, is written for two-year and four-year college students who are business or data processing majors or who are simply interested in learning about computer concepts.

How This Text Differs from Others

This textbook differs significantly from the data processing texts currently in use. It introduces the concepts of data processing as they actually relate to the business world. The degree of communication and interaction between the businessman and the computer specialist is emphasized throughout in an effort to facilitate business information flow. We do not attempt to idealize data processing. The common pitfalls and problem areas of computer processing are presented in order to familiarize the student with all facets of this field. No emphasis is placed on obsolete concepts and terminology.

The text is really a combination text-workbook which utilizes a step-by-step unit approach designed to effect an integration of material heretofore unattained. The approach is basic, neither all-encompassing nor encyclopedic, designed to provide the student with a working knowledge of data processing as it really exists, not to overwhelm him or her with independent and isolated topics.

This text is not, like many books on the market, a reference manual of computer terms and concepts. Rather it is a pedagogic tool which provides structure and organization to the teaching of computer fundamentals. Based upon our years of teaching experience and on the suggestions of our colleagues and students, we have written a text that will provide the instructor with a structured approach to the subject.

While we include recent advances in computer technology, our objective is not completeness but teaching effectiveness. Advanced concepts which require considerable computer experience to understand have been omitted or de-emphasized. What is presented, then, is a text for a semester course in the subject, not a dictionary of terms.

Rather than provide rules for all of the major programming languages in condensed form, as is characteristic of many texts, we focus on programming languages in two ways:

1. A chapter that teaches the student how to *read* a program in each of the four major programming languages: FORTRAN, BASIC, COBOL and RPG. The same applications are programmed in these languages in an effort to familiarize the student with the advantages and disadvantages of each.

2. A chapter on BASIC and a chapter on COBOL, since these are the two languages most often presented in an introductory data processing text.

   It is recommended that instructors assign *one or the other* of these chapters since emphasis on both languages in an introductory course might be too cumbersome.

   Each of these chapters is designed to familiarize students with a programming language and to enable them to actually write simple and even intermdiate-level programs.

Changes in the New Edition

1. The emphasis on programming has been changed as indicated above.

2. The text now includes review questions at the end of each chapter in addition to self-evaluating quizzes. The review questions do not include answers and thus may be assigned by the instructor for homework.

3. Recent advances in computer technology have not been appended to the text but have been integrated where appropriate. Features of mini- and microcomputers have been included; hardware and software presentations have been revised; virtual storage and other so-called "fourth-generation" concepts have been added; structured programming is included; tables and figures have been revised and updated.

4. The unit concept has been retained. Throughout each unit, there are several articles from recent computer journals which students can read to reinforce their understanding of the material presented in the unit. Each article can form the basis of classroom discussion.

5. A new chapter on the impact of computers on society has been added. The impact of computers on society is a subject that should be familiar to all students of data processing since it is so controversial and since it has, and continues to have, effects on the use of computers and the attitudes of people toward them.

6. Each chapter contains a list of key terms which are introduced or used extensively within that chapter. These terms are defined in detail in a glossary at the end of the text. This glossary does not provide formal, standard, "dictionary" definitions which are often complicated and cumbersome for students. Rather, it provides definitions which are consistent with the explanation in the text and which are easy for students to understand.

7. Some optional topics have been included. These are marked with an asterisk, both in the chapter outlines and in the text.

8. Other additions have been made which reflect the growing importance of specific advances in the field. These include point-of-sale (POS) systems, electronic funds transfer (EFT) systems, online processing concepts, word processing, electronic mail, Remote Job Entry, Computer-Assisted Instruction (CAI), and so on.

It should be noted that a Study Guide, by Richard Aukerman and John Anderson, is available for use by students in reviewing the material presented within this text.

We would like to thank Al Avins (Los Angeles Southwest College), Ida Mason (Lehigh County Community College), Richard W. Manthei (Joliet Junior College), Bob McDowell (Joliet Junior College), and Beverly Bilshausen (Oakton Community College) for their helpful reviews of the manuscript. In addition, we would like to thank Don Ford, our editor at Wiley, for his assistance and support.

Robert A. Stern
Nancy B. Stern

Contents

*Optional topic

Unit One:
Data Processing Fundamentals and Hardware

Chapter 1
An Overview of
Data Processing

1

1

I. Introduction

    A.   What Computers Can Do
    B.   Why Computers Are So Much in Demand
    C.   Types of Computers
    D.   Computer Staff
    E.   Electrical Accounting Machines

*II. The History of Computers

    A.   The Scientific Revolution, 1543–1687: The Modern Age of Science Begins
    B.   The Industrial Revolution, 1760–1830: The Modern Age of Technology Begins
    C.   American Technological Achievement: The Basis for U.S. Advances in Computer Development
    D.   Computer Generations

Important Terms Used in this Chapter

Self-Evaluating Quiz

Review Questions

    * Optional topic.

4

I. Introduction

It is hardly necessary to begin a book on data processing with a statement about the widespread use of computers in business and society in general. Table 1.1 indicates the tremendous rate at which data processing expenditures in the United States have risen since 1970 and the projected growth of these figures to 1985. More than 400,000 computers are in use today for business data processing and the annual expenditure for computing services is more than $30 billion a year.

Growth of Data Processing Industry Expenditures   Table 1.1

Year	Billions of Dollars
1970	21
1975	41
1980[a]	82
1985[a]	164

[a]Projected.

SOURCE: *Data Processing in 1980–1985: A Study of Potential Limitations to Progress*, T. A. Dolotta et al. (New York, 1976), p. 173. Reprinted with permission.

Numerous aspects of our daily lives are affected by this technology, with wide-ranging benefits for the economy and for individuals as well. By processing data quickly and efficiently, computers have greatly facilitated the flow of information in society.

But in addition to their positive value, computers have been known to cause individuals and organizations a good deal of trouble. Newspapers and textbooks frequently describe cases where computers have had negative consequences. The result is that many people view such machines with suspicion and even hostility.

Purpose of Text This book will provide the student with information on how computers typically operate in a business environment. We will consider those computer concepts and terms that are common to most systems. After reading the text, the student will understand the objectives of computers, how these objectives can be met, and the reasons why they are frequently not met.

This book has been written for three types of students:

1. The potential data processing major
2. The business major who is interested in learning how computers are used in businesses
3. The liberal arts major who is interested in learning some of the concepts of computers.

A. What Computers Can Do

Computers are capable of performing a series of fixed operations which can be described by three simple steps:

Operations that Computers Can Perform
1. Input: read incoming data
2. Processing: perform arithmetic operations, comparisons, data transfers
3. Output: produce outgoing information

---

1. Data Processing   The term *data processing* is used to describe the procedures defined above. Strictly speaking, data is a collection of incoming facts which need to be processed so that information is produced. Information is defined as structured, processed, and meaningful data. That is, data is entered as input, it is processed, and information is produced.[1] *Electronic Data Processing* (EDP) is the term used to describe the processing of data by computer.

2. Computer System (See Figure 1.1)   The term *computer system* is used to describe the group of machines which, together, perform EDP functions. That is, the actual reading of incoming data, processing, and creating of output is performed by not one, but several machines. Thus when people use the term *computer,* they are really referring to a group of machines or a system.

The actual devices that comprise a computer system depend upon the needs of the company. All such systems, however, include the following:

Elements of a Computer System
1. Input devices: machines that read the data
2. Central Processing Unit (CPU): machine that actually performs the required operations
3. Output devices: machines that produce output information

---

[1]Some texts ignore the distinction between information and data, simply equating the two terms.

Figure 1.1
Typical computer system. Courtesy Burroughs Corp.

All these devices are linked by cable so that the computer system functions as a single unit.

All operations performed by the computer consist of a series of simple instructions. A computer system, in essence, is a series of devices that are capable of reading data, performing arithmetic operations and comparisons, moving data, and producing output. Computers perform only what they are instructed to perform by a *program*.

3. Program A computer system receives a set of instructions called a *program* which indicates the specific operations to be performed. Computer specialists, called *programmers*, prepare these instructions or programs for each required application.

4. Computer Errors The term *computer error* is frequently used when output from a computer system is invalid. It can mean:

Types of Computer Errors
- The machine malfunctioned
- The processing performed by the machine was erroneous
- The data supplied as input was erroneous

Sometimes machines do malfunction but the circuitry of these devices is such that errors produced as a result of a machine malfunction are extremely rare. If they do occur, they can be easily detected and corrected.

More often, erroneous computer output is a result of human error. Recently, for example, a customer of a major department store in New York City returned merchandise worth $523. A computer-produced refund check for $523,000 was mailed to the customer, who took it to the West Coast and lived off the interest until investigators caught up with him. The company was fortunate to be able to retrieve the excess money paid by mistake. We will see that this type of erroneous computer output is, in fact, attributable to human error. Either the programmer instructed the computer incorrectly or manually prepared data was incorrectly entered.

A major emphasis of this text will be on methods that can be used to minimize such so-called "computer errors," by insuring programmer accuracy, editing incoming data, maintaining proper controls, and so on.

B. Why Computers Are So Much in Demand
There are three major reasons why computers are used:

1. Speed Electronic computers are capable of processing data at a speed typically measured in nanoseconds, or billionths of a second.[2] Since thousands of arithmetic operations can be performed in a single second by computers, they have a decided advantage over calculators and other mechanical devices.

2. Accuracy The electronic circuitry of these machines is such that when they are programmed correctly and when incoming data is error-free, the accuracy of the output is relatively assured.

Because of their speed and accuracy, computer systems are capable of processing large amounts of data more cheaply than if manual methods were used. Industrial growth rates and performance/cost ratios in companies that use computers suggest that the trend is toward greater systems reliability and productivity. (See Table 1.2.)

3. To provide capability that would otherwise be impossible Because computers can operate on data at such phenomenal speeds, they can produce results that would simply not be feasible otherwise. For example, computers can be used to provide management with up-to-the-minute figures on all aspects of its business. With this information, managers can make more meaningful decisions.

[2]The most recent large-scale computers can operate on data in picoseconds, or trillionths of a second.

Table 1.2

Summary of Data Processing Industry Trends (Normalized to 1955)

Indicator	1955	1965	1975	1985
Industry growth	1	20	80	320
Performance/cost	1	10^2	10^4	10^6
Programmer productivity	1	2.0	2.7	3.6
System reliability	1	5	24	120

SOURCE: *Data Processing in 1980–1985: A Study of Potential Limitations to Progress,* T. A. Dolotta et al. (New York, 1976), p. 175. Reprinted with permission. Figures for 1965, 1975, and 1985 represent the number of times the variables have increased since 1955.

Similarly, computers enable companies to provide customers with instantaneous services, such as airline flight availability and charge account status. The result is that these companies can offer far more customer services than would be possible without the computer.

C. Types of Computers

There are a wide variety of computers on the market today. Each type has specific capabilities which will be discussed in depth in Chapter 3. These systems can be broadly categorized as follows:

Types of Computers

SIZE	APPROXIMATE PURCHASE PRICE	APPROXIMATE MONTHLY RENTAL
Large	$2,000,000–$12,000,000	$50,000–$300,000
Medium	$ 800,000	$16,000
Small	$ 200,000	$ 4,000
Mini	$ 2,000–$20,000	usually sold, not rented
Micro	$ 500–$2,000	usually sold

Note that these figures vary greatly and change almost daily. Despite these variations, the figures do provide the student with some idea of the range of computer types.

Each computer system regardless of its size can include a wide variety of input and output devices called *hardware.* The range of possibilities is growing every day. Chapter 5 considers typical devices that are commonly used as part of a computer system.

Many companies either lease or buy a computer system to fill their own specific needs. The size and type of system will vary depending upon the requirements of the company. It should be noted that many companies cannot afford to buy or rent a computer of their own. The concept of time-sharing has therefore been developed. *Time-sharing* allows several users to share a computer, usually through the use of terminals. Chapter 12 discusses this concept in more depth.

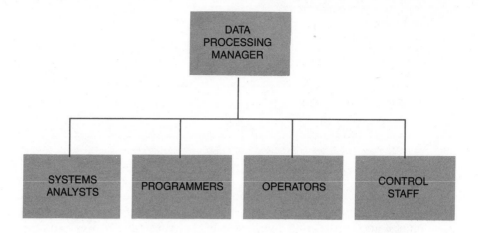

Figure 1.2
Typical organization of a data processing center.

D. Computer Staff (See Figure 1.2)
Several types of computer specialists are responsible for maintaining the computer system:

Computer Staff
1. Data Processing Manager
   Responsible for the efficient operation of the system in its entirety
2. Systems Analyst
   Plans and designs computerized business procedures after careful discussions with the businessman involved
3. Programmer
   Writes the set of instructions that reads input, processes it, and converts it to meaningful output
4. Operator
   Operates the computer system and all peripheral equipment in a data processing center.
5. Control Staff
   Maintains checks on all incoming documents and data, and on all output to ensure the proper flow of information

---

There is another professional who, while not a member of the computer staff, is essential to the smooth operation of the computer system, and that is the businessman. The businessman's role in maintaining an efficient EDP facility in a company is too often overlooked.

Communication between Businessmen and Computer Professionals One of the major sources of errors in data processing systems is the communication gap between businessmen and computer professionals. Businessmen frequently suffer from an inability to communicate their requirements to computer professionals. Similarly, computer professionals are often insensitive to the needs of the businessman.

It is a primary purpose of this text to bridge that communication gap. That is, this book has been written to assist business students in understanding data-processing functions and to assist data-processing students in understanding how one applies computer concepts to business-type problems.

It has become increasingly clear in recent years that businessmen must become active participants in the computerization of their systems. Hence, in the context of this text, they, too, will be seen as computer professionals.

E. Electrical Accounting Machines

Prior to the development of computers for commercial use in the 1950s, data processing was performed largely by special electrical accounting machines, called *EAM equipment*. These machines read data punched into cards which were produced by keypunch machines (Figure 1.3). These machines are still used in many data processing centers but they serve as peripheral equipment which

Figure 1.3
Keypunch Machine.
Courtesy IBM.

takes some of the load off computers. They are important to students since they are frequently used by them in preparation for computer processing.

Like the punched card itself, EAM equipment was invented by Herman Hollerith and James Powers, independently, both of whom developed machines for the U.S. Census Bureau. (See next section.) Years later, after several mergers, Hollerith's equipment was marketed by IBM and Powers' by Remington Rand (later Sperry Rand). These companies became the two largest manufacturers of EAM equipment.

EAM Equipment as Unit-Record Devices These devices are capable of reading only one form of input—the punched card (see Figure 1.4). Since each punched card stores a unit of information referred to as a record, EAM equipment is often called *unit-record* equipment as well.

Figure 1.4
The punched card.

Let us discuss some of the more common EAM devices.

EAM Equipment

DEVICE	FUNCTION	TYPICAL USES
1. Sorter (Figure 1.5)	Sorts cards into any sequence—alphabetic or numeric, ascending or descending	To sort cards with customer charges by account number sequence so that bills can be prepared

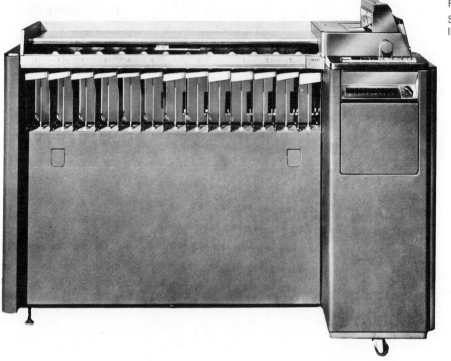

DEVICE	FUNCTION	EXAMPLE
2. Reproducer (Figure 1.6)	Reproduces all or part of a punched card	To obtain a copy of a group of card records, for the same reason that one copies documents

DEVICE	FUNCTION	EXAMPLE
3. Interpreter (Figure 1.7)	Prints on the top of the card data that has	Cards produced by most computer systems do

been punched into the card

not have printing on them; therefore, an interpreter prints data so that cards can be read by people as well as machines

Figure 1.7
Interpreter.
Courtesy IBM.

DEVICE	FUNCTIONS	EXAMPLES
4. Collator (Figure 1.8)	1. Merges two or more decks of cards into an established sequence 2. Checks sequence of cards 3. Selects cards out of a deck based on a specially coded field 4. Matches two decks of cards	1. To merge cards from different branch offices into one deck 2. To check cards that have been sorted 3. To select, for example, all females from a deck of all hourly workers 4. To insure that each deck, one for full-time employees paid last week and one for full-time employees paid this week, has cards for the same employees
5. Accounting Machine (Figure 1.9)	Prints reports; performs simple arithmetic operations	To prepare payroll and billing records; frequently used in companies that cannot afford computer systems

Figure 1.8
Collator. Courtesy
IBM.

The sorter, as indicated, can sort into various sequences, depending essentially on the manner in which the dials are positioned. The other devices are *wired* in order to perform the specific tasks required. The control panel with corresponding wires for a typical EAM device is illustrated in Figure 1.10. Note that most control panels are *not* as complex as indicated in the figure.

*II. The History of Computers

It is exceedingly useful for students of any discipline to be familiar with the history of their field. Such an awareness helps one to understand how developments have actually evolved. It also provides

Figure 1.9
Accounting
machine. Courtesy
IBM.

Figure 1.10
Control panel.
Courtesy IBM.

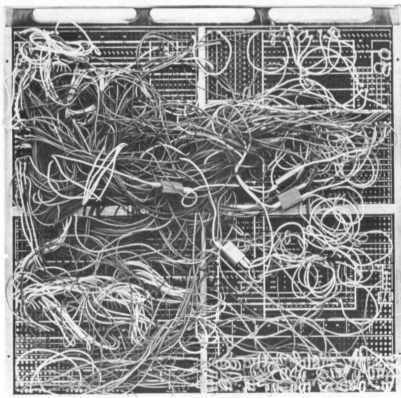

insight into the impact of those developments both within the field and on society itself. Those business and science students with a sense of historical perspective are in a far better position to understand the impact of computers in a technical and social sense.

A. The Scientific Revolution 1543–1687:
The Modern Age of Science Begins

The Scientific Revolution is a period in history which resulted in a new orientation toward science and technology, one which was so radically different from what existed before that the term *revolution* is deemed appropriate. This period begins in the mid-sixteenth century with the Copernican view of the universe, the so-called heliocentric view, and culminates with the formal definition of the laws of nature as specified by Isaac Newton in 1687.

For our purposes, it is important to note that the Scientific Revolution ushered in the era of modern science and with it, the current set of values and ideals that categorize scientific discovery and technological invention. Some of these values are as follows:

Values and Ideals that Categorize Modern Science

1. The universe functions according to specific laws that are expressed mathematically; hence all aspects of existence can be explained in terms of fixed laws
2. The universe—and everything within it—functions like a well-synchronized machine; the whole of any entity may be explained in terms of the workings of the parts
3. Science and technology are forces that have social value and are highly significant in advancing the state of civilization
4. Machines are useful in saving labor

With this new emphasis on machines and on the uses of mathematics, it is not surprising that the Scientific Revolution placed a new emphasis on scientific work, producing two important scientists who invented the first mechanical calculating machines.

1. Blaise Pascal In 1642, Blaise Pascal, a French mathematician and philosopher, devised a calculating machine that would operate by dialing a series of wheels. Around the circumference of each wheel were the numbers 0 to 9. Sums or totals appeared above the dials on indicators. (See Figure 1.11.)

2. Gotfried Liebnitz Liebnitz, like Pascal, was a seventeenth-century scientist who recognized the value of building machines that could do mathematical calculations and save labor too.

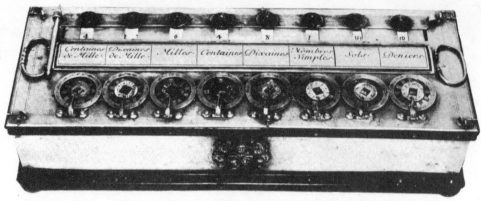

Figure 1.11
Pascal's calculator.

It is interesting to note that both these men were mathematicians who recognized the importance of calculating machines not only for mathematics but also for industry. They both tried to sell their machines to commercial firms which, at that time, were not attuned to the value of labor-saving devices.

B. The Industrial Revolution 1760–1830: The Modern Age of Technology Begins

Whereas the Scientific Revolution, for the most part, affected people's ideas toward science, the Industrial Revolution had a far greater societal impact.

The Industrial Revolution began to take shape in England around 1760 and by 1830, British society was so altered that a revolution was said to have occurred. The changes accompanying the Industrial Revolution, which quickly spread in the nineteenth century to other western countries and to the United States, may be classified as follows:

Changes Produced by Technological Growth
1. From rural to urban society
2. From hand products to mechanized manufacturing
3. From regional or local commerce to a wide-area system utilizing mass transportation
4. Attention to labor-saving machinery
5. Development of a working class

While the Industrial Revolution brought with it many civilizing influences, there are those who still maintain that its negative effects far outweigh its virtues. The fear that many associate with labor-saving machinery, and computers particularly, comes from the mass unemployment that characterized many towns in nineteenth-century England when new devices were introduced. Yet the Industrial Revolution produced several inventions that were to have an impact on the computing field.

1. Jacquard Weaving Loom In 1804, Joseph Marie Jacquard, a French inventor in the earliest years of the French Industrial Revolution, developed a method for controlling the operation of a weaving loom from coded information punched into paper cards. With punches in the appropriate positions on the card, a weaving loom could be mechanically "programmed" to weave specific patterns and to use specific colors. Jacquard's device was to become the predecessor of the punched card machine for processing data.

2. Babbage's Analytical Engine Charles Babbage, a nineteenth-century Englishman, was the first person to envision a computer, in the modern sense of the term. While building a difference engine, which was a mechanical calculator, Babbage developed the idea for an analytical engine that became the precursor to modern computers. As Babbage envisioned it, the analytical engine would be capable of performing any arithmetic operations by following instructions programmed by a programmer. These instructions would be stored within the machine. Babbage also devised a punched card similar to the one used by Jacquard as a form of input.

Babbage was a forerunner of the modern technological innovator. He was a mathematician with a considerable interest in invention inspired by the industrialization that characterized the era. He began by applying science to technology in a new and exciting way. Yet he never accomplished his goal; the machine was never built. The reasons why are diverse.

1. First, the technology was not advanced enough to render such a machine practical.
2. Babbage was not able to obtain the resources necessary to fund this project. He received an unprecedented grant from the British government to fund the difference engine but when it was not completed within the specified period of time, the government rejected further requests for funds.
3. Babbage's own, distinctive personality placed more emphasis on the development of an idea than on the construction of operable devices.

In summary, it is clear that despite Babbage's insights, the time was not ripe for the invention of a digital computer. All his ideas, however, were incorporated in modern computers.

C. American Technological Achievement:
The Basis for U.S. Advances in Computer Development

From the mid-nineteenth century on, America's technological achievement came to mean something more than simply machine development. The term "Yankee ingenuity" as it applies to the American ideal signifies a society in which technology is seen as a positive social force. In other countries, labor-saving devices signified mass unemployment, abuse of child labor, and so on. Society in the United States, however, viewed such machinery as beneficial, since the early years of industrialization were characterized by labor shortages, not unemployment.

1. Herman Hollerith Herman Hollerith is characteristic of the kind of inventor who influenced American industrialization toward the end of the nineteenth century. Hollerith was employed by the Census Bureau which was falling far behind in its ability to provide census reports. Hollerith, who was trained in engineering and had an understanding of industrial needs as well, developed a punched card (see Figure 1.4) which would contain data coded in the form of punched holes. Hollerith then built machines that could read the cards and process the data. EAM devices (discussed in the previous section) based on Hollerith's invention are still in use today.

2. World War II and Computers Many historians have suggested that wartime is a particularly fertile period for technological invention. The case of the electronic digital computer clearly supports that point of view. World War II saw the development of Howard Aiken's Mark I, an electromechanical relay computer, developed at Harvard, with engineering assistance from IBM, during the period 1939–1944. During these same war years, George Stibitz was developing a relay computer for Bell Telephone Laboratories. The fact that both inventions were developed independently of one another suggests that the time was ripe for technological advance in computational equipment.

During World War II, the U.S. government actively sought to support numerous projects that might assist in solving its diverse problems. Largely as a result of these wartime needs, the government funded a group of young engineers working at the Moore School of Electrical Engineering of the University of Pennsylvania who proposed the first electronic digital computer to solve ballistics problems. Under the direction of J. Presper Eckert, Jr. and John Mauchly, the ENIAC was developed during 1943 to 1946. It was an electronic digital computer consisting of 18,000 vacuum tubes and requiring the manual setting of switches to achieve desired results.

3. Post World War II Following the war, Eckert and Mauchly and their associates at the Moore School began work on the EDVAC, the first stored-program computer. This was built with the collaboration of the distinguished mathematician, John von Neumann, who provided the logical structure for the stored program concept. Von Neumann went on to build his own computer at the Institute for Advanced Study at Princeton, a device that was duplicated by many other universities. Eckert and Mauchly left the University of Pennsylvania to form their own company to build commercial computers.

The first such commercial computer, which was completed in 1951, was called the UNIVAC I. This machine was delivered to the Census Bureau in that year and shortly thereafter became available to business organizations. Eckert and Mauchly's company was taken over by Remington Rand in 1950 which later merged to become Sperry Rand. IBM joined Sperry in the manufacturing of commercial computers in the early 1950s and a great new industry was formed.

D. Computer Generations

Since the 1940s, the following generations of computers have evolved:

History of Electronic Digital Computers

COMPUTER TYPE	DATE	FEATURES
ENIAC	1943–1946	First electronic digital computer; programmed by manual setting of switches
EDVAC-type machines: EDVAC, EDSAC, UNIVAC	1944–1950	First computers developed with stored program concept; program was read into the computer
First generation	mid-1940s– mid-1950s	Vacuum tube computers; memory used mercury delay lines; EDVAC-type computers belong to this class
Second generation	late 1950s	Transistorized components in place of vacuum tubes; magnetic core memory; more powerful, less expensive, smaller, and more reliable than vacuum tube computers
Third generation	mid-1960s	Integrated circuits; small-scale technology, hundreds of functions wired on one small chip
Fourth generation	1970 +	Solid logic technology; semiconductor memory

It is not at all clear that the solid logic technology and the semiconductor memories of the most recent computers really represent a new generation. Hence, many professionals tend to regard the current state of the art as third generation. They attribute the concept of fourth-generation computers to the overzealous tendency of manufacturers to market their innovations in revolutionary terms. From first generation to fourth, however, the trend has been to produce more powerful, less expensive, smaller, and more reliable computers.

Important Terms Used in This Chapter

Collator	Interpreter
Control Panel	Nanosecond
Control Staff	Operator
Data	Output
Data Processing	Program
Electrical Accounting Machines (EAM)	Programmer
Electronic Data Processing (EDP)	Punched Card
Generations of Computers	Reproducer
Hardware	Sorter
Information	Systems Analyst
Input	Time-Sharing

Self-Evaluating Quiz

At the end of each chapter in this text, and sometimes at the end of a subsection, there will be a series of review questions that test the student's understanding of the information therein presented. Solutions will be provided.

The purpose of this quiz is to provide students with a method of evaluating their understanding of the chapter.

1. Computers are required in commercial organizations to perform _____.

2. When a computer produces erroneous results, it is most often because of _____.

3. (T or F) A computer is capable of far more complex "thinking" or computing than people.

4. (T or F) Computers can handle more data at a less expensive rate than can be handled by manual methods.

5. Data processing is _____.

6. The two major groups that benefit from the use of a commercial computer are _____ and _____.

7. _____ is used by companies, often too small to rent computers, who buy computer time from rental companies.

8. _____ refers to the equipment that makes up a computer system.

9. EAM is an abbreviation for _____.

10. Name and describe the functions of four EAM devices.

11. Except for the sorter, EAM devices must be _____.

12. State two major disadvantages of EAM devices.
13. Incoming data is called _____.
14. Outgoing information is called _____.
15. The main unit of a computer system is called the _____.
16. The series of instructions to the computer is called the _____.

Solutions

1 arithmetic and other clerical functions
2. human errors or the communication gap between data-processing personnel and businessmen
3. F—a machine can only do what it is instructed or "programmed" to do.
4. T—their chief asset.
5. the processing of input data to produce meaningful information
6. the manager for decision-making, the customer for quick service
7. Time-sharing
8. Hardware
9. Electrical Accounting Machines
10. SORTER—sorts cards
    INTERPRETER—prints data on the face of a punched card
    REPRODUCER—duplicates card data
    COLLATOR—collates, merges, sequence checks cards
    ACCOUNTING MACHINE—prints reports
11. wired
12. They need to be wired.
    They can operate on cards only.
    Most processing requires extensive use of many of these machines and can be performed more easily and efficiently by a single computer system.
13. input
14. output
15. Central Processing Unit (CPU)
16. program

Review Questions

I. Answer True or False

1. (T or F) A computer can solve problems that are far beyond the ability and comprehension of any individual.
2. (T or F) A computer can perform operations and procedures at a speed that is far beyond the ability of any individual.
3. (T or F) Since a computer must be programmed, its ability to solve problems is limited by the ability of the programmer to instruct it.
4. (T or F) Errors in computer-produced reports are usually a result of a machine malfunction.

5. (T or F) If incoming data such as a time card has been incorrectly recorded, the computer usually finds and corrects the error before producing the resultant output.

6. (T or F) In order for the computer's capability to be efficiently and effectively harnessed, the businessmen and computer specialists within a company must work together closely.

7. (T or F) In recent years, the number of companies acquiring computers has stabilized.

8. (T or F) In general, the more sophisticated a computer is the greater is its rental cost.

9. (T or F) Most businesses with clerical procedures that handle large volumes of data manually can usually be automated at an eventual savings to the company.

10. (T or F) Since many small companies cannot justify the expense of a computer system, the use of time-sharing has been expanding rapidly.

11. (T or F) Although the current era has been characterized as the "Age of the Computer," the ideas and concepts for computers have, in fact, developed over centuries.

12. (T or F) The punched card was developed by Herman Hollerith.

13. (T or F) Although electrical accounting machines are still in use today, they are essentially used peripherally.

14. (T or F) In order for an electrical accounting machine to perform a required operation, it must be programmed.

15. (T or F) Electrical accounting machines can process only punched card data, while computers can process other types of data as well.

16. (T or F) The main unit of a computer system is the CPU.

17. (T or F) In order to process data, the computer must be told exactly what to do in a series of instructions known as a program.

18. (T or F) Computer-produced output is always in the form of a printed report.

19. (T or F) All computer centers have the same general type of computer equipment, even though the equipment may be supplied by different manufacturers.

II. Fill in the Blanks

1. Two compelling reasons for the use of computers by large companies are _____ and _____.

2. One of the most frequent causes for computer errors is _____.

3. A computer is essentially a nonthinking machine that performs operations as it is told to, by people, in the form of _____.

4. Since computers are not rational entities they cannot, by themselves, determine if data entered is reasonable or proper. The _____ has the responsibility of controlling the quality of data entered.

5. Two major users who are served by a company's computer are _____ and _____.

6. Since many small companies do not feel they can justify the expense of a computer system, the use of _____ has been expanding rapidly.

7. The man responsible for developing a method of representing information by a series of punched holes in paper cards is _____.

8. Machines developed by Herman Hollerith and James Powers in the early part of the century used _____ to process such things as payroll, billing, and accounting data; they are still in use today.

9. Most EAM devices must be _____ to obtain the required results.

10. An EAM device that can duplicate card data is called a(n) _____.

11. An EAM device that is capable of merging cards and/or selecting cards from a deck is called a(n) _____.

12. A device used to punch data into punched card format is called a _____.

13. In many cases, a _____ can be used in place of several electrical accounting machines to perform the same tasks.

14. Incoming data entered into a computer flow is called _____.

15. Outgoing information from a computer run is called _____.

16. The main unit of a computer system is called the _____.

Chapter 2
The Punched Card
and the Printed Report

2

2

I. Characteristics of the Punched Card

    A.   The Punched Card as a Data Record
    B.   Elements of a Punched Card
           Self-Evaluating Quiz
    C.   Fields of Data
           Self-Evaluating Quiz

II. The Recording of Data on Punched Cards

    A.   Use of Keypunch Machine
    B.   Card Punch
    C.   Other Forms of Punched Cards

III. Advantages and Disadvantages of Punched Cards
        Self-Evaluating Quiz

IV. Printed Output

    A.   Characteristics of Printed Output
    B.   Continuous Forms and the Printer

Important Terms Used in this Chapter

Self-Evaluating Quiz

Review Questions

I. Characteristics of the Punched Card

This chapter will familiarize business and data processing students with one of the most common forms of computer input, the punched card, and the most common form of computer output, the printed report. With some knowledge of the fundamental nature of these media, students can begin to understand how data processing functions are performed.

The punched card is a major form of computer input and output which hardly needs an introduction. We come into contact with this form in a wide variety of ways in our everyday experiences, so much so that most of us are as familiar with punched cards as with printed documents. We see them in the form of electric bills, telephone bills, and school registration cards, just to name a few (see Figure 2.1). Each of us knows not to "bend, fold, staple, or mutilate" such cards, though few really understand why or for what purpose. It is the aim of this chapter to explain why,

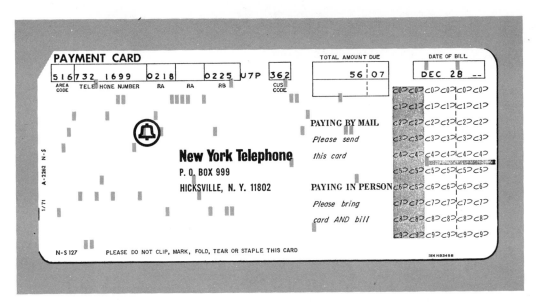

Figure 2.1
Sample telephone company punched card.

and, more importantly, to familiarize students with the basic concepts of punched card processing.

A. The Punched Card as a Data Record

The brief history of the punched card in Chapter 1 served to illustrate the fact that this data processing form has had a long and successful history. The single most important characteristic of the punched card is its use of holes punched in various positions to represent data. Beginning with Hollerith's invention in the 1880s, machines have been developed that can read, sort, merge, reproduce, and perform arithmetic operations on these cards. With the advent of the electronic digital computer in the 1940s, punched cards became an important form of input and output for this machine as well.

Most businesses today still use the punched card in some phase of their operations. These cards have the distinct advantage over more efficient forms of input and output in that they can be read by people as well as machines. Hence, consumers often see these cards in bills and orders that they receive. Utility companies, for example, supplying gas, electric, and telephone services, often bill customers with the use of punched cards, as shown in Figure 2.1. Some companies also prepare stock dividend checks on punched cards.

In general, each of these cards is used to represent a *record,* or unit of information. Because cards are usually used to represent such a unit of information, they are frequently referred to as *unit records.*

B. Elements of a Punched Card

Consider the blank card in Figure 2.2. Notice that at the very bottom of the card there are small digits numbered 1 to 80. Note also that below the first horizontal group of numbers (zero) there are the same 80 numbers. Each number corresponds to a card column. Hence, the standard punched card has 80 columns, numbered 1 to 80.[1] The card illustrated in Figure 2.2 has a shaded portion in columns 34 to 56.

Each column or position holds one character of data, where a *character* is a letter, digit, or special symbol such as a +, $, %, and so on. Thus, our standard 80-column card can hold 80 characters of data, that is, 80 letters, digits, and special symbols which, together, constitute a unit record.

Data on a card will be identified by the columns in which it is located and by the characters actually punched in the columns. You will recall that characters are represented by holes punched in the cards which are then electromechanically sensed by special equipment.

---

[1] The 96-column card will be discussed on page 47.

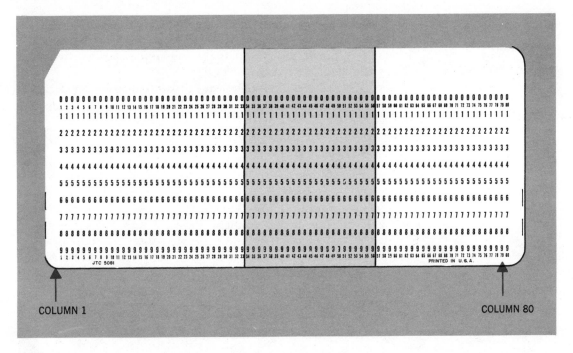

Figure 2.2
Standard punched card (columns 34–56 shaded).

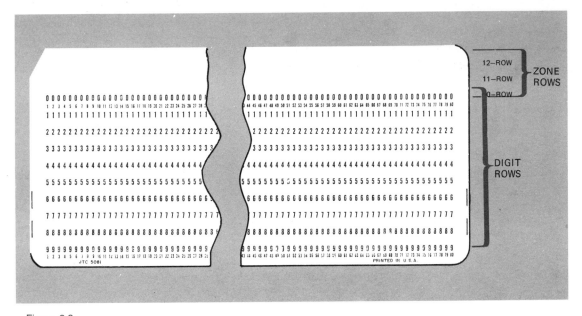

Figure 2.3
Illustration of zone and digit rows on a punched card.

1. Hollerith Code The holes are punched according to a code devised by Herman Hollerith, the inventor of the punched card. This code is called, not surprisingly, the *Hollerith Code*. We will discuss the logic behind this code.

Look again at the punched card illustrated in Figure 2.2. You will note that the numbers 0 to 9 are printed in every single column of the card along with the specific column number. These numbers 0 to 9 are called the 0 to 9 *rows,* respectively. Figure 2.3 will clarify this point.

a. Representing Digits with the Hollerith Code To code a digit or number in a particular column, a hole is punched in the corresponding row of that column. Hence, in Figure 2.4 column 54 contains a "2" because it has a punch in the 2-row. In the same figure, columns 79 and 80 contain a "05" because there is a punch in the 0-row of column 79 and a punch in the 5-row of column 80. Hence numbers are represented, according to the Hollerith Code, by a corresponding hole in the digit row of the column desired.

Figure 2.4
Time card.

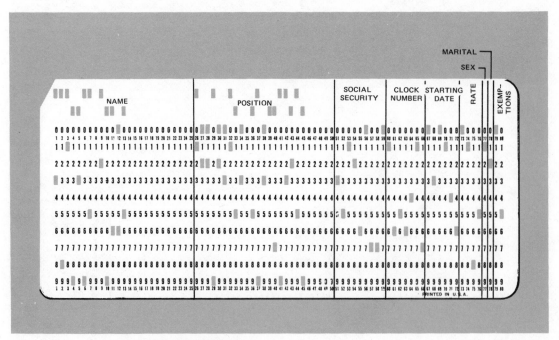

Self-Evaluating Quiz

Since many new terms have been introduced and your memory may be a little uncertain, let us review.

1. The number of characters that can be represented on a standard punched card is _____.
2. Each character is contained in one _____ of the card.
3. A character can be a number or a _____.

4. The term *punched card* means that data is represented on cards in the form of _____.

5. The code for punching characters on an 80-column card is called the _____ Code.

6. Show how the following card would look if it had a "3" in column 6.

7. Show how the card in Question 6 would look if it had a "5" in column 40.

8. Show how the card in Question 6 would look if it had a "56" in columns 23–24.

9. Indicate what area of the following card has been shaded:

10. How are punched cards "read" by data processing equipment?
11. What is a "unit record"?

Solutions

1. 80
2. column or position—these words mean the same thing, but "column" is normally used when referring to cards
3. letter or special symbol such as +, $, %—though we haven't yet learned the code for these
4. punched holes
5. Hollerith
6.

7.

9. columns 51–60
10. The holes punched in the cards are electromechanically sensed.
11. It is a term used to describe a punched card where each card is used to represent an individual record.

b. Alphabetic Data and the Hollerith Code The representation of letters and special symbols with the Hollerith Code is somewhat more complicated than the representation of numbers because we generally need to use more than one punch in a single column.

To represent alphabetic data, we must use a digit punch in conjunction with another punch. Consider again the card illustrated in Figure 2.3. There are, you will note, ten numbered rows (0 to 9) and two without printing, called the 11- and 12-rows. We use the 0-, 11-, and 12-rows in conjunction with a digit punch, in a *single* column, to represent the letters of the alphabet. Thus, the 0-, 11-, 12-rows are referred to as the *zone* rows and the 0 to 9 as the *digit* rows. For convenience, the 0-row is considered both a zone and a digit row. When used as a digit, alone, it is a digit row; when used with another digit to form a letter, it is called a zone row. The card in Figure 2.5 illustrates the coding of alphabetic characters: letters A to I are coded as 12-1, 12-2, through 12-9 punches, respectively; J to R are coded as 11-1 through 11-9, respectively; and S to Z are coded as 0–2 through 0–9, respectively. Thus, all alphabetic characters are represented with two punches, a zone punch and a digit punch, in a single column.

2. Features of a Punched Card Figure 2.6 illustrates significant facts about the punched card. The top of the card is called the

HOLLERITH CODE

		DIGIT PUNCHES								
		1	2	3	4	5	6	7	8	9
Z O N E P U N C H E S	12	A	B	C	D	E	F	G	H	I
	11	J	K	L	M	N	O	P	Q	R
	0	/	S	T	U	V	W	X	Y	Z

(a)

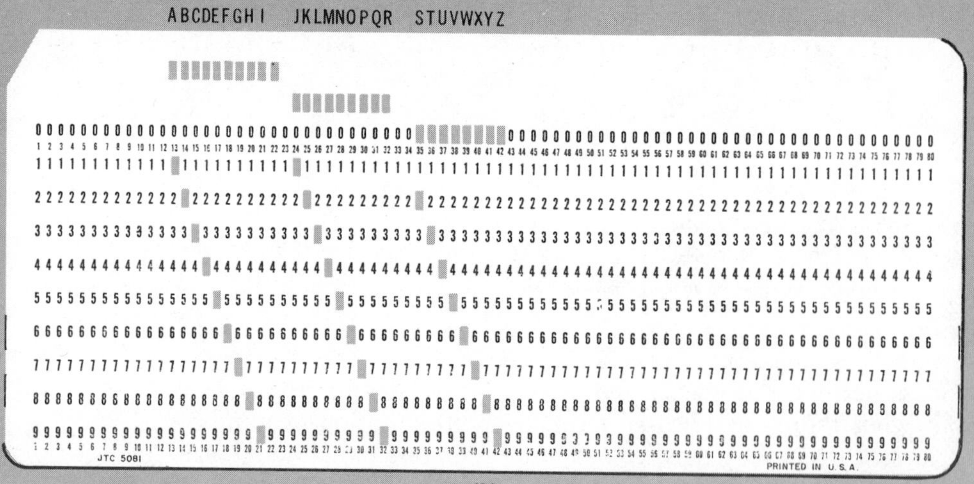

ABCDEFGHI JKLMNOPQR STUVWXYZ

(b)

Figure 2.5
(a) Hollerith Code for letters (b) The alphabet punched on a card.

12-edge, since the 12-row is located there. Similarly, the bottom of the card is called the *9-edge,* since the 9-row is at the bottom. Some punched card equipment requires cards to be entered 9-edge first; other equipment requires them to be entered 12-edge first.

The special characters that can be represented on a card are indicated in columns 51 to 76 of Figure 2.6. They each utilize 1, 2, or 3 punches in a single column. An asterisk, *, for example, (column 60) is represented by the 11-4-8 punches. An ampersand, &, is represented by a 12-punch alone (column 52). Note that the standard special characters are accepted by almost all computers, while the extended set is recognized only by the more modern ones.

It is not necessary to memorize the Hollerith Code for letters and symbols since machines, not people, do the actual punching. But it is useful to be familiar with the code for several reasons.

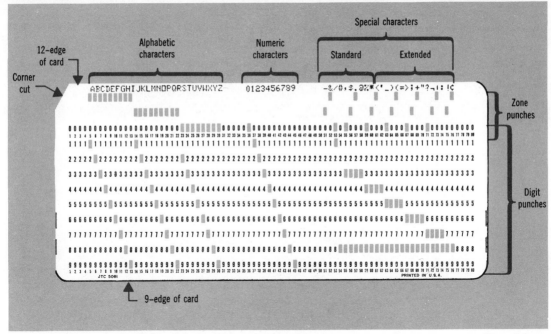

Figure 2.6
Review of
Hollerith Code.

First, it is possible for a card to be punched with data but to have no printing on the top. To identify the data, you might need to translate the punches into characters. Second, the Hollerith Code corresponds, to some extent, to the machine code used in many computers and thus is useful to know.

Self-Evaluating Quiz

1. (T or F) Data is recorded on most cards in the form of round punched holes used to represent a code.
2. (T or F) There are many machines that can mechanically sense holes on a punched card and then sort, merge, or compile the data.
3. (T or F) Characters of data on a punched card are represented by punched holes.
4. (T or F) There are 12 columns on a punched card.
5. (T or F) Each row of a card can store a character of data.
6. (T or F) Most punched cards can store 80 characters of data.
7. (T or F) The rows on a card are numbered 0 to 9.
8. (T or F) To represent alphabetic data on a card, we must use a digit punch in conjunction with another punch in the same column.
9. Data is the combination of _____ consisting of letters, digits, and symbols which result in meaningful information.
10. A vertical section of a card is called a _____, of which there are (no.) _____ for most cards.

Use Figure 2.6 to answer questions 11 to 15

11. The Hollerith Code representation for the letter V is _____.
12. The Hollerith Code representation for the letter Q is _____.

13. The Hollerith Code representation for the letter D is _____.
14. The Hollerith Code representation for the letter G is _____.
15. The Hollerith Code representation for the number 6 is _____.
16. The top of the card is generally referred to as the (no.) _____-edge and the bottom of the card is generally referred to as the (no.) _____-edge.

Solutions

1. F—holes are rectangular
2. T
3. T
4. F—there are 12 rows
5. F—Each column can store a character
6. T
7. T—But there are two more—11 and 12
8. T
9. characters
10. column, 80
11. 0-5
12. 11-8
13. 12-4
14. 12-7
15. 6
16. 12, 9

C. Fields of Data

Let us reconsider the time card illustrated in Figure 2.4. Notice that the consecutive card columns 1 to 25 in that figure represent an item of data called NAME. A set of adjacent positions used to represent such a unit is called a *field*. Hence, card columns 1 to 25 represent the NAME field, columns 26 to 50 represent the POSITION field, and so on.

On the illustrated card, each field is delineated by a broad line. This delineation is recognized by people but has no meaning to the computer, which simply senses the holes punched in the cards and pays no attention to writing or markings on the face of the cards. Hence, the computer must be instructed as to the size and type of each card field. Each field consists of characters. The NAME field has the character C in its first column (12-zone and 3-digit punches), an H in column 2 (12-8 punches), and so on. Note that if a person's name does not fill the whole field, the remainder of the field is left blank.

1. Classification of Data Data fields can be classified in three ways:

Data Classification
Numeric: digits only, such as an AMOUNT field
Alphabetic: letters and blanks only, such as a NAME field
Alphanumeric or alphameric: combination of letters, digits, and
   special symbols such as an ADDRESS field

This description of fields is important because data is placed
in fields in different ways depending upon its classification. A
computer might be instructed, for example, to expect a series of
cards to contain a NAME in columns 1 to 25, an ADDRESS in columns
26 to 50, and so on.

2. Field Sizes   Field sizes are generally established to accommodate the largest number of characters. That is, a NAME field may
be 25 characters in length because the longest name is that size.
Since most names are shorter than this, part of the field will remain blank. The manner in which unfilled characters are represented in fields depends on their classification.

   a. Numeric fields   Numeric fields, consisting of numbers
only, will contain zeros in nonfilled leftmost positions instead of
blanks. That is, the representation of the number 383 in a 5-
position AMOUNT field would be 00383 (see Figure 2.7). The representation of the number 24 in a 5-position AMOUNT field would
be 00024. We say that numeric fields are *right-justified* because the
significant digits are in the rightmost positions.

   b. Alphabetic or alphanumeric fields   Alphabetic or alphanumeric data is placed in the leftmost positions with nonfilled
rightmost positions left blank. Consider the NAME field in columns
6 to 25 in Figure 2.7. The field size is 20 characters. The data is
SMITH which consists of only 5 characters. It is placed in the
leftmost positions with nonfilled rightmost positions left blank.
We say that alphabetic and alphanumeric fields are *left-justified*.

   3. Signed Numeric Fields   Numeric fields, in addition to being
right-justified often contain plus or minus signs. These signs do
not, in general, occupy a separate position on a card. Since cards
can contain only 80 columns of data, it would be wasteful to use
one additional column each time a signed numeric field was entered. Instead, a convention has been established such that signs, if
used, are generally placed in the rightmost or *low-order position*
of a numeric field *along with the units digit*. Thus the most significant digit is in the leftmost or *high-order* position and the units
digit is placed in the low-order position along with the sign. Consequently, an AMOUNT field might contain 1234$\bar{5}$. A minus sign is a

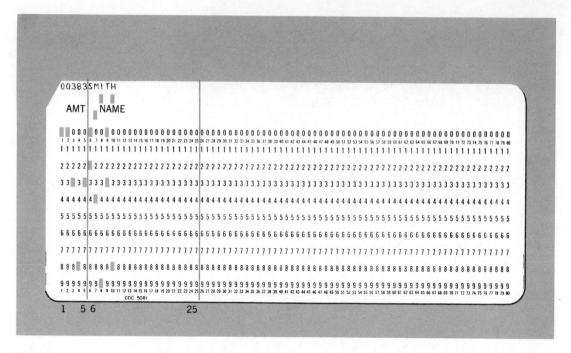

Figure 2.7

Sample data card—1.

Figure 2.8

Sample data card—2.

special character, coded as an 11-zone. Thus, the field would appear as indicated in columns 31 to 35 of Figure 2.8.

In this way, a position would be saved for each signed numeric field. The 11-5 punches in a single column can also be considered as the letter N. Thus 1234N in a field designated as numeric means

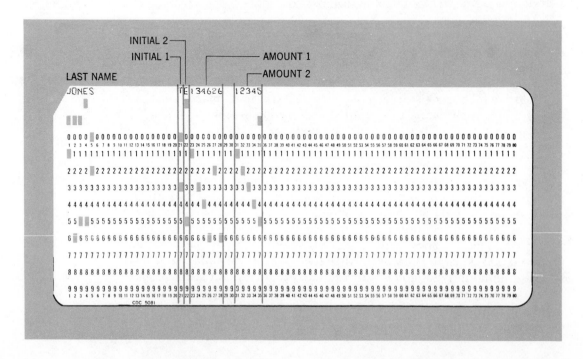

−12345 to the computer and to unit-record devices. That is, all arithmetic operations on this amount field will result in proper calculations. The computer is designed to treat 1234N in a numeric field as a negative 12345.

Similarly, 12J would be considered as −121 when coded in a numeric field. To program the computer to add 100 to this number would result in a sum of −21 or 2J.

Sometimes an operational plus sign, represented by an ampersand (12-punch), is placed in the units position of a field to represent a positive quantity. Note that the *absence* of a sign also implies a positive quantity. The use of a plus sign, however, ensures that a sign was not inadvertently or incorrectly omitted. That is, in fields where many items have negative quantities, plus signs are used to denote positive amounts. In this way, all items are signed; thus negative quantities are less likely to be incorrectly coded as positive or unsigned amounts.

A plus sign is represented in the rightmost or low-order position as a 12-punch in conjunction with the units digit. Thus 423 might be a positive quantity in an AMOUNT field. This can also be coded as 42C (12-3 punches in units position).

4. The Need for Concise Data in 80-Column Card Since most punched cards can contain only 80 characters of data, it is often necessary to condense data fields to make them more concise. Hence, unnecessary fields or characters are usually omitted. We have already seen how the placing of plus or minus signs in the units position of a numeric field saves one column for each such field. Card data is condensed in other ways as well. For example, dollar signs, decimal points, commas, and percent signs are almost never punched into data cards since the computer can be programmed to assume that they are there. That is, a four-position AMOUNT field containing 1234 can be read into the computer, with proper programming, as 12.34. In this way, only four numeric positions are needed and a column need not be wasted on a decimal point.

Similarly, some fields are *coded* in an effort to make data more concise. The use of codes on a card is an effective method of saving positions. Suppose, for example, that a retail establishment has 5000 customer accounts. The card could be designed with a 20-position field for customer name. Each customer could, however, be given a coded ACCOUNT NUMBER, by which he or she would be known within the data processing department. Thus, a four-position coded ACCOUNT NUMBER representing accounts from 1 to 5000 would save sixteen card columns. Similarly, certain payroll procedures often utilize an assigned EMPLOYEE NUMBER or a SOCIAL SECURITY NUMBER instead of NAME. This saves many storage positions and also is a more reliable identification field. Although two employees may have the same name, all employee numbers and social security numbers are unique.

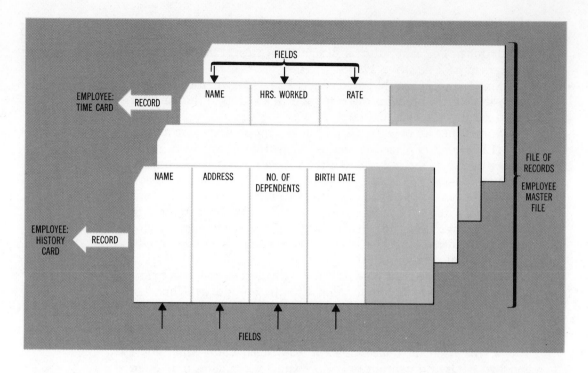

Figure 2.9
Hierarchy of data.

5. Hierarchy of Data At this point, we will indicate the hierarchy in which data is organized. We have seen that *records* are composed of related fields. For example, an employee time card is a record of data containing a NAME field, an HOURS WORKED field, and so on. A collection of related records is called a *file*. Thus, a collection of all employee time cards would constitute a file (see Figure 2.9). These definitions of fields, records, and files apply to any input/output medium.

Self-Evaluating Quiz

1. A field is a _____.
2. Field sizes are generally established to accommodate the _____ number of characters.
3. Numeric fields are _____-justified with leftmost positions generally _____-filled.
4. Alphabetic fields are _____-justified with rightmost positions _____.
5. A field that can contain a combination of letters, digits, and special characters is called a(n) _____ field.
6. Signs are often placed in the _____ position of a numeric field along with _____.
7. The number -427 would generally occupy (no.) _____ positions of a card record.
8. The number -264 could be punched in a three-position numeric field as _____.

9. How would the following data be represented in a two-position numeric field:
    a. -11
    b. -17
    c. +23
    d. +22
    e. 16
10. (T or F) A computer that adds 13 to a field would obtain the same result if it added 1C to the same field.
11. If a card has bold black lines separating items, will punched card equipment sense these lines and thus know the limits of each item?

Solutions

1. consecutive group of columns used to represent an item of data
2. largest
3. right, zero
4. left, left blank
5. alphanumeric or alphameric
6. rightmost or units or low-order
    the units digit or least significant digit or rightmost digit
7. three—there would be no extra position for the sign.
8. 26M
9. a. 1J
    b. 1P
    c. 2C
    d. 2B
    e. 16
10. T—1C is really +13 which is the same as 13
11. No—such lines are used exclusively by people who read the cards.

II. The Recording of Data on Punched Cards

Thus far, you have learned that a punched card can be used as a form of input to the computer as well as to EAM equipment such as a sorter, collator, or accounting machine. In this section, we will consider how data is actually punched into cards.

A. Use of Keypunch Machine

Data may be initially recorded on punched cards by an operator using a *keypunch machine*. The operator is called a *keypunch operator*. The keypunch operator keypunches data into a punched card usually from a report or *source document*. This keypunch machine which converts printed documents to punched cards is very similar to a typewriter. The keypunch operator presses the appropriate keys representing characters so that the machine can punch corresponding holes in the card (see Figure 2.10). Data is punched in the card according to the Hollerith Code. The operator

(a)

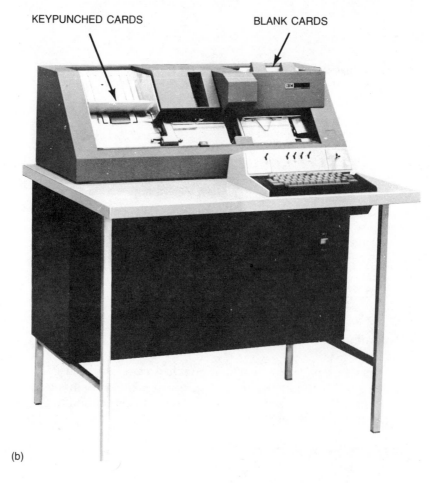

(b)

Figure 2.10

(a) Keyboard of a keypunch machine. (b) Keypunch machine. Courtesy IBM.

need not know this code, however, since he or she simply depresses the actual characters desired. Keypunch machines can print the corresponding characters on the top, or 12-edge, of each card for ease of reading.

Card Verification Just as it is possible for a typist to make typographical errors, so, too, is it possible for a keypunch operator to make mistakes. To minimize the possibility that such errors will go undetected, keypunched cards can be verified by a card verifier device which is either a separate machine or built into the keypunch machine itself.

In a verifier, the operator uses the keypunched cards instead of blank cards. He or she then depresses the verifier's keys, as in normal keypunching. If a key is depressed that has not, in fact, been punched on the card, an error light goes on.

Correctly keypunched cards are typically notched on the right side, while incorrectly keypunched ones are notched *above* the column in error. Therefore all cards with right-side notches have been verified and ones with notches on top are in error (see Figure 2.11). It should be noted, however, that even though cards are verified, it is still possible that mistakes will occur in the input data and go undetected. Consequently, programmers typically write program routines to *edit* the data to ensure that it does not contain obvious omissions, inconsistencies, or errors.

B. Card Punch

Keypunch machines are not the only devices that can produce punched cards. A card-punch machine of a computer system can be instructed to produce output in the form of punched cards. A computer system can read keypunched cards with a card reader and can punch cards with a card-punch device.

Computer-produced punched cards look exactly like keypunched cards except that they generally do not contain printing of the characters on the face of the cards. The printing mechanism is an extremely costly addition to the card punch and is therefore usually not available in most computer installations.

In short, a punched card can be created or keypunched from a source document to serve as *input* to a computer or EAM device. In addition, a punched card can serve as *output* from a computer or even an EAM device. When a card is created as output, it will usually be reentered into the data processing flow at some later date as input. Thus the utility bill or the time card is only an intermediate form of output, since it will eventually serve as input again.

C. Other Forms of Punched Cards

Consider the utility bill in the form of a punched card shown in Figure 2.12. This is a standard 80-column card which contains printed material so that it may be read by people as well as machines. It is important to note that the material printed on the face of the card is of no significance to the computer which would process this card in exactly the same manner as any other 80-column card.

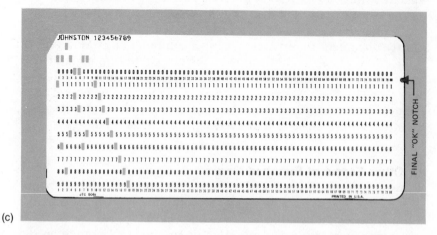

Figure 2.11

Verification of punched card. (a) Card is keypunched. (b) Card is verified: an error is detected in column 13 causing an error notch. (c) Card is re-keypunched and successfully verified, resulting in a final "OK" notch on the right side.

1. 96-Column Card In addition to the standard 80-column card, there is a 96-column card (Figure 2.13) which is used by many systems. It is a very useful variation for punched card users because it can contain 20% additional data, but it can be used only with certain computer systems.

The 96-column card is smaller than the standard 80-column card and is subdivided into three separate *tiers* or punching areas, each capable of storing 32 characters of information. The code used with this card is a variation of the Hollerith Code called BCD or

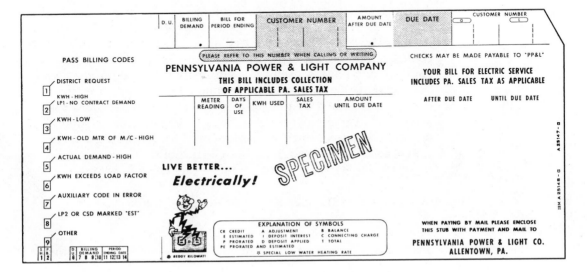

Figure 2.12

Utility bill on a punched card. Courtesy IBM.

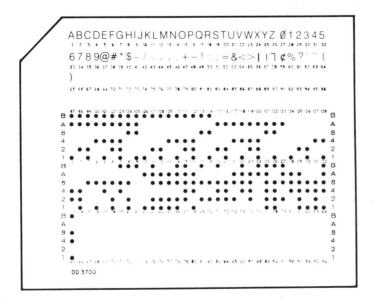

Figure 2.13

Sample 96-column card.

Binary Coded Decimal. The BCD code is a form of computer code and will be discussed in Chapter 4. Note, also, that holes punched on a 96-column card are round, not rectangular.

2. Port-A-Punch and Mark-Sensed Cards Some cards are punched *manually* by a hand device and are called Port-A-Punch cards (Figure 2.14). Other cards are manually marked by a special electrographic pencil. These marks on the card can then be interpreted by a special machine and converted to conventional punched cards. These cards are called mark-sensed cards (Figure 2.15). Many students have used these for taking multiple-choice tests. The answers are mark-sensed by the student with the special pencil. They are then converted into the appropriate Hollerith configuration, on the same card, by a special machine. Both Port-A-Punch and mark-sensed cards eliminate the need for conversion from a source document to a machine-readable form, thereby saving data processing cost. That is, the card itself serves as a source document. An employee from a water company, for example, can use either Port-A-Punch or mark-sensed cards to punch or mark water-meter figures obtained from each home meter. In this way the cards can serve as input to a data processing machine.

III. Advantages and Disadvantages of Punched Cards

Thus, we can see that the punched card has numerous uses in industry. As indicated, it is the most widely used storage medium in small-scale computer installations.

Figure 2.14

Punching a
Port-A-Punch card.

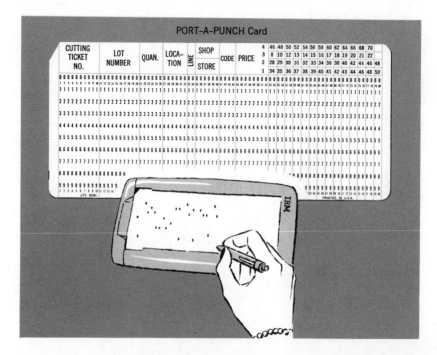

Its basic advantages and disadvantages include the following:

Advantages of Punched Cards
1. Machine and Manual Accessibility
   Computers and EAM devices can process card data, while manual methods can be utilized too, since the data punched on the card may also be printed on the face of the card. (Most keypunch machines have printing capability but most card-punch devices do not.)
2. Economy
   Cards are a relatively economical medium of storage compared to most other forms.

Disadvantages of Punched Cards
There are, however, several inherent disadvantages to card processing that must be realized by all business and data processing students.

1. Large Volume of Cards Difficult to Control
   The relative convenience of card processing decreases with increased numbers of cards.
   That is, large numbers of cards are cumbersome to process. Cards within a file can often be lost, misplaced, dropped, or missorted. Operator time is greatly increased with large numbers of cards. Operators must constantly feed these records into the appropriate machines. Magnetic tapes and disks, discussed in Chapter 5, do not have these disadvantages.
2. Mechanical Parts
   The card reader of a computer and EAM devices utilize essentially mechanical methods for sensing holes in a card. Mechanical devices often jam, causing the loss of many hours of machine time. Humid weather results in warped cards, which is a major cause of jams. These card devices, then, are not as efficient as others that rely solely on electronic equipment.
3. Speed
   Similarly, mechanical devices are notoriously slow. Some card readers, for example, can read *an average* of 1000 or more cards per minute. This speed, although seemingly fast for a layman, is very slow compared to the *billionths* of seconds in which the computer can process the data, once it is read. We shall see that other computer forms of input are much faster.
   Thus, while cost is minimal, efficiency is limited with punched cards. Similarly, physical limitations often adversely affect card processing.

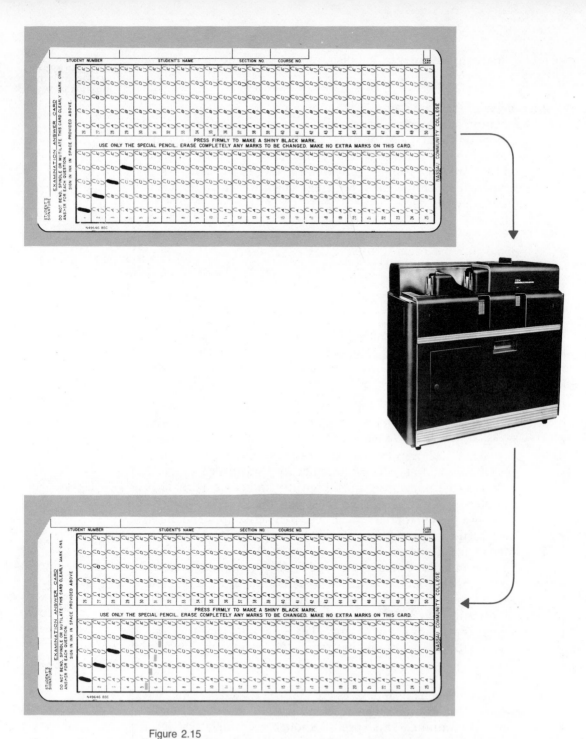

Figure 2.15

(a) Sample mark-sensed card. (b) Reproducer. Courtesy IBM. (c) Same mark-sensed card with punches.

4. 80-Column Format

The constraint of 80- or even 96-character positions per record is a distinct disadvantage. Some records do not lend themselves to 80-character formats.

In short, the punched card is the basic form of input. Most computer centers utilize the card as input, often to be converted to a more efficient medium at some later date.

Only small computer centers, however, utilize the punched card as a *primary* form of input. Such small companies usually have limited amounts of data, and for these the card remains the most economical and efficient medium. In larger companies, the disadvantages and inefficiencies of the punched card make other storage media more desirable. Table 2.1 provides a summary of typical functions commonly performed using punched cards.

Self-Evaluating Quiz

Use Figure 2.16 to answer questions 1 to 14.

1. The punched card illustrated has _____ columns.
2. Each column can hold one _____ of data.
3. A character of data consists of a _____, _____, or _____.
4. A field is a _____.

Figure 2.16

Sample punched card.

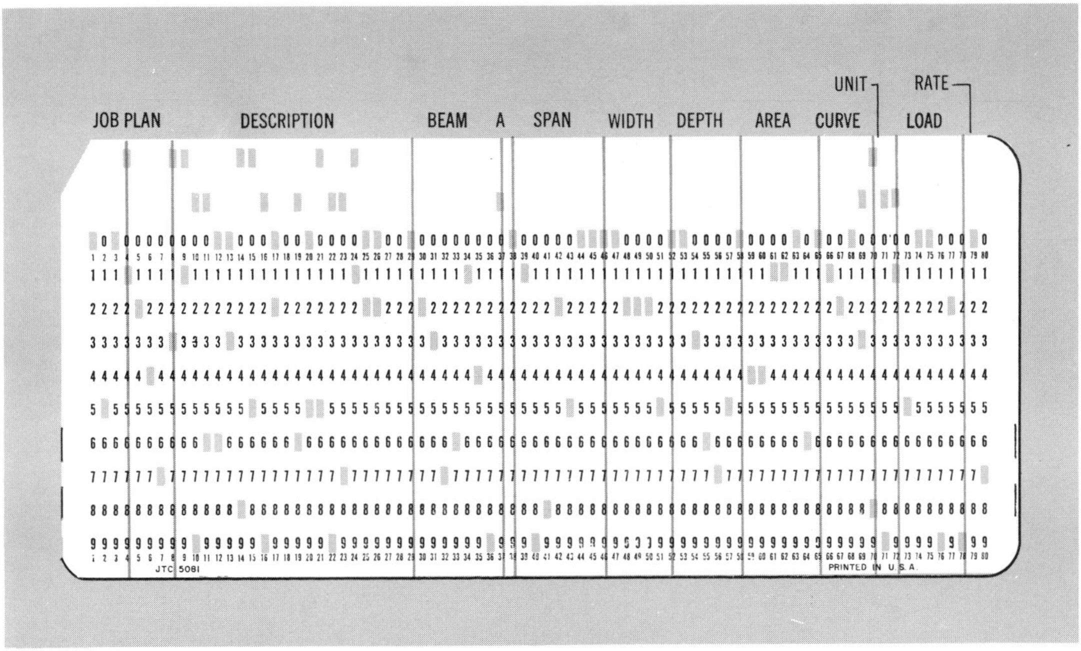

Table 2.1

Typical functions performed using punched cards.

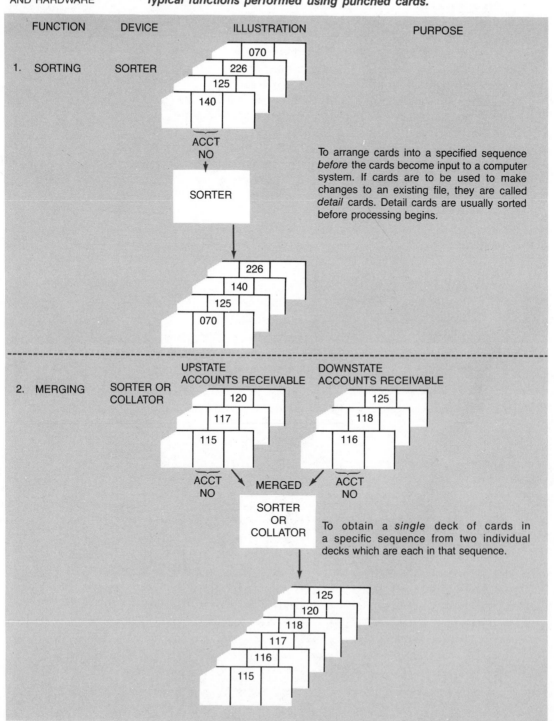

FUNCTION	DEVICE	ILLUSTRATION	PURPOSE

1. SORTING — SORTER

To arrange cards into a specified sequence *before* the cards become input to a computer system. If cards are to be used to make changes to an existing file, they are called *detail* cards. Detail cards are usually sorted before processing begins.

2. MERGING — SORTER OR COLLATOR

To obtain a *single* deck of cards in a specific sequence from two individual decks which are each in that sequence.

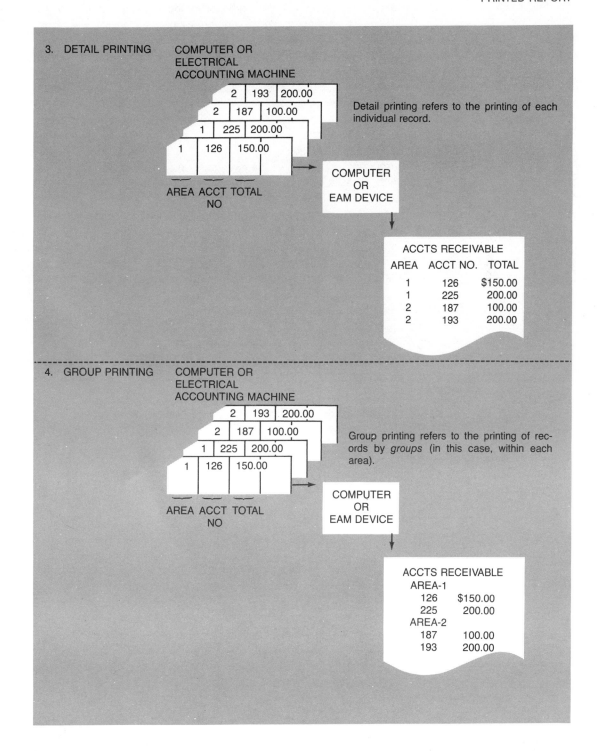

3. DETAIL PRINTING   COMPUTER OR
                      ELECTRICAL
                      ACCOUNTING MACHINE

Detail printing refers to the printing of each individual record.

AREA	ACCT NO.	TOTAL
ACCTS RECEIVABLE		
1	126	$150.00
1	225	200.00
2	187	100.00
2	193	200.00

4. GROUP PRINTING   COMPUTER OR
                     ELECTRICAL
                     ACCOUNTING MACHINE

Group printing refers to the printing of records by *groups* (in this case, within each area).

ACCTS RECEIVABLE
AREA-1
    126   $150.00
    225   200.00
AREA-2
    187   100.00
    193   200.00

5. The first three columns of the illustrated card represent the _____ field.

6. The data in the above field is _____.

7. The _____ punches are called the digit punches and the _____ punches are called zone punches.

8. A numeric field consists of _____ punches.

9. An alphabetic character consists of a _____ punch and a _____ punch in a single column.

10. An alphabetic field on the illustrated card is the _____ field.

11. An alphanumeric field is one that consists of _____.

12. _____ is a *general* example of an alphanumeric field.

13. The CURVE field is a numeric field with a _____ sign in its _____ position.

14. The high-order position of the RATE field contains a _____.

15. Punched cards can be punched by operators using a _____ machine, transcribing from a _____.

16. (T or F) While most cards can hold 80 characters, there are punched cards that can hold more.

17. Punched cards can also be created by the _____, as output.

18. Such output cards are usually reentered into the computer cycle as input at some later date. Examples of these types of cards include _____ and _____.

19. Two advantages of card processing are _____ and _____.

20. Three disadvantages of card processing are _____.

Solutions

1. 80
2. character
3. letter; digit; symbol
4. group of consecutive card columns used to indicate a unit of data, for example, JOB field, DESCRIPTION field
5. JOB
6. 050
7. 0 to 9; 0-, 11-, 12-
8. digit
9. zone; digit
10. DESCRIPTION
11. a combination of letters, digits, or special characters
12. ADDRESS
13. negative; low order or units
14. 9
15. keypunch; source document
16. T
17. computer
18. utility cards (gas, electric, telephone); time cards

19. they can be processed by machine and also be used for manual retrieval; the cost is relatively low.
20. cards warp easily, are easily dropped, misplaced, bent, etc.; card records are generally restricted to 80 columns or multiples of 80; cards are processed relatively slowly.

IV. Printed Output

The printed report is the primary form of computer output. It is the form of output that is most commonly distributed to non-data-processing businessmen.

The printed document is generally used *exclusively* as an end product. It is the final result of a computer run, often to be viewed by high-level management. It is prepared by the computer device called a *printer* (see Figure 2.17).

Other forms of output are generally intermediate products, having the ultimate function of being reentered into the computer flow as input to another job. These types of output are designed to be as efficient as possible. Fields and records of this type are condensed to make maximum use of the computer and its storage capabilities. The printed report, however, is written with the businessman in mind. Since many computer-generated reports are read by company executives, such forms must be clear, neat, and easy to interpret. The businessman should keep in mind that output reports must provide the *precise* information required within, of course, cost limitations. He or she should not be persuaded to settle for something less when the exact requirements can be obtained.

A. Characteristics of Printed Output
Several characteristics applicable only to printed output must be considered:

1. Printing of Headings Headings generally supply identifying information such as job name, date, page number, and field designations. These items are essential for clarity of presentation when creating printed output. In Figure 2.17 the lines above the actual data indicating TRIAL BALANCE and the field delineations are called headings.

2. Alignment of Printed Output Reports do not have fields of information adjacent to one another, as is the practice with cards. Printed output is more easily read and interpreted when data is spaced neatly and evenly across the page.

3. Editing of Printed Output As we have indicated, a punched card does not usually contain any edit or fill characters, since these occupy valuable card columns, not necessary for machine readabil-

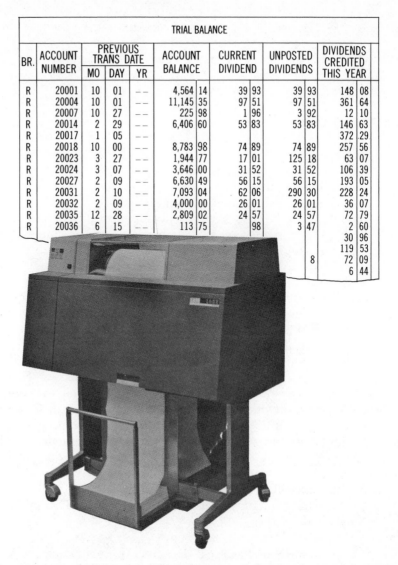

BR.	ACCOUNT NUMBER	PREVIOUS TRANS DATE			ACCOUNT BALANCE		CURRENT DIVIDEND		UNPOSTED DIVIDENDS		DIVIDENDS CREDITED THIS YEAR	
		MO	DAY	YR								
R	20001	10	01	– –	4,564	14	39	93	39	93	148	08
R	20004	10	01	– –	11,145	35	97	51	97	51	361	64
R	20007	10	27	– –	225	98	1	96	3	92	12	10
R	20014	2	29	– –	6,406	60	53	83	53	83	146	63
R	20017	1	05	– –							372	29
R	20018	10	00	– –	8,783	98	74	89	74	89	257	56
R	20023	3	27	– –	1,944	77	17	01	125	18	63	07
R	20024	3	07	– –	3,646	00	31	52	31	52	106	39
R	20027	2	09	– –	6,630	49	56	15	56	15	193	05
R	20031	2	10	– –	7,093	04	62	06	290	30	228	24
R	20032	2	09	– –	4,000	00	26	01	26	01	36	07
R	20035	12	28	– –	2,809	02	24	57	24	57	72	79
R	20036	6	15	– –	113	75		98	3	47	2	60
											30	96
											119	53
										8	72	09
											6	44

TRIAL BALANCE

ity. A printed document, however, must be as clear as possible, since it is designed to be read by individuals. While 12450 may be a typical AMOUNT field on a card, $12,450.00 is more meaningful as a printed field.

4. Spacing of Forms Printed documents, unlike other kinds of output, must be properly spaced for ease of reading. Certain entries must be single spaced, others double spaced. The printed output must have adequate margins at both the top and bottom of the form. This requires the computer to be programmed to sense the end of a form and thus to transmit the next line of information to a *new* page.

Remember that the computer-generated output report can contain any type of information. It can be an individual listing of specific records or it can be a summary report indicating only totals. It can be broken down into specific categories with control totals. It can be a statistical survey. In short, it can be compiled in any manner that is recommended by the computer specialist and deemed appropriate by the businessman.

You will recall that most cards contain 80 characters of information. The printed report typically contains 132 characters on each line, although some printers can print only 100 or 120 characters per line. Note that all positions need *not* be filled with significant characters; *many* positions on a printed line are filled with blanks or spaces. To align data on a page, we must leave numerous blank fields between significant ones. To assist in aligning printed data, a printer spacing chart sometimes called a print layout sheet (Figure 2.18) is often used. It maps out those areas of a form that are to be filled with data. Often, the computer specialist reviews these charts with the businessman prior to programming to confirm that the format is acceptable.

B. Continuous Forms and the Printer

Printed reports that serve as computer output are sometimes referred to as *continuous forms* since they are connected, separated only by perforations (see Figure 2.19). They are fed into a printer as one continuous form so that constant aligning of forms is not required. After an entire report has been printed, it is separated by a machine called a *burster* into individual sheets (see Figure 2.20). These individual sheets are then bound or transmitted to different people. Each page must have its own heading and usually a page number so that misplaced documents can be properly arranged.

Continuous forms can have additional carbon copies prepared by the computer. Standard stock continuous forms can usually be obtained as follows: 1-part (no copies), 2-part, 3-part, 4-part, or 5-part paper (4 copies). Machines that remove the carbons are called *decollators* (see Figure 2.20).

Most standard stock continuous forms are 12 inches long. Usually, 6 lines of data may be printed per inch. That is, most continuous forms may contain 72 lines of information. Sometimes, however, to condense a report, 8 lines per inch are utilized (see Figure 2.21). This is not as popular as the density of 6 lines per inch, since it is not as readable.

Note, however, that reports usually contain fewer than 72 or 96 lines per page. Generally, there are both top and bottom margins; that is, several blank lines are included at the top and bottom of each form. Similarly, many reports utilize double or triple spacing as well as single spacing to separate heading and detail lines.

Printed reports may be on plain, lined, or unlined sheets as indicated in Figure 2.19, or on special, *preprinted forms*. Bank statements, commonly printed by a computer as output, are individual preprinted forms with COMPANY NAME and other identifying

Figure 2.18
Sample printer spacing chart.

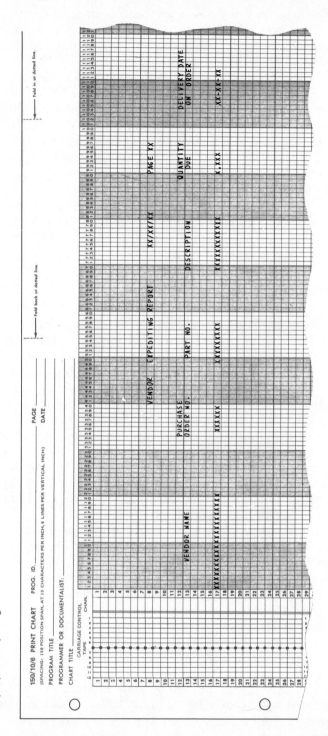

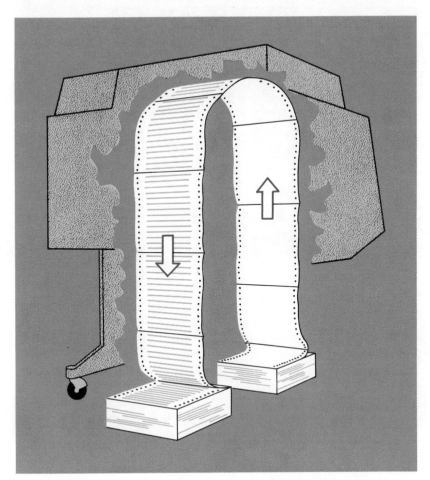

Figure 2.19
Continuous forms.
Courtesy IBM.

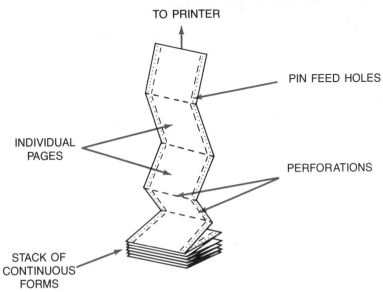

TO PRINTER

PIN FEED HOLES

INDIVIDUAL
PAGES

PERFORATIONS

STACK OF
CONTINUOUS
FORMS

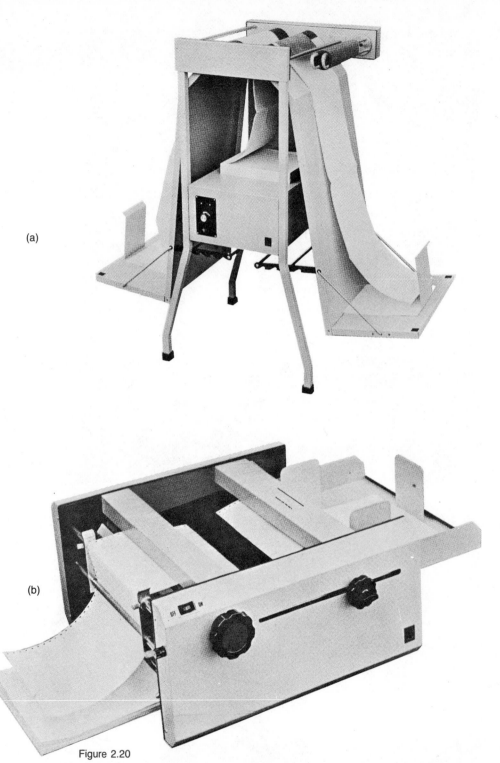

(a)

(b)

Figure 2.20

(a) Decollator, Model 620. Courtesy Monarch Co. Separates multiple-part forms and refolds them in continuous stacks, at the same time removing the carbons. (b) Burster, Model 610. Courtesy Monarch Co.

information printed on each one (see Figure 2.22). Similarly, Accounts Receivable statements may be prepared by the computer on preprinted forms (see Figure 2.23). Note, however, that the heading and the vertical and horizontal lines are preprinted on the continuous form, *prior* to entering the printer. They are *not* prepared by the computer. Keep in mind that these preprinted forms must be ordered from a company specializing in printed forms.

Thus printed reports may be produced on plain continuous forms or on preprinted continuous forms. Either may be utilized with carbons to provide additional copies. The plain 12-inch continuous forms usually can be obtained in 1, 2, 3, 4, or 5 parts. Preprinted forms may be ordered with as many copies as are required. Some manufacturers of forms specialize in carbonless paper which means that several copies of a report can be produced without the necessity of removing carbons. This type of paper is, of course, more expensive but saves the user the necessity of decollating the paper.

1. The Printer The printer is used to transmit information from the computer to the printed report. It is a device that can print generally 1000 to 1500 lines per minute, although the most modern printers can operate at more than 6000 lines per minute. It

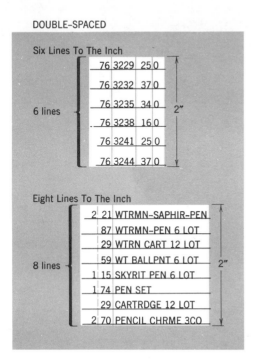

Figure 2.21

Examples of 6 lines per inch double spaced (e.g., 6 lines every two inches) and 8 lines per inch double spaced.

Figure 2.22

Example of preprinted bank statement. This statement is an example of a preprinted, side-by-side form that allows the computer to print two different bank statements at the same time by dividing the print area into two records—one for each statement. Courtesy International Business Forms, Inc.

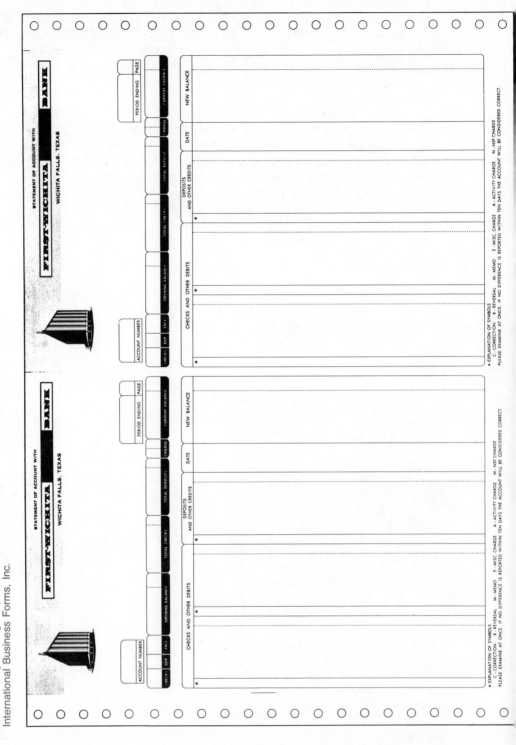

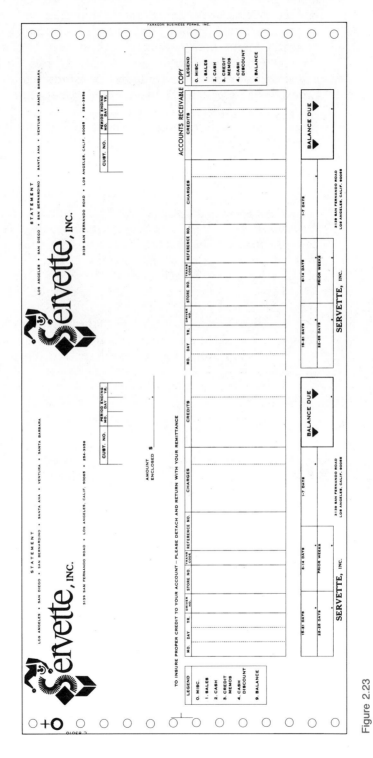

Figure 2.23

Example of a preprinted form. Courtesy International Business Forms, Inc.

is not, however, considered a high-speed device since other devices produce output at far greater rates. Note that, unlike the typewriter, most printers do not print one character at a time. Instead, a typical computer, for example, transmits 132 characters to the printer, which then prints one *line* at a time. Such printers are called *line printers*. The computer transmits a *total* line with significant characters and blanks included for spacing. The blanks are transmitted as if they were significant characters. Thus, the printer prints a line at a *constant* speed, regardless of whether the line contains 100 blanks or 5 blanks.

The device that moves the continuous forms through the printer is called the *carriage*.

2. Skipping and Spacing The continuous form may be easily programmed for *single, double,* or *triple* spacing. The programmer can also instruct the printer to *skip* to a specific line of the form. You will recall that there are generally 72 lines on a form. Any one of these lines may be accessed by the programmer for printing.

Thus, the printing of lines may be controlled by *skipping* to a specific line or by *spacing* the form 1, 2, or 3 lines.

In short, it is possible for the businessman to obtain computer-generated output records in almost any format desired, if he or she communicates the needs of the job to the computer specialist.

Important Terms Used in this Chapter

Alphanumeric Field	Keypunching
Burst	Left-Justified
Card Punch	Low-Order Position
Card Reader	Mark-Sense Card
Card Verification	Port-A-Punch Card
Character	Preprinted Form
Continuous Form	Printer
Decollate	Printer Spacing Chart
Editing	Record
Field	Right-Justified
File	Source Document
High-Order Position	Unit Record
Hollerith Code	Zone Row

Self-Evaluating Quiz

1. (T or F) A printer prints data a single character at a time.
2. _____ are needed on printed documents to ensure the proper identification of each page.

3. _____ is performed on printed data to ensure its readability.

4. A typical printer can print _____ characters per line, but many of these are _____ for ease of reading.

5. A layout form called a _____ is used by programmers and analysts, and verified by businessmen, to ensure that output data will be aligned properly.

6. The blank paper that is fed into a printer is an example of a _____.

7. Most standard stock paper is _____ inches long, and usually _____ lines may be printed per inch.

8. (T or F) Reports generally contain less than 72 lines per page because of margins.

9. In addition to standard stock continuous forms, _____ forms for special purposes may be used for printing particular reports.

10. _____, _____, or _____ spacing may be programmed, but the programmer can also instruct the printer to _____ to a specific line.

Solutions

1.	F	6.	continuous form
2.	Headings	7.	12; 6
3.	Editing	8.	T
4.	132; left blank	9.	preprinted
5.	printer spacing chart	10.	single; double; triple; skip

Review Questions

A. Punched Cards

1. Interpret the following data card:

2. Indicate how the following data would be represented in a three-position numeric field:
   a. −126
   b. −432
   c. +116
   d. +225
   e. 337

3. The top of a punched card is called the (no.) _____-edge and the bottom is called the (no.) _____-edge.

4. (T or F) A punched card may serve as a bill to a customer to be returned with the payment for further processing by the Accounts Receivable department.

5. (T or F) To represent alphabetic data on a card, we must use a digit punch in conjunction with another punch in the same column.

6. There are (no). _____ columns on a card and (no). _____ rows.

7. Each _____ of a card can store one character of data.

8. (T or F) Keypunch machines usually print the data on top of the cards while card-punch devices usually do not print data on top.

9. A _____ is used to convert written documents to punched cards.

10. To ensure that data is correctly transcribed by the keypunch operator onto a punched card a _____ is used.

11. One of the following is incorrect:
    a. The Hollerith Code for an L is an 11-3 combination of punches.
    b. The Hollerith Code for a B is a 12-2 combination of punches.
    c. The Hollerith Code for a T is a 0-2 combination of punches.
    d. The Hollerith Code representation for a −222 is a 22k in three card columns.
    e. The Hollerith Code representation for a +222 is a 22B in three card columns.

12. To represent 225 in a five-position numeric field, we would have
    a. 225 in the left three positions with two blanks in the right two positions.
    b. two blanks in the left two positions and 225 in the right three positions.
    c. two zeros in the left two positions and 225 in the right three positions.
    d. 225 in the left three positions and two zeros in the right two positions
    e. none of the above.

13. To represent ABC in a five-position alphabetic field, we would have
    a. ABC in the left three positions with two blanks in the right two positions.
    b. two blanks in the left two positions and ABC in the right three positions.
    c. two zeros in the left two positions and ABC in the right three positions.
    d. ABC in the left three positions and two zeros in the right two positions.
    e. none of the above.

14. A character of data may be represented as
    a. A single punch.
    b. Two punches.
    c. Three punches.
    d. No punches.
    e. All of the above.
15. Punched cards may be
    a. Punched by card-read devices.
    b. Punched manually with Port-A-Punch devices.
    c. Punched by card verifiers.
    d. Produced as a secondary form of output by the printer.
    e. None of the above.

B. The Printed Report

1. (T or F) Printed documents, unlike other kinds of output, must be properly spaced for ease of reading.
2. Continuous forms may be programmed to be:
    a. single spaced.
    b. double spaced.
    c. triple spaced.
    d. skipped to any line.
    e. all of the above.
3. Each page of a continuous form should generally have all of the following except one:
    a. heading.
    b. field delineators.
    c. name of department manager.
    d. page numbers.
    e. date.
4. The types of forms available for computer processing include:
    a. lined continuous forms.
    b. preprinted continuous forms.
    c. color-coordinated continuous forms with carbon copies.
    d. unlined continuous forms.
    e. all of the above.

Consider the Sales Performance Report in Figure 2.24 for the following questions. The report was produced by a computer.

5. Was this prepared on a blank continuous form or a preprinted form? Explain your answer.
6. Indicate the meaning of each field heading. Why do all the amount fields contain dashed lines?
7. Describe the report.
8. What is the significance of the two total fields at the bottom of the report?

SALES PERFORMANCE REPORT

DATE: 3/31/

DIST. NO.	OFF. NO.	SLSMN. NO.	DISTRICT, OFFICE OR SALESMAN	PRODUCT "A"	PRODUCT "B"	PRODUCT "C"	PRODUCT "D"	TOTAL BY SALESMAN	TOTAL BY OFFICE	TOTAL BY DISTRICT
1			NORTHEAST DIST							
	1		BOSTON OFFICE							
		5	J G CARGILL	231685	481937	309817	97255	1120694		
		43	A E JOHNSON	401861	362718	108536	258902	1132017		
		77	G I ROSS	400135	386992	478103	196845	1462075	3714786	
	2		NEW YORK OFFICE							
		2	P E AKERS	321398	489097	134445	186103	1131043		
		17	A K DEERING	354440	231586	398703	293223	1277952		
		36	R T INGEBRETSEN	284316	372010	281577	150432	1088335		
		79	F I RUSH	144483	231516	159147	141637	676783		
		89	T L WESTMORE	242976	340210	329514	267801	1180501	5354614	9069400 ☆
2			MID COAST DIST							
	1		BALTIMORE OFFICE							
		3	B L BARNEY	558436	471596	362093	192618	1584743		
		27	P W GOODE	323164	178041	409982	207868	1119055		
8			SOUTHWEST DIST							
	1		DALLAS OFFICE							
		51	R X MILLER	502800	185895	246831	376970	1312496		
		58	R M NORTH	233871	306630	351789	301053	1193343	2505839	
	2		EL PASO OFFICE							
		56	A R NELSON	541902	438065	372977	438091	1791035	1791035	4296874 ☆
										87210687 ☆☆

Figure 2.24
Sales performance report.

Chapter 3
The Processing of
Data by Computer

3

3

I. The Computer System

    A.   Input Units
    B.   The Central Processing Unit
    C.   Auxiliary Storage Units
    D.   Output Units
    Self-Evaluating Quiz

II. Factors Affecting Computer Capability

    A.   Memory Size
    B.   Speed
    C.   Cost
    D.   Hardware
    E.   Software
    F.   Compatibility

III. Methods of Processing Data

    A.   Batch Processing
    B.   Online Processing
    C.   Offline Processing

IV. Categories of Computers

    A.   Minicomputers
    B.   Small-Scale Computers
    C.   Medium-Scale Computers
    D.   Large-Scale Computers

V. Recent Advances in Computer Technology: Microcomputers

    A.   Purpose: Control
    B.   Microprocessor
    C.   Applications

Important Terms Used in this Chapter

Self-Evaluating Quiz

Review Questions

Appendix:

    Computer Characteristics for Selected Computer Systems

3

I. The Computer System

Each computer installation consists of a series of devices, which together operate as an integrated unit or *computer system*. Each computer system consists of separate machines that include the following:

Elements of a Computer System
1. Input units: read input data and transmit to central processing unit
2. Central processing unit: controls all operations of computer system; provides primary storage
3. Auxiliary storage units: provide auxiliary storage to augment primary storage
4. Output units: transmit processed data from CPU to output form

---

The schematic in Figure 3.1 illustrates the integration of the basic elements in a computer system.

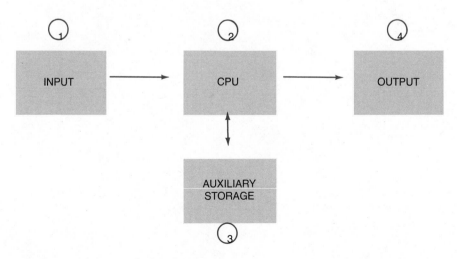

Figure 3.1
The basic elements in a computer system.

See Figure 3.2 for an illustration of a typical computer system.

Note that a computer system consists of a series of independent machines or *hardware* that function in an integrated manner to produce desired output. Note, too, that computer systems have a wide variety of input/output (I/O) devices which can be hooked up to the *mainframe* or CPU.

In this chapter we will discuss the basic characteristics of a computer system. Keep in mind that in order to process data at any given time, a computer system must be under the control of a *program*, or set of instructions indicating which units are to be used and precisely how the data is to be processed. This program, written by a programmer, is read into the CPU.

The objective of this chapter is to familiarize the student with the various methods of processing data and with the terminology used to describe those methods. Do not become overconcerned about the many terms discussed; each of them will be redefined, reinforced, and expanded in subsequent chapters.

Figure 3.2
IBM System 370.
Courtesy IBM.

A. Input Units

Each input unit of a computer system reads data from a specific form and converts it into electronic pulses. It then transmits these pulses to an input area in the CPU. A card reader, for example, is an input unit that reads punched cards with the use of mechanical brushes, converts the holes sensed to pulses, and transmits the pulses to an input storage area in the CPU. There are, of course, many other input units that can perform the same electronic conversions and transmissions with other forms of input.

Chapters 5 and 6 will discuss the following input units in depth:

Major Types of Input Units
(All convert input to electronic pulses and transmit to the CPU)

1. Card Reader: data recorded as holes in a punched card can be mechanically sensed.
2. Magnetic Tape Drive: data recorded as magnetized spots on a magnetic tape can be read.
3. Magnetic Disk Drive: data recorded as magnetized spots on a magnetic disk can be read.
4. Terminal: data is entered from remote locations usually with the use of a typewriter-like keyboard.
5. Magnetic Ink Character Reader: data recorded in magnetic ink can be read.
6. Optical Reader: data recorded on printed forms or by hand-written or typewritten methods can be read.
7. Punched Paper Tape Reader: data recorded as holes punched in a continuous paper tape can be read.
8. Computer Input Microfilm Reader: data recorded on a miniaturized photographic record can be read.
9. Console Typewriter: data keyed on a keyboard device connected to the console can be read.

Each of these devices has its own features but they all are capable of reading a form of input called an *input medium* and transmitting it to the CPU.

B. The Central Processing Unit

The *central processing unit* (CPU) is the physical device that controls the computer operations. It is the "brains" of the computer system. It is instructed by each program which specifies the functions required for a particular problem.

All operations performed by the computer system are controlled by the central processing unit. The CPU is connected by cable to each of the input/output devices and can control the I/O operations of each.

1. Components of the CPU Some CPUs contain magnetic cores to store data and programs. These cores are magnetized or demagnetized according to an internal configuration that represents a specific computer code. This code will be discussed in depth in the next chapter.

Many of the most recent CPUs contain miniaturized components such as the monolithic chip shown in Figure 3.3.

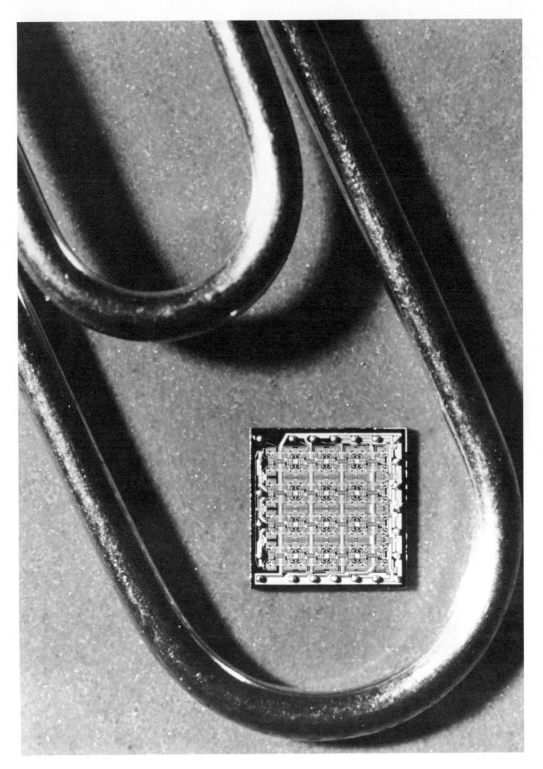

Figure 3.3
Monolithic chip—compared in size to a paper clip. Courtesy IBM.

2. Operations Performed by the CPU   The operations performed by the CPU can be categorized as follows:

```
Operations Performed by CPU
Input
Data Transfer ⎫
Arithmetic    ⎬  Processing
Logic         ⎭
Output
```

These operations are performed as called for by the programmer's instructions.

a. Input Operation   An *input operation* is one that signals an input device to read data; it then automatically transmits that data to the central processing unit. That is, each program provides an area of computer storage within the CPU to hold an input record. Thus, input operations perform two functions:

```
Input Operation
1.  Cause an input device to physically read data.
2.  Transmit the data from the input device to an input area of
    the CPU.
```

b. Processing Operations   Data transfer, arithmetic, and logic operations are *processing* functions that operate on the input data. These are the *only* operations that a computer can perform.

In order for information to be written, it must appear in an output area within the CPU that is set up by each program. The *data transfer* operation can, for example, *move* data from the input area to the output area. The *arithmetic* operations can cause the adding, multiplying, subtracting, and dividing of fields by the CPU. The *logic operations* can test or perform simple decisions such as: is one field less than, equal to, or greater than another?

c. Output Operation   An *output operation* causes information to be transmitted from the output area, provided for by each program, to an output device where it is then written out or recorded.

In short, each program that is read into the CPU generally provides for the following:

Programs Within CPU Include:
1. Input instructions to read in data and an input area into which data read by an input device is transmitted.
2. Instructions that will operate on input data to convert it to output.
3. Output instructions and an output area, from which information is transmitted when an output instruction is issued.

3. Elements of the Central Processing Unit   The Central Processing Unit is composed of three sections:

Sections of CPU
1. Primary storage
2. Control
3. Arithmetic-logic

a. Primary Storage   The *primary storage* section within the CPU contains the stored program. The program, you will recall, consists of the set of instructions necessary to read input data and convert it to output. We have expanded this definition slightly. The stored program consists of the set of instructions *and* the necessary input/output areas. Thus, if a program reads card data and converts it to printed output, storage areas will be required for the instructions, plus a minimum of 80 positions for card data and, typically, 132 positions for printed output.

Primary storage is composed of locations or addressable positions. On many computers, each position is composed of tiny ferrite rings or *cores* that are magnetized to reflect computer codes (see Figure 3.4). Thus the term *core storage* is used to denote this type of storage.

Instructions, as well as input/output areas, occupy storage positions. Each element of an instruction is placed in a storage position or storage location, called a *byte* on many computers. Primary storage capacity of minicomputers ranges from as few as 4000 characters or bytes. Small business computer systems range from approximately 32,000 bytes to 128,000 bytes, with large-scale computers possessing a primary storage capacity in excess of one million positions.[1] Thus, on average- or medium-sized computers, we can have programs with thousands of instructions, in addition to many input/output areas. The notation K is often used as an abbreviation for approximately one thousand storage positions. Thus,

---

[1] The term used for one million bytes of storage is *megabyte.*

Figure 3.4
Representation of
core storage.

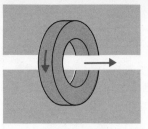
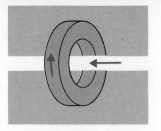

Core is magnetized.
Represents a 1,
or the presence
of a bit.

Current is reversed; the core
reverses its magnetic state.
Represents a 0,
or the absence of a bit.

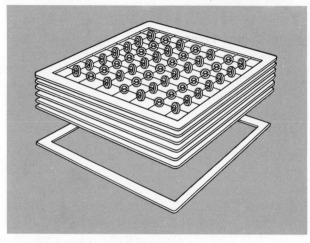

Cores in a plane.

small-sized business computers possess primary storage capacity of
from 32K to 128K.

b. Control   The control unit of the CPU supervises or
monitors the functions performed by the entire computer system.
A special program called a *supervisor* is responsible for controlling
the operations of the system. This supervisor calls in each problem
program and integrates the processing of each step.

c. Arithmetic-Logic Unit   Whenever the computer performs
arithmetic operations or makes a comparison, the CPU activates
the arithmetic-logic section. Special accumulators, or *registers,*
necessary for performing arithmetic operations are located in this
unit. These registers are internal areas used to temporarily hold
data that is being processed.

Logic operations are performed on a computer by a series of
comparisons activated by this unit. Electronic circuits called *gates*
can direct the path taken by a computer program. Depending on
whether a given quantity or field being tested is less than, equal to,
or greater than another value, specific gates or circuits are opened
or closed.

C. Auxiliary Storage Units

The total storage of a computer system is called its *memory size.*
Often, the memory size is too large to be completely housed in the

CPU. In such a case, auxiliary or secondary storage devices, linked by cables to the CPU, are used for supplemental storage. Auxiliary storage units are usually provided on tape or disk drives.

When an auxiliary storage device is linked to the CPU for supplemental storage, the CPU itself maintains control. That is, there is no need for the programmer to keep track of whether instructions or data are in primary or auxiliary storage.

D. Output Units

Each output unit of a computer system transmits information from the CPU and converts the electronic pulses to an appropriate output form. We have already seen that a printer is an output unit that transmits output from the CPU and converts it to a printed form. There are, of course, many other output devices that can perform the same electronic transmissions and conversions to produce other *output media.*

In Chapters 5 and 6 we will discuss the following devices which can serve as output units:

Major Types of Output Units
1. Card Punch: produces punched card information.
2. Line Printer: prints output reports.
3. Magnetic Tape Drive: produces magnetized spots on a magnetic tape.
4. Magnetic Disk Drive: produces magnetized spots on a magnetic disk.
5. Punched Paper Tape Device: produces punched holes on a continuous paper tape.
6. Computer Output Microfilm (COM) Device: produces output in the form of microfilm.
7. Terminal: located at remote locations and linked to the CPU by communication lines, this device can produce output in a number of different forms, depending upon the specific unit.
8. Console Typewriter; output is produced on a keyboard device connected to the console.

You will note that some computer media can serve as both input from and output to a computer system.

Self-Evaluating Quiz

1. The program that controls the operations of the entire system is called the _____ .
2. Calculations and decisions are performed in the _____ section of the CPU.

3. The _____ section within the CPU contains the stored program.

4. Primary storage is composed of _____ .

5. (T or F) Although the punched card and the printed report have been given as examples of input and output, respectively, computers can accept other forms of input and, similarly, produce other forms of output.

6. (T or F) All units of a computer system are controlled by the CPU.

7. (T or F) An input operation always accesses an input unit.

8. (T or F) Every program must contain an output operation.

9. (T or F) It is possible for some computer systems to read handwritten documents.

10. (T or F) Auxiliary storage usually consists of magnetic tape or disk devices.

Solutions

1. supervisor
2. arithmetic-logic
3. primary storage
4. locations or addressable positions called bytes on many computers
5. T
6. T
7. T
8. T
9. T
10. T

II. Factors Affecting Computer Capability

Thus far, we have seen how a computer basically operates on data. Input and output units are linked by cables to a central processing unit. The integrated activity of these devices functions as a computer system.

There are numerous commercial computer systems in use today. Among the major manufacturers of average or medium-sized computers are:

Major Computer Manufacturers
Burroughs Corp.
Control Data Corp.
Digital Equipment Corp.
Honeywell Information Systems
IBM Corp.
NCR Corp.
UNIVAC Division of Sperry Rand

Each one of these manufacturers produces computer systems designed to fit the needs of a wide variety of business organizations.

In addition, there are hundreds of data processing companies that manufacture hardware devices designed to meet specific business needs and that are *compatible* or usable with these major computer systems.

In this section we will discuss the various elements that distinguish one computer system from another. Businessmen, as well as computer specialists, must participate in the selection of new computer equipment or in the evaluation of the current computer installation at their organization. The following factors should be considered when assessing a computer system.

A. Memory Size

You will recall that a computer system can have varying memory sizes. The small-sized business computer has a storage capacity ranging from 32K to 128K, but large-scale computers can have a memory size in excess of one million characters. In general, most computer systems can be acquired with memory sizes that are designed to fit the customer's needs.

B. Speed

Early computers were measured in speeds of *milliseconds* or thousandths of a second. Second-generation computers were measured in speeds of *microseconds* or millionths of a second. Third-generation computers are measured in speeds of *nanoseconds*, or billionths of a second. Thus, we can see that each new generation of computers is designed with greatly increased speeds. Present computers perform each operation in billionths of a second, or even faster, that is in terms of *picoseconds*, or trillionths of a second. Even so, a large-volume job, such as the processing of millions of records, where hundreds of operations are needed for each, can require several computer hours. Thus the faster computers, even though they cost more, may provide a cost savings, since they result in decreased processing time.

C. Cost

Cost is a determining factor in evaluating *any* investment. Large-scale computers obviously cost much more than small-scale ones. Yet a user may require specific operations that can only be performed on large-scale computers. Thus cost, although important, is only one of several factors to be considered in selecting a computer system.

D. Hardware

Hardware, you will recall, is the term used to designate the devices associated with a particular computer system. Each business organization will have specific needs that can best be met by utilizing specific hardware with a computer system. One business, for example, may find that a device called an optical scanner, which can read printed documents and convert data directly into machine-readable codes, is best suited for its needs. Although very costly, this device may save some companies money, since keypunching of data is unnecessary.

Each computer system can be supplemented with additional hardware. That is, a device manufactured by Digital Equipment Corporation, for example, may be compatible with an IBM computer system. Thus, the businessman and computer specialist must be cognizant of the recent advances in hardware development including those that are compatible with their system. Chapters 5 and 6 discuss, in depth, various types of hardware that may be used in conjunction with a computer system.

E. Software

Software is the term used to describe the programming support supplied by the manufacturer that is designed to maximize computer efficiency. Honeywell, for instance, has various prepackaged programs that are available with Honeywell computer systems. These software packages are different from those available with NCR equipment, for example. The software support available with each computer system must be evaluated before a valid selection can be made. (Chapter 10 discusses software in more depth.)

F. Compatibility

If programs and software prepared for one computer can be utilized, without rigorous conversion, by another computer, then the two systems are compatible. Third-generation computers—for example, the IBM S/360 and S/370 series, the UNIVAC 90 series, the Burroughs 66 series, and several others—have been designed with the compatibility feature in mind. For these systems, higher model numbers within the series mean greater capability and greater cost. The IBM S/370 line, for example, consists of many models of computers; yet the 370 line is said to have *upward compatibility.* That is, a company that acquires an IBM S/370 model 148 can "trade it in" for a more sophisticated model, such as the S/370 model 158, and still maintain the same programs that were run on the model 148. With this facility, manufacturers hope to enable their users to acquire higher level computers (higher models) without requiring a complex conversion process. The computer specialist and the businessman should ascertain that the computer system acquired by their company has compatibility with other makes and models. Otherwise, extensive reprogramming effort may be required when a new system is acquired in the future.

The following table provides an indication of the amount of computer time used per week by a sample group of business firms.

Note that more than half the firms sampled use 60 or less hours of CPU time per week, but over 16% operate almost on a 24-hour basis.

The Total Number of CPU Hours Used per Week

No. of Hours	Percent of Companies Sampled
Less than 40	26.4%
41-50	17.0
51–60	10.3
61–70	7.3
71–80	5.5
81–90	5.3
91–100	5.3
101–110	3.0
111–120	3.5
121 or more	16.4

III. Methods of Processing Data

A. Batch Processing

With this method, data is entered into the information flow in large volumes, or batches. That is, the processing by computer is performed in some time interval (weekly, monthly, etc.) when large volumes are accumulated. Daily Accounts Receivable tickets, for example, may be *batch processed* on a weekly basis. Instead of being processed as they are received, the tickets are processed periodically when a sufficient volume has been accumulated.

There are several inherent disadvantages to batch processing. The system that utilizes batch processing is not especially timely, since it takes a fixed time interval before current data is added. That is, the main or master Accounts Receivable file, in our example, does not contain the current Accounts Receivable data for a full week. For this reason, a system that utilizes batch processing cannot effectively answer inquiries *between* processing intervals. The Accounts Receivable file in our example is only current on the day of the processing cycle; after that, current data will not be processed until the following week's run.

B. Online Processing

For some applications, the processing of data in batches after a fixed interval is insufficient. Airline reservation systems, for example, require immediate processing. Each time a ticket is issued or cancelled, or a plane's schedule is altered, the data must be immediately entered into a computer, processed, and made available.

Such systems utilize devices that can be manually activated, that have immediate access to a computer, and that instantaneously receive messages. This form of processing usually uses terminals linked to a CPU via telecommunication lines and is called *online processing*. This form of processing is discussed in conjunction with terminals in Chapter 12. Figure 3.5 shows a comparison of batch processing and online processing.

C. Offline Processing

Computer processing is, without question, expensive. Thus, any operation that can avoid inefficient utilization of computer equipment can save a company much money. *Offline processing* is the processing of data that is *not* directly under the control of the main CPU.

A card-to-print offline hardware device, for example, is one that can take data from a card and print it according to a specified format, *without the use of a central processing unit of a computer*. There are numerous offline devices that are compatible with most computer systems. These are discussed in chapter 6.

Hence, the type of processing utilized can directly affect the efficiency of a computer system. Each of the above processing techniques will be discussed, in depth, in subsequent chapters.

Note that offline operations often utilize auxiliary *minicomputers* to perform required conversions. Although a computer is employed, this conversion is considered offline since processing is not under the control of the *main* computer. This utilization of minicomputers for offline operations to relieve the load of full-size computers is becoming increasingly popular because it usually results in substantial monetary savings.

IV. Categories of Computers

We have thus far discussed computer systems in general. You should now be aware that computer systems can consist of many diversified devices and complex CPUs. We have also seen that computer systems vary broadly in capability and cost. The appendix to this chapter gives a broad cost and specification breakdown of most medium- and large-scale computer systems. Let us now discuss the various classes of computers.

A. Minicomputers

These computers are designed to handle simple data-processing functions. While medium- and large-scale computers are used to

BATCH PROCESSING

1. PERIODIC PROCESSING
2. INPUT DATA USUALLY SEQUENCED

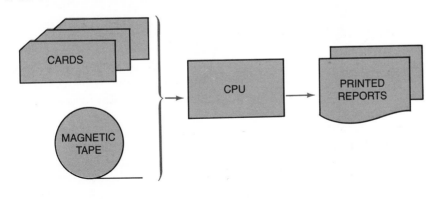

Figure 3.5
Comparison of
batch processing
and online
processing.

ONLINE PROCESSING

1. IMMEDIATE PROCESSING
2. INPUT DATA USUALLY NOT
   SEQUENCED
3. OUTPUT REPORTS
   PREPARED
   PERIODICALLY

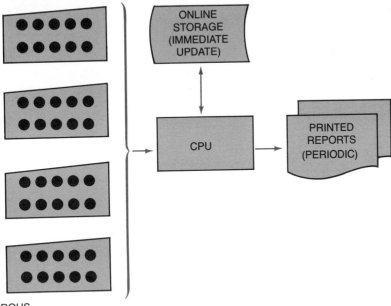

process the information flow of relatively complex systems that are then broken down into smaller aspects, minicomputers are capable of performing these independent tasks but do not lend themselves to very voluminous processing.

Minicomputers are manufactured by Digital Equipment Co., IBM, Hewlett-Packard, and Data General, just to name some of the larger manufacturers. These machines are generally small and often fit on a desk top. Some are punched-card systems capable of reading and/or producing punched cards. Most minicomputers have the ability to print data. Some just contain a keyboard, for input entries, where data is keyed in by an operator or programmer. Others can contain far more sophisticated input/output forms, but these are more costly. They are designed to be stand-alone computers, which means that they operate independently; or, they can be part of a vast network or system. Many minicomputers, for example, at different locations can amass data, edit, and verify it, perform simple calculations and then transmit them to a large-scale computer for manipulation of all the elements. Minicomputers are capable of handling typical I/O forms such as those used with much larger machines. There are, however, limitations in core capacity, speed, and functions that can be performed. They have the major advantage of being relatively inexpensive—selling for between $2,000 to $20,000.

Figure 3.6 illustrates a minicomputer manufactured by Wang Laboratories, Inc. This is a device used by insurance agents which enables them to develop a personalized statement for each client, quickly and accurately, explaining financial benefits.

This minicomputer consists of an electronic calculator and an output writer. It comes equipped with preprogrammed tape cassettes, on which the manufacturer-supplied programs are written.

Utilizing the system, an agent can custom design each client's exact insurance needs. Increased insurance sales result from this system, indirectly, because clients are impressed by an agent who can design an insurance investment portfolio on his own computer. With the use of this minicomputer, agents need not submit requests for the preparation of such personalized benefit statements for each client, which would require clerical assistance and/or the use of a large-scale computer.

A typical minicomputer manufactured by Varian Data Machines, Inc. is used in online systems for the following applications.

1. Baggage-handling systems, by maintaining data on the destination of as many as 12,000 suitcases per hour in order to make sure that passengers and their luggage depart on the same flight.
2. Teaching-machine systems, by providing computer-aided instruction *and* pupil profiles for teachers.

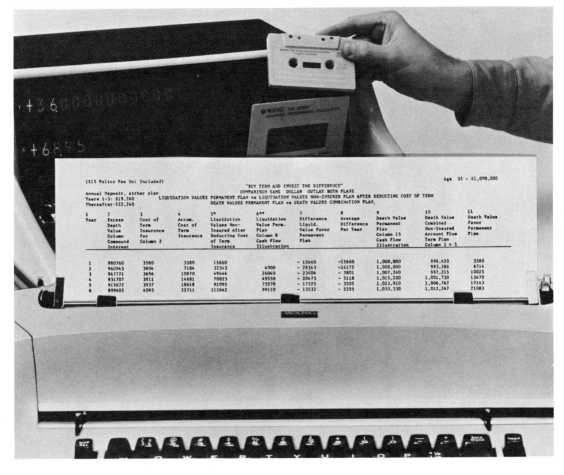

Figure 3.6

Example of a minicomputer. Courtesy Wang Laboratories, Inc.

These systems utilize a relatively inexpensive minicomputer to perform operations that were heretofore performed by large-scale expensive computer systems. These are but a few of the newer systems currently employing minicomputers.

Mini use growing fast in government—GAO

According to the General Accounting Office (GAO), minicomputer acquisition in the federal government is increasing faster than any other type of computers. About 4,777 of the 8,600 computers in use in federal agencies in 1975 were minis and small-scale computers.

The federal government uses minis primarily for scientific data processing and control of machinery, but federal managers expect they will be more widely used in the future for data entry and editing, communications and general data processing, says GAO in its report to Congress on the use of minis. GAO found that there were problems and limitations on using minis and that software costs of these small computers generally were higher than hardware costs.

"In considering minicomputers, federal managers should assess the impact of the total cost on agency operations along with assessing the impact of the hardware acquisition costs," says GAO.

The watchdog agency also found that many federal organizations were using computer programs in a language that could be used on only one manufacturer's hardware. GAO encourages users to program minis in a higher-level language that can be used on a variety of machines.

Some agencies told GAO that procurement regulations governing minicomputer acquisition were too complicated and caused them to incur excessive administrative costs and time delays. In some instances, agency officials said they obtained a more expensive alternative system instead of a mini because the procurement process was simpler and faster.

The General Services Admin. said it planned to simplify procurement requirements.

B. Small-Scale Computers

These computers are designed to perform unit-record functions in far less time and with greater accuracy than EAM equipment. IBM S32, the IBM System/3 (Figure 3.7), NCR 50, and 100, UNIVAC BC/7, Burroughs B-80, as examples, fall into this category. They utilize predominantly punched-card input and, although they have the capability of producing high-level output, they are basically used to produce printed output. The IBM System/3 uses a 96-column card designed with 20% more capacity than the 80-column card.[2] The disadvantage of this card is that it cannot be used with other data-processing equipment. Thus a company that rents such equipment and uses this card cannot use it with EAM devices or other computers that employ the standard 80-column card.

C. Medium-Scale Computers

Medium-scale computers are more widely used. They are far more capable machines. These include the IBM S/360 models 30 and 40, UNIVAC 90 series, Burroughs 3500, 4500, and 5500 series, Xerox Sigma 5, and so on. These devices are most often employed at typical business organizations throughout the country. Their average rental is approximately $10,000 to $40,000 per month and they are capable of high-speed and complex operations. They can also use the more sophisticated I/O devices indicated in the next chapters.

[2] See page 47.

They do, however, require some operator intervention, even though they utilize supervisors to handle most typical control procedures.

Figure 3.7
IBM System/3.
Courtesy IBM.

D. Large-Scale Computers

These computers are the really high-level machines that have storage capacities in the million-byte range and typically rent for more than $100,000 per month. They usually contain full control systems with minimal operator intervention. They are capable of linking up with dozens of high-level I/O devices, have storage capacity in excess of one million characters, and can perform operations at phenomenal rates. Such large-scale computers include the UNIVAC 1110, IBM S/360 models 85, 95, 195, the IBM S/370 model 165, Burroughs model 165, Honeywell 66/80, and others. Table 3.1 provides a comparison of the various categories of computers.

Categories of Computers

Table 3.1

Size	Purchase Price (Dollars)	Monthly Rental (Dollars)
Mini	2,000 to 20,000	Usually sold, not rented
Small	200,000	4,000
Medium	800,000	16,000
Large	2,000,000 to 12,000,000+	50,000 to 300,000

V. Recent Advances in Computer Technology: Microcomputers

A. Purpose: Control

As the name implies, microcomputers are very small versions of standard computers. Unlike the computers considered thus far, they are usually part of other automatic devices. Although they are frequently employed for home use, their job is mainly to provide control within a business environment.

B. Microprocessor

A built-in *microprocessor* provides the microcomputer with its capability. A microprocessor is a small chip of silicon which, because it is mass produced, costs only about $20.

C. Applications

Microcomputers are used for control purposes in a wide variety of industrial applications and for consumer products as well. In industries, they are frequently used to facilitate assembly line production. They are also used in sewing machines to control stitching operations, in electronic games such as those played on a TV screen, and are an integral control feature of some automobiles, monitoring some of the engine functions such as speed, temperature, and pollution levels to maximize operating efficiency.

In Chapter 1, we discussed the three major generations of computers. Table 3-2 provides a more detailed explanation of the features that characterize each generation.

Table 3.2

Features of Computer Generations

Generation Features	First Generation 1951–1959	Second Generation 1959–1964	Third and Fourth Generation 1964–present
Technology	Vacuum tube	Transistor	Transistor monolithic circuits semiconductor circuits
Primary Storage	Magnetic drum	Magnetic core	Magnetic core; solid state
Auxiliary Storage	Magnetic tape	Magnetic disk	Magnetic disk
Communications Capability	None	Limited	Extensive
Approximate Cost per 1700 typical dp instructions (courtesy IBM)	$14.00	$2.50–$.50	$.50–$.20 and getting less
Programming	Stored program	Batch processing; overlapped input/output	Operating system virtual storage multiprogramming (to be discussed in chapter 10)

Important Terms Used in this Chapter

Arithmetic-Logic Unit
Auxiliary Storage
Batch Processing
Byte
Central Processing Unit (CPU)
Compatibility
Control Unit
Core Storage
Data Transfer
Hardware
Input Unit
Magnetic Core
Mainframe

Memory Size
Microcomputer
Microprocessor
Minicomputer
Nanosecond
Offline Processing
Online Processing
Output Unit
Picosecond
Primary Storage
Program
Software
Supervisor

Self-Evaluating Quiz

1. The objective of a computer program is to _____.
2. The term CPU is an abbreviation for _____.
3. The unit of a computer system that transmits data to the CPU is called the _____.
4. The function of the CPU is to _____.
5. The two types of storage available in most computer systems are called _____ and _____.
6. The form of storage located in the CPU is called _____.
7. The storage capacity of a computer system is called its _____.
8. The term used to define all input and output devices in a computer system is _____.
9. (T or F) The storage capacity of large-scale computers is approximately 10,000 characters.
10. (T or F) Small-scale computers were developed essentially to handle unit-record functions.
11. Describe the major difference between batch processing and online processing.

Solutions

1. operate on input data to produce output
2. Central Processing Unit
3. input unit
4. control the operations of the computer and to provide primary storage
5. primary
   auxiliary
6. primary
7. memory size

8. hardware
9. F
10. T
11. Batch processing—data is processed in batches at fixed intervals. Online processing—data is processed as it is received.

Review Questions

I. Answer True or False

1. (T or F) A computer system consists of independent machines that function in an integrated manner to produce the desired output.
2. (T or F) All operations performed by the computer system are controlled by the CPU.
3. (T or F) All data processing centers have the same basic computer equipment.
4. (T or F) Data transfer operations cause the transmission of data from an input device to an input area of the CPU.
5. (T or F) The three main classifications of equipment at a computer center are hardware, software, and the console typewriter.
6. (T or F) The storage unit of the CPU contains the stored program.
7. (T or F) Storage is composed of locations or addressable positions.
8. (T or F) The memory size of third-generation computers cannot exceed 128K.
9. (T or F) The supervisor of a computer system is itself a program.
10. (T or F) When a system can defer the process of making a file of data current, then batch processing is utilized.

II. Fill In the Blanks

1. Most companies today utilize _____-sized computers.
2. The three sections of the central processing unit are _____, _____, and _____.
3. The stored program is contained within the _____ section of the CPU.
4. The number of storage positions available on a given computer is called its _____.
5. The program responsible for controlling the operations of the totally integrated computer system is called the _____.

Computer Characteristics for Selected Computer Systems

| Manufacturer / Model No. | Avg. Purchase Price ($1,000) | Avg. Rental Price ($/Mo.) | Central Processor | | | | | | | | | Readers | | |
| | | | Speed (usec) | | Storage | | | Typewriter Console | No. CPU I/O Channels | Data Word Length*** | Buffering | Data Collection | MICR | OCR |
			CPU Cycle Time	Add Time*	Medium**	Maximum Capacity (in characters)	Access Time (in usec)							
Basic/Four Corp. 500	38	872	1	9.6	C DI	48K	1	x	3	8	x			
Burroughs Corp. B300	240	5K	166Kc	492	C DI	19.2K	6	x		D		x	x	
B3506	510	12K	1	70	C	300K	1	x	10	B	x	x	x	x
B6715	1,987.3	41.4K	0.2	2.4	C DI	7,864K 36b	0.6 40ms		6	B	x	x		
B7748	4.440	90.2K	0.0625	0.125	C DI	7,864K 112b	1.75 40ms		56	B	x	x		
Control Data Corp. 3300	700	15K	1.2	2.75	C DR DI	262Kw 4m 838m	0.8 17ms 80ms	x	8	B D	x	x		x
3500	1,100	24K	0.9	1.2	C DR DI	202Kw 4m 838m	0.6 17ms 80ms	x	8	B D	x	x		x
Cyber 70 Model 76	9.500	220K	0.0275	0.495	C DR DI	650K 5.12m 8,200K 800m	0.0275 17ms 100ms	x	15	B D	x	x	x	x
Honeywell Information Systems 120	165	3.2K	3	69	C DR DI	32K 2.6m 149.6	1.5 27ms 75ms	x	3			x		x
415	450	9.6K	5.95	17.8	C DI	524K 120m	5.95 85ms	x	12	B D	x		x	x
2015	625	15K	1.33	15	C DI DR	262K	0.67	x	12		x		x	x
8200	2,900	40K 78K	0.75	3.12 128	C DR DI	2,096K 4.2m 300m	0.094 8.6ms 15ms	x	48-96		x		x	x
International Business Machines Corp. System/3	136-298	3.2K- 7.2K	1.52	35	C	128K	1.52m	x		B	x	x	x	x
System/360 Mod 20	99	2.2K	3.6	572	C DI	16K 10.8m	3.6 75ms	x	1	B	x	x	x	x
System/360 Mod 25	300	6K	1.8	110	C DI	49K 29m	0.9 75ms	x	1	B	x	x	x	x
System/360 Mod 30	420	8.5K	1.5	61	C DI	65K 233m	1.5 60ms	x	3	B	x	x	x	x
System/360 Mod 50	1,400	32K	2	23	C DR DI	524K 7.8m 699m	2 8.6ms 60ms	x	4	B	x	x	x	x
System/360 Mod 67	5,800	138K	0.75	3.9	C DR DI	2,096K 16.4m 699m	0.75 8.6ms 60ms	x	14	B	x			
System/360 Mod 75	3,600	80K	0.75	2.54	C DR DI	1,048K 16.4m 699m	0.75 8.6ms 60ms	x	7	B	x			

*this speed is the complete add time for two six digit numbers from memory to memory;
**C = core, DI = disc, DR = drum, IC = integrated circuit, PW = plated wire, TF = thin film;
***B = binary, D = decimal; K = thousand, m = million, b = billion, usec = microseconds,
ms = milliseconds, ns = nanosecond, w = words, x = yes, mc = megacycle.

Manufacturer/Model No.	Avg. Purchase Price ($1,000)	Avg. Rental Price ($/Mo.)	CPU Cycle Time	Add Time*	Medium**	Maximum Capacity (in characters)	Access Time (in usec)	Typewriter Console	No. CPU I/O Channels	Data Word Length***	Buffering	Data Collection	MICR	OCR
System/360 Mod 195	10,500	232K	0.54	0.154	C DR DI	1,240K 4m 233m	810 8.6ms 60ms	x	7	B	x	x		
System/370 Mod 125	377.8	8.2K	0.98	9.8	C	131K		x	16	B D				
System/370 Mod 135	472-1,020		0.75		Mono-lithic	245	0.77	x	3	B	x	x	x	x
System/370 Mod 155	1,801-3,736	37K 79K	m 2.1 ms B 115ms	C	C DI	2mb 800mb	2.1ms 300ms	x		B	x	x		
System/370 Mod 165	3,505-6,719	71K 143K	m 2ms B 80ms		C DI	3mb 800mb	2ms 300ms	x		B	x	x		
National Cash Register Co. Century 100	135	2.6K	0.8	58.4	TF DI	32K 16.8m	0.8 43.7ms	x	2	8	x		x	x
Century 200	305	6.2K	0.65	12.4	C DI	524K 1.5b	0.65 43.7ms	x	4-8	16	x		x	x
Century 300	1,170	23K	0.24	6.2	C DI	2.097m 9.2b	0.65 43.7ms	x	11	32	x		x	x
Sperry Univac Computer System 90/70	1,000	25K	0.6	20	IC DI	648K	27ms	x	22	32	x			x
1110	2,000	44K	0.12	1.5	C		0.32	x	96	96	x	x		x
9300	140	3.7K	0.6	60	PW DI	32K 12.8m	0.6 132ms	x	4 11	8	x			x
9480	350	85K	0.6	24.6	IC DI	262K	30ms	x	10	16	x	x		x
Varian Data Machines V72	43.2		0.66	12.8	C DI	64K 186.8m	10ms	x	48	B	x	x	x	
Xerox Corp. Sigma 3	200	5K	0.97	1.85	C DI	256K		x	28	B D	x			
Sigma 5	350	8.5K	0.95	3.1	C DI	512K 3b	0.9 17ms	x	256	B	x			
Sigma 9	1,000	30K	0.9	1.66	C	2,048K	0.9 17ms	x	256	32	x			
Xerox 560	700	17K	0.215	1.8	C DI		0.645 8.3ms	x	261	B D	x			

Input/Output										Software							
Printers		Magnetic Tape		Punched Cards		Punched Paper Tape		Data Communications									
Lines Per Minute	Plotter****	7-Channel K/Char. Per Sec.	9-Channel K/Char. Per Sec.	Cards Per Minute Input	Cards Per Minute Output	Charac. Per Sec. Input	Charac. Per Sec. Output	No. Transmission Lines	Visual Display	Operating System	Time Share Capability	Multiprogram	Cobol	Fortran II, IV or VI	Utilities	Communications	Other
200		10	10	400/800		300	75	8	x	x	x	x			x	x	x
1,040		72		1,400	300	1,000	100	32	x	x		x	x		x	x	
1,100		96		1,400	300	1,000	100	36	x	x	x	x	x	x	x	x	
1,040		96	240	1,400	300	1,000	100	1,024	x	x	x	x	x	x	x	x	x
1,040		96	240	1,400	300	1,000	100		x	x	x	x	x	x	x	x	x
1,200	x	120	30	1,200	250	1,000	120	512	x	x	x	x	x	x	x	x	x
1,200	x	120	30	1,200	250	1,000	120	512	x	x	x	x	x	x	x	x	x
1,200	x	120	240	1,200	250	1,000	120	unlt'd	x	x	x	x	x	x	x	x	x
300-1,100		4.8-144	37.3-149.6	1,050	100-400	600	120	1-63	x	x	x	x	x	x	x	x	x
1,200	x	7.5-120	10-160	900	100-300	500	150	120	x	x		x	x	x	x	x	x
300-1,100		5.2-144	37.3-149.3		100-400	600	120	120	x	x	x	x	x	x	x	x	x
300-1,100		5.2-144	37.3-224	1,050	100-400	600	120	1-126	x	x	x		x	x	x	x	x
1,100				500/1,000	120/260			var	x	x		x	x	x	x	x	
300-1,100		15	30	1,000	500	1,000	150	1							x	x	x
240-1,400		30	30	1,000	500	1,000	120	26	x	x		x	x	x	x	x	x
240-1,400		90	180	1,000	500	1,000	120	224	x	x		x	x	x	x	x	x
240-1,400		90	320	1,000	500	1,000	120	256	x	x		x	x	x	x	x	x
240-1,400		90	190	1,000	500	1,000		256	x	x	x	x	x	x	x	x	x
240-1,400		90	320	1,000	500			256	x	x		x	x	x	x	x	x

	Input / Output									Software							
Printers		Magnetic Tape		Punched Cards		Punched Paper Tape		Data Communications									
Lines Per Minute	Plotter****	7-Channel K/Char. Per Sec.	9-Channel K/Char. Per Sec.	Cards Per Minute Input	Cards Per Minute Output	Charac. Per Sec. Input	Charac. Per Sec. Output	No. Transmission Lines	Visual Display	Operating System	Time Share Capability	Multiprogram	Cobol	Fortran II, IV or VI	Utilities	Communications	Other
1,100		90	300	1,000	500			196	x	x		x	x	x	x	x	
x				x	x			22	x	x							
2,000	x	90	320	1,200	300	120	120	var	x	x	x	x	x	x	x	x	x
2,000		90	320	1,000	500				x	x	x	x	x	x	x	x	x
2,000		90	320	1,000	500				x	x	x	x	x	x	x	x	x
450-3,000		10-40	40-80	300-1,200	82-240	1,000-1,500	200	1-256	x	x	x	x		x	x	x	x
450-3,000		10-40	40-240	300-1,200	82-240	1,000-1,500	200	1-256	x	x	x	x	x	x	x	x	x
450-3,000		10-40	40-240	300-1,200	83-240	1,000-1,500	200	1-256	x	x	x	x	x	x	x	x	x
900-3,000		34-96	34-320	600-1,000	250	300	1,150	158		x		x	x	x	x	x	x
2,000		x	x	1,000				var	x	x	x	x	x	x	x	x	x
600-1,100		34	34-68	2,000	75/250	300	110	8	x	x		x	x	x	x	x	x
900-2,000		34-96	34-192	600-1,000	250	300	110	128		x		x	x	x	x	x	x
300-1,200		30	30	300-1,000	35-200	300	75	var	x	x	x	x		x	x	x	x
1,500		60	120	1,500	300	300	120	256		x			x	x	x	x	x
1,500	x	60	120	1,500	300	300	120	1,024	x	x	x	x	x	x	x	x	x
1,500	x	x	x	1,500	300	300	120	1,024	x	x	x	x	x	x	x	x	x
4,000		60	200	1,500	100	300	75	1,024	x	x	x	x	x	x	x	x	x

Chapter 4

Data Representation and Computer Numbering Systems

4

4

VI. Representation of Characters in Storage

    *A.   **The Binary Coded Decimal or BCD Code**
    *B.   **Parity**
    C.   **The EBCDIC Code**

Important Terms Used in this Chapter

Self-Evaluating Quiz

Review Questions

        * Optional topics.

4

4

I. Introduction

Data is entered into a computer in normal alphanumeric form as letters, digits, and special characters. Similarly, information is produced as output from the computer in the same readable, alphanumeric form. Internally, however, data is represented by a *computer code*. While this computer code varies from computer to computer, there are certain features that are standard and thus independent of the specific system. It is the purpose of this chapter to discuss just how data is represented and manipulated by computer systems in general.

All computer codes make use of the *binary numbering system* in some form or another. We shall discuss this system in detail in the following section. Note, however, that the binary numbering system uses two digits, 0 and 1, to represent every possible number. This system is ideally suited to computers for one important reason. The 0's are represented internally in the computer as an off-state and the 1's as an on-state. Hence computer circuits are on or off depending upon the binary representation of numbers. Where magnetic cores are used to denote data, the "1" state is represented by a core that is magnetized, the "0" state by a core that is demagnetized.

In this chapter, we will consider the following:

The representation of numbers in binary form
The procedures to be used in converting binary numbers to decimal form and decimal numbers to binary form
The ways in which binary numbers are added and subtracted internally by the computer
The actual computer codes that make use of binary numbers: octal and hexadecimal systems
The internal computer code that represents numbers, letters, and special characters using some form of the binary numbering system: BCD and EBCDIC

II. Review of Decimal Numbers

Let us begin by reviewing some features of our own decimal numbering system that apply to the binary numbering system as well.

103

DATA
REPRESENTATION
AND COMPUTER
NUMBERING
SYSTEMS

The decimal system, like the binary system, is a *positional* numbering system. This implies that each digit has a different significance or value depending upon its position in a sequence of numbers.

Explanation of Powers of 10   The decimal system utilizes ten distinct digits, 0–9. We sometimes refer to it as a *base 10* system. Each position can contain one of ten digits and, in addition, each position can be expressed as a factor of 10. The following is a schematic of the positional values in the decimal, or base 10, system.

Value of each position expressed as integers	1000	100	10	1
Value of each position expressed as a power of 10	10^3	10^2	10^1	10^0

Using this schematic, we can see that the fifth position in the base 10 system indicates the number of 10000's, or 10^4, and so on.

Hence, the first position has unit or 10^0 value. (Any number with exponent[1] of zero is equal to 1.) The second position has value 10, or 10 raised to the first power. The third position has value 100, or 10 raised to the second power or 10×10. The fourth position has value 1000 or 10 raised to the third power or $10 \times 10 \times 10$.

Thus the number 384 may be expressed as

10^2	10^1	10^0
100	10	1
3	8	4

$$4 \times 1 = 4$$
$$8 \times 10 = 80$$
$$3 \times 100 = \underline{300}$$
$$384$$

To obtain the value, 300 and 80 and 4, from the three digits 384, we multiply each digit by its positional value. This method of multiplying any digit by its positional value to determine the value of the entire number is the exact method we will be using to determine the decimal equivalent of binary numbers.

[1]The term exponent is used to denote a number raised to a specified power. That is, an exponent of 2 indicates a number raised to the second power, or a number multiplied by itself twice. Thus $5^2 = 5 \times 5 = 25$, and $4^3 = 4 \times 4 \times 4 = 64$.

The decimal numbering system, as indicated, has ten unique digits, 0 to 9. To represent the numbers 0 to 9 we merely use the digits 0 to 9. To represent the next number, however, we cannot use an additional digit, since no additional digit exists. Instead, we proceed with the next position (10's position) by putting a 1 there and initializing the units position at zero. Thus we have:

0
1
2
.
.
.
9 → initialize units position; add 1 to 10's position
10
11
.
.
.
19

With 1 more than 19, we initialize the units position at zero again and add 1 to the 10's position. Thus we have:

19 → initialize units position; add 1 to 10's position
20
.
.
.
29 → initialize units position; add 1 to 10's position
30
.
.
.
99 → initialize units position; initialize 10's position; add 1 to
     100's position
100

When we have utilized all digits in the units and 10's positions (99) we proceed to the next position, the 100's, and begin again by initializing units and 10's at zero: 100.

While this entire introduction may seem trite and obvious, we shall see that the basic elements are similar in all positional numbering systems.

III. Binary Numbers

The binary numbering system is a *base 2* system where only the digits 0 and 1 are used. This is ideally suited to computer processing, where, you will recall, 0 is used to represent an off-state and 1 is used to represent an on-state.

105
DATA
REPRESENTATION
AND COMPUTER
NUMBERING
SYSTEMS

Using the binary numbering system, all numbers are represented by a series of 0's and 1's. Let us consider first the logical manner in which numbers are incremented using this system and then we will proceed to the positional representation of binary numbers.

A. Numeric Representation

With only two digits, we can only represent the numbers 0 and 1 using a single digit. To represent a 2 we must use the next position and initialize the units position at 0. Thus 10 in binary, or base 2, is a 2 in decimal. A 3 would be 11; to represent a 4 we must initialize these two first positions and place a 1 in the third position. Thus 100 in binary is a 4 in decimal. A 5 would be 101. Notice that the sequence is 0, 1, then proceed to the next position and initialize (10, 11, 100, and so on).

BINARY	DECIMAL
0	0
1	1
10	2
11	3
100	4
101	5
110	6
111	7
1000	8
.	.
.	.
.	.

Notice that any decimal number can be represented by a sequence of 0's and 1's in the binary system, but that it generally takes far more digits in the binary system to represent a number than in the decimal system.

Let us now consider the *positional* attribute of binary numbers. You will recall that the decimal or base 10 system has the following positional values:

...	10^3	10^2	10^1	10^0	EXPONENTIAL VALUE OF POSITION
	1000	100	10	1	INTEGER VALUE OF POSITION

That is, a 1 in the second position and a 0 in the units position (10) is the number after 9. When there are no more single digits, we proceed to the next position, initializing the first position with 0.

Since this system has a base 10, each position has a value that is a factor of 10. The first position is 10^0 or 1, the second is 10^1 or 10, ..., the seventh position would be 10^6 or 1,000,000.

The binary numbering system has a base of 2. Thus each position has a value that is a factor of 2. We have then:

...	2^4	2^3	2^2	2^1	2^0	EXPONENTIAL VALUE OF POSITION
	16	8	4	2	1	INTEGER VALUE OF POSITION

You will recall that any number raised to the zero power is 1; 2^1 is 2; 2^2 is 2×2 or 4; 2^3 is $2 \times 2 \times 2$ or 8, and so on.

The two binary digits are 0 and 1. To represent the number 2 we must use the next position. Thus 10 in binary is 2 in decimal. That is:

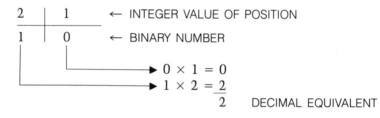

$$
\begin{array}{c|c}
2 & 1 \\
\hline
1 & 0
\end{array}
$$

← INTEGER VALUE OF POSITION

← BINARY NUMBER

$0 \times 1 = 0$
$1 \times 2 = \underline{2}$
$ 2$ DECIMAL EQUIVALENT

We say, then, $10_2 = 2_{10}$ (10 in base 2 = 2 in base 10).

B. Determining the Decimal Equivalent of a Binary Number

Thus all positional numbering systems are similar. To obtain the decimal equivalent of a number in any base, multiply the digits by their positional values and add the results.

Example 1 $1001_2 = (?)_{10}$

Find the decimal equivalent of 1001 in binary (represented as 1001_2, where the subscript denotes the base).

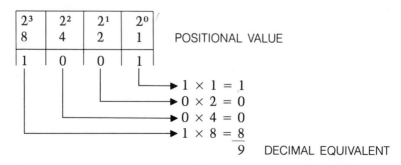

2^3	2^2	2^1	2^0	
8	4	2	1	POSITIONAL VALUE
1	0	0	1	

$1 \times 1 = 1$
$0 \times 2 = 0$
$0 \times 4 = 0$
$1 \times 8 = \underline{8}$
$ 9$ DECIMAL EQUIVALENT

Thus $1001_2 = 9_{10}$. We can simplify this calculation by eliminating all multiplications where 0 is a factor. Thus we have

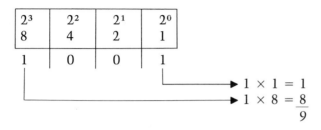

107
DATA
REPRESENTATION
AND COMPUTER
NUMBERING
SYSTEMS

In short, the binary digit 8 and the binary digit 1 are "on," the others are "off." That is, the 8-bit and the 1-bit are on, where bit is an abbreviation for *binary digit*.

Example 2 $1110_2 = (?)_{10}$

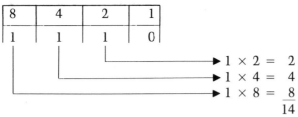

Solution: $(14)_{10}$

Example 3 $11101_2 = (?)_{10}$

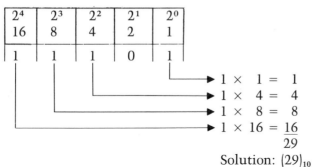

Solution: $(29)_{10}$

Thus, given any binary number we can find its decimal equivalent by the following technique.

Given Binary Number—Find Decimal Equivalent
1. Determine positional value of each digit.
2. Add the positional values for all positions that contain a 1.

Self-Evaluating Quiz

1. The decimal system has a base of (no.) _____ while the binary system has a base of (no.) _____ .

2. Since numbers are frequently represented within the computer as a series of on-off switches, the _____ numbering system is exceedingly well suited to computer processing.

3. (T or F) All numbers must be fed into the computer in binary form.

4. (T or F) There are numbers that can be expressed in base 2 that cannot be expressed in base 10.

5. (T or F) In general, more binary digits are necessary to represent a number than are necessary in the decimal numbering system.

6. $2^2 =$ _____.

7. $2^5 =$ _____.

8. $2^0 =$ _____.

9. $10^0 =$ _____.

10. Find the decimal equivalent for each of the following:
   a. 11011_2
   b. 1101_2
   c. 1111_2
   d. 11001_2
   e. 11111_2

Solutions

1. 10; 2

2. binary or base 2

3. F—decimal numbers as well as binary numbers can be entered as input.

4. F

5. T

6. $2^2 = 2 \times 2 = 4$

7. $2^5 = 2 \times 2 \times 2 \times 2 \times 2 = 32$

8. 1—any number raised to the zero power is 1.

9. 1

10. a. $11011_2 =$

2^4	2^3	2^2	2^1	2^0
16	8	4	2	1

$= 16 + 8 + 2 = 1 = 27_{10}$

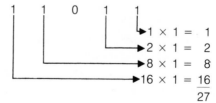

$1 \times 1 = 1$
$2 \times 1 = 2$
$8 \times 1 = 8$
$16 \times 1 = \underline{16}$
27

b. $1101_2 =$

8	4	2	1
1	1	0	1

$= 1 + 4 + 8 = 13_{10}$

c. $1111_2 =$

8	4	2	1
1	1	1	1

$= 8 + 4 + 2 + 1 = 15_{10}$

109
DATA
REPRESENTATION
AND COMPUTER
NUMBERING
SYSTEMS

d. $11001_2 =$

16	8	4	2	1
1	1	0	0	1

$= 16 + 8 + 1 = 25_{10}$

e. $11111_2 =$

16	8	4	2	1
1	1	1	1	1

$= 16 + 8 + 4 + 2 + 1 = 31_{10}$

C. Determining the Binary Equivalent of a Decimal Number

Computers generally represent numeric data in binary form or a variation of this form where digits are indicated by a series of on-off switches, circuits, or magnetized spots. Keep in mind that numeric data is entered, as input, in standard decimal form and then converted by the computer itself to a binary representation. Before the data is produced as output it is again converted to decimal form.

Thus far, we have some idea of the way in which binary numbers are converted into decimal numbers. In this section, we will learn the manner in which the binary equivalent of a decimal number may be determined.

This conversion process is a relatively simple task when small numbers are used. That is, we merely employ the positional values of binary numbers to find the right combination of digits.

Example 1 $10_{10} = (?)_2$

This example concerns itself with determining what combination of 1, 2, 4, 8, 16, 32, ... will equal 10.

It is clear that we do not need to use more than four binary digits to represent 10_{10}, since the fifth positional value is 16 which is greater than 10_{10}. Hence, we must determine what combination of 8, 4, 2, 1 will equal 10.

There is only one such combination. The numbers $8 + 2 = 10$. Thus our binary equivalent is

8	4	2	1
1	0	1	0

In order to represent the decimal number 10 in binary form, the 8-bit (or *binary digit*) and the 2-bit are on while the others are off.

Thus $10_{10} = 1010_2$.

Example 2 $(14)_{10} = (?)_2$

Here, again, we use four binary digits since the next position has value 16, which exceeds the required quantity. Again, we must determine what combination of 8, 4, 2, 1 will produce 14.

There is only one such combination: 8, 4, 2 bits are on $(8 + 4 + 2 = 14)$, while the 1-bit is off.

Thus $(14)_{10} = (1110)_2$.

Example 3 $(23)_{10} = (?)_2$

Here, we must use a combination of the numbers 16, 8, 4, 2, 1 which will produce 23. We must determine which bits are "on." The 16-bit must be on, since 8, 4, 2, 1 bits can produce a maximum decimal number of 15. Thus the 16-bit must be on to obtain a number larger than 15. The 8-bit is off since 16-8 produces 24 which exceeds the required number. Thus the 16-4-2-1 bits are on and only the 8-bit is off. We have, then,

$$(23)_{10} = (10111)_2$$

This method of determining the combination of positional values that produces the required number is useful only with small numbers. Consider the task of finding the combination of binary numbers for the decimal number 1087, for example. In short, the above method is too cumbersome for larger decimal numbers.

There is a technique called the *remainder method* which may be used to convert a decimal number to any other numbering system. The technique is as follows:

Remainder Method for Converting Decimal Numbers into any Other Base

1.   Divide the decimal number by the base (for a binary equivalent, we divide by 2).
2.   Indicate the remainder, which will be either 0 or 1 in the case of binary division.
3.   Continue dividing into each quotient (result of previous division) until the divide operation produces a zero quotient or result.
4.   The equivalent number in the base desired is the numeric *remainders* reading from the last division to the first.

Several examples will serve to clarify this procedure.

Example 4 $(38)_{10} = (?)_2$

REMAINDER

1. begin by dividing number by the base 2.

$$2 \overline{)\ 38} \quad 19$$ 0   2. Indicate the remainder.

3. divide previous result, 19, by base.

$$2 \overline{)\ 19} \quad 9$$ 1   4. Indicate the remainder.

$$2 \overline{)\ 9} \quad 4$$ 1

$$2 \overline{)\ 4} \quad 2$$ 0

111

DATA
REPRESENTATION
AND COMPUTER
NUMBERING
SYSTEMS

indicates $\quad$ 2 $\overline{|\ 2\ }^{\,1}$ $\qquad$ 0

the end ————▶ $\overline{\ 0\ }$

$\quad\quad\quad$ 2 $\overline{|\ 1\ }$ $\qquad$ 1

└——— resultant binary number
reads from bottom
to top (100110)

When the divide operation produces a quotient or result of zero, then the process is terminated. The binary equivalent, reading from the last division to the first is:

$$(38)_{10} = (100110)_2$$

We should check our result to insure its accuracy:

$(100110)_2$ should equal $(38)_{10}$

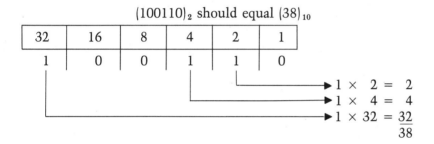

32	16	8	4	2	1
1	0	0	1	1	0

$1 \times 2 = 2$
$1 \times 4 = 4$
$1 \times 32 = \underline{32}$
$ 38$

Using the remainder method for converting from decimal to binary, it is a more efficient procedure to perform the first divide operation at the bottom of the work sheet and work up. The following is exactly equivalent to Example 4 above:

REMAINDER

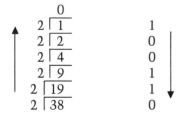

$\qquad$ $\overline{\ 0\ }$

2 $\overline{|\ 1\ }$ $\qquad$ 1

2 $\overline{|\ 2\ }$ $\qquad$ 0

2 $\overline{|\ 4\ }$ $\qquad$ 0

2 $\overline{|\ 9\ }$ $\qquad$ 1

2 $\overline{|\ 19\ }$ $\qquad$ 1

2 $\overline{|\ 38\ }$ $\qquad$ 0

In this way, the result is read from top to bottom: $(100110)_2$.

Example 5 $\quad (67)_{10} = (?)_2$

To find the binary equivalent by determining the combination of positional values can be a long and arduous procedure where the numbers are large. Instead we may use the remainder method:

REMAINDER

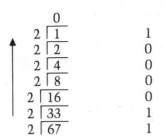

$$
\begin{array}{c|c}
 & 0 \\
2 \overline{\smash{\big)}\,1} & 1 \\
2 \overline{\smash{\big)}\,2} & 0 \\
2 \overline{\smash{\big)}\,4} & 0 \\
2 \overline{\smash{\big)}\,8} & 0 \\
2 \overline{\smash{\big)}\,16} & 0 \\
2 \overline{\smash{\big)}\,33} & 1 \\
2 \overline{\smash{\big)}\,67} & 1 \\
\end{array}
$$

Thus the result, reading from top to bottom is: $(1000011)_2 = (67)_{10}$. All operations should be checked for accuracy. Let us make certain that $(1000011)_2$ is indeed equivalent to $(67)_{10}$.

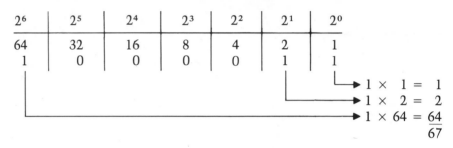

2^6	2^5	2^4	2^3	2^2	2^1	2^0
64	32	16	8	4	2	1
1	0	0	0	0	1	1

$$1 \times 1 = 1$$
$$1 \times 2 = 2$$
$$1 \times 64 = \underline{64}$$
$$67$$

Self-Evaluating Quiz

1. The binary numbering system uses _____ digits.
2. The digits used in the binary numbering system are _____ and _____.
3. The binary numbering system is ideally suited to computer processing because the digit _____ represents the _____-state and the digit _____ represents the _____-state.
4. The term *bit* is an abbreviation for _____ _____.
5. The decimal and binary numbering systems are called _____ numbering systems since the location or position of each digit is significant.
6. The binary numbering system has a base of _____.
7. The binary number 1011 is equivalent to the decimal number _____.
8. The binary number 110110 is equivalent to the decimal number _____.
9. The binary number 11101 is equivalent to the decimal number _____.
10. The largest decimal number that can be represented by four binary digits is _____.
11. The binary equivalent of the decimal number 86 is _____.
12. The binary equivalent of the decimal number 101 is _____.
13. The method used to convert a decimal number to a number in another system is called the _____ _____.

Solutions

113

DATA
REPRESENTATION
AND COMPUTER
NUMBERING
SYSTEMS

1. two
2. 0;1
3. 0; "off"
   1; "on"
4. *binary digit*
5. positional
6. *2*

7. 11:

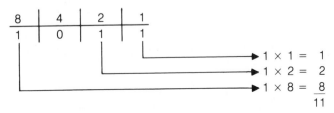

8	4	2	1
1	0	1	1

$$1 \times 1 = 1$$
$$1 \times 2 = 2$$
$$1 \times 8 = \underline{8}$$
$$11$$

8. 54:

32	16	8	4	2	1
1	1	0	1	1	0

$$1 \times 2 = 2$$
$$1 \times 4 = 4$$
$$1 \times 16 = 16$$
$$1 \times 32 = \underline{32}$$
$$54$$

9. 29:

16	8	4	2	1
1	1	1	0	1

$$16 + 8 + 4 + 1 = 29$$

10. 15

11. $(1010110)_2$ REMAINDER

```
      0
  2 | 1       1
  2 | 2       0
  2 | 5       1
  2 | 10      0
  2 | 21      1
  2 | 43      1
  2 | 86      0
```

12. $(1100101)_2$ REMAINDER

```
      0
  2 | 1       1
  2 | 3       1
  2 | 6       0
  2 | 12      0
  2 | 25      1
  2 | 50      0
  2 | 101     1
```

114

DATA
PROCESSING
FUNDAMENTALS
AND HARDWARE

13. remainder method

D. Addition and Subtraction of Binary Numbers

Thus far, we have seen that binary numbers are ideally suited to computer processing since they can be used to represent the on-off state of circuits. An "on" condition in storage can be indicated by a 1; an "off" condition by a 0.

We have learned how to convert numbers from binary to decimal by utilizing the positional values and how to convert from decimal to binary by using the remainder method.

This section will consider the addition and subtraction of binary numbers as they are handled by the computer.

The addition of binary numbers follows a simple schematic:

Addition of Binary Numbers

For each position:

1. $1 + 0 = 1$
2. $0 + 1 = 1$
3. $0 + 0 = 0$
4. $1 + 1 = 0$ with a carry of 1 to the next position.

Example 1 $10_2 + 11_2 = (?)_2$

BINARY	DECIMAL
10	2
+ 11	+3
101	5

Units position: $0 + 1 = 1$
2's position: $1 + 1 = 0$ with carry of 1
4's position: carry of 1 + zero (nothing) $= 1$

Thus, we have 101, as the sum.

Example 2 $1101_2 + 1010_2 = (?)_2$

BINARY	DECIMAL
1101	13
+ 1010	+ 10
10111	23

Notice that in each example, we checked our solution by converting the binary numbers to decimal and then determining if the decimal sum was equal to the binary total. If not, then an error was made in the binary addition.

The process of binary subtraction is somewhat more complicated than addition. Note that a computer does not perform simple subtraction in the manner that we customarily perform it. It performs subtraction by a series of negative additions. In this way, the same addition mechanisms can be used for subtraction as well.

115
DATA
REPRESENTATION
AND COMPUTER
NUMBERING
SYSTEMS

Subtraction of Binary Numbers (General Rule)

1. *Complement* the subtrahend (number to be subtracted) by converting all 1's to 0's and all 0's to 1's.
2. Proceed as in addition.
3. Cross off the high-order or leftmost digit (a 1 when the number is positive) and add a 1 to the total (called end-around-carry).

Example 3 $1101_2 - 1000_2 = (?)_2$

BINARY	DECIMAL	
1101	13	Minuend
−1000	− 8	− Subtrahend
	5	Difference

1. Complement the subtrahend or number to be subtracted:
    Complement of 1000 = 0111 converting all 0's to 1's and all 1's to 0's.

2. Proceed as in addition using complemented value as factor to be added.
    $$\begin{array}{r} 1101 \\ +0111 \\ \hline 10100 \end{array}$$

3. Cross off high-order 1 and add it to result:
    $$\begin{array}{r} \cancel{1}0100 \\ + \quad 1 \\ \hline 0101 \end{array}$$

    Answer is 0101_2 or 101_2 since leftmost 0 has no value.
    Since $101_2 = 5_{10}$, the binary subtraction solution is correct.

Example 4 $11101_2 - 11000_2 = (?)_2$

BINARY	DECIMAL
11101	29
−11000	−24
	5

1. Complement the subtrahend:
    Complement of 11000 = 00111

2. Proceed as in addition:

$$\begin{array}{r} 11101 \\ +00111 \\ \hline 100100 \end{array}$$

3. End-around-carry:

$$\begin{array}{r} 100100 \\ + \quad \longrightarrow 1 \\ \hline 0101 \end{array}$$

This procedure for subtraction, which is the method used by the computer, is called *complementation and end-around-carry.*

In the above examples, notice that the subtrahend, or number to be subtracted, was always smaller than the number to be subtracted from. If, however, the subtrahend is larger than the minuend, or number being subtracted from, we must modify Step 3 in the rules for subtraction.

Subtraction of Binary Numbers
(If subtrahend larger than minuend)
1. Complement the subtrahend (number to be subtracted) by converting all 1's to 0's and all 0's to 1's.
2. Proceed as in addition.
3. Complement the result and place a negative sign in front of the answer.

Example 5

BINARY	DECIMAL
11000	24
−11101	−29
	− 5

1. Complement the subtrahend:
    Complement of 11101 = 00010

2. Proceed as in addition:

$$\begin{array}{r} 11000 \\ +00010 \\ \hline 11010 \end{array}$$

3. Complement the result and add negative sign:
    Complement of 11010 = 00101
    Answer = −00101 or -5_{10}

Example 6

BINARY	DECIMAL
1101	13
−11001	−25
	−12

1. Complement the subtrahend:
    Complement of 11001 = 00110

117
DATA
REPRESENTATION
AND COMPUTER
NUMBERING
SYSTEMS

2. Proceed as in addition:
$$\begin{array}{r} 1101 \\ +00110 \\ \hline 10011 \end{array}$$

3. Complement the result and add negative sign:
    Complement of 10011 = 01100
    Answer = -1100 or -12_{10}

Self-Evaluating Quiz

1. The addition of 1 + 0 or 0 + 1, in binary, results in _____.
2. The addition of 1 + 1, in binary, results in _____.
3. The method used by the computer for subtraction of binary numbers is called _____.
4. $\begin{array}{r} 11011 \\ +10011 \\ \hline \end{array}$

5. $\begin{array}{r} 11111 \\ +11011 \\ \hline \end{array}$

6. $\begin{array}{r} 111 \\ +101 \\ \hline 110 \end{array}$

7. $\begin{array}{r} 11011 \\ -10011 \\ \hline \end{array}$

8. $\begin{array}{r} 111011 \\ -110001 \\ \hline \end{array}$

9. $\begin{array}{r} 010110 \\ -110001 \\ \hline \end{array}$

Solutions

1. 1
2. 0 with a carry of 1
3. complementation and end-around-carry
4. 101110 (27 + 19 = 46)
5. 111010 (31 + 27 = 58)
6. 10010 (7 + 5 + 6 = 18)
7. $\begin{array}{r} 11011 \\ +01100 \\ \hline \end{array}$ 27–19 = 8
    $\cancel{1}00111$
    $\quad\llcorner\!\!\longrightarrow 1$
    $\overline{\quad 1000}$

8.   111011
      +001110   59−49 = 10
      1001001
            →1
       1010

9.   010110
      +001110
      100100;   complement = 011011;

answer = −11011; (22 − 49 = −27)

*IV. Octal Numbers

Only on specially constructed engineering or scientific computers are pure binary codes utilized. On these computers, alphanumeric input is automatically converted by the computer to binary, all operations are performed and the data is then converted back to alphanumeric form as output. All displays of storage images and addresses are in binary.

Pure binary representation has, however, one distinct disadvantage. It requires many more positions for data than any other numbering system. To represent the two-digit decimal number 86, for example, we must use seven binary digits (1010110). Thus most commercial computers *group* binary numbers in an effort to conserve storage. IBM, specifically, utilizes the hexadecimal or base 16 system that groups four binary digits to form one hexadecimal digit. This system will be discussed in the next section.

Here we will discuss the *octal* numbering system, or base 8 system, used by other computer manufacturers. We will see that this numbering system can be used to represent *three* binary digits as a single octal number. In this way, we can significantly reduce the number of digits required to represent any number and still maintain the binary concept. That is, we can still utilize the on-off electrical impulse concept of binary numbers to represent numbers:

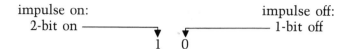

impulse on: impulse off:
  2-bit on ─────────▼ ▼───────── 1-bit off
                  1   0

It should be noted here that while some computer specialists and businessmen are unfamiliar with binary, octal, and hexadecimal numbering systems, knowledge of these concepts can be very helpful in debugging programs, understanding how a computer operates, and selecting computer equipment.

A. Representing Numeric Data with Octal Numbers

The octal numbering system uses the eight digits 0 to 7 to represent any number. The decimal numbers 0 to 7, respectively, are represented by the corresponding octal numbers 0 to 7. The decimal number 8 is equal to 10 in the octal code. In the decimal numbering system, each positional value is a factor of 10; in the binary numbering system, each positional value is a factor of 2. In the octal numbering system, as you might expect, each positional value is a factor of 8:

119
DATA
REPRESENTATION
AND COMPUTER
NUMBERING
SYSTEMS

POSITIONAL VALUES

. . .	8^2	8^1	8^0	In exponential form
. . .	64	8	1	In decimal form

In the octal numbering system, as in all such systems, we write numbers in sequence until all digits in a specific position are exhausted. Then we initialize the given position with 0 and add 1 to the next position. Consider the following pattern in the octal numbering system:

DECIMAL	OCTAL	
0	0	
1	1	
2	2	
.	.	
.	.	
.	.	
7	7	$7_8 + 1_8 = 10_8$
8	10	
9	11	
.	.	
.	.	
.	.	
15	17	$17_8 + 1_8 = 20_8$
16	20	
.	.	
.	.	
.	.	
23	27	$27_8 + 1_8 = 30_8$
24	30	
.	.	
.	.	
.	.	
63	77	$77_8 + 1_8 = 100_8$
64	100	
65	101	
.	.	

.
.
71
72

.
.
107
110

$107_8 + 1_8 = 110_8$

B. Determining the Decimal Equivalent of an Octal Number

To determine the decimal equivalent of any octal number we multiply the positional value by the represented digit and add the results:

Example 1 $(725)_8 = (?)_{10}$

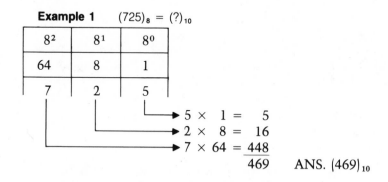

8^2	8^1	8^0
64	8	1
7	2	5

$5 \times 1 = 5$
$2 \times 8 = 16$
$7 \times 64 = \underline{448}$
469 ANS. $(469)_{10}$

Example 2 $(1436)_8 = (?)_{10}$

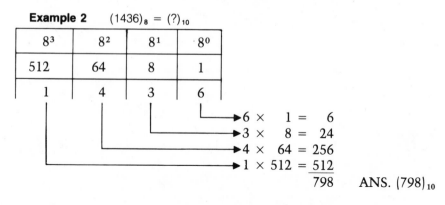

8^3	8^2	8^1	8^0
512	64	8	1
1	4	3	6

$6 \times 1 = 6$
$3 \times 8 = 24$
$4 \times 64 = 256$
$1 \times 512 = \underline{512}$
798 ANS. $(798)_{10}$

In summary, to find the decimal equivalent of an octal number, we multiply each digit by its positional value.

Self-Evaluating Quiz

Find the decimal equivalent of the following octal numbers:

1. $125_8 = (?)_{10}$
2. $236_8 = (?)_{10}$
3. $1213_8 = (?)_{10}$
4. $1419_8 = (?)_{10}$

Solutions

121
DATA
REPRESENTATION
AND COMPUTER
NUMBERING
SYSTEMS

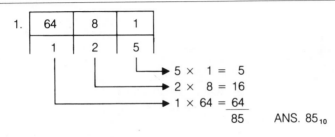

1. $\text{ANS. } 85_{10}$

$5 \times 1 = 5$
$2 \times 8 = 16$
$1 \times 64 = \underline{64}$
85

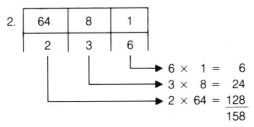

2. $\text{ANS. } 158_{10}$

$6 \times 1 = 6$
$3 \times 8 = 24$
$2 \times 64 = \underline{128}$
158

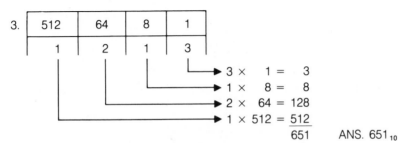

3. $\text{ANS. } 651_{10}$

$3 \times 1 = 3$
$1 \times 8 = 8$
$2 \times 64 = 128$
$1 \times 512 = \underline{512}$
651

4. This is a trick question! It should have occurred to you that 1419_8 is not a valid number since octal numbers use digits 0–7 only. Since 1419 contains a "9" it is invalid.

C. Determining the Octal Equivalent of a Decimal Number

To find the *binary* equivalent of a *decimal* number, we use the *remainder method*, dividing by the base number 2:

$$(15)_{10} = (?)_2$$

REMAINDER

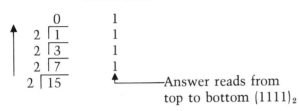

Answer reads from top to bottom $(1111)_2$

To find the *octal* equivalent of a *decimal* number, we again use the remainder method, this time dividing by the base 8:

Example 1 $(385)_{10} = (?)_8$

REMAINDER

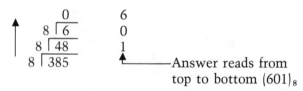

$$\begin{array}{r} 0 \\ 8\,\lceil\,6 \\ 8\,\lceil\,48 \\ 8\,\lceil\,385 \end{array} \qquad \begin{array}{l} 6 \\ 0 \\ 1 \end{array}$$

—Answer reads from
top to bottom $(601)_8$

To check our work we should determine if our octal number 601 is equal to the decimal 385:

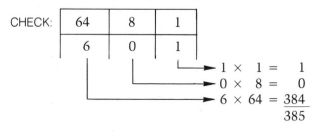

CHECK:	64	8	1
	6	0	1

$$1 \times 1 = 1$$
$$0 \times 8 = 0$$
$$6 \times 64 = \underline{384}$$
$$385$$

Example 2 $(1326)_{10} = (?)_8$

REMAINDER

$$\begin{array}{r} 0 \\ 8\,\lceil\,2 \\ 8\,\lceil\,20 \\ 8\,\lceil\,165 \\ 8\,\lceil\,1326 \end{array} \qquad \begin{array}{l} 2 \\ 4 \\ 5 \\ 6 \end{array}$$

—Answer reads from
top to bottom $(2456)_8$

Thus, to convert from the decimal numbering system to any other system, we may use the remainder method, using the base of the latter as a divisor. To convert a decimal number to an octal number, we divide by 8, using the remainder of each division to produce a solution.

Self-Evaluating Quiz

Find the octal equivalent of the following decimal numbers:

1. $221_{10} = (?)_8$
2. $143_{10} = (?)_8$
3. $206_{10} = (?)_8$

Solutions

1.

$$\begin{array}{r} 0 \\ 8\,\lceil\,3 \\ 8\,\lceil\,27 \\ 8\,\lceil\,221 \end{array} \qquad \begin{array}{l} 3 \\ 3 \\ 5 \end{array}$$

ANS. 335_8

123

DATA
REPRESENTATION
AND COMPUTER
NUMBERING
SYSTEMS

2.
$$\begin{array}{cc} 0 & 2 \\ \overline{8 \lfloor 2} & 1 \\ \overline{8 \lfloor 17} & 7 \\ \overline{8 \lfloor 143} & \end{array}$$

ANS. 217_8

3.
$$\begin{array}{cc} 0 & 3 \\ \overline{8 \lfloor 3} & 1 \\ \overline{8 \lfloor 25} & 6 \\ \overline{8 \lfloor 206} & \end{array}$$

ANS. 316_8

D. Converting Octal to Binary and Binary to Octal

At the beginning of this section, we learned that octal numbers are used to represent data on many computers in place of binary numbers. Binary numbers are uniquely suited for computers since each position can be represented as a 1 or 0, that is, an on- or off-state of an electrical impulse. Such numbers, however, are often cumbersome to deal with, since many binary numbers are required to represent relatively small decimal numbers. To represent 26, for example, we must use *five* binary digits, 11010. To make more efficient use of computer storage, we can group binary numbers in some pattern. The octal numbering system can be represented as a group of *three* binary digits, or bits. That is, any three binary digits can be represented as a single octal number.

Example 1 $(100111)_2 = (?)_8$

4	2	1	4	2	1
1	0	0	1	1	1
	4			7	

ANS. $(47)_8$

In short, we subdivide binary numbers into groups of threes, with the positional value of each group represented as 4   2   1. We then determine the octal equivalent.

Example 2 $(11011)_2 = (?)_8$
This number does not contain two complete groups of three. You will recall, however, that 11011 is the same as *0*11011, since high-order or leading zeros have no significant value. 011011 does contain two complete groups:

4	2	1	4	2	1
0	1	1	0	1	1
	3			3	

ANS. $(33)_8$

Note that a computer usually uses the binary numbering system since each circuit in storage can be represented as on or off depending on whether an electrical current or impulse is present. Data on many such computers can be represented for display purposes on core image printouts in the *octal system*. In this way, the computer can easily print out data by combining binary numbers into groups of threes. This is a relatively simple conversion and requires far less circuitry than converting binary numbers into *decimal* numbers for display purposes. Thus if a storage position contained 11111110, and the computer were asked to display this position, it would be a simple task to display it in the OCTAL system:

011	111	110
3	7	6

In short, many computers utilize the octal numbering system for displaying core image printouts to programmers and operators. That is, data that is currently in the computer can be accessed by a programmer or operator if he or she can read the octal code. Such core images are usually displayed when a program has an error.

Computers accept normal alphanumeric or decimal codes and print reports or write other forms of output in decimal, as well; but instead of converting binary numbers to *decimal*, which can be very cumbersome because of the number of digits, they convert to *octal* first and then to decimal.

Example 1 $(110111110011011)_2 = (?)_{10}$

To use the normal method of multiplying the digit by its positional value is, indeed, cumbersome:

16384	8192	4096	2048	1024	512	256	128	64	32	16	8	4	2	1
1	1	0	1	1	1	1	1	0	0	1	1	0	1	1

$$\begin{array}{r}
1 \\
2 \\
8 \\
16 \\
128 \\
256 \\
512 \\
1024 \\
2048 \\
8192 \\
\underline{16384} \\
(28,571)_{10} \quad \text{ANS.}
\end{array}$$

It would be far simpler to determine the octal equivalent of the above and then to determine the decimal number.

I. CONVERT TO OCTAL

125

DATA
REPRESENTATION
AND COMPUTER
NUMBERING
SYSTEMS

110	111	110	011	011
6	7	6	3	3

4096	512	64	8	1
6	7	6	3	3

$$3 \times 1 = 3$$
$$3 \times 8 = 24$$
$$6 \times 64 = 384$$
$$7 \times 512 = 3584$$
$$6 \times 4096 = 24576$$
$$28571$$

ANS. $(28571)_{10}$

Thus, to simplify conversions, many computers utilize the octal numbering system. In fact, most operations could be performed in the octal system, to further simplify computer procedures.

It is just as simple as the above to convert from octal back into binary. Thus a computer can convert a number from binary to octal, perform the required operations, and convert back again into binary. To convert from an octal number to a binary number, we merely represent each octal number as three binary numbers, as shown below.

Example 2 $(725)_8 = (?)_2$

7	2	5
(421)	(421)	(421)
111	010	101

ANS. $(111010101)_2$

Example 3 $(302)_8 = (?)_2$

3	0	2
011	000	010

$= (011000010)_2$ or $(11000010)_2$ since the high-order 0 has no significance.

E. Addition and Subtraction of Octal Numbers

Thus far we have seen the conversions required from any octal, binary, or decimal number to any of the other systems. Let us now see how to perform the arithmetic operations of addition and subtraction of octal numbers.

To add two octal numbers, we proceed as we do in the decimal system, keeping in mind, however, that if any addition produces an octal number in excess of 7, we must utilize the next position: $8_{10} = 10_8$, $9_{10} = 11_8$, and so on.

Example 1 $(73)_8 + (24)_8 = (?)_8$

```
   73
+  24
  117
```

ANS. $(117)_8$

Example 2 $(243)_8 + (745)_8 = (?)_8$

```
   243
+  745
  1210
```

ANS. $(1210)_8$

We should check our work by converting each of the octal numbers into the decimal system to determine if, in fact, the addition is correct.

To subtract in the octal numbering system, we may use the complementation and end-around-carry method used in the subtraction of binary numbers: $(715)_8 - (603)_8 = (?)_8$

```
   715
 - 603
```

1. COMPLEMENT THE SUBTRAHEND: 174
    603 + (ITS COMPLEMENT) = 777
    (*ANY NO.*) + (ITS COMPLEMENT) = 777

2. PROCEED AS IN ADDITION
    ```
       715
    +  174
      1111
    ```

3. END-AROUND-CARRY

```
    (1)111
       ➔1
    ─────────
       112        ANS. (112)_8
```

F. Illustration of Use

It is very useful to be able to perform arithmetic operations in the octal numbering system when utilizing a machine that employs this code. Suppose, for example, that a computer program has a "bug" or error in it. While the program is running, a computer display indicates the following:

PROGRAM CHECK INTERRUPTION 5721.

127
DATA
REPRESENTATION
AND COMPUTER
NUMBERING
SYSTEMS

This implies that at storage position 5721 there is an error.

It is possible to find this error on a program listing which indicates storage positions of each instruction. The address of the instruction often cannot, however, be determined directly. In many cases, the program listing indicates each instruction address in relative terms; that is, relative to the loading point of the program. The computer must relocate each program at the time of execution to allow room for the supervisor and any other necessary programs or subroutines. Thus while the program listing may denote instructions from storage positions 0000 to 3653, which are the available numbers at compile time, the computer may actually place the program in storage positions 3012–6665. For many computers, these addresses are noted on program listings and displayed in the octal numbering system. Thus to find the instruction at 5721, we must first subtract the starting address of the program, 3012. Since the program *listing* begins at 0000 we must find the *absolute* error point, which is determined by subtracting the actual or relocated starting address from the actual program error point.

$$\begin{array}{r} 5721 \\ -\,3012 \\ \hline \end{array}$$

1. COMPLEMENT THE SUBTRAHEND: 4765

2. PROCEED AS IN ADDITION
$$\begin{array}{r} 5721 \\ +\ 4765 \\ \hline 12706 \end{array}$$

3. END-AROUND-CARRY

(1)2706
  └──▶1
$$\overline{2707}$$

Thus 2707 on the program listing would be the error point, where the error may be found.

In short, for computer purposes, we can think of the octal numbering system as a shorthand method for representing binary numbers. Since each group of three binary numbers can be used to represent a single octal number, a computer can eliminate much of the cumbersome quality of binary numbers by representing some of its internal computer codes in the octal system.

Self-Evaluating Quiz

1. The octal numbering system has a base of _____, using numbers _____.

2. The major advantage of octal numbers for computers is _____ .

3. The use of binary numbers by computers is advantageous because _____ .

4. Binary numbers, for display purposes, however, are often _____ .

5. Three binary numbers may be used to represent _____ .

6. One octal number may be used to represent (no.) _____ binary digits or bits.

7. $(8975)_{10} = (?)_8$

8. $(7099)_{10} = (?)_8$

9. $(7576)_8 = (?)_{10}$

10. $(6607)_8 = (?)_{10}$

11. $(111011111)_2 = (?)_8$

12. $(11110000110)_2 = (?)_8$

13. $(7552)_8 = (?)_2$

14. $(66051)_8 = (?)_2$

15. $(11111111011111111)_2 = (?)_{10}$
    HINT. Convert first to the octal system.

16. Suppose you are helping to debug a program run on an octal computer that has an error at storage location 7562. The program listing has instructions that have absolute addresses beginning at 0000. The program has been relocated to start at 3300. Find the absolute error point that can then be found on the program listing.

Solutions

1. 8; 0–7
2. they may be used to represent binary numbers by combining them into groups of threes
3. each binary digit or bit can be used to represent the on (1) or off (0) state of a circuit
4. cumbersome because many digits are required to represent relatively small decimal numbers
5. a single octal number
6. three

7. $(8975)_{10} = (?)_8$

129

DATA
REPRESENTATION
AND COMPUTER
NUMBERING
SYSTEMS

```
          0        REMAINDER
     8 | 2          2
     8 | 17         1
     8 | 140        4
     8 | 1121       1
     8 | 8975       7
```

ANS. $(21417)_8$

8. $(7099)_{10} = (?)_8$

```
          0        REMAINDER
     8 | 1          1
     8 | 13         5
     8 | 110        6
     8 | 887        7
     8 | 7099       3
```

ANS. $(15673)_8$

9. $(7576)_8 = (?)_{10}$

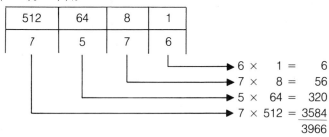

ANS. $(3966)_{10}$

10. $(6607)_8 = (?)_{10}$

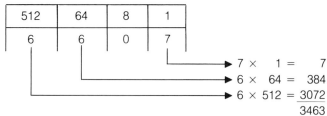

ANS. $(3463)_{10}$

11. $(111011111)_2 = (?)_8$

```
   111   |   011   |   111
    7    |    3    |    7
```

ANS. $(737)_8$

12. $(11110000110)_2 = (?)_8$

```
   011   |   110   |   000   |   110
    3    |    6    |    0    |    6
```

ANS. $(3606)_8$

13. $(7552)_8 = (?)_2$

7	5	5	2
111	101	101	010

ANS. $(111101101010)_2$

14. $(66051)_8 = (?)_2$

6	6	0	5	1
110	110	000	101	001

ANS. $(110110000101001)_2$

15. $(11111111011111111)_2 = (?)_{10}$

I. CONVERT TO OCTAL

011	111	111	011	111	111
3	7	7	3	7	7

$(377377)_8$

II. CONVERT FROM OCTAL TO DECIMAL

32768	4096	512	64	8	1
3	7	7	3	7	7

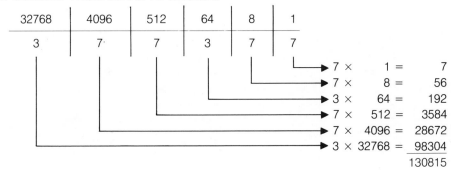

$7 \times 1 = 7$
$7 \times 8 = 56$
$3 \times 64 = 192$
$7 \times 512 = 3584$
$7 \times 4096 = 28672$
$3 \times 32768 = \underline{98304}$
130815

16.   7562
      −3300
       4262

OR USING COMPLEMENTATION AND
END-AROUND-CARRY:
 I. COMPLEMENT SUBTRAHEND 4477
 II. ADD 4477 + 7562 = 14261
 III. END-AROUND-CARRY   (1)4261
                           ──────→1
                            4262

V. Hexadecimal Numbers

A. Representing Numeric Data with Hexadecimal Numbers

We have seen that a computer uses binary numbers rather than decimal numbers to perform arithmetic operations. This is because

131

DATA
REPRESENTATION
AND COMPUTER
NUMBERING
SYSTEMS

the two binary numbers 1 and 0 can be made to correspond to the on-off state of computer circuits.

Note however that it is not feasible for the computer to utilize an entire storage position to represent one binary digit. Binary numbers utilize many positions to represent relatively small numbers. While the decimal number 23 would use two storage positions, one for the 2 and one for the 3, its binary equivalent 10111 would utilize *five* storage positions. Thus to have the computer store a single binary digit in one storage position would make inefficient use of large storage capability.

As we have seen in the previous section, the computer can group together *three* binary digits to produce a single digit in the octal or base 8 numbering system. In this section we will see that *four* binary digits can similarly be grouped together to produce a digit in the base 16 or *hexadecimal* numbering system. In computers that represent data in base 16, each storage position can store two hexadecimal digits with each such digit corresponding to four binary digits.

In base 10 there are ten unique digits 0 to 9; in base 2 there are two unique digits 0 to 1; in base 8 there are eight unique digits 0 to 7. In base 16, as you might expect, there are sixteen unique digits. Since we are familiar only with ten individual digits, the remaining six are represented as letters A to F:

HEXADECIMAL	DECIMAL
0	0
•	•
•	•
•	•
9	9
A	10
B	11
C	12
D	13
E	14
F	15

B. Determining the Decimal Equivalent of a Hexadecimal Number

Note that while the decimal numbering system has only *ten* digits 0 to 9, the hexadecimal numbering system requires six more individual characters to represent numbers 10 to 15. Arbitrarily, the letters A to F were selected to represent these numbers.

To determine the next number after F in the hexadecimal system (or 15 in decimal) we must utilize the next position. That is,

$(10)_{16} = (16)_{10}$. Since the hexadecimal numbering system has a base of 16, each positional value can be expressed as a factor of 16:

. . .	16^3	16^2	16^1	16^0
. . .	4096	256	16	1

To determine, then, $(10)_{16}$ in base 10 we have:

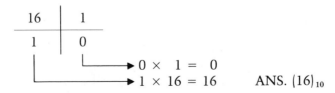

16	1
1	0

$0 \times 1 = 0$
$1 \times 16 = 16$ ANS. $(16)_{10}$

We use the same method as previously discussed to convert from any numbering system to the decimal system: multiply each digit by its positional value and then obtain the sum or total. Do not become confused by the use of hexadecimal digits A to F. When performing any arithmetic operation, merely convert them to their decimal counterpart (10 to 15, respectively).

Example 1 $(AF)_{16} = (?)_{10}$

16	1
A	F

$15 \times 1 = 15$
$10 \times 16 = 160$
175 ANS. $(175)_{10}$

Example 2 $(B6A)_{16} = (?)_{10}$

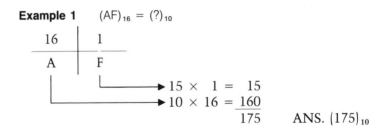

256	16	1
B	6	A

$10 \times 1 = 10$
$6 \times 16 = 96$
$11 \times 256 = 2816$
2922 ANS. $(2922)_{10}$

Self-Evaluating Quiz

Find the decimal equivalent of the following hexadecimal numbers:

1. $(2E)_{16} = (?)_{10}$
2. $(A23)_{16} = (?)_{10}$

Solutions

133

DATA
REPRESENTATION
AND COMPUTER
NUMBERING
SYSTEMS

1.
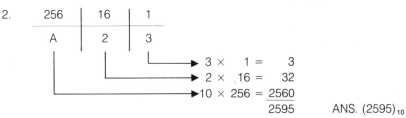

$$14 \times 1 = 14$$
$$2 \times 16 = \underline{32}$$
$$46 \qquad \text{ANS. } (46)_{10}$$

2.

256	16	1
A	2	3

$$3 \times 1 = 3$$
$$2 \times 16 = 32$$
$$10 \times 256 = \underline{2560}$$
$$2595 \qquad \text{ANS. } (2595)_{10}$$

C. Determining the Hexadecimal Equivalent of a Decimal Number

To convert from the hexadecimal numbering system to the decimal system we use the remainder method, by dividing by 16.

Example 1 $(382)_{10} = (?)_{16}$

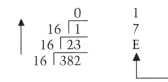

REMAINDER IN
HEX.

$$
\begin{array}{cc}
0 & 1 \\
16\,\overline{\rvert\,1} & 7 \\
16\,\overline{\rvert\,23} & E \\
16\,\overline{\rvert\,382} &
\end{array}
$$

Reading from top to bottom

ANS. $(17E)_{16}$

Example 2 $(1583)_{10} = (?)_{16}$

REMAINDER IN
HEX.

$$
\begin{array}{cc}
0 & 6 \\
16\,\overline{\rvert\,6} & 2 \\
16\,\overline{\rvert\,98} & F \\
16\,\overline{\rvert\,1583} &
\end{array}
$$

ANS. $(62F)_{16}$

Self-Evaluating Quiz

Find the hexadecimal equivalent of the following decimal numbers:

1. $(132)_{10} = (?)_{16}$
2. $(214)_{10} = (?)_{16}$

Solutions

1.

$$\begin{array}{cc} 0 & 8 \\ 16\,\overline{\big|\,8} & 4 \\ 16\,\overline{\big|\,132} & \end{array}$$

ANS. $(84)_{16}$

2.

$$\begin{array}{cc} 0 & D \\ 16\,\overline{\big|\,13} & 6 \\ 16\,\overline{\big|\,214} & \text{ANS. } (D6)_{16} \end{array}$$

D. Addition and Subtraction of Hexadecimal Numbers

Arithmetic operations in hexadecimal are similar to those in other numbering systems. Perform the operation on each column decimally, convert the decimal number to hexadecimal, and proceed.

Example 1 $(BAD)_{16} + (431)_{16} = (?)_{16}$

$$\begin{array}{ccc} B & A & D \\ 4 & 3 & 1 \\ \hline F & D & E \end{array}$$

$11 + 4 = 15 \longrightarrow \uparrow \quad \llcorner\!\!\!\!\!\!\!\!\quad 13 + 1 = 14$
$\quad = F \qquad 10 + 3 = 13 \qquad\qquad = E \qquad$ ANS. $(FDE)_{16}$
$\qquad\qquad\qquad\quad = D$

Example 2 $(CBA)_{16} + (627)_{16} = (?)_{16}$

$$\begin{array}{ccc} & C & B & A \\ + & 6 & 2 & 7 \\ \hline 1 & 2 & E & 1 \end{array}$$

$12 + 6 = 18_{10} \longrightarrow \qquad \llcorner\!\!\!\!\!\quad 10 + 7 = 17_{10} = 11_{16} \text{ (carry 1)}$
$\quad = 12_{16}$

ANS. $(12E1)_{16}$

Keep in mind that the carrying of hexadecimal numbers to the next position is performed in exactly the same manner as in the decimal numbering system. A sum of 16 results in a carry of 1 ($10_{16} = 16_{10}$).

Example 3 $(83E)_{16} + (F6F)_{16} = (?)_{16}$

$$\begin{array}{cccc} & 8 & 3 & E \\ & F & 6 & F \\ \hline 1 & 7 & A & D \end{array}$$

$14 + 15 = (29)_{10} = (1D)_{16} \text{ (carry 1)}$

ANS. $(17AD)_{16}$

135

DATA
REPRESENTATION
AND COMPUTER
NUMBERING
SYSTEMS

We can subtract hexadecimal numbers by again converting each digit to decimal for each position and then converting the difference obtained back to hexadecimal. Note that the system of borrowing from or exchanging with the next position results in an exchange of 16 rather than 10.

Example 4 $(26)_{16} - (7)_{16} = (?)_{16}$

$$
\begin{array}{ccll}
26 & 1 & (16 + 6) & \text{(16 borrowed from 2nd position)} \\
-7 & = & - 7 & \\
\hline
& 1 & F & \text{ANS. } (1F)_{16}
\end{array}
$$

On some computers, specifically the IBM line, computer printouts *of storage locations* and their contents are specified in hexadecimal. While the normal program output is printed decimally, any program specifications are indicated in hexadecimal. Thus programmers are required to understand positional numbering theory to assist in computer processing.

When errors or "bugs" exist in a program or when programmers wish to pinpoint the contents of specific storage locations for testing purposes, they must be able to perform hexadecimal arithmetic.

Core dumps, or displays of storage contents, are given in hexadecimal. Thus a programmer may be advised that a program began at hexadecimal location 28E6 and that an error occurred at location 3EF2. The program listing has the address of each instruction, but only in relative terms, that is, from address 0000 on with no relation to where the program began. Thus to obtain the absolute error point and to find the corresponding instruction the starting point, 28E6, must be subtracted from 3EF2 to obtain the absolute error point.

In order to extract items from storage, then, the average programmer must understand hexadecimal arithmetic:

$$
\begin{array}{l}
3EF2 \\
-28E6 \\
\hline
160C \qquad \text{ABSOLUTE ERROR POINT}
\end{array}
$$

E. Converting from Hexadecimal to Binary and from Binary to Hexadecimal

At the start of this section, we indicated that hexadecimal numbers are used by some computers because they effectively reduce 4 binary digits to a single digit in base 16. That is, we can represent any four binary digits by a single hexadecimal digit.

Given any binary number, regardless of its size, we can convert it to a hexadecimal number by dividing it into groups of four digits and representing each group with a single hexadecimal digit.

Example 1 $(1101001101110111)_2 = (?)_{16}$

8421	8421	8421	8421
1101	0011	0111	0111
D	3	7	7

ANS. $(D377)_{16}$

Example 2 $(101101111)_2 = (?)_{16}$

0001	0110	1111
2	6	F

ANS. $(16F)_{16}$

Note that when the binary number does not consist of a multiple of four digits, it can be enlarged by using high-order or insignificant zeros. That is, 11 is the same as 0011, which has four digits. Because of the simple relation between binary and hexadecimal digits, the computer can represent data in hexadecimal, by still maintaining the binary (on-off state) configuration.

Notice also that it is sometimes easier to determine the *decimal* equivalent of a *binary* number by first finding its hexadecimal equivalent. A large binary number requires numerous calculations to determine the positional values, and then to convert to decimal. The conversion process is simplified from hexadecimal to decimal and since we can easily represent binary numbers as hexadecimal numbers, the double conversion often simplifies the operation.

Let us consider the binary number in Example 2 directly above.

$(101101111)_2$

Suppose we wish to find its decimal equivalent. We can use the standard method by determining each positional value and then adding all "on" positions. Or we can convert the number to hexadecimal and obtain 16F as in the example. Then we can convert:

256	16	1
1	6	F

$$15 \times 1 = 15$$
$$6 \times 16 = 96$$
$$1 \times 256 = \underline{256}$$
$$367$$

ANS. $(367)_{10}$

Often we find that the time it takes to convert large binary numbers to the decimal numbering system is significantly reduced by performing the intermediate conversion to hexadecimal.

Self-Evaluating Quiz

137
DATA
REPRESENTATION
AND COMPUTER
NUMBERING
SYSTEMS

1. $(8E6)_{16} = (?)_{10}$

2. $(9FC)_{16} = (?)_{10}$

3. $(1387)_{10} = (?)_{16}$

4. $(8365)_{10} = (?)_{16}$

5. $\begin{array}{r} 8EC \\ +DE2 \\ \hline \end{array}$

6. $\begin{array}{r} 9CC \\ +DEE \\ \hline \end{array}$

7. $\begin{array}{r} 9CE \\ -8DF \\ \hline \end{array}$

8. $\begin{array}{r} AEC \\ -932 \\ \hline \end{array}$

9. $(11011111110111)_2 = (?)_{16}$

10. $(111111101111)_2 = (?)_{16}$

Solutions

1. $(8E6)_{16} = (?)_{10}$

256	16	1
8	E	6

$$6 \times 1 = 6$$
$$14 \times 16 = 224$$
$$8 \times 256 = \underline{2048}$$
$$2278 \qquad \text{ANS. } 2278$$

2. $(9FC)_{16} = (?)_{10}$

256	16	1
9	F	C

$$12 \times 1 = 12$$
$$15 \times 16 = 240$$
$$9 \times 256 = \underline{2304}$$
$$2556 \qquad \text{ANS. } 2556$$

3. $(1387)_{10} = (?)_{16}$

REMAINDER IN HEX.

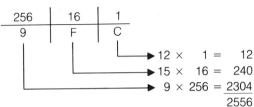

$$\begin{array}{rl} & 0 \qquad\quad 5 \\ 16\overline{)\,5} & \qquad 6 \\ 16\overline{)\,86} & \qquad B \\ 16\overline{)\,1387} & \end{array}$$

ANS. 56B

4. $(8365)_{10} = (?)_{16}$

REMAINDER IN HEX.

```
                    0        2
              16 | 2         0
              16 | 32        A
              16 | 522       D
              16 | 8365
```

ANS. 20AD

5.   8EC
     DE2

     16CE

6.   9CC
     DEE

     17BA

7.   9CE
    −8DF

     EF

8   AEC
    −932

     1BA

9    $(11011111110111)_2 = (?)_{16}$

0011	0111	1111	0111
3	7	F	7

ANS. $(37F7)_{16}$

10. $(111111101111)_2 = (?)_{16}$

1111	1110	1111
F	E	F

ANS. $(FEF)_{16}$

VI. Representation of Characters in Storage

We have seen that through a combination of on-off bits, or binary digits, it is possible to represent any number. Many computers group binary numbers in an effort to conserve storage so that data may be represented internally in the octal numbering system, where three binary numbers are grouped, or in the hexadecimal numbering system, where four binary numbers are grouped.

Most computer systems use some variation of the binary representation to store all characters including letters and special symbols. We shall discuss the two most widely used computer codes to familiarize the student with the principle involved.

*A. The Binary Coded Decimal or BCD Code

Binary Coded Decimal or BCD is a computer code, or method of data representation, which was very common on early computers.

It is still frequently used, particularly as a means of coding data on external media such as tapes.[2]

139
DATA
REPRESENTATION
AND COMPUTER
NUMBERING
SYSTEMS

Each storage position can be viewed as in Figure 4.1. Every character is represented as a series of "on-off" bits in bit-positions BA8421.

The digit portion of this code is already familiar to you since it includes the characters 8-4-2-1 or 2^3-2^2-2^1-2^0. Each decimal digit 0 to 9 can be represented by some combination of 8-4-2-1 "on" bits.

Zones are "off" for digit representation. Hence each decimal digit is represented as follows in BCD:

DECIMAL DIGIT	BCD CONFIGURATION							
	B	A	8	4	2	1		
1	0	0	0	0	0	1	1	bit
2	0	0	0	0	1	0	2	bit
3	0	0	0	0	1	1	2-1	bits
4	0	0	0	1	0	0	4	bit
5	0	0	0	1	0	1	4-1	bits
6	0	0	0	1	1	0	4-2	bits
7	0	0	0	1	1	1	4-2-1	bits
8	0	0	1	0	0	0	8	bit
9	0	0	1	0	0	1	8-1	bits
0	0	0	1	0	1	0	8-2	bits

The representation for digits 1 to 9 is the standard binary representation. Zero, you will note, has a bit-configuration of 8-2. You might have expected zero to be represented as all zeros but that is the configuration for a blank character. To distinguish between a blank and a zero, the 8-2 or 001010 BCD representation is used for the latter.

Bits B and A are used to represent the Hollerith zones 12-11-0. You will recall that the Hollerith zones are used as follows:

$$12 + \text{digit} = A - I$$
$$11 + \text{digit} = J - R$$
$$0 + \text{digit} = S - T$$

In BCD we have the following:

ZONE	B-A BITS	
12	B – A	on
11	B	on
0	A	on

Hollerith Codes are then directly convertible to BCD Codes. The zone portion converts as above and the digit portion is represented

[2] See chapter 5.

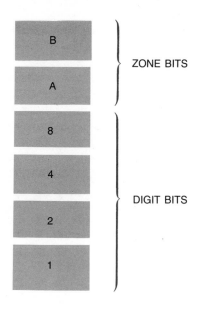

ONE STORAGE POSITION

Figure 4.1

Representation of BCD code in each storage position.

in binary form. Hence, the BCD configuration in one storage position for the letter A, which is 12-1 in Hollerith, is

B	A	8	4	2	1
1	1	0	0	0	1

or B-A-1

The BCD configuration for the letter C, which is 12-3 in Hollerith, is:

B	A	8	4	2	1
1	1	0	0	1	1

or B-A-2-1

Similarly, the BCD configuration for the letter N, which is 11-5 in Hollerith, is:

B	A	8	4	2	1
1	0	0	1	0	1

or B-4-1

*B. Parity

There is one more element necessary to complete the BCD Code, an element called a *parity* or check bit denoted as C. The purpose of this bit is to provide an internal check on the validity of the character represented. There exists a slight possibility, although it is very slight indeed, that the computer could lose or gain a bit during processing; that is, a circuit might accidentally go off or on. To prevent such an occurrence from going unnoticed, computer codes generally include an *extra* parity or check bit. Using BCD, the check bit is employed to ensure that there are always an odd number of bits on in a particular position. Hence: E which is represented by the four bits BA41 would require an additional bit to make it have an odd number of bits on. Thus E is represented in its complete BCD form as CBA41, where C is the check bit. The letter D which is represented by BA4 already uses an odd number of bits. Hence the check or parity bit would be off in this case. Figure 4.2 illustrates how a sample punched card would be represented in storage in BCD.

141
DATA
REPRESENTATION
AND COMPUTER
NUMBERING
SYSTEMS

Figure 4.2
Punched card data and its BCD equivalent in storage positions 801 to 808.

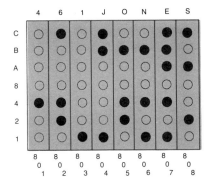

NOTE: ODD-PARITY MACHINE

Computers that use BCD codes are generally classified as odd-parity machines, since there must always be an odd number of bits on at a given time. If the computer gains or loses a bit during processing, that is, inadvertently magnetizes or demagnetizes a core or circuit, the bit configuration would be invalid since there would then be an even number of bits on, an occurrence that would automatically stop the machine.

You might well ask, at this point, what happens if two bits, instead of one, are inadvertently turned on or off in a storage position. That would still leave an odd number of bits and the machine would not recognize an error. It is true, in fact, that the computer is capable of recognizing only a *single* error for each position, a possibility that itself can best be described as remote. The possibility of *two* errors in a single position is, however, so unlikely that it is not even provided for. The use of a parity system takes care of practically all possible errors.

Some machines are called even-parity computers, meaning that an even number of bits are required in a given position at all times. The principle is exactly the same as described above with the check bit being used to ensure an even number of bits.

As a summary, look carefully at Table 4.1 which provides the BCD configuration for numbers, letters, and some of the more common special characters.

C. The EBCDIC Code

More recent computers often use an internal computer code which is an extension of the BCD code described above. It is called EBCDIC which means *Extended Binary Coded Decimal Interchange Code* and is pronounced eb-ce-dick. Using the BCD Code, it is possible to represent 64 characters. Using EBCDIC, it is possible to represent 256 characters. The additional characters that can be represented in EBCDIC include lower case letters (as well as upper case or capital letters), many additional special symbols, and control characters.

Using the EBCDIC Code, each storage position consists of eight bits. On many machines, including the IBM 360/370 systems, a single storage position consisting of eight bits is called a *byte*.

Each byte is divided into a zone portion, consisting of four bits and a digit portion consisting of four bits, producing what is referred to as the zoned decimal format.

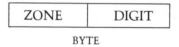

There are no BA bits in EBCDIC as in BCD. Instead, the zone portion of the byte is represented in exactly the same manner as the digit portion.

Table 4.1

BCD Code for Numbers, Letters, and Selected Special Characters

Character	C	B	A	8	4	2	1	Character	C	B	A	8	4	2	1
0	C			8		2		A		B	A				1
1							1	B		B	A				2
2						2		C	C	B	A			2	1
3	C					2	1	D		B	A		4		
4					4			E	C	B	A		4		1
5	C				4		1	F	C	B	A		4	2	
6	C				4	2		G		B	A		4	2	1
7					4	2	1	H		B	A	8			
8				8				I	C	B	A	8			1
9	C			8			1	J	C	B					1
								K	C	B				2	
BLANK	C							L		B				2	1
—		B						M	C	B			4		
&	C	B	A					N		B			4		1
$	C	B		8		2	1	0		B			4	2	
*		B		8	4			P	C	B			4	2	1
•		B	A	8		2	1	Q	C	B		8			
								R		B		8			1
								S	C		A			2	
								T			A			2	1
								U	C		A		4		
								V			A		4		1
								W			A		4	2	
								X	C		A		4	2	1
								Y	C		A	8			
								Z			A	8			1

BYTE

ZONE				DIGIT			
8	4	2	1	8	4	2	1

The digit portion is used in exactly the same manner as described for BCD. For the zone portion, a 12-zone is represented as 8-4, an 11-zone as 8-4-1 and a 0-zone as 8-4-2.

Thus the letter A in Hollerith, a 12-zone and a 1-punch, is:

ZONE				DIGIT				
8	4	2	1	8	4	2	1	POSITIONAL VALUE
1	1	0	0	0	0	0	1	BITS

BYTE

The 12-zone corresponds to 1100, a 12 in binary, and the 1 is 0001. A hexadecimal printout of this byte would be C1 (8 + 4 in the hexadecimal system is a C). That is, the zone and digit portions are treated independently for printout purposes.

The letter T corresponding to 0–3 punches is represented as:

HEX PRINTOUT	ZONE				DIGIT				CHARACTER
E3	8	4	2	1	8	4	2	1	T
	1	1	1	0	0	0	1	1	

0-ZONE   3-DIGIT

In a hexadecimal printout, the T would be represented as E3. Numeric characters are also represented in this form. For *unsigned* numbers, all zone bits are on. Thus we have 1111 as the zone portion of all numbers. The number 8 then is represented in a byte as:

ZONE				DIGIT			
8	4	2	1	8	4	2	1
1	1	1	1	1	0	0	0

ACTUAL VALUE   +   8

HEXADECIMAL REPRESENTATION   F   8

The 1111 in the zone portion of a byte is used to denote an unsigned number which is assumed to be positive. The selection of 1111 was based on the fact that it would make unsigned numbers the highest in the collating or sorting sequence. Note that an unsigned 5 in a hexadecimal printout of storage would read as F5.

A definitive positive sign is denoted by 1100 (hex C) and a minus sign by 1101 (hex D).

The following chart summarizes the representation of the zone portion of characters in EBCDIC and hexadecimal.

145

DATA
REPRESENTATION
AND COMPUTER
NUMBERING
SYSTEMS

Summary of Zone Representation

HOLLERITH	EBCDIC	HEXADECIMAL
12	1100	C
11	1101	D
0	1110	E
no zone (unsigned numbers)	1111	F

Note that, as indicated in the previous section, each group of four bits or binary digits can be used to represent a single hexadecimal digit. Thus a shorthand method for representing characters in EBCDIC is to represent them as *two* hexadecimal digits. Since each hexadecimal digit is used to represent four binary digits, two hexadecimal digits are needed to represent one byte or eight bits.

E6 in hexadecimal represents the EBCDIC code for W:

ZONE				DIGIT			
1	1	1	0	0	1	1	0

0-ZONE   6-DIGIT

This is equivalent to 0–6 in Hollerith or the letter W.

F5 in hexadecimal represents the zoned decimal format in EBCDIC for a positive 5:

ZONE	DIGIT
F	5
1111	0101

All unsigned numbers in zoned decimal format are represented hexadecimally with an F followed by a digit.

Table 4.2 provides a summary of the EBCDIC representation of numbers and letters.

The EBCDIC code also has provision for a parity or check bit called a P-bit in this system.[3] Many third-generation computers are *even-parity* machines. Hence the P-bit is used to ensure that an even number of bits is always on. EBCDIC is thus a nine-bit code. Figure 4.3 illustrates how sample punched card data would be represented in storage in EBCDIC.

---

[3] See page 181 for a further discussion of the check bit.

Table 4.2

EBCDIC and Hollerith Codes for Numbers and Letters

| Character | EBCDIC | | Hollerith |
	Zone	Digit	
A	1100	0001	12-1
B	1100	0010	12-2
C	1100	0011	12-3
D	1100	0100	12-4
E	1100	0101	12-5
F	1100	0110	12-6
G	1100	0111	12-7
H	1100	1000	12-8
I	1100	1001	12-9
J	1101	0001	11-1
K	1101	0010	11-2
L	1101	0011	11-3
M	1101	0100	11-4
N	1101	0101	11-5
O	1101	0110	11-5
P	1101	0111	11-6
Q	1101	1000	11-8
R	1101	1001	11-9
S	1110	0010	0-2
T	1110	0011	0-3
U	1110	0100	0-4
V	1110	0101	0-5
W	1110	0110	0-6
X	1110	0111	0-7
Y	1110	1000	0-8
Z	1110	1001	0-9
0	1111	0000	0
1	1111	0001	1
2	1111	0010	2
3	1111	0011	3
4	1111	0100	4
5	1111	0101	5
6	1111	0110	6
7	1111	0111	7
8	1111	1000	8
9	1111	1001	9

We have, by no means, exhausted all the variations on computer codes. To do so would require a text for that purpose only. Rather, we have provided the principles used in most computer codes. Other codes are merely variations on this theme and after reading the fundamentals in this chapter you would require only a minimal amount of effort to understand them.

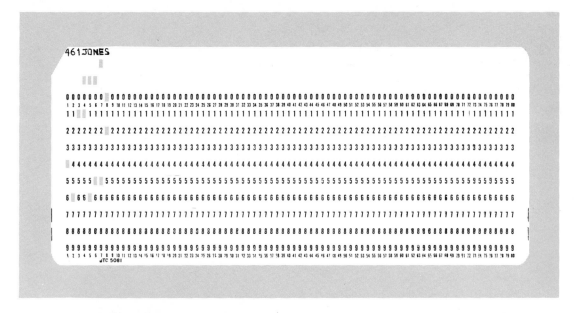

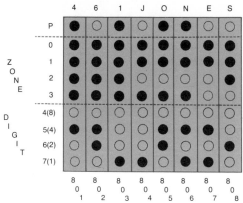

NOTE: EVEN-PARITY MACHINE

Figure 4.3
Punched card data and its EBCDIC equivalent in storage positions 801 to 808.

Important Terms Used in this Chapter

Binary Coded Decimal (BCD)
Binary Number
Bit
Byte
Check Bit
Extended Binary Coded Decimal Interchange Code (EBCDIC)
Hexadecimal Numbering System
Octal Numbering System

Parity
Positional Numbering System
Zoned Decimal Format

Self-Evaluating Quiz

Find the BCD Code for the following. Use the chart on page 143 if necessary. There is no need to memorize configurations.

1. A
2. 8
3. 5
4. T
5. K

Find the EBCDIC Code for the following. Use the chart on page 146 if necessary. There is no need to memorize configurations.

6. A
7. 8
8. 5
9. T
10. K

Solutions

1. BA1
2. 8
3. C41 (C is the check bit)
4. A21
5. CB2

	ZONE	DIGIT	HEX
6.	1100	0001	C1
7.	1111	1000	F8
8.	1111	0101	F5
9.	1110	0011	E3
10.	1101	0010	D2

Review Questions

1. $721_8 = (?)_2$
2. $677_8 = (?)_{10}$
3. $101101_2 = (?)_{10}$
4. $423_{10} = (?)_8 = (?)_2$
5. $E27D_{16} = (?)_{10}$
6. $1739_{10} = (?)_{16}$
7. $110110_2 + 11101_2 = (?)_2$

149

DATA
REPRESENTATION
AND COMPUTER
NUMBERING
SYSTEMS

8. $11110_2 - 11001_2 = (?)_2$

9. $8FC_{16} + 9EE_{16} = (?)_{16}$

10. $E8FD_{16} = (?)_2$

11. Find the BCD Code for the following:
   a. 7
   b. Q
   c. F
   d. V

12. Find the EBCDIC Code for the following:
   a. 7
   b. Q
   c. F
   d. V

13. Determine the decimal equivalents of the following binary numbers:
   a. 1001111
   b. 11100
   c. 110011

14. Determine the binary equivalents of the following decimal numbers:
   a. 234
   b. 435
   c. 333

15. Add the following binary numbers and indicate the sum in binary form. Check your work by converting each number back into decimal form:
   a. 11101111 + 1111101111
   b. 111111011101 + 1111011
   c. 1110111 + 111111

16. Determine the decimal equivalents of the following hexadecimal numbers:
   a. 6FFE
   b. 70FD
   c. 67EE

17. Determine the hexadecimal equivalents of the following decimal numbers:
   a. 10678
   b. 16745
   c. 2345

18. Add the following hexadecimal numbers. Check your answers:
   a. 45EE + FE34
   b. 3355 + FDE2
   c. 897F + 5FFF

19. Represent the following in EBCDIC form:
   a. G
   b. M
   c. −3
   d. +6
   e. W
   f. D

Chapter 5
Common Computer Media and Input/Output Devices

5

5

I. Types of Media and Devices

*II. Representation of Data on Magnetic Tape and Disk

Important Terms Used in this Chapter

Self-Evaluating Quiz

* Optional topic.

Computer systems consist of the following:

> 1. Input devices: accept data and transmit it to the CPU
> 2. Central Processing Unit (CPU): processes incoming data
> 3. Output devices: transmit processed data from CPU to an output form

The most simplified computer system could function with a card reader, a CPU, and a printer. That is, the system utilizes card input only and produces printed reports as the sole form of output. Most computer centers, however, use more diversified equipment to handle files of data for a varied list of business applications.

I. Types of Media and Devices

Hardware is the term used to describe all the devices in a computer system. Hardware is categorized as

> **Types of Devices**
> 1. Input only
> 2. Output only
> 3. Combination input/output

A card reader is an example of an input device; a printer is an example of an output device; a card read/punch is a combination device that can read cards and also punch output cards.

Linkage Between Device and CPU   Each device is linked to the CPU by cables which electronically transmit data from input devices to the CPU and from the CPU to the output devices.

Each device is capable of reading or writing a single form of computer input or output. Hence, a card read/punch can only process punched cards, a printer can only print reports, and so on. Figure 5.1 illustrates the most common storage media used to store data files.

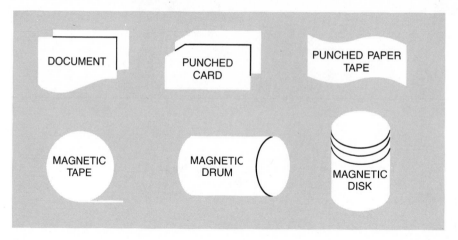

Figure 5.1

The most common storage media used to store data files.

The types of I/O devices used in a given computer installation are usually determined by the systems analyst who, communicating with businessmen, determines the company's needs.

For each program to be run on the computer, the programmer, systems analyst, and businessman must decide the file types to be included. These are generally limited to those devices already in use at the installation or those that can be acquired on a cost-justified basis.

We will subdivide our discussion into two units:

1. The most frequently used devices—this chapter
2. Specialized equipment—Chapter 6

A. Card Read/Punch (Figure 5.2)

Since the punched card is a common computer medium, the card read/punch is an integral part of most computer systems.

The device is used to read card data and transmit it to the CPU. It can also punch output cards with information transmitted from the CPU.

While some manufacturers produce independent card read and card punch devices, the combination card read/punch is the most common type.

The card read/punch is a single device which houses two separate units: a card reader and a card punch. A typical card reader section reads punched card input by mechanically sensing the punched holes with the use of wire brushes (see Figure 5.3). The data is then electronically transmitted to the CPU. Some card readers use photoelectric methods to electronically sense the holes. The card punch section punches output cards from data that has been transmitted to it by the CPU, converting the computer's codes to Hollerith Code. The *punch hopper* contains blank cards which are then punched and transferred to the *punch stacker.*

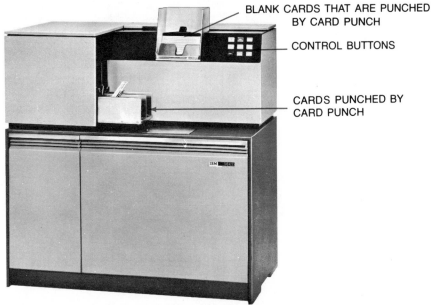

Figure 5.2
Card read/punch.
Courtesy IBM.

BLANK CARDS THAT ARE PUNCHED
BY CARD PUNCH

CONTROL BUTTONS

CARDS PUNCHED BY
CARD PUNCH

Figure 5.3
How punched cards
are mechanically
sensed.

"1" punched
in column 1

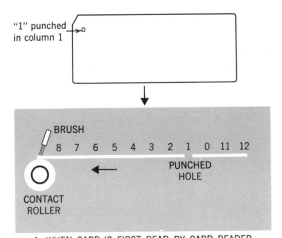

BRUSH

8 7 6 5 4 3 2 1 0 11 12

PUNCHED
HOLE

CONTACT
ROLLER

1. WHEN CARD IS FIRST READ BY CARD READER

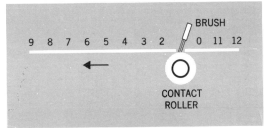

BRUSH

9 8 7 6 5 4 3 2 0 11 12

CONTACT
ROLLER

2. WHEN 1-PUNCH IS SENSED

HOLE IN THE 1-ROW IS SENSED: A CIRCUIT
IS COMPLETED WHEN CONTACT ROLLER
MAKES CONTACT WITH BRUSH

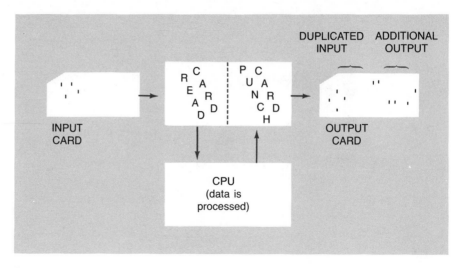

Figure 5.4
Reading cards as input and punching additional data into duplicated cards.

Since the card read and card punch units are completely separate in this device, it is not generally possible to read cards as input and then punch additional data into them. While there are devices that have this capability, they are very costly. Hence, if input cards require additional information the card is usually duplicated and the additions made on a new punched card (see Figure 5.4).

Cards can be *read* at an average rate of 800 to 1200 cards per minute. Output cards are punched at a much slower rate, approximately 300 to 600 cards per minute.

Note that computer-produced output cards do not usually contain the imprinting of the data on the face of the card. Although card punch units can be equipped with special print features, such features are very costly and thus rarely used.

A special EAM machine called an *interpreter* can print on the face of a card the data that has been punched in it.

Recall that there are two common methods for obtaining punched card data.

Methods of Producing Punched Cards
1. Keypunch the data manually
2. Program a computer to punch data automatically

A comparison of cards as a computer medium with other I/O media appears in Table 5.1 on page 172.

B. The Printer

A printer is the most common output device used in business applications. Characteristics of printed reports have already been discussed in Chapter 2. In this unit we will consider the types of printers that can be used to produce such reports.

The printer converts information transmitted from the CPU to a permanent or *hard copy* typewritten form. Typically printers are capable of printing 100, 120, or 132 characters per line depending upon the model. The output is on *continuous forms*.

1. Line Printers These devices use an impact printing method where *one line* is printed at a time. Standard line printers can create output at rates from 150 lines per minute to 2500 lines per minute. This is the most common form of printer (see Figure 5.5).

2. Nonimpact Printers These are more costly devices which use electronic or photoelectric methods to produce reports at extremely fast rates.

3. Character Printers Like typewriters, these devices print one *character* at a time at rates of approximately 30 characters per second, too slow for high-volume output. Character printers sometimes use the *wire matrix* format for representing data. Each character is printed as a pattern of dots arranged in a group of 35 wires in a 5 × 7 matrix. See Figure 5.6.

157
COMMON
COMPUTER
MEDIA AND
INPUT/OUTPUT
DEVICES

WINDOW
TO VIEW PRINTED
OUTPUT

PRINT
MECHANISM

CONTINUOUS
FORMS (BLANK)

Figure 5.5
Line printer.
Courtesy
Honeywell.

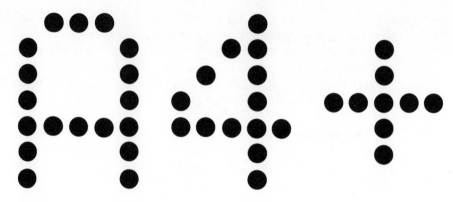

Figure 5.6
Sample characters printed in a matrix format.

C. Magnetic Tape and Drive (Figure 5.7)

We will begin our discussion of high-speed input and output with magnetic tape. A magnetic tape is a *high-speed* medium that can serve as input to, or output from, a computer. It is one of the most common file types for storing high-volume files.

A magnetic tape drive is the device that can either read a tape or write onto a tape. Each tape drive has a read/write head that is accessed by the computer for either reading or writing.

Magnetic tape drives function like home tape recorders. Data can be recorded, or written, onto a tape and "played back," or read, from the same tape at a later date. If data is written on a tape, previous data in that area is written over or destroyed. For this reason, computer centers must take precautions to protect important tapes from being destroyed inadvertently.

1. Features of Magnetic Tape A typical magnetic tape is generally 2400 to 3600 feet long and ½ inch wide. The tape is made of plastic with an iron oxide coating that can be magnetized to represent data. Since the magnetized spots or *bits* are extremely small and not visible to the human eye, large volumes of data can be condensed into a relatively small area of tape. Information from an entire 80-column card, for example, can typically be stored in one tenth of an inch of magnetic tape, or less. The average tape, which costs approximately $25, can store as many as 20 million characters.[1] After a tape file has been processed and is no longer needed, the same tape may be reused repeatedly to store other information.

---

[1] The more technical aspects of magnetic tape are presented in section II of this chapter.

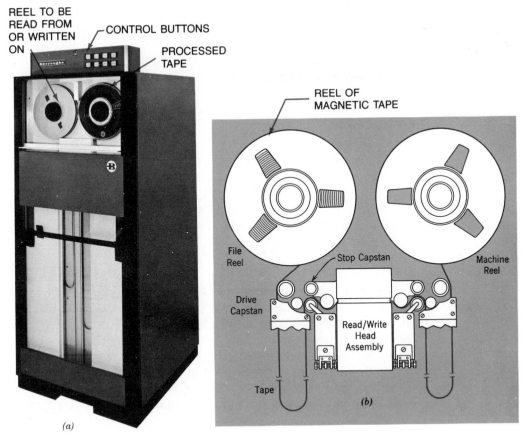

REEL TO BE READ FROM OR WRITTEN ON

CONTROL BUTTONS

PROCESSED TAPE

REEL OF MAGNETIC TAPE

File Reel

Stop Capstan

Machine Reel

Drive Capstan

Read/Write Head Assembly

Tape

(b)

(a)

Figure 5.7

(a) Magnetic tape drive. Courtesy Burroughs Corp. (b) Read/write head on tape drive. Courtesy IBM.

2. High-Speed Capability of Tape Drives Because tape drives read data *electronically* by sensing magnetized areas, and write data electronically by magnetizing areas, tapes may be processed at very high speeds. Data can be read or written at speeds of from 100,000 to 300,000 characters *per second.*

Thus tape files are frequently used for large volumes of data. One tape can store hundreds of thousands of records, transmit and receive data at very high speeds, and store the data in a compact form. In many medium- or large-scale companies, *master files* for Payroll, Accounts Receivable, Accounts Payable, Inventory, and so on are stored on tape. A master file is the main data file that holds all current information for a specific department or system.

A record on a tape may be any size, as long as it is physically consistent with the size of storage. That is, it is not feasible to create 5000-position records using a 4000-position computer, since the output area (5000 positions) must be located in storage. Aside from this limitation, tape records may usually be any size. Keep in mind, however, that extremely large record sizes are more difficult to process.

3. Tapes for Batch Processing   Because of a tape's capacity to handle large volumes of data in a relatively short time, it is ideally suited for *batch processing,* or processing groups of data at fixed intervals.

4. Tapes as Input/Output   Like punched cards, tapes can be read as input to a computer and can be produced as output from a computer system. Just as a card read/punch can both read and punch card data so, too, can a tape drive read and write tape data.

Cards can be created by a keypunch machine as well as by a card punch. Similarly, *key-to-tape encoders* can be used to create tapes.

5. Key-To-Tape Encoder   A key-to-tape encoder or converter (Figure 5.8) is a device similar to a keypunch machine. It requires an operator to code data from a source document to a magnetic tape via a typewriter-like keyboard. The operator depresses a key for a specific character and the device converts it to the appropriate magnetized coding. Tapes encoded in this manner may be verified by the same device to ensure their accuracy. Key-to-tape encoders thus eliminate the need for punched card input by transcribing data *directly* onto magnetic tape.

6. Tapes for Sequential Processing   In short, tape is a very common file medium for high-speed, voluminous processing. It does, however, have several inherent disadvantages.

Data recorded on a tape may only be processed *sequentially.* That is, to access a record with TRANSACTION NUMBER 254 from a tape file that is maintained in TRANSACTION NUMBER sequence, we must read past the first 253 records. We instruct the computer to read a record; test if it contains TRANSACTION NUMBER 254; and, if it does not, to read the next record. Thus, 254 records are read. There is no convenient method to instruct the tape drive to skip the first few inches of tape or to go directly to the middle of the tape.

Thus, unless all or most records from a tape file are required for processing *most of the time,* this method could become inefficient and costly.

If an INVENTORY FILE is created on tape with 100,000 records and only a handful of these are required to print a report, then tapes may not provide the best file type. Processing time and, thus cost, would be excessive, since most of the file must be read even to process only a small number of records. Sequential processing is beneficial only when *most* records on a high-volume file are required for normal processing.

161
COMMON
COMPUTER
MEDIA AND
INPUT/OUTPUT
DEVICES

Figure 5.8
Key-to-tape encoder. Courtesy Honeywell.

7. Read/Write Feature of Tape Drives Another disadvantage of tape processing is that a particular tape cannot usually be read from, and then written onto, during the same run. As with cards, if tape records are to be changed, a new record must be created on an output file which duplicates the old records and makes the necessary changes. In this procedure, two tape drives are needed, one to read a file as input and the other to write an output file.

8. Identification Problem with Tape Drives A third disadvantage of tape processing is the identification problem. Most medium- and large-scale computer installations have hundreds or even thousands of magnetic tapes, each utilized for a specific application.

Because data recorded on these tapes is not "readable" or visible to the naked eye, it is often difficult to maintain control. If a master Accounts Receivable tape is inadvertently "written over," or used as *output* for some other job, for example, the result could be an expensive re-creation process, since the writing of output would destroy the existing information. Several steps have been implemented at most installations to prevent such occurrences, or to reduce the extent of damage, should they occur.

9. Methods Used to Ease Tape Identification Problem

a. External Tape Labels External gummed labels are placed on the face of each tape (see Figure 5.9), identifying it and indicating its *retention cycle*, or how long it should be maintained. These labels are clearly visible to anyone, so that chances of inadvertent misuse of a valuable tape are reduced. The problem with gummed labels, however, is that they sometimes become unglued. Their effectiveness is also directly related to the effort and training

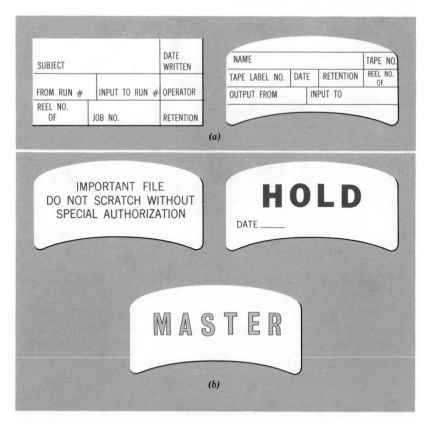

Figure 5.9

External tape labels: (a) Two commonly used external labels. (b) Three commonly used special-purpose tape labels.

of the computer staff. If operators are negligent, then the labels are sometimes ignored.

163

COMMON
COMPUTER
MEDIA AND
INPUT/OUTPUT
DEVICES

b. Tape Librarian Most medium- and large-scale companies have numerous tapes that must be filed or stored and released for reuse when no longer required. Such companies employ a *tape librarian* to maintain the tape files. If he or she performs the job properly, there will be less misuse or misplacing of tapes.

c. Internal Tape Labels To make the identification of tapes more reliable, most programs include a built-in routine which, for output tapes, creates a *tape label record* that is produced as any other tape record, with magnetized bits. The label is the *first* record on the tape. When the tape is used as input, at some later date, then this first label record, called a *header label,* is checked as part of the program, to ascertain that the correct tape is being used.

Thus header labels are created on output tapes and later checked on input tapes. This label creation for output and label checking for input is a standard procedure in most programs. Since it uses the computer to verify that the correct tapes are being used, there is less danger of errors resulting from carelessness.

d. File Protection Ring (Figure 5.10) Those available tapes that may be written on, or used as output, have a *file protection ring* inserted in the back. The tape drive is electronically sensitized so that it will *not* create an output record unless this ring is in its proper place. For those tapes that are to be maintained and not "written over" the ring has been removed. Thus if an operator erroneously uses such a tape for an output operation, the computer prints a message that states, in effect, "NO RING—NO WRITE." If the operator is cautious, he or she will examine the external label and realize that the wrong tape is being used. Sometimes, however, an operator will merely place a ring on the tape (any file protection ring fits all tapes) and restart the job. Thus this method, alone, deters the misuse of tapes but does not totally alleviate the problem.

e. Backup Tapes Since tapes can sometimes be written over or even become physically damaged, it is necessary to maintain backup tapes so that the re-creation process, should it become necessary, is not enormously costly and cumbersome.

Suppose a new master tape is created each month. After processing, it is best to store the old master tape and update transactions *along with* the new master tape. In this way, if some mishap should befall the new master tape, it is a simple task to re-create. Normally, operators maintain *two* previous tapes as backup in addition to the present one, in order to prevent any serious problem. Hence, the three *generations* of tapes maintained for important files are called the *grandfather-father-son* tapes (see Figure 5.11).

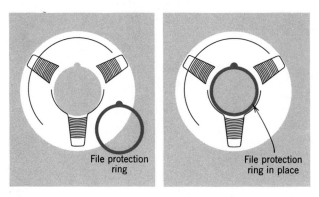

Figure 5.10

File protection ring. This is a plastic ring that fits into a groove in the tape reel. When the ring is in place, both reading and writing of tape records can occur. When the ring is removed, only reading can occur. In this way, the file is protected from accidental erasures.

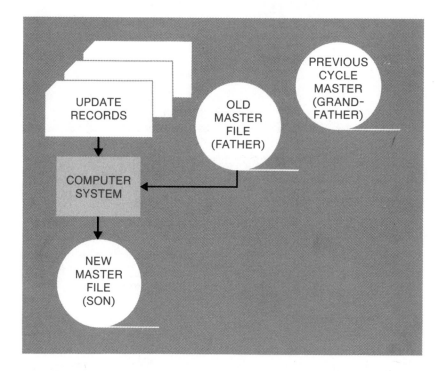

Figure 5.11

Grandfather-father-son method of file backup.

D. Magnetic Disk and Drive (Figure 5.12)

The magnetic disk is another high-speed medium that can serve as either input to, or output from a computer system. Like tape, it has an iron oxide coating that is used to store millions of characters of data, typically 6 to 70 million. The magnetic disk drive is used to record information onto the disk and to read information from it.

(b)

(a)

Figure 5.12

(a) Disk drive. (b) Disk pack. Courtesy Burroughs.

Figure 5.12 illustrates a typical disk pack. The pack resembles a series of disks similar to phonograph records that rotate on a vertical shaft.

Each surface of each disk consists of numbered concentric tracks. Each track is used to store information. A read-write head is used to read information from, and record information onto, any of the tracks.[2]

Disk processing has many of the same advantages as tape processing. It can store large numbers of records in a condensed area. The disk drive, like the tape drive, reads and records information electronically and thus is a high-speed device. Records on a disk can essentially be any length. They are not fixed, as is the case with 80-column cards, for example.

1. Direct Access Disk processing, however, has some additional features that are not available with tape processing. A disk may be used for either *direct or sequential* processing.

In addition to handling records in sequence, a disk has the facility to access records in some order other than the one in which they were originally recorded. The processing of records on disk is similar to the accessing of phonograph records from a juke box. By indicating that phonograph record 106 is required, for example, the

[2]For a more thorough description of the physical characteristics of a disk, see section II of this chapter.

mechanism is capable of accessing 106 *directly* without first reading records 1 to 105, as is required with tape processing.

2. Index on a Disk   The most common method for accessing magnetic disk records directly (or randomly) is with the use of an *index*. During the creation of records, the computer establishes an index on the disk itself. The index essentially indicates where each record is located. This is similar in concept to the index found at the end of a book, which indicates the page where each item of information can be located.

The disk index indicates the *addresses* or locations of records that are stored on the disk. The address, in basic terms, refers to the surface number and track where a particular record can be found. A *key data field* in each record, as indicated by the programmer, is used by the computer as the basis for establishing address information in the index. As an example, if a Payroll file is stored on disk, a key field would probably be SOCIAL SECURITY NUMBER or EMPLOYEE NUMBER, if this is to be used as a means of identification.

To access any disk record, then, the user need only supply a particular key data field, such as EMPLOYEE NUMBER 17537. The computer then "looks up" the corresponding disk address for this record in the index and seeks that record directly.

3. Input/Output Disks   In addition, disks have the added advantage of permitting updates or changes to existing records *on the same disk*. In this way, a new disk need not be created to incorporate the current changes, as is usually required with tape processing. That is, the same disk may be used for *both* input and output. We can read a record from a disk and make changes to that record on the same disk; we can add records to the disk; we can delete records from the disk.

4. On-Line Applications of Disk   This type of processing is extremely advantageous for specific applications. Suppose, for example, that a police department wishes to obtain information on three known criminals immediately. Suppose, too, that the department maintains a 100,000-record criminal file. If the criminal file were on tape (a sequential medium) each tape record would be read, in sequence, until the appropriate ones were found.

To read 100,000 data records would require considerable time. If, however, the file were on a disk pack, then each of the three records could be accessed directly, in a much shorter time. We merely supply the key data field, which may be MAN NUMBER or PRISON RECORD NUMBER.

Where time is critical and random processing is frequently required, disks are far more suitable than tapes. For *online* processing, or immediate processing of data, a disk file is usually used, since individual detail records can be used to update the disk file quickly and easily.

167

COMMON
COMPUTER
MEDIA AND
INPUT/OUTPUT
DEVICES

In recent years, more flexible disk packs have become available. Disk packs that are currently marketed range from the small *floppy disks* which resemble phonograph records and are used extensively with minicomputers to much larger units (see Figure 5.13).

5. Disadvantages of Disk   In short, a disk is extremely advantageous for processing records directly (or randomly), as well as sequentially. Disks do, however, possess some inherent limitations:

- Disk packs are relatively expensive compared to other media such as tape or cards. The purchase price for a typical disk pack ranges from approximately $400 to $3000, depending upon the model.
- The identification of disk files, just as with tapes, often results in some problems. Since disk files, like tape files, cannot be visibly read, labels, both external (physically glued to the pack) or internal (programmed data labels) are required.
- Tape update procedures usually result in a new master file that is created from the previous master file and a series of change records; the previous master can always be used as backup, should the new master be defective and a re-creation process deemed necessary. Since update procedures on a master disk file add to or delete from the one master, re-creation, if it becomes necessary, is very difficult.

6. Key-to-Disk Encoders   Most disk files are created by computer output, although key-to-disk devices, such as keypunch machines and key-to-tape encoders, are available. Since key-to-disk devices are relatively expensive, most businesses create disk files only as output from a computer system. That is, disks are less frequently created directly from a source document than are cards and tape.

E. Other Types of Direct-Access Devices

1. Magnetic Drum (Figure 5.14)   Magnetic drum is another type of random or direct-access device that has characteristics similar to a magnetic disk. It has a smaller storage capacity than disk but a faster access time.

2. Data Cell (Figure 5.15)   A data cell is a direct-access medium which is also capable of storing large volumes of data. It has an extremely large storage capacity but a slower access time than disk. Information is stored on *magnetic strips.* The magnetic strips move through the data cell and are read or written by stationary read/write heads. Because of the mechanical action of the device, the access time is considerably slower than with other direct-access devices.

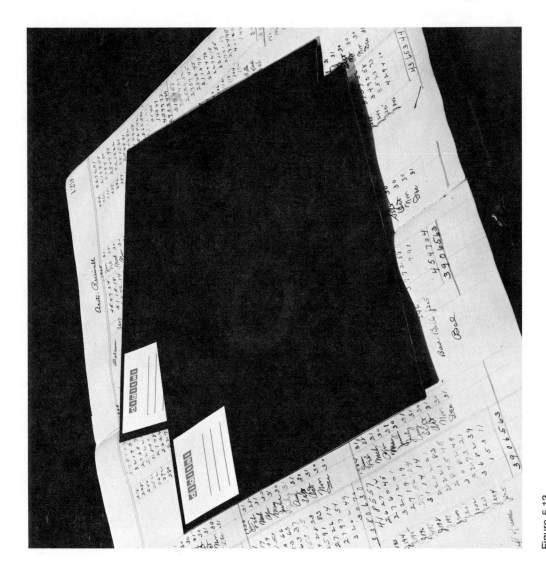

Figure 5.13
Floppy disk. Courtesy Digital Equipment Corp.

Figure 5.14
A drum storage
device.

F. Terminals

The terminal is one of the newest and most important additions to computer hardware. The major feature of such a device is that it can access a computer from a remote location. That is, with the use of telephone lines, a terminal can be linked to a CPU located anywhere in the country.

These terminals enable the user to:

- Enter data from remote locations
- Enter jobs—programs and data—from remote locations
- Make inquiries into the current status of central files from remote locations

The types of systems that make use of terminal processing are diverse. An airlines reservation system is perhaps the most common illustration of an application where terminals located throughout the country access a central CPU.

Figure 5.15
(a) Data cell drive. Courtesy IBM.

The type of terminal equipment available is also diverse. Most have typewriter-like keyboards which an operator can use to access the CPU.

The output from the terminal may be:

- Printed form
- Visual display on a television-like screen called a cathode ray tube (CRT)
- Audio response—recorded messages
- Graphs from a graph plotter

(b) Data cell. Courtesy IBM.

Terminals have become an important aspect of most data processing centers and are extremely significant in providing flexibility for online, real-time, and time-sharing systems. They are discussed in depth in Chapter 12.

G. Comparing Cards, Tape, and Disk as File Types

The businessman, along with the computer specialist, plays an integral role in determining the most efficient files to be used for systems. Selecting an inefficient medium would be extremely costly in the end. Thus every attempt must be made to find the appropriate file types. Table 5.1 summarizes the major characteristics of card, tape, and disk files. This table should serve as a review of the previous sections.

Table 5.1

Characteristics of the Three Major File Types

File Type	Characteristics	Advantages	Disadvantages
Punched Card	80 columns; data recorded by keypunch machine or card punch of computer.	Utilized by electrical accounting machines to supplement computer use; relatively inexpensive in small volume jobs; can be maintained by operator because data is visual.	Warps easily; easily mishandled; very inefficient for large-volume jobs because of relatively slow I/O capability.
Magnetic Tape	Data represented as magnetized bits on an iron-oxide coating; data recorded by computer via tape drive or a keytape converter.	Efficient for large-volume jobs; any size record can be stored; stores millions of characters on a single tape.	Information not visible to the naked eye; strictly sequential processing; no easy reading and writing possible from the same tape during a single operation.
Direct Access Files	Includes magnetic disk, drum, and data cell; addresses of disk records may be "looked up" on an index; data recorded by computer via disk drive or key-to-disk recorders.	Efficient for large-volume jobs; any size record can be stored; stores millions of characters on a single disk; random and sequential processing; can read and write from one disk during a single operation.	Data usually recorded by computer only—keying devices relatively expensive; disk packs expensive; requires much software.

Let us use the following examples to illustrate how file types are selected.

Example 1

A Payroll system, servicing 75,000 employees, produces weekly payroll checks in social security number sequence. Two reports are also produced, both in social security number sequence.

Since the volume is relatively large and the output must be produced as efficiently and in as timely a manner as possible, card processing would not be adequate. Since records in a Payroll file would generally be processed in a fixed sequence (social security

173

COMMON
COMPUTER
MEDIA AND
INPUT/OUTPUT
DEVICES

number, usually), the direct access feature of disk would not be applicable. Thus tape is the best medium for a Payroll file, such as the one above.

Example 2

A small-scale company has 500 customers and wishes to maintain a single Accounts Receivable file that can be used by the computer to produce monthly bills and that can be used by the clerks to answer inquiries.

Since the volume is relatively small, cards would be a suitable medium. They can be entered as input to the computer and also manually read to answer inquiries.

Example 3

A large department store has 200,000 charge customers and wishes to maintain a computerized Accounts Receivable File. The file is used once a month to prepare customer bills. In addition, a program has been written that would utilize inquiry cards as input, search the file, and print answers to the inquiry. Inquiries are made at the volume of 15,000 daily and are fed into the computer on cards that are entered in no specified sequence.

A direct-access file is the only viable alternative for this system. The volume of the file necessitates a high-speed device. The inquiry cards necessitate a file search in random sequence. Thus, a direct-access file would be required.

Example 4

A medium-sized company now maintains an inventory on 2000 stock parts. The company plans to merge with another organization in the near future and will maintain an inventory on all parts currently held by both companies.

Ordinarily, if only 2000 records on parts are to be stored on a file, a card file could be the least costly. But since the company expects rapid growth shortly, a tape file would probably be a better alternative.

Important Terms Used in this Section

Backup Tape	Header Label	Magnetic Tape Drive
Batch Processing	Index	Nonimpact Printer
Card Read/Punch	Key-to-Disk Encoder	Read/Write Head
Character Printer	Key-to-Tape Encoder	Retention Cycle
Data Cell	Line Printer	Sequential Processing
Direct Access	Magnetic Disk	Tape Librarian
File Protection Ring	Magnetic Disk Drive	
Hard Copy	Magnetic Drum	
Hardware	Magnetic Tape	

Self-Evaluating Quiz

1. Three physical components that are generally required for any computer application are _____, _____, and _____.

2. The CPU is a machine that _____.

3. An input device _____.

4. An output device _____.

5. Each input or output device is linked to the Central Processing Unit by _____.

6. Batch processing is _____.

7. The term _____ is used to denote computer input/output devices.

8. The card read/punch is a single device that houses (no.) _____ separate units.

9. (T or F) Most card read/punch devices can read card data and punch additional data into the same card.

10. (T or F) Cards are generally punched at a much slower rate than they are read.

11. (T or F) Computer-produced punched cards generally contain the imprinting of data on the face of the card.

12. (T or F) Keypunched cards generally contain the imprinting of data on the face of the card.

13. An EAM device called an _____ imprints data punched into a card on the face of the card.

14. The basic advantages of card processing are _____ and _____.

15. Two disadvantages of card processing are _____ and _____.

16. Each line of a computer printed report generally contains a maximum of _____ or _____ characters per line.

17. A _____ is the device most often used to produce computer printouts.

18. One of the most common master file types in medium- or large-scale computer centers is _____.

19. (T or F) A magnetic tape can serve as either input to or output from a computer system.

20. A magnetic tape drive resembles a home _____.

21. (T or F) After a tape has been processed and is no longer needed, the same tape may be reused to store other data.

22. The three major advantages of tape processing as compared to card processing are: _____, _____, and _____.

23. Two methods of recording data onto a magnetic tape are with the use of a _____ and a _____.

24. Because of a tape's capacity to handle large volumes of data in a relatively short time, it is ideally suited for _____ processing.

25. A disadvantage of tapes is that they can only be processed _____

26. The sequential method of processing tape records creates no time problem when _____.

27. Because of the vast numbers of magnetic tapes in many installations, _____ often becomes a problem.

28. The creation of _____ on output tapes in a program is used for checking purposes when the tapes are used as input.

29. Most computer installations employ _____ to ensure proper handling of tapes.

30. Three advantages of disk processing that are common to tape processing are _____, _____ and, _____.

31. An advantage of disk processing that makes it more suitable for some applications than tape processing is the _____.

32. The most common method for accessing magnetic disk records directly is with the use of an _____.

33. Direct processing is advantageous where _____.

34. A major disadvantage of disk processing is _____.

175

COMMON
COMPUTER
MEDIA AND
INPUT/OUTPUT
DEVICES

Solutions

1. Central Processing Unit (CPU); input device; output device
2. processes data by performing arithmetic operations, logic functions, and manipulating data to produce output
3. accepts data and transmits it to the CPU
4. transmits information or processed data from the CPU to an output medium
5. cables
6. the collection of groups or batches of records to be processed, collectively, by a computer run at periodic intervals
7. hardware
8. two
9. F
10. T
11. F
12. T
13. Interpreter
14. its relatively low cost; its ability to be read both manually and electronically
15. its relative lack of durability; its relatively slow speed
16. 100; 132
17. line printer
18. tape or disk
19. T
20. tape recorder
21. T
22. speed; storage space is saved; records can be any size
23. tape drive of a computer system; key-to-tape encoder
24. batch

25. sequentially
26. all or most of the records on a tape must be processed in sequence
27. identification
28. header labels
29. tape librarians
30. speed; storage space is saved; records can be any size
31. direct processing capability
32. index
33. small numbers of records from a large file are required for processing in a random sequence
34. its cost

Review Questions

I. Answer True or False

1. (T or F) Major files in most data processing installations are stored on cards.
2. (T or F) A tape file is generally used when most records from a large master file are required for sequential processing during each run.
3. (T or F) Punched cards are a high-speed medium that can serve as input to, or output from, a computer.
4. (T or F) A very small computer center could operate with just a card reader, CPU and printer.
5. (T or F) Some devices are equipped to process records directly while others can only process them sequentially.
6. (T or F) Batch-processing refers to the accumulation of data prior to its entry into the computer flow.
7. (T or F) Batch-processing is most often utilized with direct-access files.
8. (T or F) A card reader unit and a card punch unit are always housed in the same device called a card read/punch.
9. (T or F) A record on a tape may be read by a computer system and additional information may then be added to that record.
10. (T or F) If a tape is used as output (that is "written over"), then information that was originally recorded on it will be destroyed.
11. (T or F) A file protection ring is used to ensure that a tape is not inadvertently destroyed.
12. (T or F) Information can be more densely stored on a magnetic tape than on a punched card.

II. Fill in the Blanks

1. The basic advantages of card processing are _____ and _____.
2. A record on a tape may be any _____, as long as it is physically consistent with the size of primary storage.
3. A _____ is a device that requires an operator to code data from a source document onto a magnetic tape via a typewriter-like keyboard.

177

COMMON
COMPUTER
MEDIA AND
INPUT/OUTPUT
DEVICES

4. When most records are required for processing in a specified sequence then _____ is considered the most suitable file type.
5. Two disadvantages of tape processing are _____ and _____.
6. The creation of a header label record on a tape is required because _____.
7. A tape librarian is employed by many companies because _____.
8. A disk index is used to _____.
9. Two disadvantages of disk processing are _____ and _____.

*II. Representation of Data on Magnetic Tape and Disk

Magnetic tape and magnetic disk are the two most frequently used high-speed storage media. This chapter has outlined the utilization of these two as they relate to the businessman and to the computer specialist.

Although businessmen are not required to understand the exact representation of data on these media, familiarity with this topic often helps to establish a proper perspective on how magnetic tape and magnetic disk are used. Thus, in this section, we will attempt to familiarize business and data processing students with representation of tape and disk data.

A. Representation of Data on Magnetic Tape

1. Magnetic Tape Code   Data is recorded on magnetic tape on a thin film of iron oxide coating. Each tape is subdivided into a series of tracks where each track can contain one magnetized bit. This is analogous to a punched card which consists of 12 rows where combinations of row-punches in a given position represent a specific character (see Figure 5.16).

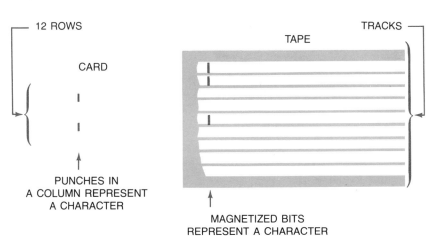

12 ROWS

CARD

PUNCHES IN
A COLUMN REPRESENT
A CHARACTER

TAPE

TRACKS

MAGNETIZED BITS
REPRESENT A CHARACTER

Figure 5.16

Representation of data on punched cards and magnetic tape.

Figure 5.17
Review of EBCDIC.

ZONE PORTION

| BITS / ZONE | 0 | 1 | 2 | 3 | ← BIT NUMBER |
	8	4	2	1	← POSITIONAL VALUE
12 (for letters A-I)	1	1	0	0	
11 (for letters J-R)	1	1	0	1	
0 (for letters S-Z)	1	1	1	0	
DIGITS	1	1	1	1	

DIGIT PORTION

| BITS / DIGIT | 4 | 5 | 6 | 7 | ← BIT NUMBER |
	8	4	2	1	← POSITIONAL VALUE
0	0	0	0	0	
1	0	0	0	1	
2	0	0	1	0	
3	0	0	1	1	
4	0	1	0	0	
5	0	1	0	1	
6	0	1	1	0	
7	0	1	1	1	
8	1	0	0	0	
9	1	0	0	1	

Each of these tracks on a tape can be magnetized or demagnetized depending upon the data to be represented.

Magnetic tapes typically consist of either 9 tracks or 7 tracks; 9-track tapes produce characters in EBCDIC form and 7 track tapes produce characters in BCD form.

179

COMMON
COMPUTER
MEDIA AND
INPUT/OUTPUT
DEVICES

Magnetic Tape Configurations

TYPE	USE	CORRESPONDING CODE
9-track	Compatible with third-generation computers	EBCDIC (eight data bits + check bit)
7-track	Invented for second-generation computers; can be used with third-generation as well.	BCD (six data bits + check bit)

a. 9-Track Magnetic Tape   Data is represented on 9-track tapes in EBCDIC form. EBCDIC, you will recall, is an abbreviation for Extended Binary Coded Decimal Interchange Code. Figure 5.17 reviews this code which was discussed in detail in Chapter 4.

The bit configuration for EBCDIC data on 9-track magnetic tape is shown in Figure 5.18. Notice that bit numbers 0 to 3 are used for the zone portion of a character, while bits 4 to 7 are used for the digit position.

Disregarding the P-bit momentarily, we may represent any character using this combination of four zone and four digit bits.

The letter A, a combination of a 12-zone and a 1-digit in Hollerith, would be represented on tape as indicated in Figure 5.19.

Similarly, the letter L is represented on 9-track tape as shown in Figure 5.20.

A typical way to represent any *integer* on magnetic tape would be to use 1111 in the zone positions in addition to the corresponding digit representation. Thus the number 172 in a numeric field will be represented in three positions of tape as shown in Figure 5.21.

Note that the illustrated codes are the *same* as the ones the computer uses for internal representation of data. The 1's denote magnetized positions or bits "on." The 0's denote demagnetized

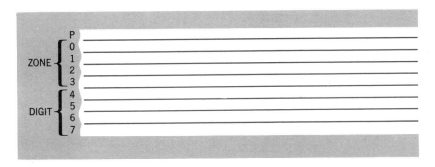

Figure 5.18

Bit configuration on a 9-track magnetic tape.

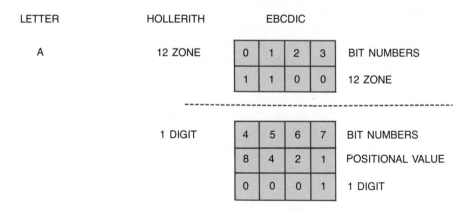

LETTER	HOLLERITH	EBCDIC				
A	12 ZONE	0	1	2	3	BIT NUMBERS
		1	1	0	0	12 ZONE
	1 DIGIT	4	5	6	7	BIT NUMBERS
		8	4	2	1	POSITIONAL VALUE
		0	0	0	1	1 DIGIT

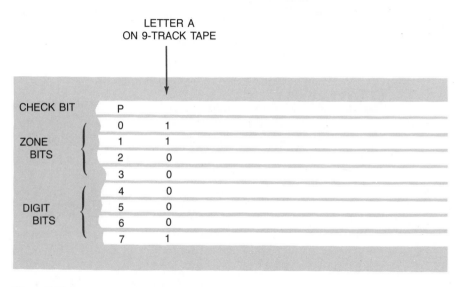

LETTER A
ON 9-TRACK TAPE

CHECK BIT	P	
ZONE BITS	0	1
	1	1
	2	0
	3	0
DIGIT BITS	4	0
	5	0
	6	0
	7	1

Figure 5.19
Representation of the letter A on a 9-track tape.

positions or bits "off." Magnetic tape can be processed quickly by computer because no code conversion is required. Data is represented on tape in 9-track form, with each track having current "on" or "off," in the same manner as each character is represented internally in the computer by nine bits per position or byte. Thus, for the computer to read from or write onto magnetic tape is a high-speed process.

Parity The P-bit corresponds to a *Parity* or check bit and is used to check the coded representation of data.

When data is coded, both internally in the computer and on magnetic tape, there is a remote possibility that a single bit posi-

181
COMMON
COMPUTER
MEDIA AND
INPUT/OUTPUT
DEVICES

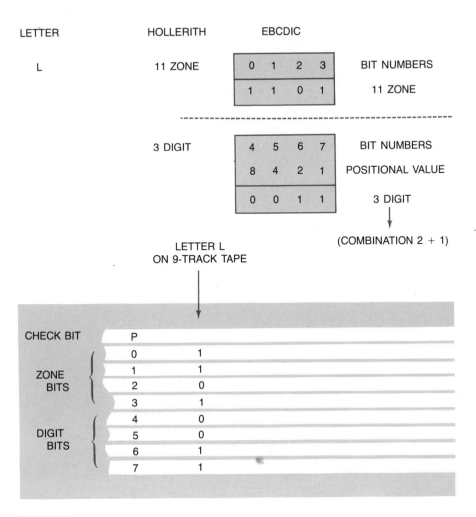

Figure 5.20
Representation of the letter L on a 9-track tape.

tion can sometimes become demagnetized, or an "off" position can become magnetized. The parity or P-bit is used to determine if this error has occurred.

Odd Parity   *Odd parity* is the utilization of an odd number of on-bits to represent *any* character. Thus Figure 5.22 illustrates how the digit 5 is represented on tape.

Note that there are *six* bits on, not counting the P-bit. Using the concept of odd parity, the machine would automatically magnetize or "turn on" the P-bit.

Thus, the complete codes for the number 7 and the letter A are denoted also in Figure 5.22.

	1								7								2						
BIT NUMBER	0	1	2	3	4	5	6	7	0	1	2	3	4	5	6	7	0	1	2	3	4	5	6	7
POSITIONAL VALUE	8	4	2	1	8	4	2	1	8	4	2	1	8	4	2	1	8	4	2	1	8	4	2	1
	1	1	1	1	0	0	0	1	1	1	1	1	0	1	1	1	1	1	1	1	0	0	1	0

		Col 1	Col 2	Col 3
	P			
ZONE	0	1	1	1
	1	1	1	1
	2	1	1	1
	3	1	1	1
DIGIT	4	0	0	0
	5	0	1	0
	6	0	1	1
	7	1	1	0
		1	7	2

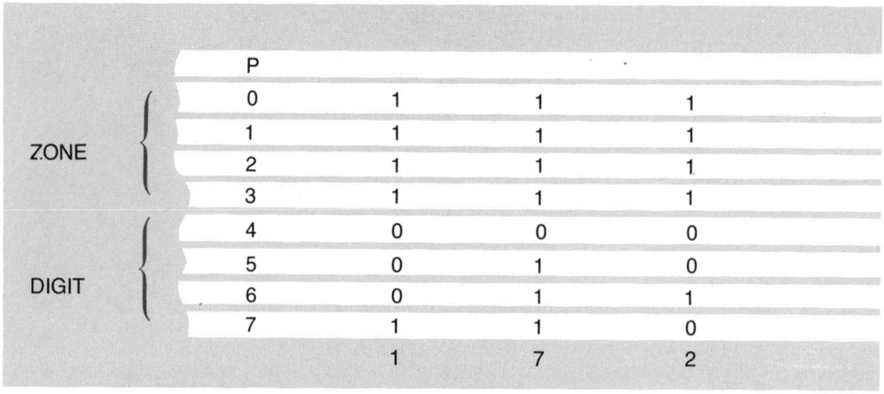

Figure 5.21

Representation of the number 172 on a 9-track tape.

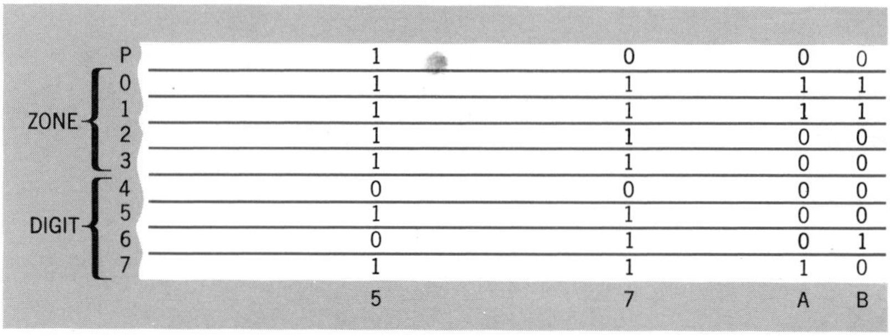

		Col 1	Col 2	Col 3	Col 4
	P	1	0	0	0
ZONE	0	1	1	1	1
	1	1	1	1	1
	2	1	1	0	0
	3	1	1	0	0
DIGIT	4	0	0	0	0
	5	1	1	0	0
	6	0	1	0	1
	7	1	1	1	0
		5	7	A	B

Figure 5.22

Representation of the characters 5, 7, A, B on 9-track tape.

The P-bit is used to ensure that an odd number of bits is always on for the computer that uses odd-parity checking.

Even Parity   For *even-parity* computers, the P-bit is used to ensure that an *even* number of bits is always on.

In short, the number of bits on must always be *odd* for odd-parity computers. Thus magnetic tapes typically utilize an odd number of bits for each character. During the reading of a magnetic tape, the number of bits on is checked to determine if, in fact, an odd number exists. If a single bit were inadvertently demagnetized or the current turned "off," or similarly an extra bit were magnetized, this would result in a parity error. The computer would not continue processing this tape until the problem was located.

Notice that this technique of parity checking only works when a *single* bit for a specific character is inadvertently misrepresented. If two bits are demagnetized, an odd number would still exist and no parity error would occur. Keep in mind, however, that the loss or gain of a single bit during processing is a remote possibility, but one that must nonetheless be properly handled; the loss of two bits, however, has almost no probability of occurring during processing and thus is simply not handled by most computers.

183
COMMON
COMPUTER
MEDIA AND
INPUT/OUTPUT
DEVICES

Self-Evaluating Quiz

Indicate the 9-track configuration for the following characters using odd parity:

1. E
2. Q
3. 6
4. T
5. V

```
P
0
1
2
3
4
5
6
7
        E      Q        6        T        V
```

	P	1	1	1	0	0
ZONE {	0	1	1	1	1	1
	1	1	1	1	1	1
	2	0	0	1	1	1
	3	0	1	1	0	0
DIGIT {	4	0	1	0	0	0
	5	1	0	1	0	1
	6	0	0	1	1	0
	7	1	0	0	1	1
		E	Q	6	T	V

Solutions

> *b. 7-Track Tapes* The code used on 7-track tapes corresponds to BCD (Binary Coded Decimal) and also used a check bit.

7-Track Configuration

BITS	MEANING	USE
C	Check bit	Turned on to make an odd or even number of bits, depending upon parity of machine
B-A	Zone bits	B-A 12 zone B 11 zone A 0 zone
8 4 2 1	Digit bits	Combination of 8-4-2-1 to make digit

Examples of characters represented on 7-track even-parity tape are shown in Figure 5.23.

2. Density We have seen that millions of characters can be recorded as magnetized bits on a single magnetic tape. The primary

Figure 5.23

Representation of characters on 7-track, even-parity tape.

reason for this storage capability is the fact that bits are exceedingly small so that hundreds of them can be placed on a very small area of tape. The actual number of characters that can be represented in an inch of tape is called the *density*. Since each character is represented by a series of bits in a specific position, tape densities are measured in *bits per inch* (bpi). The most common tape densities are 800 bpi or 1600 bpi but some tapes have densities of 6000 or more bits per inch. This means that on most tapes 800 to 1600 characters of data or 10 to 20 cards of data can be represented in a single inch of tape. This storage capacity is one reason why magnetic tapes are so frequently used at computer installations.

185

COMMON
COMPUTER
MEDIA AND
INPUT/OUTPUT
DEVICES

3. Blocking Another major advantage of tape processing is that tape records are not restricted, like cards, to an 80-position format but can be practically any size, restricted only by the physical limitations of the computer.

a. Tape Record Size Thus we may have 100-position tape records, 500-position tape records, or any size desired within the limitations of the computer system. When all records in a single tape file are the same size, we say that the file employs *fixed-length* records. When records in a single tape file have different sizes depending on the format of each record, we say that the file employs *variable-length* records.

Programming effort is simplified by using fixed-length records on a tape. Variable-length tape records require far more sophisticated programming and thus are not usually employed unless there is some overriding reason.

We will, therefore, restrict our discussion to fixed-length tape records, where each record is the same size. The specific size of each record, however, is determined for each application by the systems and programming staff.

b. Interblock Gaps Between physical tape records the computer automatically reserves a fraction of an inch of blank tape called an *Interblock Gap (IBG)*. Thus when a tape is created as computer output, it is created as indicated in Figure 5.24.

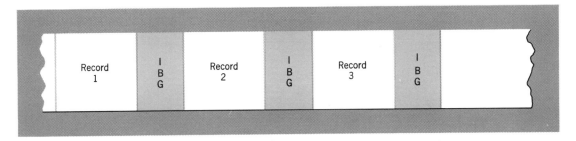

Figure 5.24
Physical tape records separated by interblock gaps (IBGs).

For some tape drives, this interblock gap between records is ¾ inch, for others it is ³/₅ inch. The smaller the IBG, the less wasted tape there is.

The IBG is necessary for processing. When a computer reads from a tape, it reads at very high speeds of more than 100 inches per second. Because of that speed, the computer requires a fraction of a second for the equipment to physically stop when the end of a record is sensed. This concept is called *inertia*. It is similar to the automobile traveling at 60 miles per hour which, after the brake has been applied, requires a braking distance before actually coming to a full stop.

Thus a magnetic tape that is read or written at tremendous speeds needs a fraction of a second to physically stop after reaching the end of a record. In this fraction of a second, a fraction of an inch of tape has been bypassed. That is, in the time it takes the read/write head of a tape drive to stop, an extra fraction of an inch of tape has been passed.

To accommodate this inertia, each record, upon creation, is automatically written with a blank area of tape next to it. This blank area, or IBG, is the exact size necessary for the inertia, so that when the fraction of an inch of tape has been bypassed, no significant data has been lost.

Let us assume the size of the IBG is 0.6 inches. If each tape record were 100 characters long, and the tape had a density of 800 bpi, we would have data represented on tape as indicated in Figure 5.25.

You will note that while each record occupies ⅛ (0.125) of an inch, each IBG adjacent to it uses ³/₅ (0.6) inches. In effect, we would have more blank tape than recorded areas.

To alleviate this problem, the computer systems allow us to "*block*" or group tape records to make maximum use of the tape area. The systems and programming staff determines the size of the block, or the *blocking factor*, as indicated in Figure 5.26.

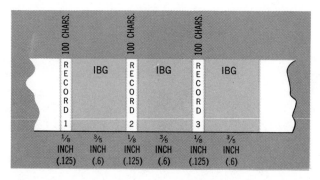

Figure 5.25

Representation of data on tape without blocking.

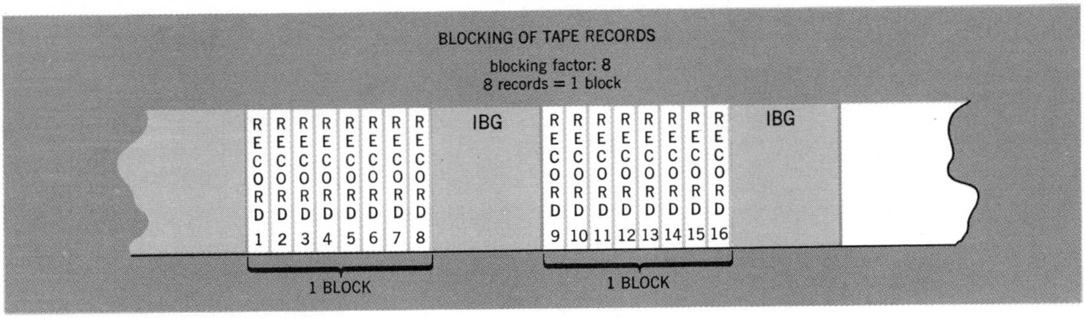

BLOCKING OF TAPE RECORDS
blocking factor: 8
8 records = 1 block

Figure 5.26
Blocking of tape records.

In Figure 5.26, the computer processes eight records as a group. If each record contained 100 characters, the physical record or block would contain 800 characters. At 800 bpi that would be 1 inch of tape. Thus we would have our 0.6-inch IBG between each inch of data. This is a distinct improvement over our previous example where we had substantially more blank area than recorded data.

c. Programming Tape Problems The blocking of data on tape does *not* represent very much increase of programming effort. The programmer is merely required to supply the blocking factor and the record size and the computer itself will perform the specific input/output functions. When a computer is instructed to read from a tape, for example, it reads a *physical record* or *block* into storage (see Figure 5.27).

Physical and Logical Records It then makes the first *logical record*, Record 1, available for processing. When it is instructed to read a second record, it does *not* go to the tape again, but makes Record 2 *from storage* available for processing. Thus for the first three READ TAPE commands, the computer accesses the tape only *once*. It then makes each of the logical records available *from storage* as they are called on by a READ TAPE command. On the fourth READ TAPE command, the computer must physically access the next block of three records, and place it in storage overlaying the previous three records.

The creation of output tape records operates similarly. If the blocking factor is again three, the computer will accumulate three logical records in storage before it physically writes a block. Thus the first three WRITE TAPE commands merely result in the accumulation of three logical records *in storage*. The fourth WRITE TAPE command causes the previous block of three records to be created on tape and the fourth logical record placed in storage. Here, again, the computer accesses the tape only after every three records have been processed.

188

DATA
PROCESSING
FUNDAMENTALS
AND HARDWARE

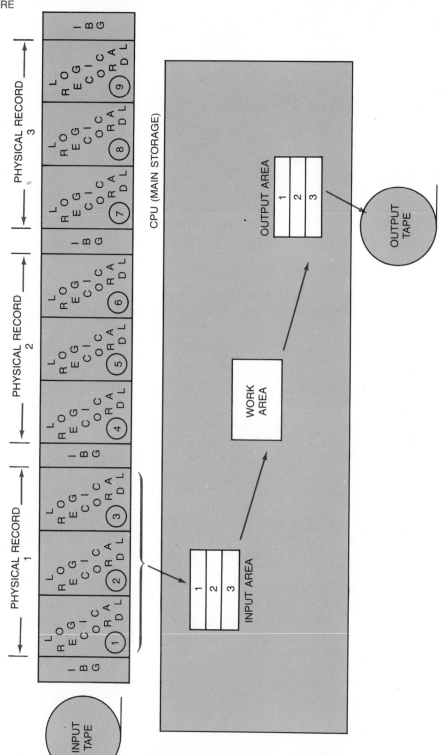

Figure 5.27
Processing of blocked records (three logical records = one physical record).

189

COMMON
COMPUTER
MEDIA AND
INPUT/OUTPUT
DEVICES

I/O Control The programming effort required for blocking records is not very great, since the computer's I/O control system is capable of handling many of the details. The programmer is required to supply the record size and the blocking factor and the computer can perform much of the internal processing. The programmer need only supply READ and WRITE commands and the blocking and deblocking is automatically handled.

The complex coding of the following can usually be eliminated by utilizing the computer's control system:

1. Tape labels (header labels for identification, trailer labels for summary or total information)
2. Creation of IBGs
3. Blocking of records
4. End-of-file conditions
5. End-of-reel conditions (where a specific file requires more than one physical tape reel)
6. Wrong length record errors (where programming or transmission errors result in a record that is not of the specified length)

The programmer need only specify the length of a logical record, and the control system will incorporate in the program a wrong length record check. Similarly, the programmer need only specify the blocking factor, and blocking techniques will also be included.

d. Limitations on Block Size The blocking factor is determined by the systems and programming staff and is subject only to the physical limitations of the computer. A record size of 1000 and a blocking factor of 50, for example, would simply be too cumbersome or too large to be effectively handled by many computers. In addition, the larger the physical block, the more chance there is for transmission errors.

4. Utility Programs for Tape Processing Since many types of tape programs require the same or similar coding, computer manufacturers make available standard, prepackaged *utility* programs which can be used by many different users. Since the programming required to sort a tape, for example, is somewhat cumbersome, the existence of sort-utility packages saves a significant amount of programming effort. Utility programs require the programmer to supply certain specifications which may vary from user to user. In the case of sorts, for example, the field to be sorted would be different for each application; hence the sort field is a required specification.

Typical utility programs include:

Sample Utility Programs

TYPE	FUNCTION	TYPICAL SPECIFICATIONS REQUIRED
Sort	Sorts a tape	Sort fields; sequence desired: ascending or descending, alphabetic or numeric
Merge	Merges two or more tapes	Merge fields
Card-to-tape	Converts card data to a tape	Tape format desired
Tape-to-print	Prints data on a tape	Tape format; output format desired

B. Basic Features of the Magnetic Disk Pack

We have already discussed the primary feature of magnetic disk—the *direct-access* capability. We will now discuss, in greater depth, the distinguishing facets of a disk storage unit in order to present a comprehensive understanding of this important storage medium.

A typical disk storage unit consists of *six* platters, or *disks*, arranged in a vertical stack, called a *disk pack*, shown in Figure 5.28.

Data may be recorded on both sides of the disks. There are, however, only *ten* recording surfaces, since the upper surface of the top disk and the under surface of the bottom disk cannot be utilized. Each of the ten recording surfaces is accessed by its own individual read/write head, which is capable of both retrieving and storing information.

Technically, the ten recording surfaces are numbered from 0 to 9. The corresponding read/write heads, which access each of these surfaces, are similarly numbered. Figure 5.29 illustrates the relationship of the read/write heads to the disk pack.

Figure 5.28
Typical disk pack.

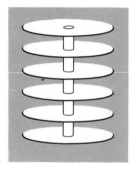

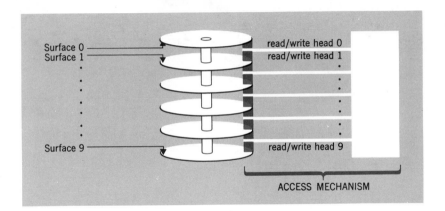

Figure 5.29
Accessing data from
a disk pack.

Surface 0 ——— read/write head 0
Surface 1 ——— read/write head 1

read/write head 9
Surface 9 ———

ACCESS MECHANISM

Let us outline the characteristics of a typical disk surface:

Disk Surface
1. 203 tracks: each track stores data as magnetized bits
2. Tracks are numbered 000 to 202 (see Figure 5.30)
3. Each track stores 3625 characters
4. Only 200 of 203 tracks are available for processing. Three are held in reserve for use in place of defective tracks.

This disk pack can therefore store approximately 7.25 million characters: 10 surfaces × 200 tracks × 3625 characters/track. Records on disk are blocked in much the same way and for the same reasons as for tape processing (see Figure 5.31). Thus several logical disk records are often blocked into a physical record with physical records separated by an IBG.

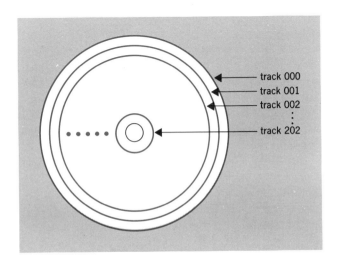

track 000
track 001
track 002
track 202

Figure 5.30

Tracks on a disk
surface.

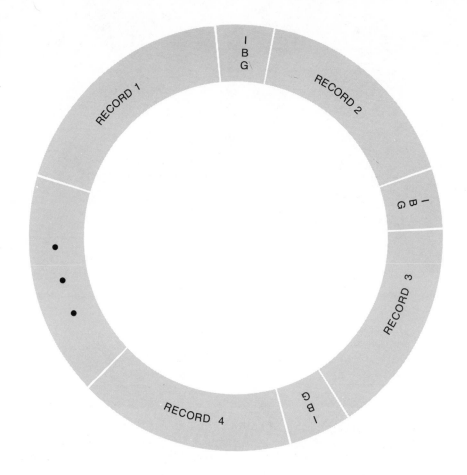

Figure 5.31
Storing several data records on a disk track.

A series of vertical tracks constitutes a *cylinder*. The above disk pack therefore has 203 cylinders (see Figure 5.32). When a specific track has been filled, data is then stored on the next surface but within the same track. Hence data is stored on the same cylinder. The advantage of storing data in this manner as opposed to moving to the next track is that time is saved in both storing and retrieving data. Since all read/write heads on the access mechanism move in and out *together*, rather than independently, after writing data on a particular track it would be easy to access the same track on the next surface. If a particular track has just been filled with data, there is no need to reposition the access mechanism in order to proceed with the recording of additional data within the same cylinder. All that is required is that a different read/write head, *which is already in position*, be activated to continue the processing on the next surface. No movement of the

193
COMMON
COMPUTER
MEDIA AND
INPUT/OUTPUT
DEVICES

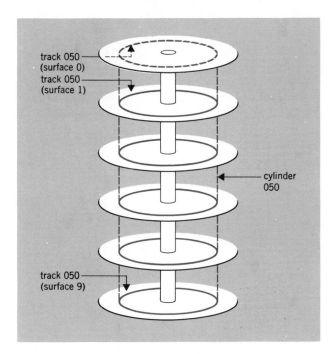

Figure 5.32
The cylinder concept using magnetic disk.

access arm is required, as would be the case if the adjacent track were used instead.

On some disks the track is further subdivided into even smaller segments called *sectors*. In this case, the address of any disk record includes a cylinder number, track number, and sector number.

Important Terms Used in this Section

BCD	IBG (Interblock Gap)
Bit	Logical Record
Bpi (Bits per inch)	9-Track Tape
Blocking	Parity
Check Bit	Physical Record
Cylinder	7-Track Tape
Density	Track
EBCDIC	Utility Program
Fixed-Length Records	Variable-Length Records

Self-Evaluating Quiz

1. Data is recorded on magnetic tape on a thin film of _____.
2. Most computer centers use (no.) _____ or (no.) _____ track tapes.

3. The tracks of a 9-track tape are labeled (no.) _____ to (no.) _____ and (letter) _____.

4. Four bits are used to represent the _____ and four bits are used to represent the _____.

5. To represent any integer on magnetic tape we typically use _____ in the zone positions.

6. The digit positions of bits 4 to 7 represent the integers (no.) _____, (no.) _____, (no.) _____, and (no.) _____, respectively.

7. The P-bit corresponds to a _____ or _____ bit.

8. _____ is the term used to represent the utilization of an odd number of on-bits for any character.

9. The number of characters per inch of tape is called _____.

10. The most frequently used densities are _____ and _____, although some tapes have densities in excess of _____.

11. When records on a single tape file have different sizes depending on the format of each record, then the file uses _____ records.

12. Between tape records the computer automatically reserves a fraction of an inch of blank tape called an _____.

13. This fraction of an inch is necessary to provide for the physical concept of _____.

14. To make maximum use of the tape area so that less tape is wasted, logical records are often grouped or _____.

15. (T or F) Suppose an input file is blocked 8. The computer physically reads from the tape after every READ command.

16. (T or F) If an input file is blocked 8, after every eight READ commands a physical record is read into storage.

17. (T or F) The programmer is required to handle most of the sophisticated tape routines in his or her program.

18. Packaged programs to handle many types of tape processing are called _____.

19. An example of a packaged tape program is a _____.

20. A tape-to-print utility performs the operation of _____.

Solutions

1. iron-oxide coating
2. 7 or 9
3. 0; 7; P
4. zone; digit
5. 1111
6. 8, 4, 2, 1
7. parity; check
8. Odd parity
9. density
10. 800; 1600; 6000

11. variable-length
12. interblock gap (IBG)
13. inertia
14. blocked
15. F
16. T
17. F
18. utility programs
19. SORT utility
20. printing the data that is written on a tape

195

COMMON
COMPUTER
MEDIA AND
INPUT/OUTPUT
DEVICES

Chapter 6
Specialized Computer Media and Equipment

6

6

I. Devices That Can Read Source Documents

The computer hardware described in the previous chapter represent the most commonly used devices in a computer system.

A. The Conversion Process

Notice, however, that cards, tapes, and disks, the media most often used as input, require *conversion from a source document.* This conversion process, using devices such as keypunch machines or key-to-tape encoders with operators, can be extremely costly and time-consuming. In addition, it requires a major control procedure. Source documents must be counted and the result compared against the number of input records created by the conversion to ensure that records have not been misplaced. Manual procedures must be employed to physically transport source documents to an operations or control staff, and then to transport the machine-readable input records to the computer room.

As computer equipment becomes even faster and more sophisticated, this conversion process consumes a greater percentage of total data processing time. In many companies, where inputs are voluminous, this conversion process can require up to 35% of the total operation time.

In an effort to alleviate the increased cost and time allotted to conversion, manufacturers have sought to produce equipment that will accept source input without requiring extensive conversion. The major devices thus far in use today include:

Devices that Eliminate the Conversion Process
1. Magnetic Ink Character Recognition (MICR) equipment
2. Optical Character Recognition (OCR) equipment
3. Punched paper tape read/punch
4. Terminal devices.

Terminal equipment requires special consideration because it functions most typically in an online environment. Terminals will be discussed in depth in Chapter 12. (Table 6.1 on page 214 provides a synopsis of file types discussed in this chapter.)

The first three device types indicated above usually employ *batch-processing* procedures. That is, they are best suited for applications that utilize large volumes of data, processed in a group at fixed intervals. For batch-processing procedures, conversion from a source document is relatively costly. The above devices are capable of reading a source document and converting it to a machine-readable form *directly*, as discussed below.

B. MICR (*Magnetic Ink Character Recognition*)

The banking industry is the largest user of this equipment, which is capable of reading bank checks (see Figure 6.1). The checks have account numbers, recorded in special type characters of magnetic ink, imprinted on the bottom. When a check is cashed, the amount is also imprinted by a special device. A MICR reader-sorter can interpret the data on checks, sort it into account number or branch number sequence, and transfer the data to a CPU of a computer system or to an offline device.

C. OCR (*Optical Character Recognition*)

An OCR device, commonly referred to as an *optical scanner*, reads characters from printed documents (see Figure 6.2). No special ink or typing is required. Some devices can read handwritten as well as typed data.

The optical scanner senses data with the use of a photoelectric device. The data is read by a light source, which converts these characters into electrical impulses. On many devices, the input document must have characters or marks in designated positions in order to be properly sensed, as shown in Figure 6.3. The computer, then, must be instructed as to which positions will contain the data.

1. Uses of OCR Equipment A major use of optical scanners is in conjunction with gasoline company credit card receipts. Credit card identification from a plastic plate is imprinted on the receipt along with the amount of the purchase. These receipts are then read into a computer with the use of an optical scanner that senses the amount and customer account number. Other major users include department stores which batch-process handwritten receipts that are read by OCR equipment (see Figure 6.4). Consider the tremendous advantage of reducing the need for a large and costly operations staff by using the source document as machine-readable input.

Speed OCR equipment varies in speed from approximately 50 characters per second, for devices that can read handwritten letters, to 2400 characters per second, and from 200 to 1200 documents per minute. Most page readers are very costly, however, ranging in price from $160,000 to $400,000 on the average, with

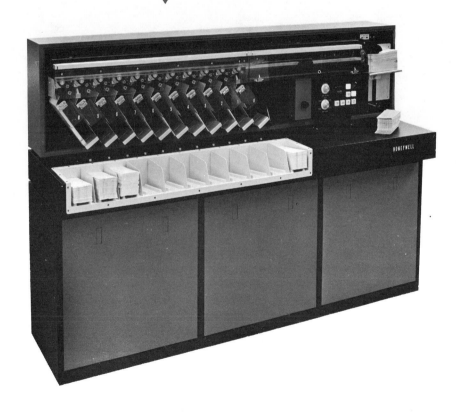

207025

ON   SHARES • PAY $

THE
SOUTHLAND
CORPORATION
DALLAS TEXAS

TO
THE
ORDER
OF

VOID

CHASE MANHATTAN BANK
NEW YORK, NEW YORK

PRESIDENT

⑆207025⑆ ⑉0210⑈0002⑉ 910⑈4⑈012373⑈

Figure 6.1

MICR reader-sorter. This low-cost document reader-sorter is used most frequently in banks. It reads magnetic ink encoded documents at speeds up to 600 documents per minute and sorts them into 11 different pockets. Courtesy Honeywell.

Figure 6.2
Optical character reader. Courtesy IBM.

monthly rentals from $2500 to $6000. For many applications, it is still cheaper to utilize the traditional conversion process. In one company, a systems analyst performed a cost study to determine the feasibility of acquiring an OCR device for a billing system. It was determined that an OCR device could only be monetarily justified where the system processed 20,000 documents per day. With fewer documents, the standard conversion process would be more economical. Thus we can see that such a device is relatively costly and is justifiable only when processing a voluminous quantity of input.

2. Reliability Problem In addition to cost, OCR equipment has one other disadvantage, one that results in limited reliability. Characters that are sensed by this device often must *rigidly* conform to the standard. Typing erasures, overlapping of positions, and

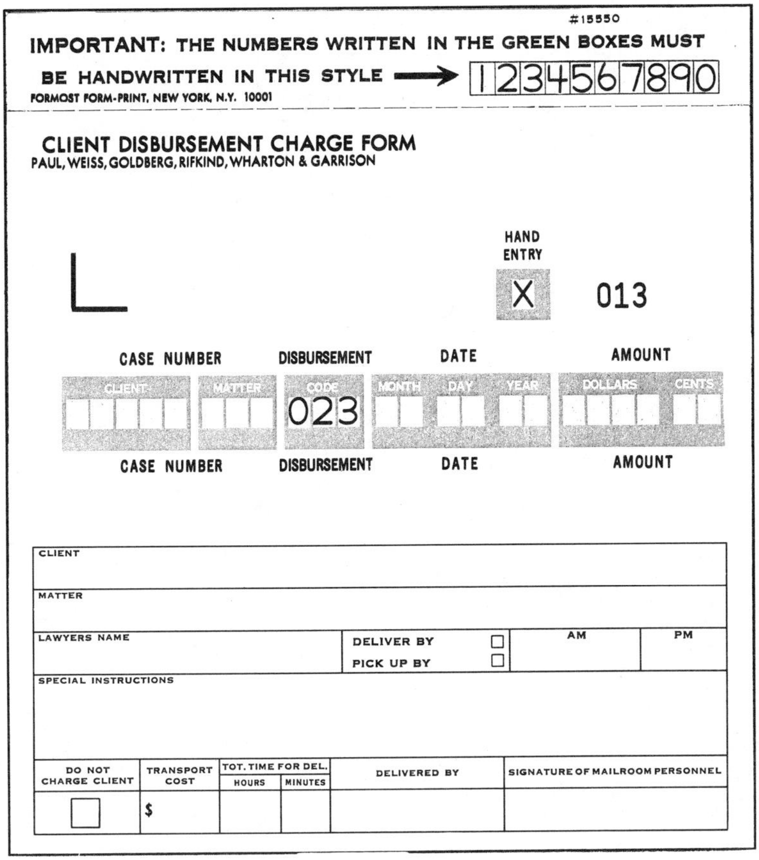

#15550

IMPORTANT: THE NUMBERS WRITTEN IN THE GREEN BOXES MUST BE HANDWRITTEN IN THIS STYLE → 1 2 3 4 5 6 7 8 9 0

FORMOST FORM-PRINT, NEW YORK, N.Y. 10001

CLIENT DISBURSEMENT CHARGE FORM

PAUL, WEISS, GOLDBERG, RIFKIND, WHARTON & GARRISON

HAND ENTRY X 013

CASE NUMBER		DISBURSEMENT	DATE			AMOUNT	
CLIENT	MATTER	CODE	MONTH	DAY	YEAR	DOLLARS	CENTS
		023					
CASE NUMBER		DISBURSEMENT	DATE			AMOUNT	

CLIENT

MATTER

LAWYERS NAME — DELIVER BY ☐ / PICK UP BY ☐ — AM — PM

SPECIAL INSTRUCTIONS

DO NOT CHARGE CLIENT	TRANSPORT COST	TOT. TIME FOR DEL. HOURS	MINUTES	DELIVERED BY	SIGNATURE OF MAILROOM PERSONNEL
☐	$				

Figure 6.3

Sample input. Courtesy International Business Forms.

so on can cause the erroneous transmission of data. In some applications, as much as 10% of the input data is unreadable because of such errors. In short, the promise of increased reliability and decreased cost in future years will make OCR equipment more widespread than it is today.

3. Mark-Sense Devices as Optical Readers A mark-sense reader detects the presence of pencil marks on predetermined grids. The typical documents to be mark-sensed are computer-scored test papers, where students are required to indicate the correct answer by pencilling in grid A, B, C, D, or E. Note that the mark-sensed cards discussed in Chapter 2 are examples of input documents that can be read by mark-sense readers. Here again, the data can be transformed into an input medium. Note that while these are optical readers, they have limited facility and therefore limited use. Their capability is much less than optical scanners, where actual

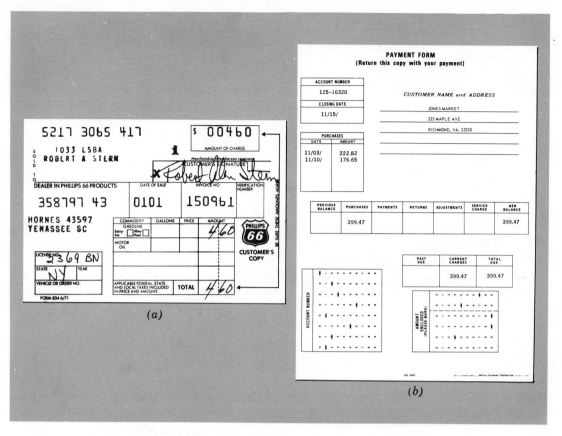

Figure 6.4
Sample input to optical reader. (a) On gasoline credit slip, only imprinted data is read by optical reader. (b) Payment form serves as a statement to the customer. When returned with payment, the account number and amount enclosed (marked at the bottom of the form) serve as input to an optical scanner. Courtesy Optical Scanning Corporation.

handwritten or typed data can be read. But their reliability and cost are less problematic than more versatile optical readers.

D. Punched Paper Tape Read/Punch (Figure 6.5)
A punched paper tape (Figure 6.6) is a paper tape that, like a card, is punched with holes in specified rows and columns. A paper tape read/punch is, like a card read/punch, two separate units that can read from a paper tape or punch data into one.

1. No Source Document Necessary Punched paper tape may be produced by special adding machines, accounting machines, and cash registers. With the aid of the read/punch it can then be used, as a source document, by the computer system.

2. Advantages The punched paper tape has several advantages that make it more suitable for some applications than card

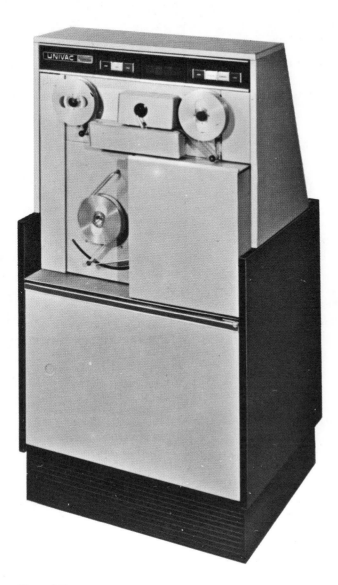

Figure 6.5
Punched paper tape read/punch. Courtesy UNIVAC.

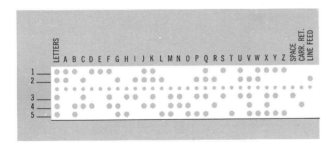

Figure 6.6
Punched paper tape.

processing. A file can be represented on a continuous tape; thus there is no limitation on record size as with punched cards. Punched paper tape equipment is less expensive than card equipment. It is easier to store and transport paper tapes than large volumes of cards. There is no problem with sequencing the tape records, since the file can be represented on one contiguous tape.

3. Disadvantages There are, however, several limitations to paper tape processing. Paper tape is not as durable as cards. Paper tape devices are slower than card equipment. Typical paper tape read/punch devices can read 300 characters per second and punch 110 characters per second. In general, only applications that use cash register or adding machine tapes, teletypes or other specialized systems employ paper tape devices.

Summary In short, there are several computer devices available that can read source documents directly without requiring a conversion to some other medium, such as cards, tape, or disk. Terminal devices are also included in this category, but because they are utilized in an online environment, they require special consideration, which will be discussed in Chapter 12.

II. Microfilm

A. Advantages of Microfilm

Microfilm has had a long and successful history as primarily a non-computerized storage medium. It is a photographed record or document in miniature requiring special devices to read. It is an exceedingly useful method of storing information. Hundreds or even thousands of records can be stored on a single unit and high-speed readers are capable of accessing specific records in relatively short periods.

Libraries are one of the most common users of microfilm, storing many editions of a journal or newspaper on one unit and making it accessible to readers with the use of microfilm readers.

B. Computers and Microfilm

In recent years, the computer industry has come to recognize the distinct advantages of microfilm. Since storing a large number of cards or printed reports has proven cumbersome, computer devices capable of creating output on microfilm have become increasingly popular.

C. Computer Output Microfilm: COM

Computer Output Microfilm (COM) devices include those that when linked to a CPU can create output on microfilm at very great speeds (see Figure 6.7). Other COM devices create microfilm from computer-produced magnetic tapes (see Figure 6.8). Printed

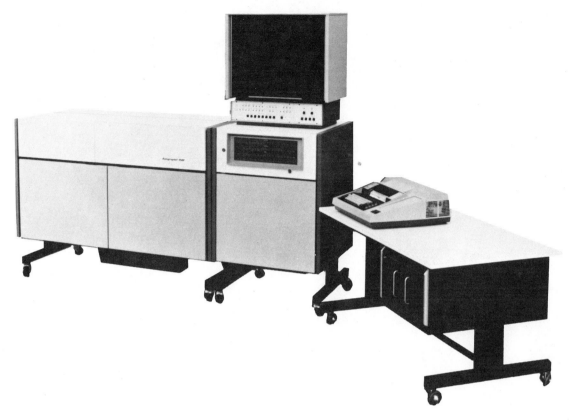

Figure 6.7
Example of a minicomputer controlled microfilm recorder. Courtesy DatagraphiX, Inc.

reports can be produced at enormous speeds on microfilm, rather than on paper by relatively slow printers. To access these COM reports, microfilm readers would be used (see Figure 6.9). Figure 6.10 illustrates how COM works when information is on computer-produced magnetic tapes.

1. Advantages of COM Microfilm output, produced instead of standard printed reports or punched cards, has the following advantages:

Advantages of COM
1. Output is produced at far greater speeds: microfilm output can be created at speeds in excess of 120,000 characters per second or 21,800 lines per minute.
2. Output is in miniaturized, compact form: this can typically save the user 98% of the storage space required to store cards or reports.

Figure 6.8
Tape-to-film recorder creates microfilm from computer-produced magnetic tapes.
Courtesy DatagraphiX.

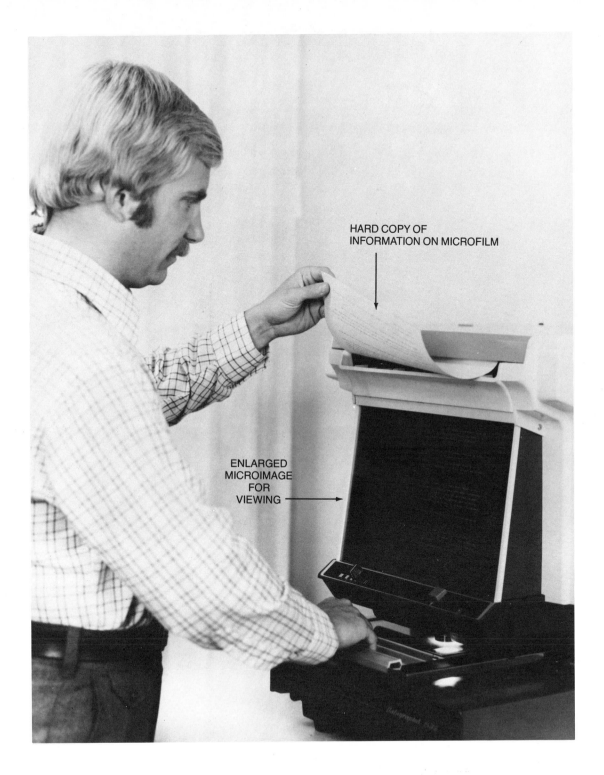

HARD COPY OF
INFORMATION ON MICROFILM

ENLARGED
MICROIMAGE
FOR
VIEWING

Figure 6.9
Example of a microfilm reader with capability of printing copies of desired information.
Courtesy DatagraphiX.

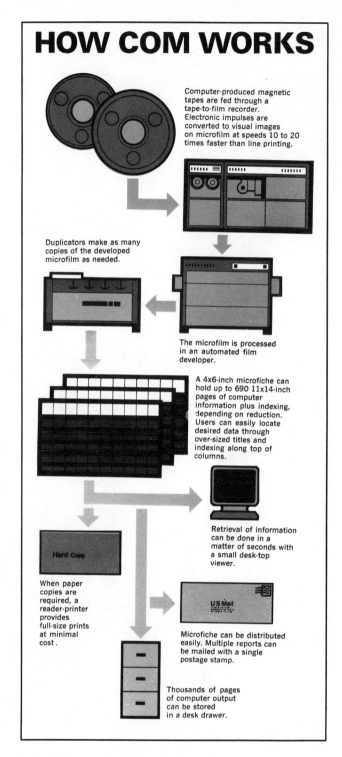

HOW COM WORKS

Computer-produced magnetic tapes are fed through a tape-to-film recorder. Electronic impulses are converted to visual images on microfilm at speeds 10 to 20 times faster than line printing.

Duplicators make as many copies of the developed microfilm as needed.

The microfilm is processed in an automated film developer.

A 4x6-inch microfiche can hold up to 690 11x14-inch pages of computer information plus indexing, depending on reduction. Users can easily locate desired data through over-sized titles and indexing along top of columns.

Retrieval of information can be done in a matter of seconds with a small desk-top viewer.

Hard Copy

When paper copies are required, a reader-printer provides full-size prints at minimal cost.

US Mail

Microfiche can be distributed easily. Multiple reports can be mailed with a single postage stamp.

Thousands of pages of computer output can be stored in a desk drawer.

Figure 6.10

Illustration of COM procedure when information is on magnetic tape. Courtesy DATACORP.

In short, COM is sometimes used by companies that produce a significant number of reports for in-house use.

2. Forms of COM Microfilm, the most common form of COM, refers to rolled film on reels. *Microform* is the generalized term used to describe microfilm as well as other forms of miniaturized records. The following list provides a summary of the microforms currently available as COM:

Microforms (Figure 6.11)
1. Microfiche card: each frame stores one printed document; requires microfiche reader to access
2. Aperture card: unit record concept; standard punched card with provision for filmed report, picture, graph, etc.; requires microfiche reader to access; punched data on card can be read by card machines
3. Microfilm: rolled film—16mm, 35mm, or 105mm—requires microfilm reader to access

---

3. Reading COM When companies use COM in place of printed records or punched cards, a special reader is required to access or read the material. Microfilm and microfiche readers can access specific records in a matter of seconds. Most of them can

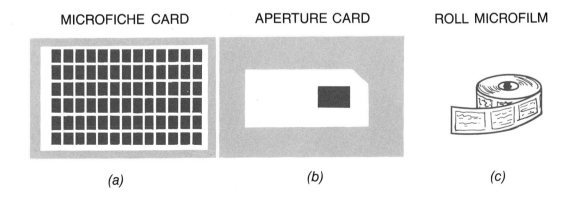

MICROFICHE CARD   APERTURE CARD   ROLL MICROFILM

(a)   *(b)*   *(c)*

Figure 6.11

Examples of microforms. (a) Microfiche card. Each microfiche card contains dozens of microfilm images. To access an individual record, a microfiche viewer must be used. (b) Aperture card. Each aperture card contains punched card data with an individual microfilm image. (c) Roll microfilm. Up to 2,000 pages of information can be stored in 100 feet of 16-mm. microfilm.

also provide hard-copy printouts of any desired record or illustration (see Figure 6.9 again).

D. Computer Input Microfilm: CIM

With the increasing use of COM equipment, there has been a corresponding interest in computer input devices that can *read* microfilm. With the development of such input devices, it would be possible to use microfilm in place of magnetic tape or disk as a high-speed, high-volume storage medium. Microfilm has one major advantage over magnetic tape or disk. It can be read by people with the use of a microfilm reader as well as by computers.

CIM or *C*omputer *I*nput *M*icrofilm is the term used to describe the devices capable of reading microfilm and transmitting data to the CPU. Note that most operations involving computer-produced microfilm currently utilize this medium to store finalized output records that do not usually reenter the data flow. Hence, the ability of inputting microfilm has not yet become really significant. Computer input microfilm thus far has had less applicability and less success than COM.

On COM

For decades, The Reuben H. Donnelley Corp., in its New York region, maintained records on as many as a half-million Yellow Pages advertisers in hard copy. To maintain this mountain of paper, 56 giant rotor files, operated by 26 employees, were needed. This required 15,000 sq. ft. of expensive floor space.

Two recent situations brought this cumbersome old system under close scrutiny by Donnelley. One was the increase in Yellow Pages directories servicing the New York area—which required even more file space. The other was the present physical condition of the rotor files. Worn and dilapidated, they would soon have to be replaced, with the addition of add-on equipment for new books. So, a systems study was conducted which resulted in a recommendation to convert to computer output microfilm.

Conversion was accomplished over a three-day holiday weekend. Data was drawn from Donnelley's computerized contract file, put on microfilm in a matter of hours and the system was ready for operation when the staff returned the next work day.

The new system uses COM supported by both microfiche and microfilm cassettes. The microfiche provides an index to the cassette containing the actual account record, plus back-up information.

In operation, the operator checks the microfiche index for the account being processed. If a copy of the master record is required, she turns to the cassette to retrieve the actual record. The computer system has been designed to format the record so that it exactly follows the familiar, old record in appearance to minimize retraining on procedural changes. If the operator's visual review does not satisfy the request, she can then obtain a hard copy by the simple press of a button.

On CIM

CIM (BETTER YOU SHOULDN'T ASK!)

"Computer input microfilm is a boring subject and too much has been said about it already," states Information International, Inc. (III) President Al Fenaughty. The III chief officer, whose firm is one of the few companies capable of producing CIM at present, would rather call for a "users revolt against the poor quality of all forms of printing—on COM, paper and CRTs—which people are forced to look at today."

Fenaughty, nevertheless, concedes CIM will have its place. Currently, III is performing a feasibility study for the British Government on one form of CIM which would replace data stored on mag tape.

The III executive points out that reels of tape have to be recycled periodically, about every two years, to maintain integrity of data. He adds that data stored on film would last for more than 100 years. "In this particular type of CIM, the user would want to retain data for possible future study. We can go from tape to film, formatted in a manner which will drive the computer to produce the necessary output."

A second form of CIM involves starting off with data stored in computer memory. III has done a study on this for the Dept. of Agriculture, and proven the feasibility of translating digital data to human-readable form on microfilm, with the capability of returning the data to the computer.

Still a third form of CIM starts off with source documents of various sizes and conditions, with this information microfilmed, subsequently processed through an optical character recognition system and digitized to drive a computer.

"Any CIM procedure is expensive and the market will develop slowly," III's Fenaughty says. He explains that his firm would contract to put data on microfilm for archival or other purposes only to prove feasibility, in order to sell equipment. "Now can we talk about the quality of printing? For example, with our COM recorder . . ."

E. COM and CIM Disadvantage: Cost

As with any new computer storage medium, the use of COM and CIM equipment is currently very costly, a factor that thus far has greatly inhibited their use. In addition, the "human factor" plays a part in the reluctance of many companies to use microfilm. Since machines are required to both read and create this medium, they are viewed with some trepidation by people who would rather read a printed report directly, even if the preparation of that report takes more time.

Table 6.1

Major Characteristics of Specialized Devices and File Types

File Type	Characteristics	Advantages	Disadvantages	Major Uses
MAGNETIC INK CHARACTER RECOGNITION (MICR) FILES	Data recorded in special characters of magnetic ink; data may be read and sorted by MICR devices used with computer systems.	Source documents imprinted with magnetic numbers can be read without a conversion process; devices are highly accurate even if an input document is bent or slightly mutilated; devices can handle any size document.	MICR devices can only detect numbers.	Banking systems utilize checks with MICR numbers imprinted on bottom as ACCOUNT NUMBER and AMOUNT (after check has been processed).
PRINTED DOCUMENTS READ BY OPTICAL CHARACTER RECOGNITION (OCR) EQUIPMENT	Data recorded in regular type or handwritten form; no conversion process necessary; for some machines, characters must be printed or typed in designated positions.	Saves considerable time and expense by eliminating the conversion process.	Rigid conformance to standard type fonts is required; erasures and slight overlapping of positions cause errors in transmission; extremely expensive compared to other input/output devices.	Department stores utilize OCR devices to read handwritten sales slips for charge customers. The sales slips are meticulously prepared by trained sales personnel; they are then read by OCR equipment which transmits the data to the computer which then updates the Accounts Receivable file.
PUNCHED PAPER TAPE	Tape is punched by machine (computer device, cash registers, adding machines) with holes in specified rows and columns; it then is read by a PAPER TAPE READ/PUNCH of a computer system.	File can be represented on a continuous tape without record length restrictions; easier to transport and store paper tape than cards; no sequencing problem with a continuous tape.	Not as durable as card files; the punched paper tape read/punches are slower than card devices.	Cash register receipts, adding machine tapes can be read by computer. Telephone companies can maintain records of all calls from a given area on paper tape.
MICROFILM	A microfilm is a photographed record in miniature—1/24 to 1/42 of its original size; devices that create microfilm records as a result of a computer run are called Computer Output Microfilm (COM) equipment; there are special viewers that may then be used to read the microfilm records and/or convert them to a printed report; computer devices that can read microfilm are called Computer Input Microfilm (CIM) equipment.	A major advantage of microfilm is the greatly reduced storage area required to maintain computer output (as opposed to the printed report which is the most common output form); the ability of high-speed microfilm readers to access this computer output quickly is another advantage.	The use of microfilm as a file type requires additional computer hardware and viewers that are relatively costly.	Firms that must store large amounts of printed information and be able to retrieve it speedily use microfilm. Motor vehicle bureaus, which maintain millions of records and which also need quick access to these records in case of accidents, stolen cars, etc., sometimes use microfilm. Similarly, personnel records, accounting ledgers, etc., at large companies are stored on microfilm.

Table 6.1 provides a summary of the major characteristics of the devices and file types discussed in this chapter. Table 6.2 provides a summary of the features of the input and output devices themselves.

Table 6.2

Features of Input and Output Devices

Device	Medium	Characteristics	Type	Speed class
Card reader	Punched cards	Reads 200 to 2000 cards (16,000 to 160,000 characters) per minute (average 800–1200)	Input	Low speed
Card punch	Punched cards	Punches 50 to 600 cards (4000 to 48,000 characters) per minute (average 300–600)	Output	Low speed
Line printer	Paper forms	Prints 150 to 3000 lines per minute	Output	Low Speed
Magnetic tape drive	Magnetic tape	Transfers 15,000 to 500,000 characters per second (average 100,000–300,000)	Input, output, storage	High speed
Magnetic disk drive	Magnetic disk	Transfers 100,000 to 3 million characters per second	Input, output, storage	High speed
Magnetic drum drive	Magnetic drum	Transfers 100,000 to 1.5 million characters per second	Input, output, storage	High speed
Magnetic ink character reader (MICR)	Documents printed with ferrite-impregnated ink	Reads approximately 1000 documents per minute	Input	Low speed
Optical character reader	Printed documents	Reads approximately 1000 documents per minute	Input	Low speed
Paper tape reader	Punched tape	Reads up to 1000 characters per second	Input	Low speed
Paper tape punch	Punched tape	Punches up to 150 characters per second	Output	Low speed
Computer-output microfiche or microfilm (COM) recorder	Photosensitive film	Records 500 to 40,000 pages per minute (average 21,000 lines per minute)	Output	High speed
Terminal/control console	Visual display, voice response, hardcopy	Transfers in excess of 2000 characters per second	Input, output	Low to medium speed

Important Terms Used in this Chapter

Aperture Card
CIM (Computer Input Microfilm)
COM (Computer Output Microfilm)
Conversion
Mark Sense
MICR (Magnetic Ink Character Recognition)
Microfiche

Microfilm
Microform
OCR (Optical Character
 Recognition)
Punched Paper Tape
Source Document
Terminal

Self-Evaluating Quiz

1. The process of _____, although mainly a manual operation, utilizes much time in data processing installations.
2. The banking industry uses _____ devices to minimize the conversion process.
3. Computer-processed checks and deposit slips have special _____ on the bottom that can be read by MICR devices.
4. (T or F) MICR equipment can handle almost any size check or deposit slip so that an industry-wide standard size is not required.
5. (T or F) Letters and numbers can be read by MICR devices.
6. The device that can read printed characters typed in regular ink is called a(n) _____ or a(n) _____ .
7. The OCR device is used to eliminate the manual _____ process from source documents to a computer medium.
8. (T or F) With some OCR devices, handwritten material can be read.
9. OCR equipment is monetarily justifiable when _____.
10. (T or F) OCR equipment is slow compared to devices such as tape and disk drives.
11. Major disadvantages of OCR equipment include _____.
12. Punched paper tapes commonly produced by special _____ and _____ can be used as input to a computer.
13. (T or F) Paper tape read/punch devices are slower than card read/punch devices.
14. Microfilm is a _____.
15. The two major computer advantages of microfilm are in the areas of _____ and _____.
16. Two forms of computer output microfilm are _____ and _____.

Solutions

1. conversion
2. Magnetic Ink Character Recognition (MICR)
3. magnetic ink digits
4. T
5. F—only numbers

6. optical character recognition (OCR) device; optical scanner
7. conversion
8. T
9. voluminous input records need to be processed frequently
10. T
11. its lack of reliability because of typing erasures; overlapping of charac-
    ters; its expense
12. adding machines; cash registers; accounting machines
13. T
14. photographed document or record in miniature
15. conserving storage; automated retrieval of data
16. rolled film; aperture or microfiche cards

Review Questions

I. True or False

1. (T or F) All business systems require conversion of a source document
    into machine-readable form.
2. (T or F) Banking systems use optical scanners to read the digits on the
    bottom of checks.
3. (T or F) A major disadvantage of optical character recognition equip-
    ment is that input to this device must rigidly conform to a standard.
4. (T or F) Specially prepared cash register tapes may be entered as input
    to a punched paper tape read/punch.

II. Fill in the Blanks

1. The conversion process refers to the conversion from a _____
    to a _____.
2. Two frequently used devices that eliminate the need for a conversion
    process are _____ and _____.
3. MICR equipment can read characters on checks that have been im-
    printed with _____.
4. MICR equipment senses *(letters or digits)* that have been imprinted on
    source documents.
5. A disadvantage of MICR equipment is _____.
6. OCR equipment is used by companies which _____.
7. Microfilm equipment is used by companies which _____.
8. A major disadvantage of microfilm equipment is _____.

Unit One: Selected Bibliography

History

1. "Preliminary Discussion of the Logical Design of an Electronic Computing Instrument," A. W. Burks, H. H. Goldstine and John von Neumann; "Planning and Coding of Problems for an Electronic Computing Instrument," H. H. Goldstine and John von Neumann in John von Neumann, *Collected Works*, vol. V (Oxford: 1963).
    (a) These are the first major works on the logical structure of an automatic digital computer.
    (b) Provide the student with an understanding of the original design of computers as proposed by John von Neumann.
2. *The Computer From Pascal to von Neumann*, Herman Goldstine (Princeton: 1972).
    (a) Provides an excellent account of the history of computers focussing specifically on von Neumann's role.
    (b) Provides the student with some understanding of how scientific and technical ideas are generated and disseminated.
3. *The Origins of Digital Computers*, Brian Randall, (New York: 1975).
    (a) Includes a series of primary source documents written by major figures in the history of computers beginning with Charles Babbage.
    (b) Provides the student with an interesting perspective on the history of computers.

Types of Computers

1. "Supercomputer Development—The Pleasure and the Pain," Neil R. Lincoln, *Datamation*, vol. 23, May 1977, p. 221.
    (a) Focusses on some of the problems faced by both manufacturers and users of large-scale computers.
    (b) Provides students with information on some of the common "myths" about these machines.
2. "The Top 50 U.S. Companies in the Data Processing Industry," Oscar H. Rothenbuecher, *Datamation*, vol. 23, June 1977, p. 61.
    (a) Focusses on IBM's share of the computer market and the share of the market held by other manufacturers as well.
    (b) Provides students with some insight into the state of the art.

Common Input/Output

"Non-Impact Printers Speed Veterans Administration Report Processing with Added Convenience," *Infosystems*, vol. 24, January 1977, p. 21.

(a) Focusses on the recent advances in and utility of non-impact printers.
(b) Provides students with a readable account of sophisticated hardware.

Magnetic Tape
"Matching Magnetic Media with Modern Machines," Bob Katzive, *Digital Design*, June 1977.
(a) Focusses on the recent innovations in magnetic media.
(b) Familiarizes the student with the language and terminology of computer specialists.

Minicomputers
"Mini Computers, Their Expanding Role," C. W. Spangle, *Computers and People*, December 1976.

Computer Arithmetic: Text
Background Math for a Computer World, Ruth Ashley, (New York: 1973).

Chapter 7
Steps Involved in Programming a Computer

7

Unit Two

Computer Programming Fundamentals and Software

7

Thus far, we have introduced the student to the general features of a computer system. This chapter will focus on the detailed steps involved in actually instructing a computer to produce desired output.

Problems in Communication   You will note that one of the most serious problems that arises in the effort to computerize business functions is communication. Business people are often uninformed about the programmer's responsibilities and limitations. Similarly, programmers are often unfamiliar with business problems and with the responsibilities and limitations of the business manager. The result is a decided gap in communication which results in computerized systems that are not as efficient or as effective as they could be.

It is the purpose of this chapter to shed sufficient light on the nature of programming in a business setting so that such problems in communication between computer specialists and business people will be minimized.

Why Business People Need to Understand the Complexities of Programming   A business person with an appreciation of programming tasks and problems can assist in:

1. Determining what specific details must be imparted to the data processing staff so that their complete understanding of the output required is assured.
2. Ensuring that meaningful data is maintained and that extraneous input data is eliminated in the computerized system.
3. Assisting in combining and condensing output data so that the efficiency of each program is maximized.

By discussing all the steps involved in instructing a computer to produce desired output, we hope to give business and data processing students a greater understanding of why procedures require weeks and even months to automate. We also hope that they will realize how errors can easily manifest themselves in the same phase or aspect of the programming cycle and how these errors can be avoided.

In short, a businessman with a keen awareness of the programmer's responsibilities will have realistic expectations of automated procedures. That is, the steps involved in computerizing an application will be more completely understood. In this way, there will be less likelihood of facing disappointment and annoyance, should a problem arise. Similarly, the computer specialist who can communicate effectively with the businessman is in a better position to understand the problems that might arise.

I. Systems Preparation—Prior to Programming

When business procedures are to be computerized, the *systems analyst* is called in first to study the department's needs. The role of the systems analyst will be discussed in more detail in Chapter 14. At this point, it is important simply for the student to know that the analyst is responsible for studying company procedures, and for designing, where feasible, computerized alternatives.

Once the analyst understands every phase of the application or job that must be performed, the steps involved in achieving the desired result must be defined. The analyst prepares a formalized document called a *problem definition* that describes, in detail, the operations to be performed for the job. The businessman, or department manager, should, if possible, approve this *problem definition*, indicating that he or she concurs with the job description.

The result of this step, then, is a formal document, written by the analyst and approved, where possible, by the businessman, which specifies, in detail, what the program will achieve.

The analyst then supplies the programmer with the problem definition, and data layouts. The data layouts are pictorial representations of how input and output will appear (Figure 7.1). The problem definition is usually in the form of a narrative and indicates what operations must be performed to achieve desired output.

II. Program Preparation

Once the programmer understands the basic requirements of the job and how they will be integrated into the system as a whole, he or she often needs to reinforce this understanding by communicating with the businessman. The programmer must be sure to understand every facet of the job. The following items must be clearly ascertained:

Items to Be Determined Before Programming Begins
1. Field descriptions for input data.
2. Frequency of input data, control of the data, and the form in which data will enter the data processing facility.

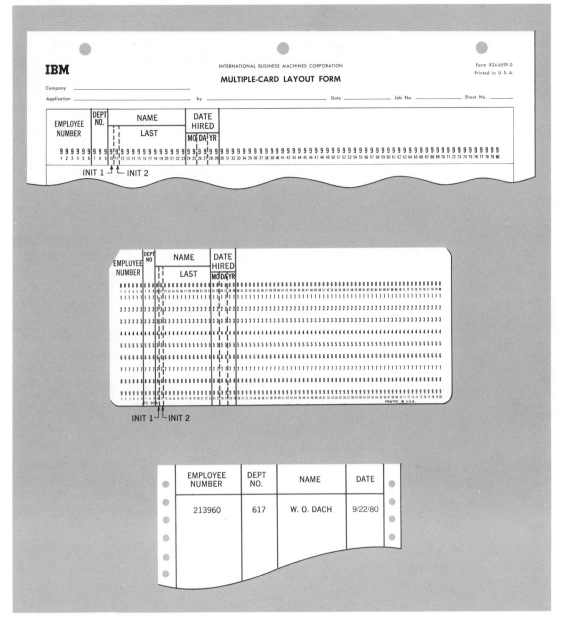

3. Arithmetic operations required.
4. Edit procedures required.
5. Error procedures required.
6. Field descriptions for output data.
7. Frequency of output and its control.

Figure 7.1
Sample data
layouts.

Any element overlooked or misunderstood might require significant reprogramming effort later on. To insert changes in a program

after it is running is never as efficient, productive, or satisfactory as programming these elements from the beginning.

Figure 7.2 illustrates in pictorial form the major steps that are involved in program preparation. We will discuss each in detail.

A. Flowcharting

Often the steps involved in achieving a job's requirements are intricate and detailed. *Prior* to writing the set of instructions, it is imperative that the programmer outline the logic to be employed. In this way, the omission of instructions or the inclusion of illogical functions will be avoided or at least minimized.

A *standardized* method for outlining the logic to be utilized in a program has been employed for many years in the data processing industry. This is a pictorial representation called a *program flowchart*. It indicates, in diagram form, the program elements and how they will logically integrate. This flowchart contains symbols denoting specific functions, with explanatory notes inside. Each symbol is connected by flowlines indicating the flow of logic. Figure 7.3 illustrates a sample flowchart. Chapter 8 describes, in detail, the steps involved in flowcharting.

Keep in mind that the objective of the program flowchart is to map out all the logical steps to be programmed *prior to* the actual writing of the set of instructions. The process is analogous to the formulation of a blueprint prior to the construction of a building. The blueprint, like the flowchart, ensures that all elements will logically integrate.

More and more businessmen today are becoming familiar with flowcharting techniques. The flowchart provides an excellent vehicle of communication between business people and data processing personnel. The specific steps to be utilized in a program and their logical integration are clearly detailed and easily seen. Thus a businessman who is able to scrutinize a flowchart is in a far better position to understand the programmer's concept of the procedures involved. Moreover, any omissions or flaws in the programmer's logic can be more easily seen by a businessman who understands flowcharting concepts.

B. Coding the Program

Once the steps of a program have been outlined in a flowchart and the programmer is satisfied that they integrate logically, the set of instructions can be written. The writing of these instructions is called *coding the program*.

Programs are coded on sheets of paper called coding or program sheets. See Figure 7.4 for a sample coding sheet.

When the program has been completely coded on coding sheets, it must be converted to a form that can be accepted by the computer. Typically, programs are keypunched onto cards. Each line of a coding sheet is keypunched into a single punched card.

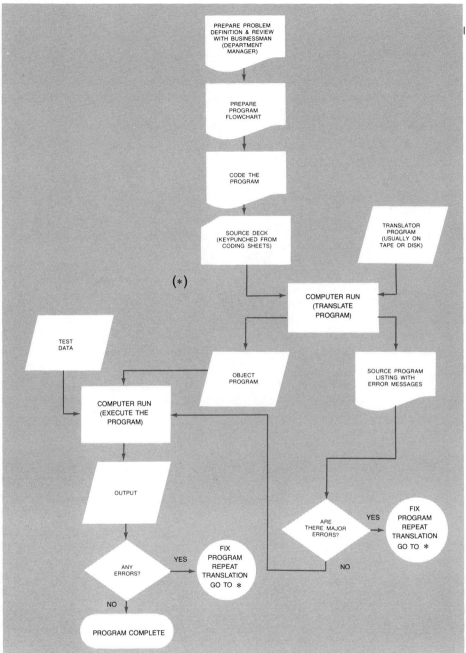

Figure 7.2
Steps involved in producing a computer program.

The entire deck of program cards is then read by the computer. Another common method of entering a program is on a terminal where the programmer simply types the program, line by line, from the coding sheets.

Figure 7.3
A sample flowchart.

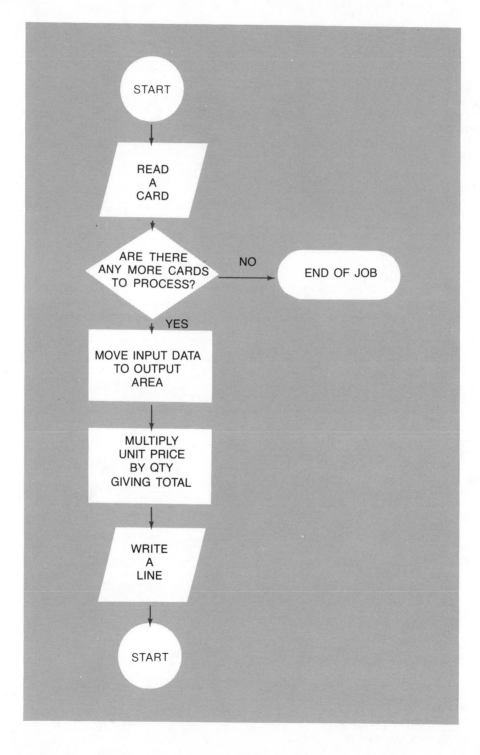

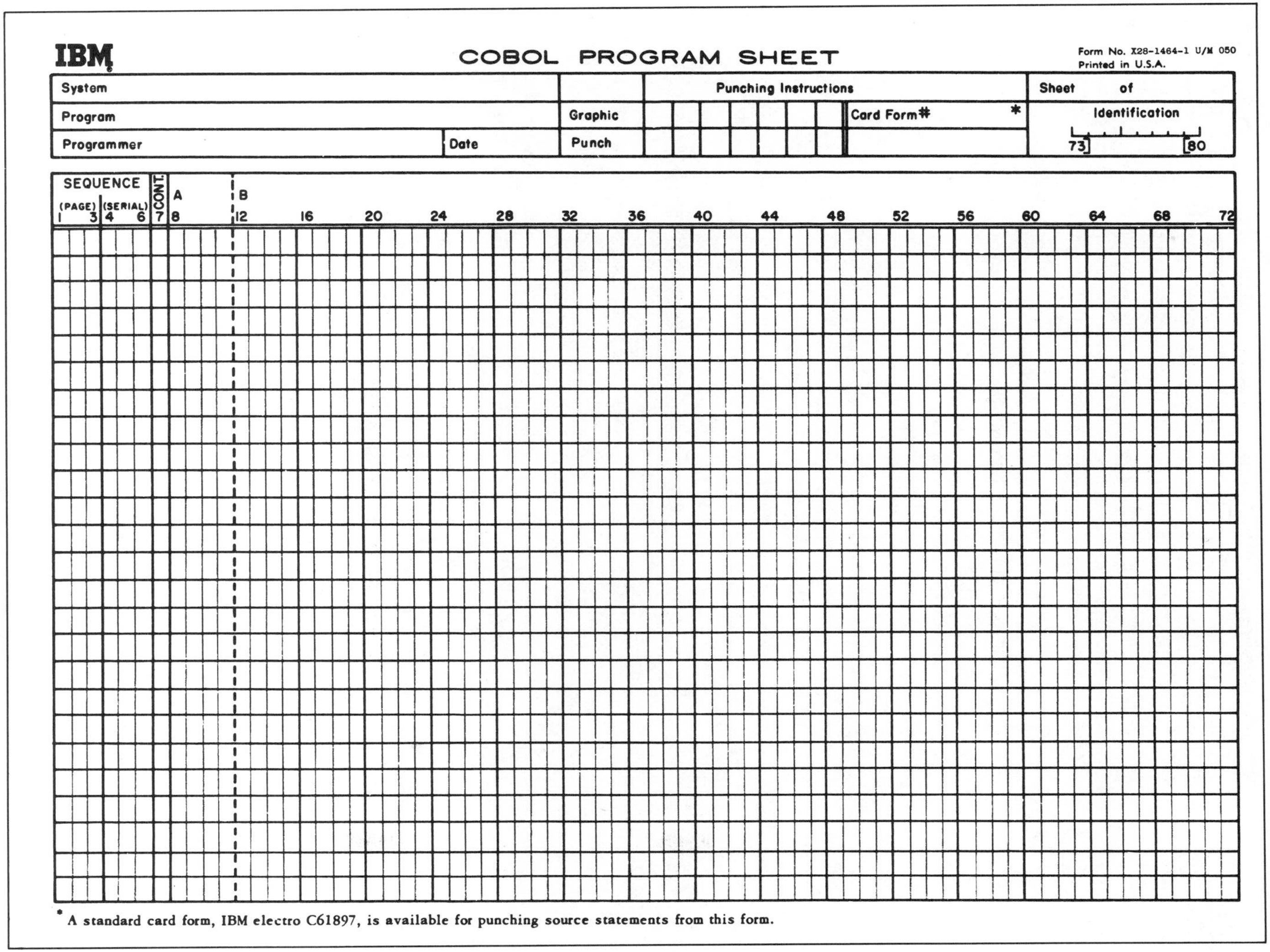

Figure 7.4
Sample coding sheet.

Here again, businessmen with an appreciation for and an understanding of program coding can communicate on a more detailed level with the programmer. Keep in mind that it is the main purpose of this unit to familiarize data processing and business students with the fundamentals of programming to facilitate both their jobs and to improve the flow of communication between them.

1. Actual Machine Language Computers can operate on or *execute* programs only if they are in the computer's own code, that is, in *actual machine language.* This language is rarely used in business applications because:

1. Machine language uses complex operation codes.

    An ADD instruction, for example, may be a 58 code in absolute machine language; a MULTIPLY may be a 4J. For the programmer to code a program in actual machine language, he or she must remember such complex codes, a rather cumbersome task.

2. Machine language uses actual machine addresses.

    An ADD instruction, for example, which adds two input fields, can place the result or sum in a third field. In absolute machine language, all three fields must be actual machine locations. To program, then, in this language, requires the programmer to keep track of actual machine locations, also a cumbersome and difficult task, since addresses can be numbered from 1 to over 100,000, depending upon the storage capacity of the computer.

2. Symbolic Programming It is obvious, then, that programming in actual machine language is complex and cumbersome. Few programmers actually code in the machine's own language. An alternative to absolute machine language coding is *symbolic programming.*

A symbolic programming language is one that is far easier for the programmer to code. It uses *symbolic* operation codes, such as ADD or +, and *symbolic* addresses such as HOLD, RESULT, SUM. Thus we can say ADD TAX TO TOTAL rather than something like 2R 406803. The overwhelming majority of programs are coded in a symbolic language as opposed to machine language.

3. Converting Symbolic Programs Note that a symbolic program, although easier for the programmer to code, is *not* executable. That is, it cannot be run or executed by the computer. It must first be *converted* to machine language code so that the computer can understand the instructions.

Thus a program in symbolic language requires two phases:

Two Phases of Symbolic Programming
1. Translation phase: the program is translated to machine language.
2. Execution phase: once translated, the program is run, or executed.

---

4. Source Program   As indicated, most programs are coded in a symbolic language. This symbolic program, written on coding sheets, must be converted to a form that can be accepted by the computer, such as cards or tape. This program written by the programmer is called a *source program*. A source program keypunched onto cards is called a *source deck*. Source programs are nonexecutable—they must first be translated into machine language before they can be run. The computer itself is programmed to perform this translation process.

Note that there are numerous symbolic languages, each serving a specific purpose.

Symbolic Programming Languages

CHARACTERISTICS   LANGUAGES

High-level languages: Englishlike;   COBOL
easier to program; more difficult   FORTRAN ⎫
to translate   PL/1   } High-level
                                      RPG   ⎬ languages
                                      BASIC   ⎭

Low-level languages: Machinelike;   Assembler languages
more difficult to program;
easier to translate.

We will discuss the features of each language later on in the chapter.

C. Translating Source Programs

All symbolic languages must be translated into machine language before they can be run or executed. The computer itself performs this translation. That is, the machine reads the source program as input, and converts it to output, which is the machine-language program.

1. Compiling Source Programs   High-level symbolic languages are those that are very simple to code but very difficult for the machine to translate. High-level languages require complex translations while low-level ones require simple translations. With high-level languages, such as COBOL, FORTRAN, RPG, PL/1, and BASIC, this translation process is called a *compilation.*

A special program, supplied by the computer manufacturer, called a *compiler,* reads the source program written in a symbolic language and produces, as output, a machine-language equivalent called the *object program.*

Thus the compiler is merely a program that reads in as input the source program and translates it to output which is a machine-language program.

FORTRAN, COBOL and, indeed, all high-level languages require separate compilers. That is, a FORTRAN compiler must be used to translate FORTRAN programs; a COBOL compiler must be used to translate COBOL programs, and so on.

Each computer requires a compiler program that can read the specific symbolic program and convert it to its *own* machine language. Since individual computers have their own unique machine language, each compiler for each machine will be different. In every case, however, the result is the same: a machine-language program called an *object* program.

2. Assembling Source Programs   Low-level programming languages (assembler languages) are similar to machine language and do *not* require complex translations. They require a simplified translation called an *assembly.* A special program called the *assembler* translates an assembler-language program into machine language. Keep in mind that assembler language, the language requiring the simplest translation, entails more complex programming effort. The programming effort required by high-level languages is less, but the conversion process is more complex.

Since each computer has its own independent machine language, the translation or compilation will produce unique programs for each computer. Thus, a COBOL compiler for IBM S/370 will be different from a COBOL compiler for a Honeywell machine.

The translator (assembler or compiler) is a program that is usually on a tape or disk *file of programs,* ready to be accessed by the computer. The control system of the computer calls for these programs, as required. When a translator is read into the CPU, it then calls for the source program as input and begins the translation.

Once a program is translated (either compiled or assembled) three types of output usually result (see Figure 7.5).

Any *major* error will result in an incomplete or erroneous object program. In such cases, the source program must be corrected and the translation process repeated. The object program originally created cannot be used, since it contains errors generated in the source program. Note that most programmers must translate their programs several times before they are "debugged," or free from rule violations. Thus numerous translations of source programs are

Results of Translation Process

1. Object program: the machine-language equivalent of the source program.
2. A source program listing: this listing makes it far easier to follow program logic than if coding sheets or the source deck is used. The programmer uses the program listing to flag errors and check the logic.
3. A listing of diagnostics, or rule violations: Any rules that have been violated by the programmer will cause the computer to print an error message. If the add operation is spelled AD instead of ADD, for example, an error message will print.

often required. The detail and precision required in programming makes errors a commonplace occurrence.

Notice, also, that the list of diagnostics will indicate violations of rules but will *not* tag an error in logic. Logic errors can only be found by running or testing the program with sample data.

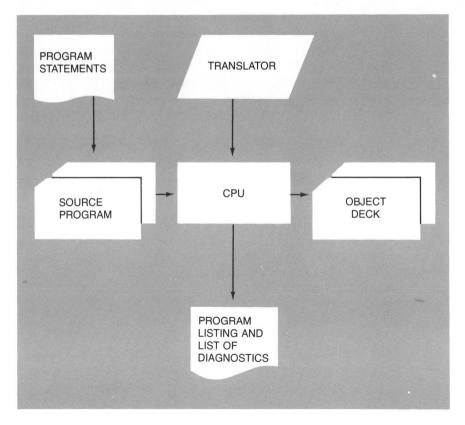

Figure 7.5

Translation process (assembly and compilation).

Self-Evaluating Quiz

1. A standardized method for outlining the logic to be utilized in a program is called a(n) _____.
2. Once the steps of a program have been outlined and the programmer is satisfied that they logically integrate, the next step is to _____.
3. A program is written on _____.
4. After a program is written, it must be _____.
5. Computers can execute programs only if they are in _____ form.
6. A(n) _____ language is one which is far easier for the programmer to code but which requires a translation phase.
7. Three examples of high-level programming languages are _____, _____, and _____.
8. High-level programming languages require a complex translation phase, called a(n) _____, while low-level programming languages require a simpler translation phase, called a(n) _____.
9. A _____ must be carefully prepared by the programmer to ensure that his or her program tests for all possible conditions.
10. (T or F) Programs are coded on coding sheets which are sometimes keypunched into cards called the source deck.
11. (T or F) Programs may be executed when they are either in absolute or symbolic machine language.
12. (T or F) Absolute or actual machine language requires complex operation codes and actual machine addresses too cumbersome for the average programmer to utilize.
13. (T or F) A program in symbolic language requires both a translation and an execution phase.
14. (T or F) A program written in COBOL is called the object program.

Solutions

1. program flowchart
2. code the program
3. coding sheets
4. compiled or assembled or translated
5. actual machine language
6. symbolic
7. PL/1, COBOL, FORTRAN, BASIC, RPG
8. compilation
   assembly
9. flowchart
10. T
11. F
12. T
13. T
14. F—it is called the source program

D. Execution Phase—Testing the Program

After a machine-language program (that contains no rule violations) has been produced the execution phase can begin. In this phase, we test the program to determine if it performs all required operations and if it produces the desired output. Although the program contains no rule violations, it may contain logic errors. The *execution phase* is used to "debug" a program or to eliminate all such errors.

1. Test Data   We run or execute the program with *test* or *sample data*. The output produced is then compared against the output that has been manually prepared from the same data. If everything checks, then the program is considered debugged, or free from errors. It is then ready to be run on a scheduled basis.

Note that test data must be carefully prepared to incorporate *all possible conditions*. Any condition that is feasible must be included. In this way, the program tests for all possibilities and it is then unlikely that future scheduled runs of the program will result in errors. When programming errors are detected as a result of the test, the source program must be corrected, retranslated, and the test performed again.

2. Example of Logic Error   Any condition that is inadvertently omitted from the test data can produce major errors later on. Suppose, for example, a program allows for from 1 to 10 transaction cards for each account within an Accounts Receivable file. The programmer should include test data that has accounts with 1 card, 2 cards, and so on up to 10 cards. In this way, every condition possible would be included within the test data. To assume that because the program works properly for 2 cards in an account it will therefore work for 10 cards in an account may be fallacious.

Suppose, for example, that the program provides only one position for the NUMBER OF CARDS field. Then when there are *10* (2 digits) cards for an account, erroneous processing will occur. Unless the test data includes an account with 10 cards, this erroneous condition will not be discovered until the program is run on a scheduled basis. At that time the necessity for corrections would result in a disruption of the normal computer processing and would waste valuable computer time.

It is also imperative that the programmer incorporate procedures for handling errors in input. The program should contain error procedures for invalid cards and test data should contain invalid cards to ensure their proper treatment. There is an adage in data processing that because of the large volume, anything that could *possibly* go wrong with input data *will* eventually go wrong. Thus, error tests must be built into the program.

E. Program Documentation

Once the program is finalized and running properly, it must be prepared for the operations staff to be run on a regularly scheduled

basis. That is, the programmer must provide the operations staff
with enough detail and information about the program so that it
can be run at regular intervals. The *program documentation* is a
series of written documents that ensures a smooth transition from
the programming staff to the operations staff. If it is thorough and
precise, it will eliminate the need for a computer operator to constantly question the programmer and the business people involved
about aspects of the run. Many programmers have been plagued by
numerous phone calls from the operations staff requiring explana-
tions of the run and the output, because documentation was not
properly provided.

Documentation should include:

Documentation
1. Problem Definition: indicating a narrative on what the program accomplishes.
2. Program Flowchart: indicating the logic flow of the program.
3. Data Layout Sheets of Required Input and Output: denoting
   precisely what the input and output look like.
4. Control Procedures: indicating from whom input data is received and to whom output should be sent, how totals should
   be specified for control of documents, and so on.
5. Scheduling Procedures: indicating when runs are to be performed.
6. Format for Control Cards: indicating date, or type of run (such
   as monthly or weekly) if required.
7. Operation Procedures: indicating precisely what the operator
   must do for each phase of the run; for example, mount tape on
   Tape Drive 1, use five-part paper on printer, and so on.
8. Specifications Required for Tape and Disk: indicating formats
   for any external labels or header labels required.
9. Error Sheet: indicating what the operator should do in case
   specific errors occur.
10. Halt Sheet: indicating what the operator should do in case
    specified programmed halts occur.

In short, every detail should be included so that once the job
is "turned over" to the operations staff, the programmer is not constantly besieged with numerous questions. Too often, a programmer supplies a program with minimum documentation only to be
called at 2:00 A.M. by an irate computer operator who does not
know what to do because an unspecified condition has occurred.

F. Conversion or Cut-Over
Conversion or *cut-over* is the process of running a program, for the
first time, with real or "live" data after it has been tested and de-
clared debugged. Sometimes, however, programming errors occur

during conversion that were not found during testing. This is often embarrassing to the programmer, since the conversion process is undertaken only after the program has been rendered complete and adequate. For this reason, the necessity for including detailed test data prior to the conversion process cannot be overstated.

During the conversion process, the programmer works closely with the operations staff to ensure that (1) the program functions smoothly, and (2) the operators understand the requirements and specifications of the program.

Parallel Run   Usually the program is run during conversion at the same time that the manual procedure is performed to produce the same result. This is called a *parallel run*. The computer-prepared output is then compared with the manually prepared output and, barring minor discrepancies, they should be consistent. If not, the program must be rechecked to determine why errors have occurred.

Once the conversion process is complete, the manual method for preparing output is abandoned. The operations staff is then responsible for the periodic computer run and the programmer's job is considered to be completed.

III. Major Programming Languages

You will recall that source programs, written by the programmer, must be translated into machine language before they can be executed. There are many programming languages that can be used on many different computers that serve varied business needs. In this section we describe some of the major languages in use today.

A. COBOL

COBOL, an acronym for *Common Business Oriented Language* is, as the name implies, a business language. It has been created to satisfy normal business needs. It utilizes business terminology.

Since most business-oriented problems operate on vast amounts of data, requiring high-speed processing, a business language must be capable of easily and effectively handling high-speed storage media such as magnetic tape and disk. COBOL uses instructions that make programming for these high-level devices a simple task. That is, we can perform header label routines, blocking functions, indexing of disk records, and so on with relative ease in COBOL.[1] Since most business problems do not require complex mathematical routines, a business language is not required to handle complex mathematics. Hence, simple arithmetic operations are easily performed in COBOL, whereas mathematical functions such as square-root and trigonometric routines require more extensive coding.

[1]See Chapter 5 for a discussion of these terms.

1. The Nature of Business-Oriented Problems Thus, business-oriented problems are generally those that require large amounts of input/output with relatively simple arithmetic functions. Payroll jobs, for example, are typical business problems; they utilize great numbers of records with simple arithmetic routines. COBOL is a symbolic language ideally suited for such business problems.

2. Features of COBOL COBOL is considered a universal language because it has been standardized. That is, it can be run on many computer makes and models. The same COBOL program, with little modification, can be run as effectively on an IBM S/370 as on a Honeywell computer. Similarly, both the IBM S/370 model 155 and the IBM S/370 model 168 can operate on the same COBOL program with little change.

COBOL is an Englishlike language. The similarity to English makes it easy to train programmers. To add two fields, we say ADD; to read a card, we say READ, and so forth. Since instructions read like English statements, it is easy to both understand and code COBOL programs. Chapter 11 presents the fundamentals of CO-BOL in depth.

B. FORTRAN

The symbolic programming language FORTRAN is an abbreviation for *Formula Trans*lator. FORTRAN is a mathematical language that is particularly suited to setting down formulas. To add two fields A and B, for example, and place the answer in a field called C, we use the FORTRAN expression:

$$C = A + B$$

Note that this is equivalent to a mathematical formula.

FORTRAN is most often used for scientific or engineering applications because of its mathematical nature. It includes features for determining logarithms, trigonometric functions, and so on. It, like COBOL, has been standardized so that it can be used on many different computers.

Although FORTRAN can easily handle complex mathematical problems, it is not as well suited for high-level input/output operations as are some other languages.

The Nature of Scientific Problems Most scientific applications utilize numerous high-level mathematical problems with little input/output. That is, several numbers fed into a computer pinpointing a moon trajectory can result in hours of computer calculations.

For mathematical problems, we generally use many calculations and comparatively little input/output. FORTRAN, as a mathematical language, was created for handling complex calculations but sacrifices some of the ease with which high-level input/output, such as disk, can be handled.

Note that FORTRAN is used predominantly in business applications where mathematics is required. Sales forecasting and inventory control are operations that most often use FORTRAN. In short, COBOL is a more effective language when dealing with business-oriented problems that include large amounts of input/output with relatively simple calculating. FORTRAN is a more effective language when dealing with scientific or business-oriented problems that include complex calculating routines with relatively simplified input/output.

C. PL/1

PL/1, an abbreviation for Programming Language/1, is a symbolic language that is designed to meet the needs of both scientific and commercial computer users. That is, it is designed to combine essentially the major advantages and features of COBOL and FORTRAN so that a user can employ it for both scientific and commercial problems.

PL/1 is a most effective and necessary tool in companies that require both scientific and commercial applications. An engineering firm, for example, that has one large computer that processes engineering and business (Payroll, Accounts Receivable, and Accounts Payable) applications might best utilize PL/1 for its prime programming language. In this way, the company need not hire two types of programmers, those with knowledge of FORTRAN and those with knowledge of COBOL. Similarly, employee transfers between the scientific programming staff and the commercial programming staff can easily be made.

There are, then, many advantages to adopting a single programming language for companies that possess both scientific and commercial applications. In this way, *both* high-level mathematics and high-level input/output can be effectively handled using one language and even one program. Its one main disadvantage is its complexity.

D. RPG

Many business organizations, particularly small-scale ones, do not need the extensive options available with COBOL or PL/1. Their needs could be satisfied with a simplified language that is most often used to print output from cards or tape or disk. There is usually very little high-level programming involved to produce printed output.

RPG, an abbreviation for *R*eport *P*rogram *G*enerator, is a symbolic language ideally suited for creating printed reports from input media. There is a minimum of programming effort required with RPG. That is, it is a very simple language. Page numbers, page headings, field names on primary page breaks, editing, and printing final totals are performed in RPG with minimum programming effort.

Thus, it is relatively easy to train RPG programmers, since the various options of COBOL, FORTRAN, or PL/1 need not be learned. Since the prime purpose of this language is to create printed reports, few logic problems are encountered. Thus, RPG is an ideal language for individuals with little or no programming expertise.

Keep in mind, however, that RPG has one primary function and that is to create printed output with minimum effort. It cannot perform complex decision or logic functions. It is a semistandard language in that it may be used on *some* computers, but not all.

E. Basic

BASIC is an acronym for *B*eginner's *A*ll-purpose *S*ymbolic *In*struction *C*ode. It is a symbolic language that is most often used to program from terminals. It is essentially a simplified version of FORTRAN. Because of its simplicity, this language can be learned in a matter of hours. We will discuss BASIC in more detail in Chapter 13.

Table 7.1 provides a summary of the programming languages discussed so far.

Table 7.1

High-Level Programming Languages

Name	Meaning	Features
COBOL	*Common Business Oriented Language*	For business applications; universal language; Englishlike
FORTRAN	*Formula Translator*	For scientific applications; universal language; uses mathematical symbols
PL/1	*Programming Language One*	Combines features of COBOL and FORTRAN
RPG	*Report Program Generator*	Simplified language most suited for creating printed output
BASIC	*Beginner's All-purpose Symbolic Instruction Code*	Simplified version of FORTRAN; ideally suited for terminal programming

F. Assembler Language

Assembler Language is a very complicated programming language that is similar to machine-language programming, with only minor variations to simplify programming effort. It is used usually when great programming efficiency is required to save storage or to perform complex functions. Each machine has its own *individual* Assembler Language. That is, although the above five languages are relatively standard regardless of the computer on which they are run, each computer has its own independent Assembler Language that is usually different from that of *another computer.*

Most companies would not have an Assembler Language as their main programming language because of its complexity. For that reason, it is not discussed in detail in this text.

Summary The symbolic language utilized at a data processing installation will depend on the type of applications or jobs generally required. That is, an organization that usually requires business-oriented programs and that has several different computers would probably utilize COBOL as a main language. A company that utilizes scientific applications or business functions with high-level mathematics to be included would probably use FORTRAN. Table 7.2 provides a summary of language characteristics.

Summary of Language Characteristics   Table 7.2

Language Type	Characteristics
Machine Language	1. Machine dependent 2. Involves the use of special codes and the assignment of storage addresses
Assembly Language	1. Machine dependent 2. Uses symbolic operation codes (called mnemonics) and symbolic storage addresses (called operands) 3. For every assembly language instruction, one machine language instruction is generated (1-to-1 language)
High-Level Language	1. Machine independent 2. Uses Englishlike instructions 3. One instruction may result in several machine language statements (1-to-many language)

In summary, the programming cycle includes:

Programming Cycle
1. Preparing the Problem Definition: to ensure complete understanding of the job requirements.
2. Preparing the Program Flowchart: to formalize the logical integration of elements to be written in the program.
3. Coding the Source Program.
4. Translating the Source Program into Machine Language: to permit execution, the program must be translated; this phase

also produces a listing of rule violations (diagnostics) that must be corrected before execution can begin.

5. Testing the Program: to ensure that there are no errors in logic; any such errors that occur must be corrected and the program then translated again.

6. Preparing the Program Documentation.

7. Conversion or Cut-Over of Program.

Business people and programmers should note that each of these steps involves detail and precision. Every facet is subject to errors which, because of the nature of the tasks involved, frequently occur. Programmers often require weeks or even months to complete applications. In addition to the expected programming errors that must be anticipated, revisions to the problem definition or unexpected computer "down" time (when the computer is being repaired or checked) cause further delays. The student should note that a definition of the problem ought to be complete and precise *before* the undertaking of any programming effort. Changes to aspects of the job *after* programming has begun often cause extensive delays. Thus business people and data processing personnel must work closely to ensure that they both have a total picture of the job requirements.

Important Terms Used in this Chapter

Actual Machine Language	High-Level Language
Assembler (Assembly)	Low-Level Language
Assembler Language	Object Program (Object Deck)
BASIC	Parallel Run
COBOL	PL/1
Compiler (Compilation)	Problem Definition
Conversion Process	Program
Cut-Over	Program Coding
Debug	RPG
Diagnostics	Source Program (Source Deck)
Documentation	Symbolic Program
Execution	Test Data
Flowchart—Program	Translation
FORTRAN	

Self-Evaluating Quiz

1. Programs are rarely written in _____ language because of its _____.

2. Programs are generally written in a _____ language that must be converted or translated into machine language.

3. COBOL is an acronym for _____.

4. COBOL is a common language in the sense that _____.

5. COBOL is a business language in the sense that _____.

6. Business problems have need for _____ but usually do not involve complex _____.

7. (T or F) Logarithmic functions and other complex mathematical routines can easily be handled in COBOL.

8. COBOL is a(n) _____-like language, which makes it easy to train programmers.

9. FORTRAN is an abbreviation for _____.

10. Complex _____ routines can easily be performed in FORTRAN while large amounts of _____ can best be handled in COBOL.

11. An Inventory program for a department store would probably be written in the _____ language.

12. (T or F) Because of all the steps involved, a programmer may require many weeks to complete a program.

13. (T or F) The systems analyst provides the programmer with job requirements from which the programmer must create his or her program.

14. (T or F) Any aspect of an application that the programmer finds confusing he or she should question after completing the basic program.

15. A formalized document called a _____ describes, in detail, the operations to be performed.

16. This document should be approved by _____ to ensure _____.

17. The program flowchart indicates _____.

18. The process of writing the actual computer instructions is called _____.

19. Each line of a coding sheet converts to _____ in the _____.

20. In order for programs to be executed, they must be in _____.

21. Programmers rarely code in actual machine language because of its _____.

22. Most programmers code in a _____ _____ _____.

23. Symbolic programs must be _____ before they can be _____.

24. A source program is _____.

25. Four examples of symbolic programming languages are _____, _____, _____, and _____.

26. RPG is an abbreviation for _____.

27. PL/1 combines the advantages of _____ and _____.

28. _____ is a language most often used with terminals.

29. _____ is a language that is similar to machine language with only minor variations to simplify programming effort.

30. A business function usually requires _____ input/output with relatively _____ mathematical operations.

31. A scientific function usually requires _____ input/output with _____ mathematical operations.
32. _____ is a programming language ideally suited for business applications, while _____ handles complex mathematical functions with relative ease.
33. A compiler is a _____.
34. An object program is _____.
35. The output from a compilation is _____, _____, and _____.
36. After a program has been compiled successfully, with no errors, then the _____ phase is undertaken.
37. The execution phase will determine if there are _____ in the program.
38. The _____ is a series of written documents that ensures a smooth transition from the programming staff to the operations staff.
39. The _____ process is the running of a program for the first time with "live" data.

Solutions

1. actual (or absolute) machine; complexity
2. symbolic
3. *Common Business Oriented Language*
4. it can be run on many different makes and models of computers
5. it is especially suited to handling business-type problems such as Payroll and Accounts Receivable
6. large volumes of input/output; mathematical functions
7. F
8. English
9. *Formula Translator*
10. mathematical; input/output
11. COBOL
12. T
13. T
14. F—*before* completion
15. problem definition
16. businessmen; that the computer specialist's understanding of every facet and detail of the procedure is correct
17. the logical integration of the flow of data in a program
18. coding the program
19. a single punched card; source deck
20. actual machine language
21. complexity
22. symbolic programming language
23. translated; run or executed
24. a program written in a symbolic language
25. RPG; FORTRAN; BASIC; COBOL; PL/1; Assembler Language
26. *Report Program Generator*

27. FORTRAN; COBOL
28. BASIC
29. Assembler Language
30. large volume *or* high-level; simple or low-level
31. low volume or low-level; high-level
32. COBOL; FORTRAN
33. translator program that converts an input source deck in a symbolic language to an output object program in machine language
34. the machine language equivalent of the source deck
35. an object program; a listing of rule violations; a program listing
36. execution
37. logic errors
38. program documentation
39. conversion

Review Questions

1. A standardized method for outlining the logic to be utilized in a program is called a(n) _____.
2. Once the steps of a program have been outlined and the programmer is satisfied that they logically integrate, he or she may begin to _____.
3. A program is written on _____.
4. After a program is written, it must be _____.
5. Computers can execute programs only if they are in _____.
6. A(n) _____ language is one which is far easier for the programmer to code but which requires a translation phase.
7. Three examples of high-level programming languages are _____, _____, and _____.
8. High-level programming languages require a complex translation phase called a(n) _____, while low-level programming languages require a simpler translation phase, called a(n) _____.
9. _____ must be carefully prepared by the programmer to ensure that his or her program tests for all possible conditions.
10. If _____ is thorough and precise, the need for computer operators to constantly question the programmer about aspects of the program will be eliminated.
11. _____ is the process of running a program for the first time with real or "live" data after it has been tested.
12. The process of running a program during conversion, at the same time that the manual procedure is performed, is referred to as a _____.
13. A programming language designed to fill normal business needs, utilizing business terminology, is _____, an abbreviation for _____.
14. A business application typically operates on relatively (large, small) _____ amounts of input while requiring relatively (few, many) _____ calculations.

15. A scientific application typically operates on relatively (large, small) _____ amounts of input while requiring relatively (few, many) _____ calculations.

16. A programming language designed to fill normal scientific needs, utilizing mathematical formulas, is _____, an abbreviation for _____.

17. A programming language designed to meet the needs of both scientific and commercial computer users is _____, an abbreviation for _____.

18. An advantage of PL/1 programming is _____.

19. A programming language that is ideally suited for creating printed reports from input media is _____, an abbreviation for _____.

20. A programming language that is most often used for terminal processing is _____.

21. A programming language that is often used for writing control programs, translators, and other advanced programs is _____.

22. COBOL is a relatively easy language to learn because it is _____.

23. A programming language is considered common if it can be _____.

24. PL/1 combines the advantages of _____ and _____.

25. BASIC is a programming language very similar to _____.

Program Flowcharting

8

8

A major aspect of the data processing function is the logical integration of programming elements so that the flow of data proceeds simply and accurately. In fact, it is no overstatement to suggest that logic is the very crux of computer programming and data processing in general.

The best method for clearly representing the logical flow of data in a data processing environment is with the use of a *flowchart*, a technique used to pictorially represent computer logic.

The purpose of this chapter is to

1. Provide the business and data processing student with the fundamentals necessary to read, interpret, and draw program flowcharts.
2. Enable business and data processing students to communicate their understanding of a data processing function with the use of a flowchart.
3. Enable the student to use the flowchart as a tool for understanding computer logic.

I. Elements of a Program Flowchart

A program flowchart is a diagram, or pictorial representation, of the logical flow of data in a particular program.[1] Its relative position in the programmer's sequence of activities is indicated in Figure 8.1.

The flowchart is drawn *before* the program is written to ensure that the instructions in a program will be logically integrated. The concept is not unlike that used by architects who prepare pictorial representations, called blueprints, prior to the actual design of a building. Blueprints verify and integrate elements of a building before construction. Similarly, flowcharts verify and integrate elements of a program prior to coding.

The flowchart is drawn by the programmer to ensure that his or her interpretation of the logic required in the program is accurate. Notice that the writing of the instructions is only part of a program; the sequence in which these instructions are executed represents the *logic* of the program. Coding errors similar to typo-

---

[1] The systems flowchart, a more general representation of data flow in a system, as a whole, will be discussed in Chapter 15.

DETAILED BREAKDOWN OF OPERATIONS	TOOL
ANALYST FORMULATES PROBLEM FOR PROGRAMMER	SYSTEMS DESIGN PACKAGE
PROGRAMMER FORMULATES HIS CONCEPTION OF THE PROBLEM	PROGRAMMER'S PROBLEM DEFINITION
PROGRAMMER PREPARES PROGRAM FLOWCHART TO DEPICT LOGIC	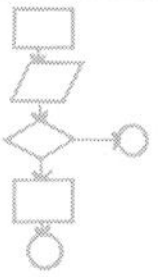
PROGRAMMER REVIEWS FLOWCHART WITH ANALYST & BUSINESSMEN	INTERVIEW
PROGRAMMER CODES THE PROBLEM	CODING SHEET 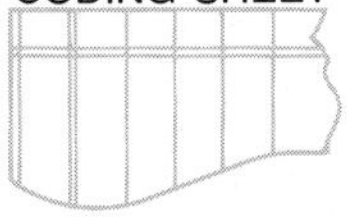

Figure 8.1

The sequence of programmer activities.

graphical erorrs are easily detected by the computer during program translation; errors in logic, however, are harder to find and require more intricate and rigorous revamping. These logic errors can often be avoided when precise program flowcharts are drawn beforehand.

The businessman and the programmer often work closely in refining the flowchart. Any discrepancies, misconceptions, or lack of detail, will become apparent when the logic is represented in flowchart form. The flowchart, then, provides a common foundation with which computer specialists and businessmen can bridge communication gaps. In the end, the flowchart should be approved by businessmen and programmers before detailed coding is undertaken.

Most flowcharts can be effectively drawn using the five basic symbols shown in Table 8.1. Note that these symbols conform to a data processing standard and are universally used throughout the computer industry. Thus data processing personnel in diversified areas can understand the symbols and the logic used in any flowchart. To facilitate the drawing of a flowchart, a flowcharting template (Figure 8.2) is used to draw the symbols representing each

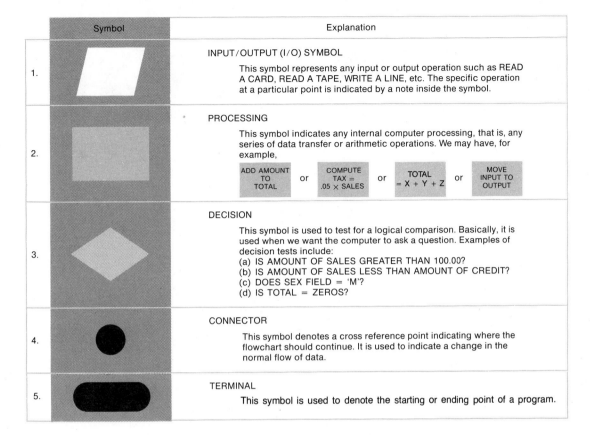

	Symbol	Explanation
1.		**INPUT/OUTPUT (I/O) SYMBOL** This symbol represents any input or output operation such as READ A CARD, READ A TAPE, WRITE A LINE, etc. The specific operation at a particular point is indicated by a note inside the symbol.
2.		**PROCESSING** This symbol indicates any internal computer processing, that is, any series of data transfer or arithmetic operations. We may have, for example, ADD AMOUNT TO TOTAL or COMPUTE TAX = .05 × SALES or TOTAL = X + Y + Z or MOVE INPUT TO OUTPUT
3.		**DECISION** This symbol is used to test for a logical comparison. Basically, it is used when we want the computer to ask a question. Examples of decision tests include: (a) IS AMOUNT OF SALES GREATER THAN 100.00? (b) IS AMOUNT OF SALES LESS THAN AMOUNT OF CREDIT? (c) DOES SEX FIELD = 'M'? (d) IS TOTAL = ZEROS?
4.		**CONNECTOR** This symbol denotes a cross reference point indicating where the flowchart should continue. It is used to indicate a change in the normal flow of data.
5.		**TERMINAL** This symbol is used to denote the starting or ending point of a program.

Table 8.1
Major Flowcharting Symbols.

of the specified functions to be included in a particular logic diagram.

Let us consider the following problem to see what a program flowchart looks like. Assume that we have a deck of punched cards, each with the format shown in Figure 8.3. The code field will contain either a "1" to denote a male or a "2" to denote a female. We would like the computer to process this deck and produce a report that lists only the names and telephone numbers of females. An example of the desired output is shown in Figure 8.4. We will assume that the cards are already in alphabetical sequence by last name.

The logic for this problem consists of the following steps:

1. Read a card.
2. Determine if the card pertains to a female (that is, determine if the code field is equal to 2).
3. If the code field is not equal to 2, then do not process this card any further, since it contains data for a male. Instead, read in the next card; that is, go back to Step 1.

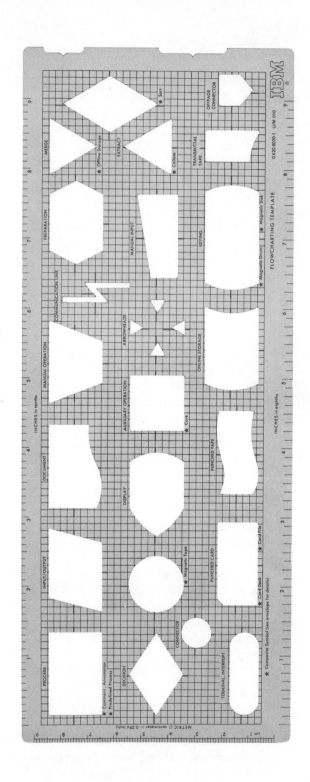

Figure 8.2
Flowcharting template.

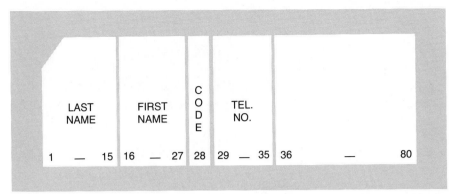

Figure 8.3
Card format—
Example 1.

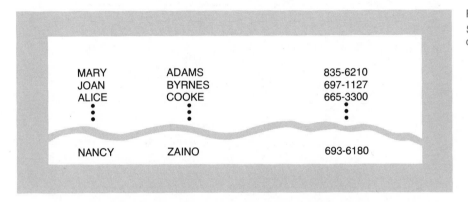

Figure 8.4
Sample
output—Example 1.

4. If the card contains data for a female (that is, code is equal to 2), then print out the following fields: first name, last name, telephone number.

5. Go back to Step 1 to read the next card.

The flowchart depicting this logic is illustrated in Figure 8.5. Notice how much simpler it is to represent the logic of this problem by a flowchart rather than with the use of a narrative.

The following points should also be noted:

1. Generally, flowcharts show the logic necessary to read in *one* input record, process it, and then go back to read in the next input record. Each symbol indicates the operation to be performed. "Read A Card," for example is an input/output operation; "Is CODE = 2" is a decision, etc.

2. By convention, the logic of a flowchart is read from top to bottom, and from left to right, unless there are arrows used to indicate otherwise. The lines used to connect the symbols are called *flowlines*. In the above flowchart, notice that the arrowheads are superfluous, since the logic normally flows from top to bottom and from left to right.

3. Connectors are used to indicate where the logic in a particular path should continue. In the above flowchart,

Figure 8.5
Flowchart for
Example 1.

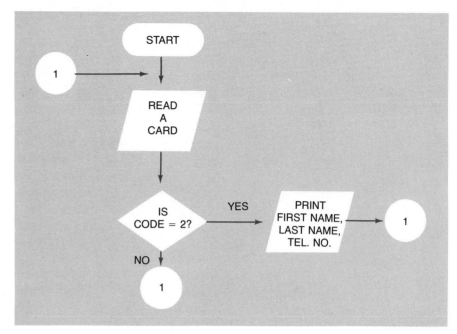

notice that after the name and telephone number for a particular female are printed out, the path to be followed continues where we find a connector with the number 1 in it. That is, the next instruction is to read a card again. Note that a branch to 1 *without* printing data occurs only when code is *not* equal to 2.

Although the above flowchart correctly depicts the logic required, it lacks many details that are generally found in flowcharts of typical business problems. For example, reports generally have title and column headings for identification purposes. In addition, many business reports contain some sort of statistical information such as the total number of cards processed, the percentage of cards that contain data on females, and so on. We will now consider these additional items.

Let us first consider the method used to produce a report with a title and column headings, such as shown in Figure 8.6. Since the title and the column headings appear at the beginning of the report, we can expect that in our flowchart we will print these items at the beginning of our logic flow. Figure 8.7 shows the logic necessary to accomplish this. Notice the difference between

both of which appear in the flowchart. The first I/O symbol indicates that we want the computer to print out the *words* that appear in the quote marks. To print the word "NAME", for example, is to call for a field heading. The second I/O symbol indicates that we want the contents of the fields indicated to be printed out. To print NAME, for example, is to print the *field* called NAME.

Now let us consider the logic necessarv to get the computer to print the same report but with a message at the end indicating the total number of females processed. This message might appear as:

THE TOTAL NUMBER OF FEMALES IS 576

Since we only want this message to print out when all the cards have been processed, we must include in our logic a test to see if the last data card has already been processed. This test is often referred to as the "last card" test, abbreviated by programmers as the L/C test, and typically appearing after the step that reads in an input record, as shown in Figure 8.8.[2] The dotted lines indicate

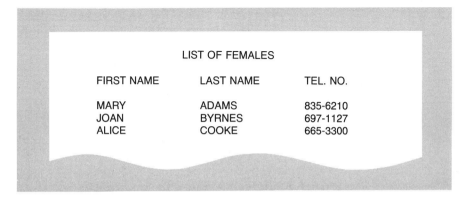

LIST OF FEMALES

FIRST NAME	LAST NAME	TEL. NO.
MARY	ADAMS	835-6210
JOAN	BYRNES	697-1127
ALICE	COOKE	665-3300

Figure 8.6

Sample output with headings.

[2] We will see in later chapters exactly how the last card test is programmed. Typically, for example, when a card file is being read in, a blank card with a /* in the first two columns is placed behind the last data card. We can then program the computer to proceed to an end-of-job sequence when it detects this card.

Figure 8.7
Revised flowchart
for Example 1.

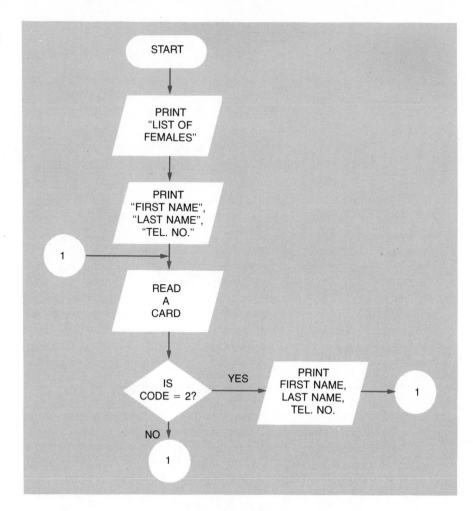

other parts of the flowchart which are not shown. Notice that when the last card (L/C) has already been processed, the computer is instructed to print out the message in quote marks, THE TOTAL NUMBER OF FEMALES IS. This message is followed by the actual number accumulated in the field called COUNT in the CPU. We will see next how COUNT is established and used in our logic.

In order to print out a count of the number of females, it is necessary for us at the *beginning* of our logic to indicate that a special area must be set up in the CPU. The purpose of this area is to keep a running total of the number of females as the cards are being processed. In addition to setting up a field in the CPU for counting purposes, we must also make sure that this field is set equal to zero. Otherwise, we will get an incorrect answer, since the field may contain data from the previous program that was run. To set up a counting area in the CPU, we can use the logic shown at the beginning of the flowchart in Figure 8.9. When drawing a flow-chart, any name may be arbitrarily used to establish (label) a field.

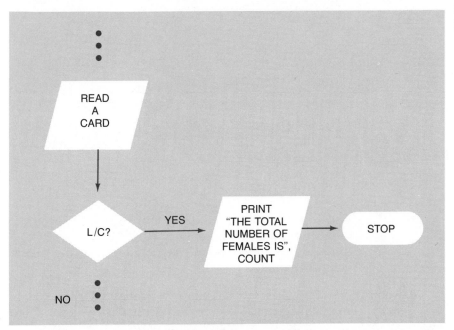

Figure 8.8
Last card test.

When you actually write the program, however, you must set up field names according to the rules for each specific language. The above step will accomplish three things in our logic:

1. It will set aside an area in the CPU for counting.
2. It will initialize or clear that area so that it starts out with a contents of zero.
3. It will provide us with a name, COUNT, by which we can refer to this particular area later on in our program.

Having now established an area for counting, we must indicate in our program every time we want to add to this counter. Since, in this program, we want to find the total number of females, each time the computer finds a female card the field should be incremented by 1. The flowchart segment that indicates this part of the logic is shown in Figure 8.10. Notice that when a "female" card is found, two steps must be performed:

Figure 8.9
Setting up a counter.

COUNT = 0

Figure 8.10

Incrementing the
counter.

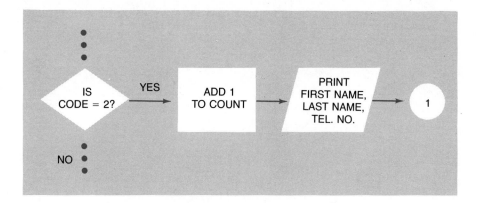

1. Add 1 to the counter, called COUNT, which is keeping a running total of the number of females.
2. Print out the name and telephone number of the female just processed.

It should be noted that the flowchart segment in Figure 8.11 is equally correct, since it also accomplishes the desired logic. Note that there are frequently several ways to write a flowchart, all of which will result in correct logic. Many times, programmers write the step to add one to COUNT in a flowchart as follows:

$$COUNT = COUNT + 1$$

Although this is not a valid equation, it is valid in computer logic. In fact, in many programming languages this is the type of instruction actually used. Simply stated, the computer does what is indicated to the right of the equal sign first and then stores the result in the field listed to the left. Hence, 1 is added to the current value of COUNT in the CPU and the new total replaces the old value of the field COUNT. Thus, COUNT is incremented by 1.

We are now ready to put together all the segments of the flowchart to accomplish our objective of printing a heading, the

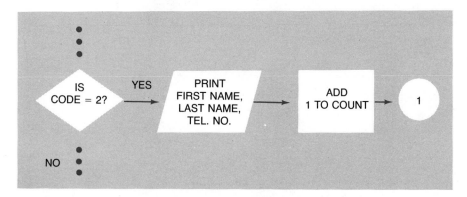

Figure 8.11

Alternative logic for incrementing the counter.

names and telephone numbers of all females from a deck of cards and, at the end of the report, the total number of females processed. Figure 8.12 illustrates this flowchart.

To ensure that you understand the fundamental concepts of flowcharting, examine the following illustrative problems and suggested flowcharts.

Example 1

Note the following about the flowchart in Figure 8.13. We wish to print (1) the total number of students processed and (2) the percentage of students who are female.

1. We do not have a step at the beginning to print out a title or message, since in this problem, we will simply print out two messages which are produced only after all cards have been processed.
2. We have set up two areas to accumulate results—F and T. These names have been arbitrarily chosen and must be used consistently throughout. T will contain total number of students and F will contain total female students.
3. Since we need a total number of students, we increment counter T after a card is read and we have determined that it is not a last card indicator.
4. After the last card (L/C) has been read, we must indicate how the desired percentage is to be computed. You will recall that the computer does nothing unless it is instructed. It must be given detailed instructions for all the operations to be performed.

In this case, the percentage is computed by (1) dividing the number of females by the total number of students, which will produce a decimal number, and (2) then multiplying by 100 to obtain an actual percent. The literal, or constant "THE PERCENTAGE OF FEMALES IS " will accompany the actual number. In addition, the literal "THE TOTAL NUMBER OF STUDENTS IS " along with the actual number T will print.

Example 2

The basic logic for each card read in Figure 8.14 is as follows:

If HOURS WORKED is in excess of 40, we proceed to the step labeled OVERTIME, where we multiply 40 by RATE, subtract 40 from HOURS WORKED to obtain the OVERTIME-HRS, and then multiply OVERTIME-HRS by 1.5 times the RATE. We then add the amounts and continue with the check-processing functions. If the HOURS WORKED is not in excess of 40, then we simply multiply HOURS WORKED by RATE to obtain the TOTAL AMOUNT. After the TOTAL AMOUNT is calculated, we print the person's name and gross salary. For the sake of simplicity, the process of computing payroll deductions for tax purposes has not been included.

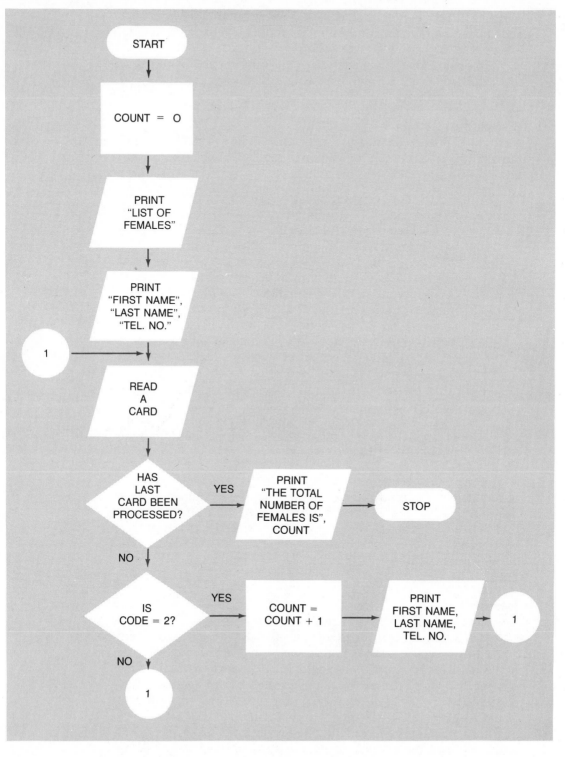

Figure 8.12
Completed flowchart for Example 1.

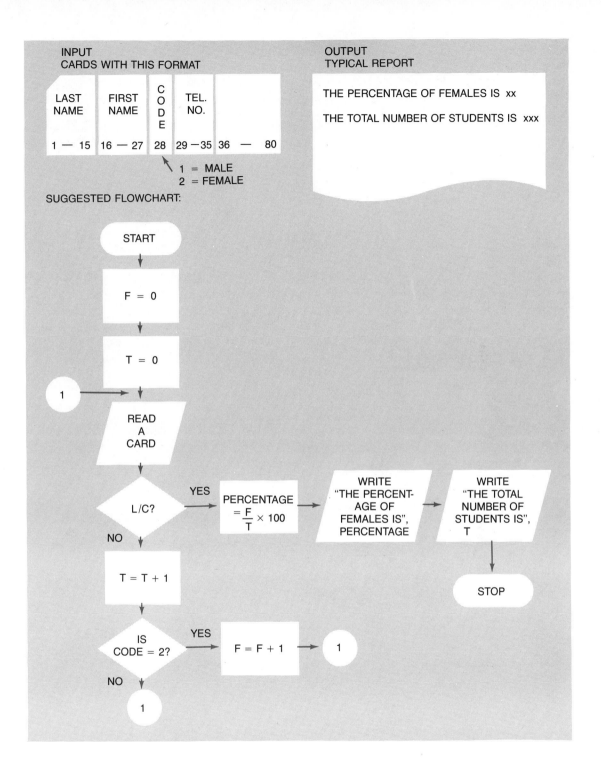

Figure 8.13

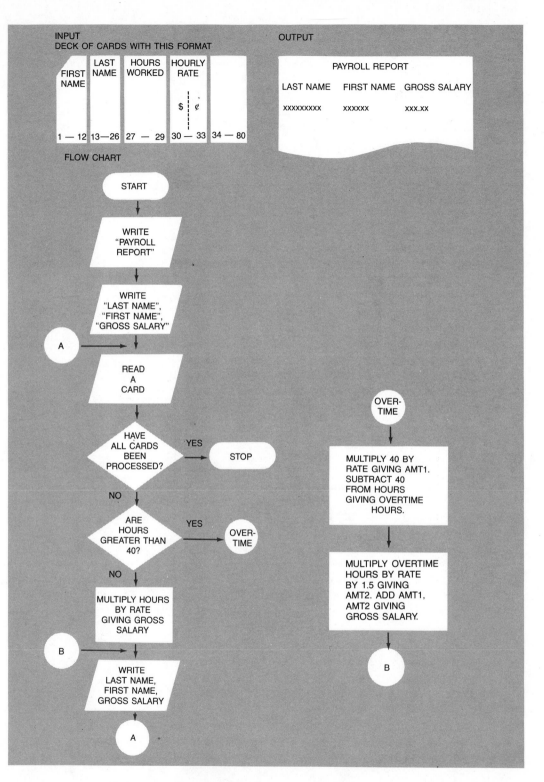

Figure 8.14
Gross salary is computed, with time-and-a-half paid for overtime.

Notice that the above flowchart is not really complete. Conditions could occur for which we have not provided. Suppose, for example, that specific time cards do not have name fields, or that HOURS WORKED or RATE is erroneously blank. What should be done?

To adequately describe a set of procedures, a flowchart must be thorough and include *every possible detail* by testing for every possible contingency. The businessman who outlines the manual procedures so that every possible condition and associated action is accounted for will not be plagued later by numerous erroneous results. Thus the system must be described in every facet. The revised flowchart in Figure 8.15 is more efficient than the preceding because it provides for the possibilities discussed above.

Observe that this flowchart utilizes the three types of connectors shown in Table 8.2. Note that connector symbols may be identified by any notational insert. Some programmers prefer to use notes

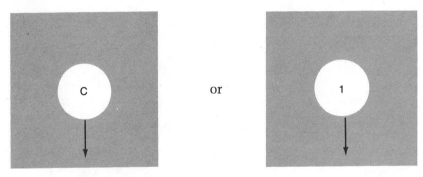

while others use explanatory notation,

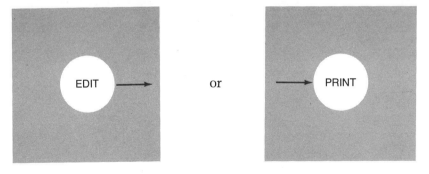

Notice, too, that the unconditional branch connector is always the *last* element in a sequence. Once we issue an instruction that causes the flow to proceed elsewhere, there is no need for further instruction at that point. The flowchart excerpt in Figure 8.15a is *invalid* and meaningless.

Once an unconditional branch to BEGIN is executed, the instruction following the connector cannot be completed.

Keep in mind that the decision symbol and the conditional branch connector are always coded together.

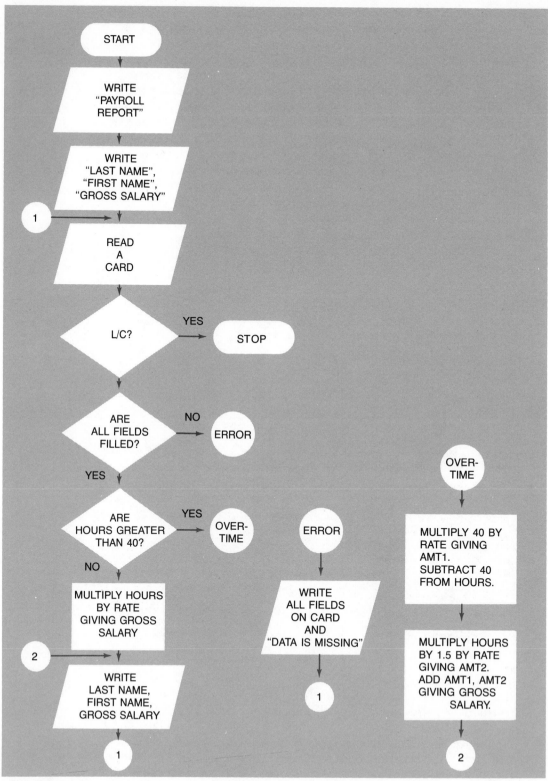

Figure 8.15
Revised flowchart for preparation of a payroll report.

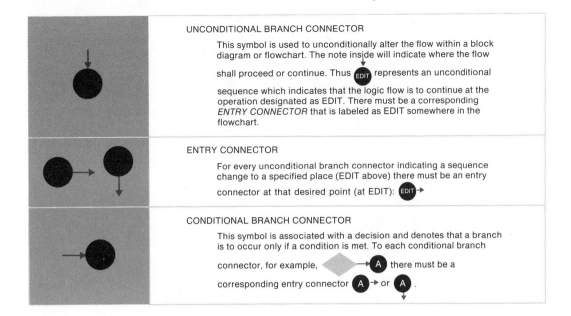

UNCONDITIONAL BRANCH CONNECTOR

This symbol is used to unconditionally alter the flow within a block diagram or flowchart. The note inside will indicate where the flow shall proceed or continue. Thus EDIT represents an unconditional sequence which indicates that logic flow is to continue at the operation designated as EDIT. There must be a corresponding *ENTRY CONNECTOR* that is labeled as EDIT somewhere in the flowchart.

ENTRY CONNECTOR

For every unconditional branch connector indicating a sequence change to a specified place (EDIT above) there must be an entry connector at that desired point (at EDIT): EDIT

CONDITIONAL BRANCH CONNECTOR

This symbol is associated with a decision and denotes that a branch is to occur only if a condition is met. To each conditional branch connector, for example, A there must be a corresponding entry connector A or A .

Table 8.2
Types of Connectors

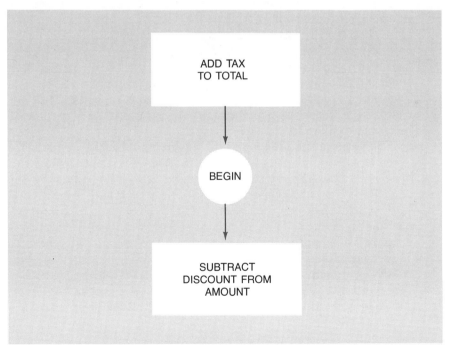

Figure 8.15a
Erroneous
Flowchart Excerpt.

This indicates that *if* a condition is met, then a branch to the entry point indicated should occur. Otherwise, the flow continues with the next sequential step. Every conditional branch connector must have an entry connector associated with it:

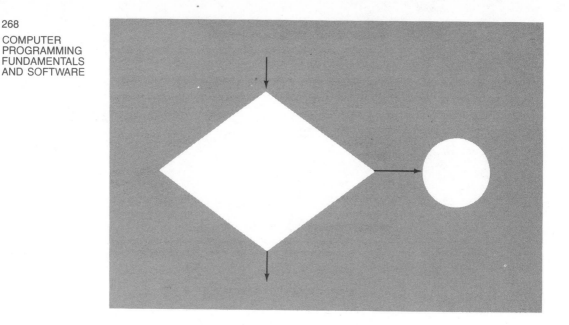

In short, a flowchart is a pictorial representation of the logical integration of elements in a procedure. We have seen that in order to be meaningful, a flowchart must be thorough and include every possible condition. A program flowchart that maps out the logical flow of data in a program also requires the utmost precision. Any condition not tested will, in the subsequent execution of the program, create problems that will require major revision. Thus, in analyzing and designing procedures, we use flowcharts that must be thorough, detailed, and precise.

Because of the blocks in a flowchart, the diagram is often referred to as a *block diagram*. Note that the flowchart depicts the logic of the program. It performs this by illustrating the steps involved and the order of steps with the use of standardized symbols.

Each of the operations indicated above converts to a program step during coding. Thus it is a relatively simple task to code a program from a flowchart, where the logic is clearly indicated. Those programmers who do not write flowcharts prior to coding complex programs often find that their logic is incorrect or that they did not provide for all possible conditions. Flowcharts provide a means of illustrating the sequence of instructions prior to writing the program.

Example 3
Suppose we wish to punch five output cards for every input card read. That is, we wish to perform a punch *routine*, or *sequence*,

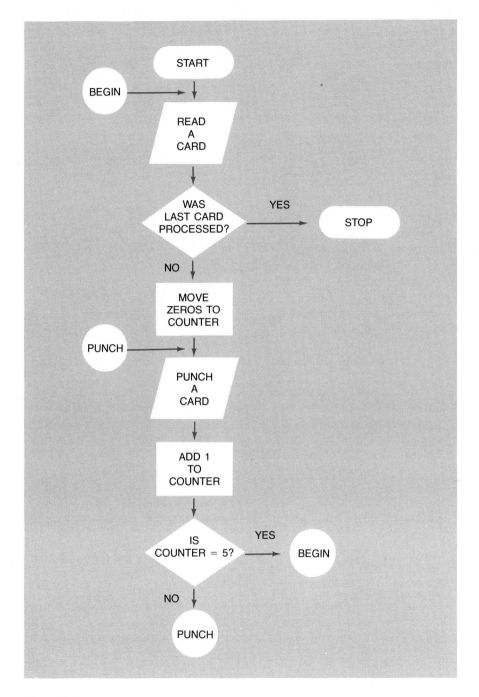

Figure 8.16
Flowchart of a looping routine to punch five output cards for each input card.

five times. A sequence of steps to be executed a fixed number of
times is referred to as a *loop*. Generally, for looping operations, we:

Loop Rules

GENERAL	EXAMPLE—FIGURE 8.16
1. Establish a counter with zero contents.	1. MOVE ZEROS TO COUNTER (SAME AS COUNTER = 0).
2. Perform operation(s) required.	2. PUNCH A CARD.
3. Add 1 to counter. Every time the operation is performed, 1 is added to the counter. Thus the counter reflects the number of times the operation has been performed.	3. ADD 1 TO COUNTER.
4. Test the counter to see if the operation was performed the required number of times.	4. IS COUNTER = 5?
5. Branch if counter equals required number, otherwise repeat sequence.	5. Branch to BEGIN if COUNTER = 5, otherwise branch to PUNCH.

Note that we cannot merely tell the computer to punch a card five times. The looping routine is required to perform an operation a fixed number of times, as in Figure 8.16.

You will recall that a program residing in storage includes the set of instructions and the necessary input/output areas. In addition a program must provide for constants and work areas that may be required. COUNTER, for example, in the above flowchart, would have to be defined as a work area in the corresponding program, while the number 1 would be a constant that would also require a storage area.

Self-Evaluating Quiz

1. A flowchart is a diagram that illustrates the _____ of _____ in a _____.

2. A sequence of steps in a flowchart consists of _____ connected by _____.

3. The direction of flow in a flowchart is usually from _____ to _____.

4. A symbol represents _____.

5. All symbols must be connected by _____; each symbol contains a _____ inside it.

6. A flowcharting tool called a _____ contains all the standard symbols used to draw flowcharts.

Identify each of the symbols in Questions 7 to 14:

7.

8.

9.

10.

11.

12.

13.

14.

15. Arithmetic operations are coded in _____ symbols.

16. Each symbol can generally be used to code a program _____.

17. If a decision is *met,* then the _____ indicates where the flow is to continue; otherwise the program proceeds with the _____.

18. When the flow of a sequence is interrupted and is to continue at some step other than the next sequential step, a(n) _____ is said to occur.

19. Consider the following:

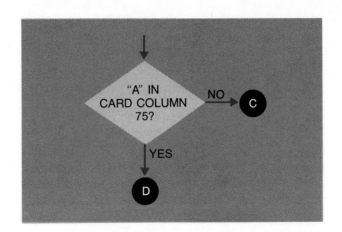

If there is *not* an A in card column 75, a _____ to _____ will occur.

20. The unconditional branch connector must be the _____ step in a sequence.

21. To every branch connector, there must correspond a(n) _____.

22. (T or F) A branch to one entry point may occur from several different points in a flowchart.

23. A _____ is a group of integrated steps connected by flowlines.

24. Consider the flowchart in Figure 8.17. The flowchart depicts the logic in an automobile insurance company procedure. Column 18 denotes marital status (M = married, S = single, O = other, such as widowed, divorced, separated). Column 19 denotes sex (M = male, F = female, blank denotes that sex is unknown). The procedure or *routine* determines the total number of individuals who will receive discounts because they are either:

   (1) female, or
   (2) married and male

   It has been determined by several studies that female drivers and married, male drivers have fewer accidents than other people. Because of this fact, this insurance company will issue discounts to those categories of people. With the following input cards, what will be the contents of TOTAL at the end of all operations?

CARD NO.	CONTENTS OF COLUMN 18	CONTENTS OF COLUMN 19
1	M	M
2	M	F
3	S	M
4	M	F
5	O	F
6	M	—
7	S	F
8	M	M

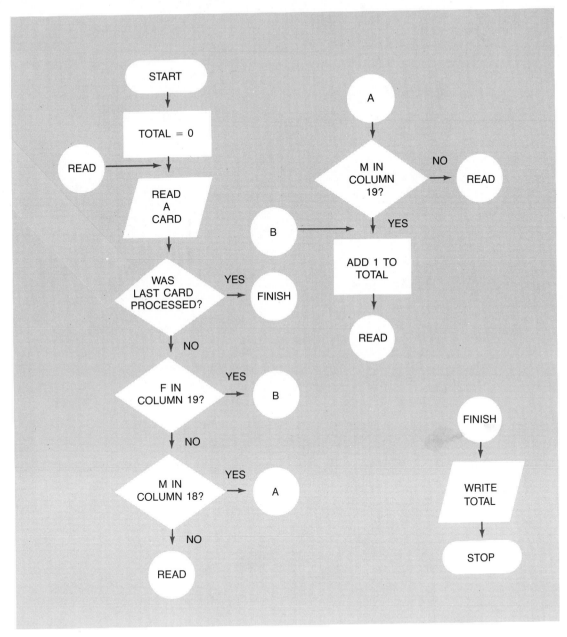

Figure 8.17
Flowchart for Question 24.

Consider the flowchart in Figure 8.18 for questions 25 to 32.

25. For every (no.) _____ cards read, 1 line is printed.

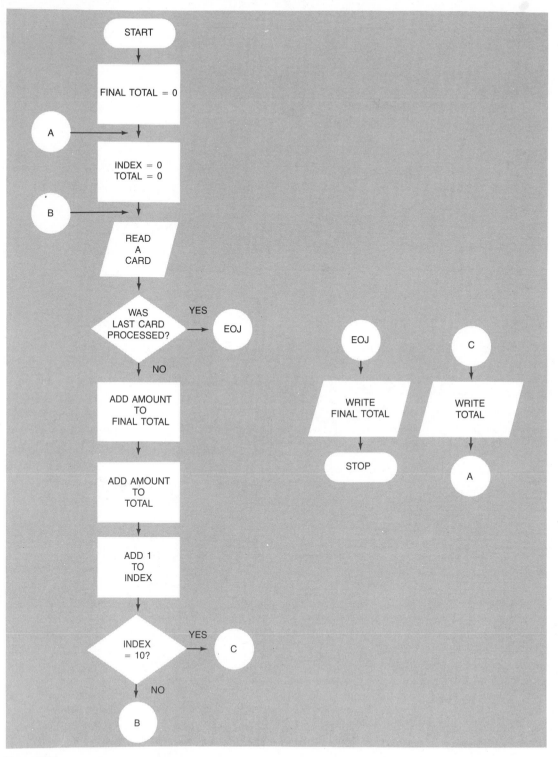

Figure 8.18
Flowchart for Questions 25-32.

26. When there are no more cards, a(n) _____ to _____ occurs.
27. At EOJ _____ is printed which is obtained from the total of all _____ .
28. INDEX is a field used as a _____ for _____ .
29. After 10 cards have been read and added, a branch to _____ occurs.
30. After the data has been printed for each group of 10 cards, _____ and _____ must be initialized, or restarted at zero.
31. Each time a card is read and an amount is added to TOTAL, (no.) _____ is added to INDEX.

Solutions

1. order (logic); functions; program
2. symbols; flowlines
3. top; bottom
4. a function
5. flowlines; note
6. template
7. processing
8. input/output (I/O)
9. decision
10. unconditional branch connector
11. entry connector
12. entry connector
13. conditional branch connector
14. terminal
15. processing
16. instruction
17. conditional branch connector; next sequential step
18. branch
19. branch; C
20. last
21. entry connector
22. T
23. sequence
24. 6
25. 10
26. branch; EOJ
27. a final total; amount fields
28. counter; looping
29. C
30. INDEX; TOTAL
31. 1

II. Illustrative Flowcharting Procedures

At this juncture, you have learned the symbols and some of the techniques that may be used in a program flowchart. You have also been given many examples that emphasize the reading of program flowcharts. This section will provide additional examples designed to assist you in learning to draw your own flowcharts.

Example 1

Draw a flowchart that prints the names of all employees whose salary is less than $5,000 and creates a tape file of the names of all employees whose salary is greater than $20,000. Assume that there are two input fields, NAME and SALARY, for each input employee record.

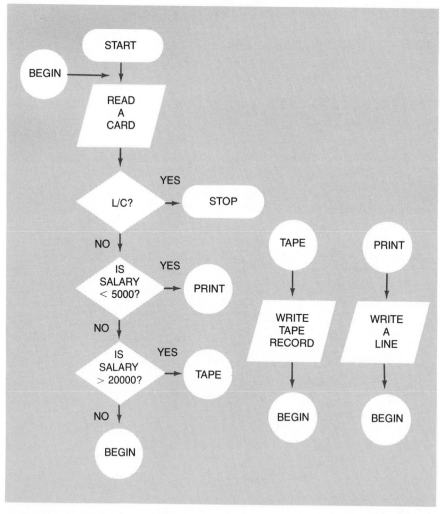

Figure 8.19
Flowchart for Example 1.

Note: The creation of tape files is depicted in a program flow-chart in exactly the same way as the creation of print files. Instead of saying WRITE A LINE or PRINT A LINE we say WRITE A TAPE RECORD. Try drawing the flowchart on scrap paper. Then compare your results with the flowchart in Figure 8.19.

Your sequence of symbols should be similar to the one above but your notes inside the symbols may, of course, vary. The translation of these notes into proper programming form will be discussed in the next chapter.

Note, also, that the mathematical symbols for less than and greater than are commonly used in flowcharts as they are in actual programs. These symbols are:

<   LESS THAN

>   GREATER THAN

Example 2
Draw a flowchart to do the following:

1.   If CODE of a card is 1, AMT is added to TOTAL and TOTAL is printed
2.   If CODE of a card is 2, AMT is subtracted from TOTAL and TOTAL is printed
3.   If CODE is neither 1 nor 2, the error message "INVALID CODE" is printed

Each card contains fields for CODE, AMT, and TOTAL. Your flowchart should look like Figure 8.20. Note that this flowchart shows two decision symbols in succession. There's a special art to the order of logical comparisons; you'll learn more about that (and about codes) as we get into more complex decision-making. If your flowchart differs substantially from the one above, check the sequence of the illustrated flowchart to make certain you understand the logic flow.

Example 3
Using a loop procedure, draw a flowchart to read in cards and print the total number of cards read.

Hint: By adding 1 to a counter each time a card is read, we can accumulate the total number of cards read.

Notice that in the flowchart in Figure 8.21 a single total will print without any reference to the meaning of that number. To prevent any misinterpretation of output, it is considered good programming form to include a literal which explains the meaning of the printed number. Thus, the following would represent a somewhat more meaningful sequence at EOJ:

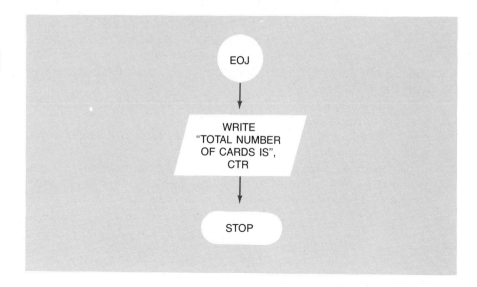

Figure 8.20
Flowchart for
Example 2.

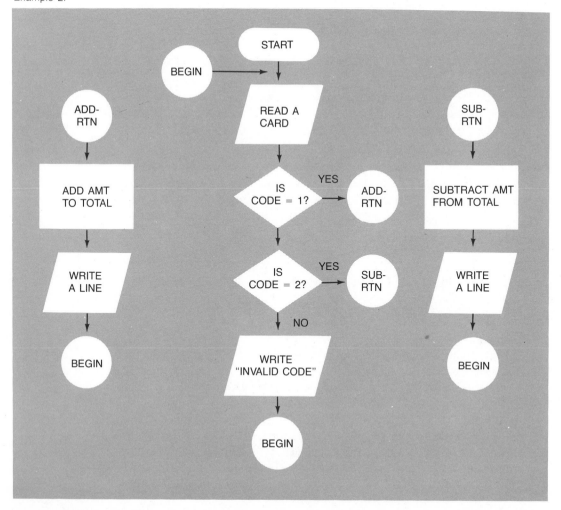

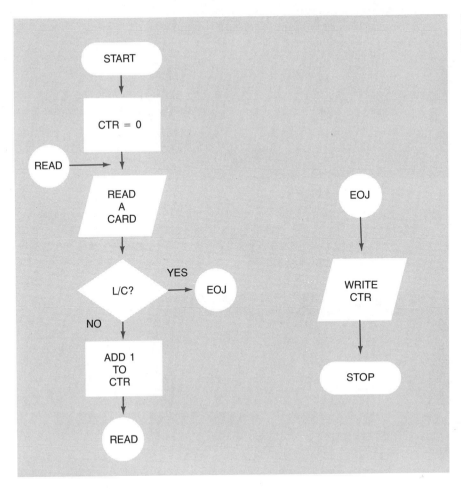

Figure 8.21
Flowchart for
Example 3.

START

CTR = 0

READ →

READ
A
CARD

L/C? — YES → EOJ

NO

ADD 1
TO
CTR

READ

EOJ

WRITE
CTR

STOP

Example 4

Draw a flowchart that will sum the odd numbers from 1 to 101. (*Hint:* start CTR at 1 and add 2 each time. See Figure 8.22.)

III. Flowcharting Business Applications

Now that we have noted the basic flowcharting symbols and how they are used to create simple block diagrams, let us study illustrative business applications.

Example 5: A Banking Operation

A banking organization uses punched cards to store all transaction data for the week. The card format is indicated at the top of page 280.

Cards are in sequence by ACCOUNT NUMBER. Each customer has one type "B" card (balance on hand at beginning of week). This will be the *first* card for each account or customer. In addition, there *may* be several "D" (deposit) or "W" (withdrawal) cards following a "B" card for a customer, depending on the number of transactions

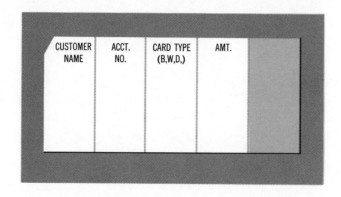

during the week. Thus, all cards for a single account will appear together, with the "B" card being the first for the group.

The output of the program will be a printed report with the following information:

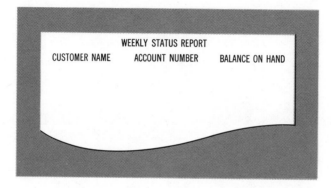

BALANCE ON HAND = BALANCE (from "B" card) + DEPOSITS (from "D" cards) − WITHDRAWALS (from "W" cards)

The flowchart is illustrated in Figure 8.23. Note that the headings are printed first, prior to any card processing. In some programming languages, information to be printed must first be *moved* to the print area *before* it is printed; in other languages the MOVE statement is *not* necessary. We have included the MOVE here for the sake of completeness.

Since the first card read is a "B" card, a branch to NEW-ACCT occurs, where a line is printed. For normal processing this line contains the data for the previous account. That is, a "B" card signals the start of a new account and thus the previous one must be printed. For the first card, however, there is no previous account. Since no data was moved to the print area, a blank line is in effect printed. The total area is cleared and data from this new balance card is moved to the print area. More cards are read. Deposits, denoted by "D" cards are added to the TOTAL, and withdrawals, de-

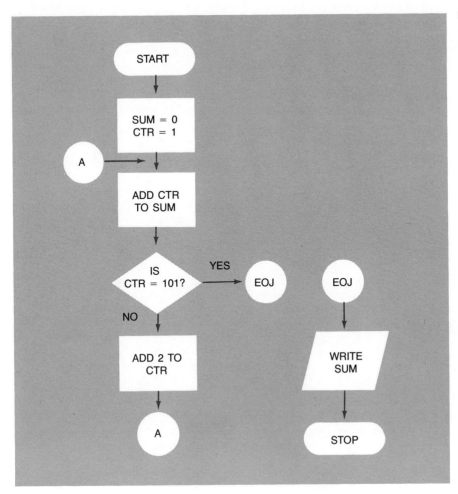

Figure 8.22
Flowchart for
Example 4.

noted by "W" cards, are subtracted. There may be many "D" and "W" cards for a specific account, depending on the number of transactions for the week. When a "B" card is read, the previous data (NAME, ACCOUNT NUMBER, and BALANCE ON HAND) is printed, the print area is cleared, and the new data is read.

Each card read is tested for a "B," "D," or "W." If it is a "B" card, it signals a new account, since the first card of an account must be a "B" card. If it is a "D" or "W" card, the amount is added or subtracted, correspondingly. If it is not a "B," "D," or "W" card, then an error message is printed. It is always good practice to test for validity in a card program, since keypunching errors are relatively frequent.

When there are no more cards to be read, a branch to EOJ occurs. At EOJ, we must print the *last* account group. Since accounts are only printed when a *new* account number (a "B" card) is read, the last account must be "forced." That is, the last account

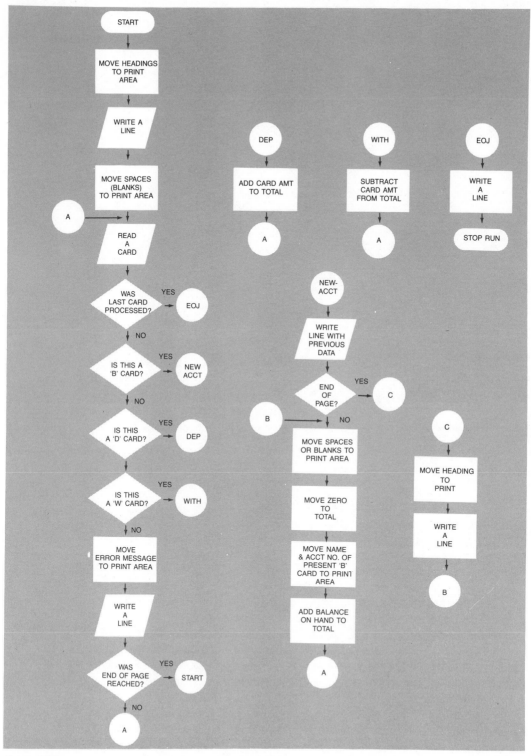

Figure 8.23
Flowchart for Example 5.

group does not have a "B" card following it to signal a print routine. Thus at EOJ, a print routine must be performed.

Note, too, that print programs test for the end of the page. When the end of a page has been reached, we generally wish to print headings on top of the next page.

Example 6: Simplified Accounts Receivable Billing Program

This program will utilize, as input, a master file with information on all charge accounts for a particular department store. The input is on tape:

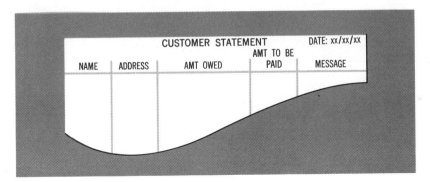

The output is a monthly statement or bill submitted to the customer:

Note that the bills are produced on a series of preprinted continuous forms that contain headings. The programmer must merely insert the date and required data.

The operations to be performed are as follows:

Compilation of Billing Data

If TYPE OF ACCOUNT contains a 1 (regular charge), the *entire* bill is to be paid each month. In this case, AMT OWED is transmitted to the output field, AMT TO BE PAID, with no interest computed.

If TYPE OF ACCOUNT is a 2 (budget charge) then $1/12$ of AMT OWED + INTEREST CHARGE (1% of entire AMT OWED) is recorded on the bill as AMT TO BE PAID.

In each case, NAME, ADDRESS, and AMT OWED are placed directly on the customer statement from the master tape. DATE is obtained

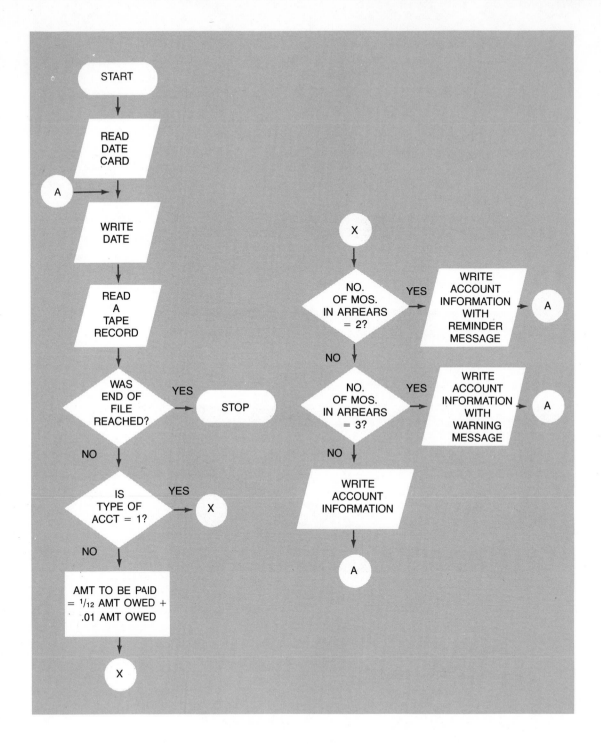

Figure 8.24
Flowchart for
Example 6.

from a control card, which is the only card read. The information from this control card is placed in the computer in a field called DATE.

Determination of Charge Status

The field called NO. OF MOS. THAT ACCT IS IN ARREARS denotes the number of months since a payment has been made to an account that has a balance. If 2 months have elapsed (a 2 is in the field) then a message: REMINDER—YOUR ACCOUNT IS IN ARREARS is to print on the statement. If 3 months have elapsed (a 3 is in the field) then a message: WARNING—YOUR CHARGE PRIVILEGES HAVE BEEN SUSPENDED is to print. A separate monthly run provides a listing of all customers that have not made payments in three months. This list is then distributed to sales personnel who are told not to honor the customers' charge cards.

The flowchart is indicated in Figure 8.24.

Important Terms Used in this Chapter

Conditional Branch Connector	Loop
Decision Symbol	Processing Symbol
End-of-Job Routine	Routine
Entry Connector	Template
Flowchart	Terminal Symbol
Flowlines	Unconditional Branch Connector
Input/Output Symbol	

Self-Evaluating Quiz

1. (T or F) A flowchart is read sequentially from top to bottom.
2. (T or F) If a programmer writes a flowchart before he or she codes a program, the program will run flawlessly.
3. (T or F) A flowchart is a group of symbols connected by flowlines that depict the logic that will be used in a program.
4. (T or F) A flowchart is a standard method of representing the flow of data.
5. (T or F) A terminal symbol is usually the end point in an end-of-job routine.
6. (T or F) A flowchart indicates the steps involved in a problem, the sequence or order of these steps, and the number of input records.
7. (T or F) Each operation denoted in a flowchart converts to a program step during coding.
8. (T or F) Each decision symbol must be associated with a conditional branch connector.
9. (T or F) There is no standard method for flowcharting.

Use Figure 8.25 to answer Questions 10–13.

Figure 8.25

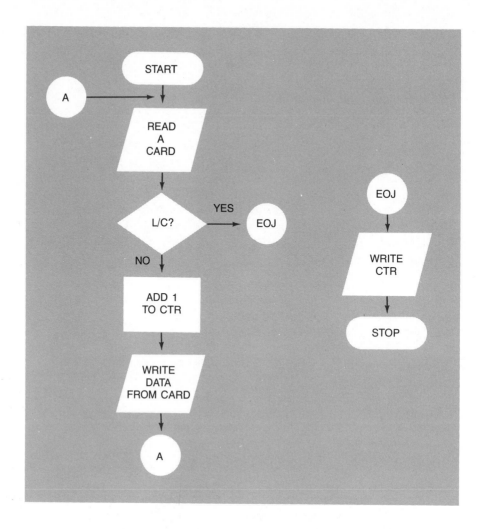

10. (T or F) Each READ instruction should be associated with an end-of-file test.
11. (T or F) At the end of the job, CTR will always contain 10.
12. (T or F) For each card read, two lines are printed.
13. (T or F) The program flowchart contains a logically correct set of procedures.

    Use Figure 8.26 to answer Questions 14–16.

14. (T or F) The program flowchart contains a logically correct set of procedures.
15. (T or F) Only one card is read according to this flowchart.
16. (T or F) Unless the program is terminated by a computer operator, the logic depicted will cause the printing of the same data indefinitely.

    Use Figure 8.27 to answer Questions 17–19.

Figure 8.26

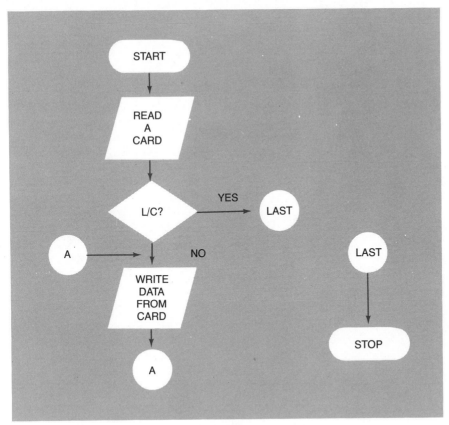

17. (T or F) The flowchart depicted contains a logically sound set of procedures.

18. (T or F) The total number of drivers will print if the program written from this flowchart is executed.

19. (T or F) Only two lines of data print as a result of the logic depicted.

Solutions

1. T
2. F—the chances are improved that it will run smoothly but no one can guarantee a flawless run
3. T
4. T
5. T
6. F—it does not indicate the number of input records
7. T
8. T

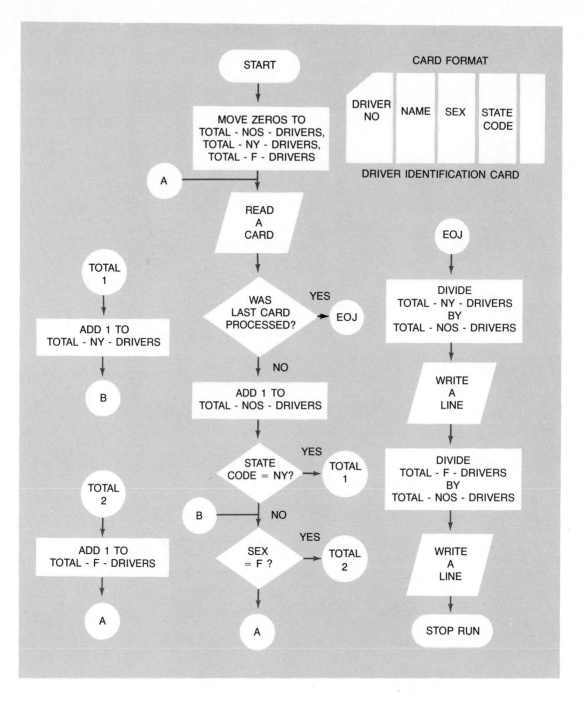

Figure 8.27

9. F
10. T
11. F—CTR will indicate the number of cards processed
12. F—for each card, one line is printed
13. T

14. F—it prints the same input record over and over
15. T
16. T
17. T
18. F—it is computed but it does not print
19. T

Review Questions

1. A flowchart depicts the _____ that will be used in the program.
2. Each symbol in a flowchart represents a(n) _____.
3. The programmer writes _____ within each symbol.
4. Another name for a flowchart is a(n) _____.
5. For each entry connector there is either a corresponding _____ or a(n) _____.
6. An end-of-job condition usually occurs when _____.
7. An example of what a decision symbol may be used to denote is: _____.
8. In order to perform a looping operation, a(n) _____ must be established with an initial value of _____.
9. The symbol used to denote a processing step is a _____.
10. The symbol used to denote an input step is a _____.
11. The symbol used to denote an unconditional branch connector is a _____.

Use Figure 8.25 to answer Questions 12–15.

12. The field CTR prints when _____.
13. Each time a card is read, _____.
14. The purpose of the flowchart is to _____.
15. The number of output lines that print is equal to _____.

Use Figure 8.26 to answer Questions 16–19.

16. The number of lines that will print is dependent upon _____.
17. The data that will print is the same as _____.
18. The end-of-job routine performs a _____.
19. The symbol with the note _____ corresponds to an entry connector.

Use Figure 8.27 to answer Questions 20–22.

20. The data that prints as a result of these operations is _____.
21. In order to execute the TOTAL1 routine, a card must contain _____.
22. In order to execute the TOTAL2 routine, a card must contain _____.

Programming in High-Level Languages: An Overview

9

9

The purpose of this chapter is to familiarize the student with some of the features of the most commonly used programming languages. The following languages will be considered:

COBOL
FORTRAN
BASIC
RPG

We will focus on the basic structure of the languages and provide an illustration and in-depth explanation of the same task programmed in each language. This will provide the student with a basic understanding of the advantages and disadvantages of each language. In Chapters 11 and 13 respectively, COBOL and BASIC will be considered in more detail in an effort to provide the student with enough information so that he or she can actually program in these languages.

I. COBOL

A. The Nature of COBOL

COBOL is the most widespread commercial programming language in use today. You will recall that COBOL is an abbreviation for *CO*mmon *B*usiness *O*riented *L*anguage. It is a business-oriented language designed specifically for commercial applications. It is also a computer language that is universal, or common to many computers. The universality of COBOL allows computer users great flexibility. A company is free to use computers of different manufacturers while retaining a single programming language. Similarly, conversion from one model computer to a more advanced or newer one presents no great problem. Computers of a future generation will also be equipped to use COBOL.

Thus the meaning of the word COBOL suggests two of its basic advantages. It is common to most computers and it is commercially oriented. There are, however, additional reasons for its being such a popular language.

COBOL is an Englishlike language. All instructions are coded using English words rather than complex codes. To add two numbers together, for example, we use the word ADD. Similarly, the rules for programming in COBOL conform to many of the rules for

9

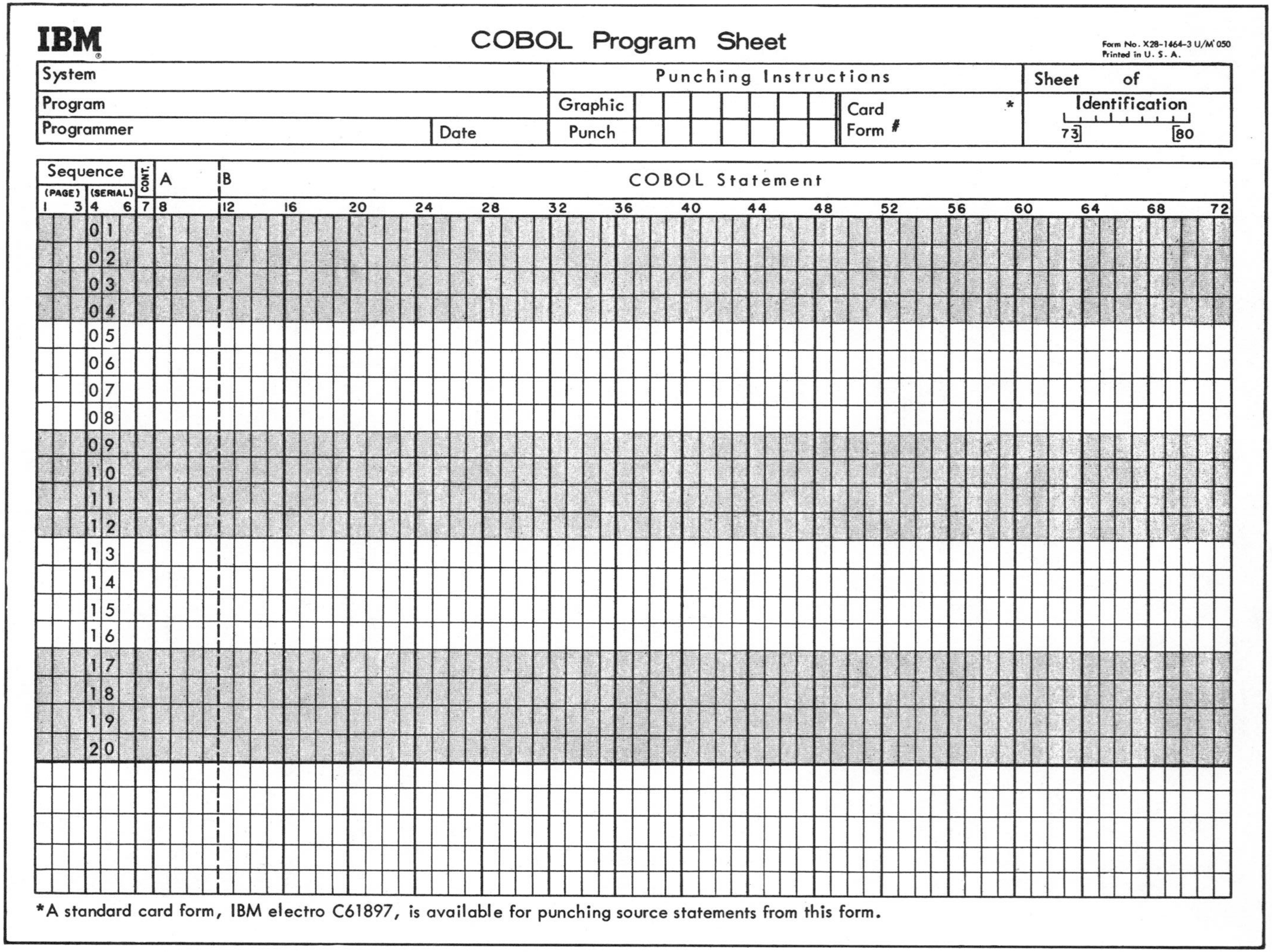

Figure 9.1
COBOL coding sheet.

writing in English, making it a relatively simple language to learn. It therefore becomes significantly easier to train programmers. In addition, COBOL programs are generally written and tested in far less time than programs written in most other computer languages.

Thus the Englishlike quality of COBOL makes it easy to *write* programs. Similarly, this quality makes COBOL programs easier to *read*. Such programs can generally be understood by non-data-processing personnel. The businessman who is not an expert on computers can better understand the nature of a programming job simply by reading a COBOL program.

With a brief introduction to the language, a student can effectively read a program and understand its nature. This significantly reduces the communications gap between the programmer and the businessman. Both can work jointly to correct or improve the logic of a COBOL program.

B. Basic Structure of a COBOL Program

1. The Coding Sheet COBOL programs are written on coding or program sheets (Figure 9.1). The coding sheet has space for 80 columns of information. Each line of a program sheet will be keypunched into *one* punched card. Usually the standard COBOL card (Figure 9.2) is used for this purpose.

Thus, for every *line* written on the coding sheet, we will obtain *one punched card*. The entire deck of cards keypunched from the coding sheets is called the *COBOL SOURCE PROGRAM*. Note that *all* programming languages utilize specially designed

Figure 9.2
COBOL source
program card.

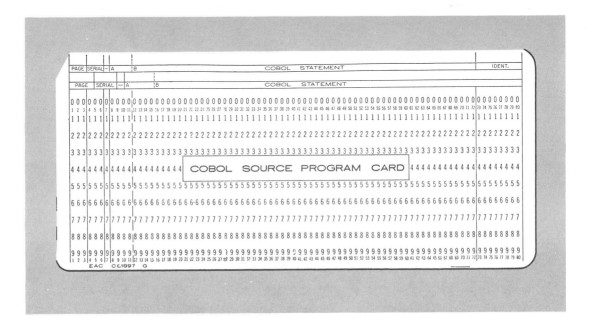

coding sheets, except PL/1—a free-form language that does not require characters to be in any specific positions. Similarly, all source decks consist of cards keypunched from coding sheets, where one line is punched into one card.

Let us examine the COBOL program sheet more closely. The top of the form has identifying fields such as System, Program, etc. which are used to maintain control of the coding sheets but which actually have no effect on the program. Only the numbered items become part of the program.

COBOL Program Sheets

ITEM	MEANING	KEYPUNCHED INTO CARD COLUMNS
Sequence	Includes page and line number—optional, with no effect on program	1–6
COBOL Statement	Includes actual instructions	8–72
Identification (Upper Rt. Corner)	Includes an identifying code, usually a number; optional	73–80

The identification number, positions 73 to 80, and the page and serial number, positions 1 to 6, are optional entries in a COBOL program, and in *all* other programming languages. Both fields, however, can be extremely useful, should cards in the source deck be misplaced or lost.

Page and serial (line) numbers on each line, and therefore, on each punched card are advisable, since cards are sometimes inadvertently dropped. In such cases, resequencing of the deck is necessary. If page and serial numbers are supplied, it is also an easy task to insert cards in their proper place. Note that some coding sheets preprint the serial numbers to assist the programmer.

2. The Four Divisions Every COBOL program consists of four separate *divisions*. Each division is written in an Englishlike manner designed to decrease programming effort and to facilitate the understanding of a program by non-data-processing or business personnel. Each of the four divisions has a specific function.

Four Divisions of a COBOL Program

NAME	FUNCTION
Identification	• Identifies the program to the computer

Division	• Provides documentary information that assists businessmen in understanding nature of program and techniques it will employ
Environment Division	• Describes computer equipment and features to be used in program
Data Division	• Describes input and output formats used in program • Defines constants and storage areas necessary for processing of data
Procedure Division	• Contains instructions and logic flow necessary to create output from input data • Coded directly from flowchart

C. Illustrative COBOL Program

1. Definition of the Problem   A computer center of a large company is assigned the task of calculating weekly wages for all nonsalaried personnel. You recall that to process data, the incoming data or input must be in a form that is acceptable or understandable to the computer. Punched cards, magnetic tape, and magnetic disk are common forms of input to a computer system.

Thus the employee data will be received from the Payroll Department in the form of time cards. These time cards will contain three fields as indicated in Figure 9.3. For purposes of a COBOL program these fields will be called:

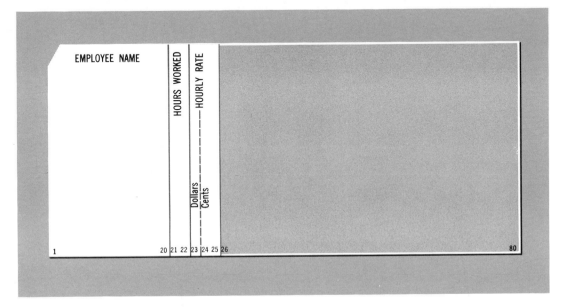

Figure 9.3
Input card format for sample program.

FIELD	LENGTH
EMPLOYEE-NAME	20
HOURS-WORKED	2
HOURLY-RATE	3 (1 integer decimal)

The three fields of data will be transcribed or keypunched onto a punched card that will be accepted as input to the data processing system.

Card columns 1 to 20 are reserved for each EMPLOYEE-NAME. If any name contains less than 20 characters, the low-order, or rightmost, positions are left blank. Similarly, HOURS-WORKED will be placed in columns 21 to 22 and HOURLY-RATE in columns 23 to 25. The HOURLY-RATE figure, as a dollars and cents amount, is to be interpreted as a two-decimal field. That is, 125 in columns 23 to 25 is to be interpreted by the computer as 1.25. The decimal point is not generally punched into a card used for commercial applications since it would waste a column. We will see that this method of implying or assuming decimal points is easily handled in COBOL.

A deck of employee cards, with the above format, will be keypunched and then read as input to the computer. WEEKLY-WAGES will be calculated by the computer, as

$$\text{WEEKLY-WAGES} = \text{HOURS-WORKED} \times \text{HOURLY-RATE}$$

The computed figure, however, *cannot* generally be added to the input record. That is, with card or tape processing we cannot easily create output data on an input record.[1]

We will create, then, an output file that contains all input data in addition to the computed wage figure for each record. The output PAYROLL-FILE will be placed on a magnetic tape with the record format shown in Figure 9.4. At a later date, the tape will be used to create payroll checks.

Figure 9.4

Output tape format for sample program.

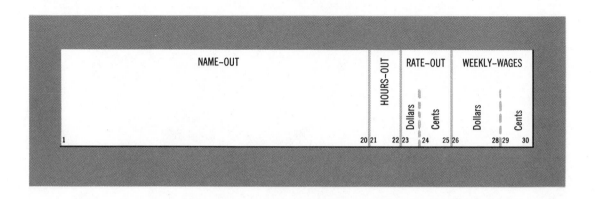

---

[1]Disk processing can be used to simply add additional data to input records.

Thus the input to the system will be called EMPLOYEE-CARDS. The computer will calculate WEEKLY-WAGES from the two input fields HOURS-WORKED and HOURLY-RATE. The input data along with the computed figure will be used to create the output tape called PAYROLL-FILE. Figure 9.5 represents the flowchart for the problem.

2. The Program   Once the input and output record formats have been clearly and precisely defined as in Figures 9.3 and 9.4, and the logic has been determined and represented by a flowchart, as in Figure 9.5, the program may be written. You will recall that a program is a set of instructions and specifications that operates on input to produce output. Figure 9.6 is a simplified COBOL program that will operate on employee cards to create a payroll tape file with the computed wages.

Notice that the program is written in an Englishlike language. Note also that the program is divided into *four major divisions.* The IDENTIFICATION, ENVIRONMENT, DATA, and PROCEDURE DIVISIONS are coded on lines 01, 03, and 07 of page 1, and line 01 of page 2, respectively. Every COBOL program must contain these four divisions in the above order. Each must appear on a line by itself, with no other entries, and must be followed by a period. Punctuation in COBOL is just as important as it is in English.

a. Identification Division   In this program, the IDENTIFICATION DIVISION has, as its only entry, the PROGRAM-ID. That is, the IDENTIFICATION DIVISION of this program merely serves to identify the program.

b. Environment Division   The ENVIRONMENT DIVISION assigns the input and output files to specific devices in the INPUT-OUTPUT SECTION. EMPLOYEE-CARDS, the name assigned to the input file, will be processed by a card reader. Similarly, PAYROLL-FILE is the output file assigned to a specific tape drive.

c. Data Division   The DATA DIVISION describes, in detail, the type of files and the field designations within each record. The input and output areas in the CPU are fully described in the DATA DIVISION in the FILE SECTION. The File Description, or FD, for EMPLOYEE-CARDS indicates that labels[2] are not needed, that the record mode is F for fixed, and that the card format will be called EMPLOYEE-RECORD. This record includes three input fields called EMPLOYEE-NAME, HOURS-WORKED, and HOURLY-RATE. The fourth field called FILLER is just the blank area at the end of the card. FILLER, a COBOL RESERVED WORD, denotes that the field has no significance in the program. Each field has a corresponding PICTURE clause denoting the size and type of data that will appear in the field:

----

[2]For a complete discussion of label use, see Chapter 5.

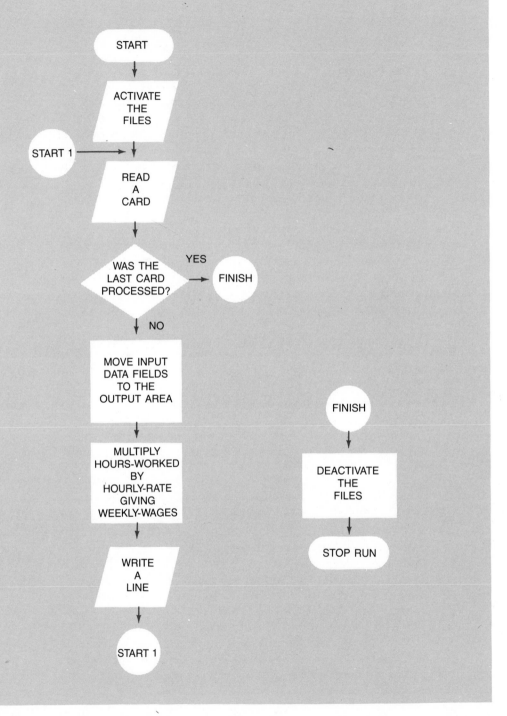

Figure 9.5
Flowchart for sample program.

Input File: Employee Cards

FIELD	PICTURE	MEANING
EMPLOYEE-NAME	A(20)	A—alphabetic field (20)—20 positions
HOURS-WORKED	99	9—numeric field 99—two positions *Note:* 99 is same as 9(2)
HOURLY-RATE	9V99	Numeric—3 positions V—implied or assumed decimal point after first digit (e.g., 125 will be interpreted by computer as 1.25) *Note:* Decimal point does not appear on the input card but is nonetheless implied

Similarly, the output file called PAYROLL-FILE has:

> Standard labels
> Fixed record format called PAYROLL-RECORD

PAYROLL-RECORD is subdivided into four fields, each with an appropriate PICTURE clause. The first three fields, NAME-OUT, HOURS-OUT, and RATE-OUT will be taken directly from each input record, using a MOVE statement. The last field, WEEKLY-WAGES with three integer, or dollar, positions, and two decimal or cents positions must be computed. Since HOURS-WORKED has two integer positions and HOURLY-RATE has one, *three* integer positions are needed for the product of these two fields.

If any constants or work areas were required in the program, they, too, would be described in the DATA DIVISION.

d. Procedure Division The PROCEDURE DIVISION contains the set of instructions or operations to be performed by the computer. Each instruction is executed in the order in which it appears, unless a GO TO statement, or branch, alters the sequence. You will note that the PROCEDURE DIVISION may be coded directly from the flowchart. The meaning of each statement is as follows:

LINE NUMBER	INSTRUCTION	MEANING
2	OPEN statement	Prior to execution, all files must be opened, or prepared for processing.

COMPUTER
PROGRAMMING
FUNDAMENTALS
AND SOFTWARE

Figure 9.6
Coding for sample program.

COBOL PROGRAM SHEET

Form No. X28-1464-1 U/M 050
Printed in U.S.A.

Sheet 1 of 2

System

Program SAMPLE

Programmer N. STERN

SEQUENCE (PAGE) (SERIAL)	A B	COBOL STATEMENT
001 01		IDENTIFICATION DIVISION.
02		PROGRAM-ID. 'SAMPLE'.
03		ENVIRONMENT DIVISION.
04		INPUT-OUTPUT SECTION.
05		FILE-CONTROL. SELECT EMPLOYEE-CARDS ASSIGN TO READER.
06		SELECT PAYROLL-FILE ASSIGN TO TAPE-1.
07		DATA DIVISION.
08		FILE SECTION.
09		FD EMPLOYEE-CARDS
10		LABEL RECORDS ARE OMITTED, RECORDING MODE IS F,
11		DATA RECORD IS EMPLOYEE-RECORD.
12		01 EMPLOYEE-RECORD.
13		02 EMPLOYEE-NAME PICTURE A(20).
14		02 HOURS-WORKED PICTURE 99.
15		02 HOURLY-RATE PICTURE 9V99.
16		02 FILLER PICTURE X(55).
17		FD PAYROLL-FILE
18		LABEL RECORDS ARE STANDARD, RECORDING MODE IS F,
19		DATA RECORD IS PAYROLL-RECORD.
20		01 PAYROLL-RECORD.
21		02 NAME-OUT PICTURE A(20).
22		02 HOURS-OUT PICTURE 9(2).
23		02 RATE-OUT PICTURE 9V99.
24		02 WEEKLY-WAGES PICTURE 999V99.
001 025		

* A standard card form, IBM electro C61897, is available for punching source statements from this form.

IBM

COBOL PROGRAM SHEET

System	
Program	
Programmer		Date

| Graphic | | | | Punching Instructions | Card Form # | | * |
| Punch | | | |

Form No. X28-1464-1 U/M 050
Printed in U.S.A.

Sheet 2 of 2

Identification
73 [ ] 80

SEQUENCE (PAGE) 1-3 (SERIAL) 4-6	CONT 7	A 8	B 12	Statement
00201				PROCEDURE DIVISION.
02				OPEN INPUT EMPLOYEE-CARDS OUTPUT PAYROLL-FILE.
03				START1.
04				READ EMPLOYEE-CARDS AT END GO TO FINISH.
05				MOVE EMPLOYEE-NAME TO NAME-OUT.
06				MOVE HOURS-WORKED TO HOURS-OUT.
07				MOVE HOURLY-RATE TO RATE-OUT.
08				MULTIPLY HOURS-WORKED BY HOURLY-RATE GIVING WEEKLY-WAGES.
09				WRITE PAYROLL-RECORD.
10				GO TO START1.
11				FINISH.
12				CLOSE EMPLOYEE-CARDS, PAYROLL-FILE.
00213				STOP RUN.

* A standard card form, IBM electro C61897, is available for punching source statements from this form.

4	READ statement	Reads card data from card reader into storage. AT END GO TO FINISH is a clause which causes the computer to branch to the paragraph called FINISH when there are no more cards to be processed.
5–7	MOVE statements	Input fields are moved to output areas
8	MULTIPLY statement	Weekly wages are calculated by multiplying HOURS-WORKED by HOURLY-RATE and placing the answer in the output field called WEEKLY-WAGES
9	WRITE statement	Takes the data in the output area and writes it on magnetic tape
10	GO TO statement	Permits the program to repeat the sequence of operations for succeeding cards
11	FINISH—a paragraph name	Execution continues in the above sequence until there are no more cards, at which point a branch to FINISH occurs
12	CLOSE statement	Files are deactivated
13	STOP RUN statement	Program is terminated

Figure 9.6, then, represents a sample COBOL program in its entirety. This program will run on any commercial computer with only slight modifications possibly required in the ENVIRONMENT DIVISION. Since this division indicates the computer equipment utilized in the program, it is frequently machine-dependent, that is, non-standard.

Figure 9.6 is an illustration of the program coded by the programmer. These sheets must then be transcribed into a machine-readable form (cards, tape, etc.) and then run on the computer.

Figure 9.7 is a sample program listing as prepared by a computer from the source deck during compilation or translation into machine-language.

An analysis of the program reveals several essential points. The Englishlike manner and the structural organization of a COBOL program make it comparatively easy to learn. Similarly, the ease with which a COBOL program may be read by businessmen with only minimal exposure to the language makes it a distinct asset to most data processing installations. Note, however, that COBOL, unlike the remaining languages we will consider, is very wordy, requiring much writing. Other languages are more compact, requiring fewer rules and words to be coded by the programmer.

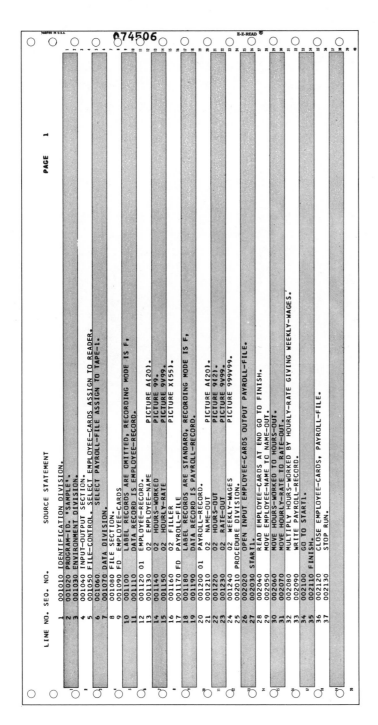

```
LINE NO. SEQ. NO.        SOURCE STATEMENT

  1      001010 IDENTIFICATION DIVISION.
  2      001020 PROGRAM-ID. 'SAMPLE'.
  3      001030 ENVIRONMENT DIVISION.
  4      001040 INPUT-OUTPUT SECTION.
  5      001050 FILE-CONTROL. SELECT EMPLOYEE-CARDS ASSIGN TO READER.
  6      0C1060         SELECT PAYROLL-FILE ASSIGN TO TAPE-1.
  7      001070 DATA DIVISION.
  8      001080 FILE SECTION.
  9      001090 FD  EMPLOYEE-CARDS
 10      001100     LABEL RECORDS ARE OMITTED, RECORDING MODE IS F,
 11      001110     DATA RECORD IS EMPLOYEE-RECORD.
 12      001120 01  EMPLOYEE-RECORD.
 13      001130     02 EMPLOYEE-NAME              PICTURE A(20).
 14      001140     02 HOURS-WORKED               PICTURE 99.
 15      001150     02 HOURLY-RATE                PICTURE 9V99.
 16      001160     02 FILLER                     PICTURE X(55).
 17      001170 FD  PAYROLL-FILE
 18      001180     LABEL RECORDS ARE STANDARD, RECORDING MODE IS F,
 19      001190     DATA RECORD IS PAYROLL-RECORD.
 20      001200 01  PAYROLL-RECORD.
 21      001210     02 NAME-OUT                   PICTURE A(20).
 22      001220     02 HOURS-OUT                  PICTURE 9(2).
 23      001230     02 RATE-OUT                   PICTURE 9V99.
 24      001240     02 WEEKLY-WAGES               PICTURE 999V99.
 25      002010 PROCEDURE DIVISION.
 26      002020     OPEN INPUT EMPLOYEE-CARDS OUTPUT PAYROLL-FILE.
 27      002030 START1.
 28      002040     READ EMPLOYEE-CARDS AT END GO TO FINISH.
 29      002050     MOVE EMPLOYEE-NAME TO NAME-OUT.
 30      002060     MOVE HOURS-WORKED TO HOURS-OUT.
 31      002070     MOVE HOURLY-RATE TO RATE-OUT.
 32      002080     MULTIPLY HOURS-WORKED BY HOURLY-RATE GIVING WEEKLY-WAGES.
 33      002090     WRITE PAYROLL-RECORD.
 34      002100     GO TO START1.
 35      002110 FINISH.
 36      002120     CLOSE EMPLOYEE-CARDS, PAYROLL-FILE.
 37      002130     STOP RUN.
```

PAGE 1

Figure 9.7
COBOL program listing.

Since COBOL is so commonly used for business applications, we have included an entire chapter, Chapter 11, on the fundamentals of this language.

Self-Evaluating Quiz

1. The word COBOL is an abbreviation for _____.
2. COBOL is a common language in the sense that _____.
3. COBOL is a business-oriented language in the sense that _____.
4. All COBOL programs are composed of _____.
5. The names of these four divisions in the order in which they must be coded are _____, _____, _____, and _____.
6. The function of the IDENTIFICATION DIVISION is to _____.
7. The function of the ENVIRONMENT DIVISION is to _____.
8. The function of the DATA DIVISION is to _____.
9. The function of the PROCEDURE DIVISION is to _____.

Solutions

1. *COmmon Business Oriented Language*
2. it may be used on many different computers
3. it makes use of ordinary business terminology
4. four divisions
5. IDENTIFICATION; ENVIRONMENT; DATA; PROCEDURE
6. identify the program
7. describe the equipment to be used in the program
8. describe the input, output, constants, and work areas used in the program
9. define the instructions and operations necessary to convert input data to output

II. FORTRAN

FORTRAN is a computer language which, like COBOL, is universal, or common to many computers. The name FORTRAN is an acronym for *FOR*mula *TRAN*slator. This suggests that this language is particularly suited for writing programs that deal primarily with formulas. FORTRAN is widely used for scientific and engineering applications. Notwithstanding this fact, it is also true that FORTRAN is utilized to program many traditional business applications.

The purpose of this chapter is twofold:

1. To enable a student to read and understand simple FORTRAN programs.
2. To explore typical business applications that are programmed in FORTRAN.

A. The Nature of FORTRAN

The essence of the FORTRAN language is that most instructions are written in terms of mathematical formulas or expressions. Whereas, in COBOL we might say:

MULTIPLY HOURS-WORKED BY HOURLY-RATE GIVING WEEKLY-WAGES

in FORTRAN we would use the following instruction to accomplish the same result:

WAGES = HOURS * RATE

Notice that in COBOL the instruction reads like an English sentence, while in FORTRAN we have what appears to be an equation.

To demonstrate the nature of this language, we will present, in Figure 9.8, a simplified FORTRAN program to calculate weekly wages for employees. This program is equivalent to the COBOL program presented at the beginning of this chapter.

An explanation of this program is as follows:

Line	Statement and Explanation

1st and 2nd

```
C  THIS FORTRAN PROGRAM ACCOMPLISHES THE SAME THING AS
C  THE COBOL PROGRAM PRESENTED AT THE BEGINNING OF THIS CHAPTER
```

The "C" in column 1 of each card indicates that these cards contain only Comments for the purpose of clarification for someone reading the program. These lines have *no* effect on the logic of the program itself.

3rd

```
DIMENSION NAME (5)
```

This instruction is technically necessary, since FORTRAN compilers generally do not allow an alphanumeric field as large as 20 positions to be read in and stored in *one* field. It is therefore necessary in this program to instruct the computer to set up several adjacent fields to hold all of the characters from the input field (NAME). We will use five adjacent fields, each four positions long.

4th

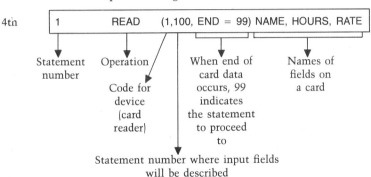

FORTRAN CODING FORM

Form X28-7327-4
Printed in U.S.A.

IBM							
Program	SAMPLE			Punching Instructions		Page 1 of 1	
Programmer	R. STERN	Date	Graphic	Punch	Card Form #	*	Identification 73 80

FORTRAN STATEMENT

STATEMENT NUMBER		FORTRAN STATEMENT
C FOR COMMENT		
C		THIS FORTRAN PROGRAM ACCOMPLISHES THE SAME THING AS
C		THE COBOL PROGRAM PRESENTED AT THE BEGINNING OF THIS CHAPTER
		DIMENSION NAME(5)
	1	READ (1,100,END=99) NAME,HOURS,RATE
		WAGES = HOURS * RATE
		WRITE (6,110) NAME,HOURS,RATE,WAGES
		GO TO 1
99		END FILE 6
		STOP
100		FORMAT (5A4,F2.0,F3.2)
110		FORMAT (5A4,F3.0,F4.2,F6.2)
		END

* A standard card form, IBM electro 888157, is available for punching source statements from this form.

Figure 9.8
Coding for sample
problem 1.

5th

> WAGES = HOURS * RATE

Formula to perform desired calculation. Note the use of the asterisk in place of the multiplication sign.

6th

> WRITE   (6,110) NAME, HOURS, RATE, WAGES

Instruction to tell computer to write on tape unit 6, the following fields: NAME, HOURS, RATE, and WAGES, which are further described as to field specifications in statement number 110.

7th

> GO TO 1

A branch back to statement number 1 to repeat the process if there are cards left.

8th

> 99   END FILE 6

This statement is the one to which a branch occurs after there are no more cards to be processed. That is, the END = 99 in statement 1 causes a branch to statement number 99 after all cards have been processed. The END FILE command in this statement is an instruction which causes the computer to place an end of file indicator on the tape.

9th

> STOP

We are now ready to stop the program, since all cards have been processed.

10th

> 100   FORMAT (5A4, F2.0, F3.2)

The purpose of the FORMAT statement is to describe the specifications or format of the input or output, in detail. This FORMAT, numbered 100, is associated with the input cards (READ(1,100 . . .)). The *first* specification of 5A4 indicates that the first five adjacent groups of four positions each contain alphanumeric (A) data pertaining to NAME, the first field listed in the READ statement. That is, columns 1–20 in the card contain this data. Since the FORTRAN compiler does not ordinarily allow for an alphanumeric specification larger than four positions, such as A20, we must accommodate large fields by grouping the data in some manner that will yield the desired size. A specification of 10A2, for example, would achieve the same result as the specification used above. However, a different statement (DIMENSION NAME(10)) would have to be put at the beginning of the program. The next specification is the F, or floating-point, specification which indicates the length of the field *on the card* and the number of decimal positions. In this case, the F2.0 indicates that the second field (HOURS) will be two positions long with no (0) decimal positions. The last specification, F3.2, indicates that the third field (RATE) will be three positions long, and should be stored with a decimal point and 2 digits to the right of the point.

11th

> 110   FORMAT (5A4, F3.0, F4.2, F6.2)

This FORMAT describes the output listed in the WRITE statement: WRITE (6,110) NAME, HOURS, RATE, WAGES. We are asking the computer to store NAME, HOURS, RATE, and WAGES on tape for the card just processed. The FORMAT statement describes each of these fields. The specification 5A4 has the same meaning as in the previous FORMAT. The second specification (F3.0) indicates that HOURS is to occupy three positions on the tape—two integers *and* the decimal point, with no (0) decimal digits after it. The next specification of F4.2 indicates that RATE is to occupy four positions on the tape, including the decimal point with two digits to the right. The last specification of F6.2 describes how WAGES is to be stored. It is to occupy six positions, including a decimal point with two digits to the right. Note that in FORTRAN, unlike COBOL, there is no convenient way of storing a field on tape, for example, with an implied decimal point to separate dollars from cents. In FORTRAN, such a field is usually stored with the decimal point actually included.

12th

> END

The END statement signifies to the computer that there are no more statements in this program.

Now that we have seen the structure of a FORTRAN program, we will discuss some programs that involve slightly more sophisticated logic in order to illustrate some of the common types of FORTRAN statements. As the next illustration, we will read in cards with the weekly sales figures for each salesman, and produce a report which shows commissions that have been earned. The sales cards and the sales report have the formats shown in Figure 9.9.

Figure 9.10 shows the coding for this program.

This program points out some interesting features of FORTRAN not encountered in Figure 9.8.

1. The first WRITE instruction tells the computer to print out a specified heading. Notice that there are no field names indicated next to the WRITE statement. However, the associated format, statement number 5, tells the computer what to do. The first specification, '1', is a code for carriage control purposes that tells the computer to begin the report on the first line of a new page. The next specification, 56X, tells the computer to skip 56 positions on the first line and then begin the heading (between quotation marks) in the 57th print position.

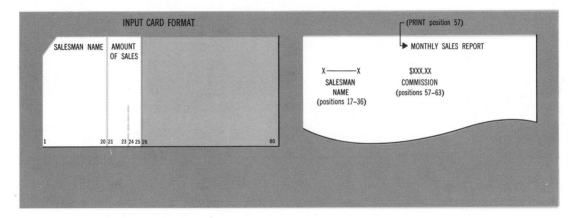

Figure 9.9
Input and output formats for sample problem 2.

2. After the READ instruction and the associated FORMAT statement, we tell the computer that IF SALES are greater than (.GT.) 100.00, a branch to statement 20 should be executed. If it is not, the computer automatically goes to the next instruction, which, in this case, is another test.

3. Statement 40 instructs the computer to write out the values for NAME and COMMIS in accordance with the specifications in statement 50. This statement shown below, is explained as follows:

50   FORMAT ('0', 16X, 5A4, 20X, '$', F6.2)

The first specification, '0', is a code for carriage control purposes that tells the computer to double space before printing the line. The 16X tells the computer to skip the first 16 print positions on the line and then print the NAME field, which is a 20-position alphanumeric (A) field. After the NAME field, 20 positions are skipped (20X), a dollar sign is printed, and right next to the dollar sign, COMMIS will print out with three integers, a decimal point and two decimal positions.

B. Comparison of FORTRAN and COBOL

At this point, we can make several observations about FORTRAN as compared to COBOL.

1. COBOL is a more structured language than FORTRAN, in the sense that COBOL has four DIVISIONS (IDENTIFICATION, ENVIRONMENT, DATA, and PROCEDURE) that *must* be included in every program in the sequence specified. FORTRAN, on the other hand, is more flexible. There are no particular statements that must be included.

IBM

Form X28-7327-4
Printed in U.S.A.

FORTRAN CODING FORM

Program	SAMPLE PROGRAM 2		Punching Instructions: Graphic	Card Form # *	Page 1 of 1
Programmer	R. STERN	Date	Punch		Identification 73–80

C FOR COMMENT

STATEMENT NUMBER (1–5)	Cont. (6)	FORTRAN STATEMENT (7–72)
C		THIS PROGRAM TAKES CARDS WITH THE WEEKLY SALES
C		FIGURES FOR EACH SALESMAN, AND PRODUCES A REPORT
C		WHICH SHOWS COMMISSIONS THAT HAVE BEEN EARNED.
		DIMENSION NAME(5)
		WRITE (3,5)
5		FORMAT ('1', 56X, 'MONTHLY SALES REPORT')
7		READ (1,10,END=100)NAME,SALES
10		FORMAT (5A4,F5.2)
		IF(SALES.GT.100.00)GO TO 20
		IF(SALES.GT.50.00)GO TO 30
		COMMIS = 000.00
		GO TO 40
20		COMMIS=SALES * .03
		GO TO 40
30		COMMIS = SALES * .02
40		WRITE (3,50) NAME,COMMIS
50		FORMAT ('0',16X,5A4,20X,'$',F6.2)
		GO TO 7
100		STOP
		END

* A standard card form, IBM electro 888157, is available for punching source statements from this form.

Figure 9.10
Coding for sample problem 2.

2. A program in FORTRAN, being generally more mathematical in nature, may not be as easy for a businessman to understand as one in COBOL, which is similar to English. The following comparison dramatizes this point.

COBOL

IF SALES-AMT IS GREATER THAN
100.00 MULTIPLY .03 BY SALES-AMT
GIVING COMMISSION.

FORTRAN

IF (SALES .GT. 100.00) GO TO 20
⋮
20 COMMIS = SALES * .03

Notice for example, that the code .GT. in FORTRAN is not as easy to read as the words GREATER THAN in COBOL. That is, it requires prior familiarity with a code rather than simple understanding of English.

3. In FORTRAN, the rules of the language limit to six the maximum number of characters used to identify a field, whereas in COBOL, the maximum is 30 characters. This often results in abbreviated field names in FORTRAN that may not be as self-explanatory for the businessman as corresponding names in COBOL. For example, in COBOL we might call a field YEAR-TO-DATE-GROSS-EARNINGS or perhaps Y-T-D-GROSS-EARN. In FORTRAN, the best we can do is something like YTDGRS.

4. From the examples presented in FORTRAN, you may have noticed the amount of effort required by the programmer to code FORMAT statements that precisely specify what the input or output looks like. In COBOL, with the aid of PICTURE clauses, it is usually easier to describe input or output specifications. However, although FORTRAN is considered to be cumbersome in the area of input/output specifications, it is much easier to code arithmetic operations. That is, arithmetic instructions are less verbose and easier to write in FORTRAN than in COBOL. In addition, FORTRAN enables the programmer to include complex mathematical functions that cannot be included in a COBOL program. In some business applications, such as sales forecasting, or inventory control, there is often the need to use mathematical concepts such as trigonometric functions; that is, a formula might require the computer to find the cosine of a particular angle. In FORTRAN, we can easily write an instruction such as:

$$Y = COS (X)$$

and the FORTRAN compiler, or translator, will recognize what is meant by the operation "COS." In COBOL, this cannot be done very easily, since the COBOL compiler is not equipped to recognize the code COS, or most other mathematical functions.

Although a programmer can write instructions that will allow the COBOL compiler to compute the cosine, it obviously takes more effort than in FORTRAN, where it can be performed with the use of a function. Note that it is possible to write part of a program in COBOL and part in FORTRAN assuming that the computer used has both compilers.

C. Understanding More Advanced FORTRAN Programs

In the following paragraphs, we will present some additional concepts of FORTRAN that will allow the student to more easily understand and review FORTRAN programs for business applications.

1. Mathematical Operations   The following list shows the fundamental mathematical operations and the symbols used in FORTRAN:

SYMBOL	OPERATION
**	Exponentiation
*	Multiplication
/	Division
+	Addition
−	Subtraction

Exponentiation involves raising some number to a power, or multiplying a number by itself a specified number of times. That is, 2^3 is represented as 2 ** 3 in FORTRAN and is calculated as the number 2 multiplied by itself 3 times ($2^3 = 2 \times 2 \times 2 = 8$). For example, if a programmer wishes the computer to add A^2 and B^2 to obtain the result X, where A, B, and X are fields, the following instruction would be indicated in FORTRAN:

$$X = A ** 2 + B ** 2$$

Similarly, the FORTRAN expression:

$$ANSWER = (AMT1 + AMT2 + AMT3)/3.0$$

calculates the average of the three fields—AMT1, AMT2, AMT3. Suppose the parentheses were omitted from the above arithmetic expression. The question is whether this instruction would still calculate the average. That is, the expression:

$$ANSWER = AMT1 + AMT2 + AMT3/3.0$$

might reduce to either of the following two formulas

$$\text{ANSWER} = \frac{\text{AMT1} + \text{AMT2} + \text{AMT3}}{3.0}$$

or

$$\text{ANSWER} = \text{AMT1} + \text{AMT2} + \frac{\text{AMT3}}{3.0}$$

If the parentheses were not included, the average would *not* be calculated properly. ANSWER would, in fact, equal

$$\text{AMT1} + \text{AMT2} + \frac{\text{AMT3}}{3.0}$$

The reason has to do with the *hierarchy of operations:* that is, the computer does not necessarily perform operations in the order in which the expression is read. The basic rules of hierarchy are as follows:

1.   Any operations within parentheses, if included, are performed first, in accordance with the rules below.
2.   In the absence of parentheses, operations are normally performed in the following order:
     I. Exponentiation (**)
     II and III. Multiplication (*) or Division (/), whichever appears first.
     IV and V. Addition (+) or Subtraction (−), whichever appears first.

Exponentiation is ordinarily performed first. After that, the computer looks at the mathematical expression beginning at the equal sign and proceeds to the right. It finds the next highest operation in the formula according to the hierarchy rules, and then it performs that operation. Therefore, the following FORTRAN statement mentioned above is evaluated as follows:

ANSWER =   AMT1 + AMT2   +   AMT3/3.0
           ⎵⎵⎵⎵⎵⎵⎵⎵⎵   ⎵⎵⎵   ⎵⎵⎵⎵⎵⎵⎵
           2nd operation   3rd operation   1st operation

Thus, we have:

$$\frac{\text{AMT3}}{3.0} + \text{AMT1} + \text{AMT2}$$

This explains why parentheses are required to obtain the correct formula for the average. As indicated in the hierarchy list above, multiplication and division both have equal priority below exponentiation, while addition and subtraction both have equal priority below multiplication and division. It is sometimes best to include parentheses around complex calculations when there is some doubt as to how the computer will evaluate the operations.

2. Understanding Why Equations are not Equations A very common FORTRAN statement is of the following type:

$$N = N + 1$$

This is obviously not a valid equation in the mathematical sense. That is, N = N and N cannot be equal to 1 more than N. However, the above *is* a valid FORTRAN statement. That is, we set N equal to one more than the original N. Thus, if N = 5 and the FORTRAN statement N = N + 1 is executed, N is then set equal to 6. The FORTRAN statement does not make the two items (N) and (N + 1) equal; it sets the field on the left side of the equal sign equal to the result calculated on the right side.

Thus, in FORTRAN, for an arithmetic statement, the computer:

1. Performs all computations that are indicated to the right of the equal sign.
2. Takes the final result and moves it to the field whose name is specified to the left of the equal sign. Therefore, the statement N = N + 1 has the following meaning to the computer:
    a. Add 1 to the current value of the field called N.
    b. Take this result and move it to N. In other words, add 1 to N. The statement N = 0 technically abides by the same rules. Since there are no computations involved, the computer simply takes the result indicated at the right of the equal sign (zero) and moves it to the field called N. In essence, N = (constant) is a data transfer operation that moves the constant to the field name. The above method is used to establish counters. If, in a FORTRAN program, the programmer wants the computer to count the number of cards processed, we might expect to find the following instructions:

```
N = 0
READ (1,3) NAME, SALES
N = N + 1
```

After every card is read, 1 is added to the field N. Thus, at the end of the run N reflects the number of cards read.

Self-Evaluating Quiz

317

PROGRAMMING
IN HIGH-LEVEL
LANGUAGES:
AN OVERVIEW

1. The name FORTRAN is an acronym for _____ .
2. FORTRAN is widely used for _____ problems.
3. While COBOL uses words such as ADD, MULTIPLY, SUBTRACT, DIVIDE to indicate mathematical expressions, FORTRAN uses _____ .
4. COBOL instructions read like sentences, while in FORTRAN instructions read like _____ .
5. In business areas such as _____ , where advanced mathematical concepts are employed, FORTRAN is most often used.
6. (T or F) The expression $X = X + 1$, although not a valid mathematical expression, is a valid FORTRAN expression.

Solutions

1. *FOR*mula *TRAN*slator
2. scientific or mathematical
3. mathematical symbols
4. mathematical equations
5. sales forecasting
6. T

III. BASIC

A. The Nature of BASIC

The processing of data with the use of terminals is fast becoming an exceedingly popular mode of data entry. In addition to entering data, it is possible to write and debug programs with the use of terminals. Commercial organizations, as well as many colleges and universities, have found programming with the use of terminals to be, in many cases, profitable and efficient.

Some programming languages are better suited for terminal processing than others. COBOL, for example, is a language that is not frequently programmed with the use of terminals because it requires long statements and sentences. Such coding with the use of a terminal connected to a CPU would generally be inefficient since lengthy instructions would have to be entered slowly, taking up terminal time as well as CPU time. Hence, languages such as COBOL are best suited for card or tape entry where the program is first converted to a machine-readable form offline and then entered for processing.

Since a terminal is a relatively slow method of data entry, BASIC was designed to require minimum coding or keying. Instructions and data formats are simple and require less programming effort than in most other languages. Similarly, BASIC was not designed to handle sophisticated routines that are required in other languages. Thus, this language may be learned in a relatively short time.

In short, BASIC is the programming language ideally suited for terminal processing in a time-sharing environment. The term BASIC is an abbreviation for *Beginner's All-Purpose Symbolic Instruction Code*, which, by its very name, suggests the major feature of the language—simplicity.

BASIC is becoming an increasingly popular language just as terminals are becoming increasingly popular in data processing environments. BASIC is currently being used extensively for the following applications:

Applications of BASIC

1. College Campuses: many colleges have acquired terminals connected to their central computer system. Programming with the use of these terminals affords the student the unique learning experience of interacting directly with the computer.
2. Businesses: increasing numbers of business people are provided with access to terminals connected to main computer systems. These people can learn BASIC in a relatively short period and can then write short programs to extract or otherwise process data that is needed quickly.
3. Engineering or Scientific Applications: BASIC is used extensively by engineers and scientists to solve problems and perform calculations that are necessary for their work.

BASIC can be regarded as a simplified version of FORTRAN, similar to the latter in format but without all the intricate or sophisticated options. Both languages utilize mathematical notation and, as such, are generally regarded as somewhat scientific in nature. But, like FORTRAN, BASIC may be used effectively for simplified business applications. In addition, FORTRAN and BASIC are ideally suited for business applications where mathematical or scientific notations are used, such as forecasting and graph plotting.

Note that the programmer communicates *directly* with the computer when coding on a terminal in BASIC. Since such programs are almost always short and simplified, they often contain *data* as well as *instructions*. That is, programs in most other languages are usually written so that they can be run by the operations staff in periodic intervals with voluminous input. A Payroll program written in COBOL, for example, may be implemented so that it will be run on a monthly basis with a large number of records. When a programmer, scientist, or businessman codes a BASIC program on a terminal, it is often a "one-shot" job. That is, a simple BASIC program is coded merely to obtain an output listing and *not* to be run periodically. It also requires minimal input since the keyboard device is far too slow to transmit a voluminous amount of data.

Note, however, that BASIC can be run on a computer *without* the use of a terminal. Thus a program in BASIC can be compiled and translated and utilized for periodic runs in the same manner as COBOL or FORTRAN programs, although a BASIC program is not commonly used for this purpose. Because BASIC is so widely used and is simplified enough to serve as an ideal language for the beginner, we have included an entire chapter on it, Chapter 13, which provides the fundamentals of this programming language. For now, we will simply illustrate a sample program to demonstrate the relative simplicity of BASIC.

B. Illustrative BASIC Program

We have seen sample COBOL and FORTRAN programs that create a tape from employee time cards. The employee cards have the format indicated in Figure 9.3 and the tape has the format indicated in Figure 9.4, where

WEEKLY-WAGES = HOURS-WORKED × HOURLY-RATE.

A simple BASIC program run with the use of a terminal cannot usually accept card input nor can it create tape output unless the terminal system contains a card reader as input and a tape drive as output. Usually, the terminal has only a keyboard and some print or visual display. We will, then, examine a BASIC program that reads data in from a terminal, determines WEEKLY-WAGES (W), and prints the result on the same terminal:

```
100   INPUT N$, H, R
105   IF H = 99 THEN 999
110   LET W = H * R
120   PRINT N$, H, R, W
130   GO TO 100
999   END
```

Notice that the BASIC program has significantly fewer steps than the program in the other languages. However, although coding is simplified in BASIC, the form of input and output is somewhat limited.

Notice that BASIC is a free-form language which means that there are no special positions in which instructions must be entered. We can enter instructions anywhere on the line and need not adhere to any formal rules in this regard.

Line Numbers The left-hand numbers associated with each instruction are called line numbers. Essentially, any numbers may be used, but it is recommended that the numbers selected not be continuous. That is, if during debugging we discover that an instruction was inadvertently omitted between line 100 and 105, we can key in 101, for example, and the computer will automatically insert the instruction in its proper place. Hence line numbers in BASIC are not merely, as in other languages, for sequencing in case the source program is dropped or mis-sorted; they actually are an important part of the program. Line number 999 is typically used, as a convention, for the last instruction. Let us examine each instruction more carefully:

INPUT Statement: INPUT   N$, H, R

After the program has been entered, compiled and listed, it is ready for execution. An executed INPUT statement causes the computer to request the keying in of some input data. Typically, a question mark or a requesting statement prints, which is a signal to the programmer that some data must be entered.

The names of input fields in this sample program are N$, H, R for name, hours worked, and hourly rate respectively. Note that field names are generally more concise and less informative than in other languages. The dollar sign, $, associated with the name field, N$, establishes it as an alphanumeric field. We separate input fields by commas. Hence a sample input entry of name, hours worked, and hourly rate might be:

PAUL NEWMAN,15,9.98

Note that the rate, R, may be keyed in *with* the decimal point. For example, 1.25 is a valid entry for rate; that is, the decimal point is coded rather than implied or assumed, as in COBOL and other languages.

END-OF-JOB INDICATOR: IF H = 99 THEN 999

Statement 105 is a conditional statement. It causes a branch to statement number 999, the end of the job, if H, hourly rate, contains "99." Hence, to signal the computer that there is no more input or to cause the computer to terminate the run, we enter a value of H equal to 99.

LET Statement: LET W = H * R

This is an arithmetic statement, with * signifying multiplication, as it does in FORTRAN.

PRINT Statement: PRINT N$, H, R, W

The name, hours worked, hourly rate, and computed wage figure will print for the input supplied.

GO TO Statement: GO TO 100

This statement causes a branch back to statement 100, the INPUT statement, and the series of steps is then repeated. This processing continues until a "99" is keyed in for hours worked which signals a branch to the END statement.

END Statement

This statement results in the termination of the run.

Self-Evaluating Quiz

1. (T or F) Terminal devices are ideally suited for high-speed interaction with the computer.
2. (T or F) BASIC is a language that is specifically designed for terminal processing in a time-sharing environment.
3. (T or F) BASIC is ideally suited for programming complex business applications, such as Accounts Receivable and Payroll.
4. (T or F) Many programs written in BASIC are used only once to obtain an answer to a specific question or problem.
5. (T or F) In BASIC, a statement requires a line number only when a branch will be made to that statement.
6. In the statement 20 IF A = 100 THEN 50, the significance of THEN 50 is
_____ .
7. An INPUT statement causes the computer to print a _____ to signal the user that _____ .

Solutions

1. F
2. T
3. F
4. T
5. F—each instruction requires a line number
6. a branch to statement 50 will occur if A is equal to 100
7. ? or some request for data, data must be entered

IV. RPG

A. The Nature of RPG
RPG is an abbreviation for *Report Program Generator.* It is a high-level language in which the programmer codes specifications for a problem and the computer generates a program. That is, coding in

RPG does not result in a source program but in a set of specifications that will be used to generate a program. The advantages of RPG include:

1. Easy to Code: since RPG consists, basically, of a series of specifications, it is relatively simple to code and is generally regarded as the highest level or least machinelike language offered. Because of the ease with which RPG can be learned, it is used in many colleges and businesses.

2. Requires Minimal Storage: since RPG consists of only a set of specifications, it requires minimal storage capacity. Thus small-scale computers, such as the IBM S/360 model 20, that do not have adequate primary storage to run large COBOL or PL/1 programs, often utilize RPG.

3. Ideal for Report Output: RPG, as a program generator, is used primarily to produce reports or report-type output. Although it may create tape or disk output, it is not as effective a language for handling complex input/output tasks, such as creating nonstandard header labels or employing key fields for indexing. In short, it is an excellent business tool for producing reports and report-type output.

The disadvantages of RPG include:

1. Cannot Easily Handle Complex Logic: note, however, that RPG is usually used for simple applications, where complex logic is not required and report-type output is needed. Whenever the logic becomes complicated, the programmer would probably code in a more powerful language such as PL/1, COBOL, or FORTRAN.

2. Difficult to Debug: keep in mind that coding in RPG does *not* result in a source program. The coded specifications must be used to *generate* a source program. Thus any logic errors made by the programmer are difficult to find and debug since they require evaluation of a new source program.

Let us consider a data processing installation with a personnel system that is computerized. Suppose the Personnel Department frequently requests special reports that require data from the computerized personnel file. For example, a listing of all employees who are college graduates with degrees in Industrial Engineering may be required one day while a listing and tabulation of all employees who have been employed at least 10 years may be necessary the next day. RPG is an appropriate language for coding the above types of problems to produce the desired output. It is a relatively simple language and since no complex computations are required, it is ideal in the above case. Programmers can code the problems in a matter of minutes and obtain the desired output very quickly. Similarly, businessmen with some exposure to data processing can learn the RPG specifications in a matter of hours and code such special programs themselves. This is often done in large companies where the programming staff is already overburdened.

In short, RPG has real advantages in small data processing installations where the computers are not large enough to run COBOL, PL/1, or FORTRAN programs, and in companies where report-type problems utilizing relatively simple logic are handled.

A simple RPG program is coded on four specification forms (see Figure 9.11).

RPG Coding Sheets

NAME	DESCRIPTION
1. Control Card and File Description Specifications	Lists the files to be used, the devices they will employ and special features to be included
2. Input Specifications	Describes format of input files
3. Calculation Specifications	Describes arithmetic and logic operations to be performed
4. Output Format Specifications	Describes format of output files

The deck of cards created from all the forms comprises the *RPG program or source deck,* which must be compiled, or translated, into machine language before it can be run or executed.

B. Basic Structure of an RPG Program

RPG programs are generally written on the above four specification sheets, in the order indicated. There are additional sheets, not discussed in the text, which are required for specialized processing.

You will note that on the same sheet used for File Description Specifications, there is provision for Control Card Specifications (see Figure 9.11). RPG, for most computers, requires a special card, called a control card, as its first card. Different versions of RPG have different requirements for this card. For most installations, all that is required is an H in column 6, denoting a Heading card. Thus control card specifications for our illustration will merely have an H in column 6.

Each specification sheet has space for 80 columns of information. As indicated, each *line* of a sheet is keypunched into one punched card.

Let us examine the coding sheets more closely:

Figure 9.11
RPG specification sheets.

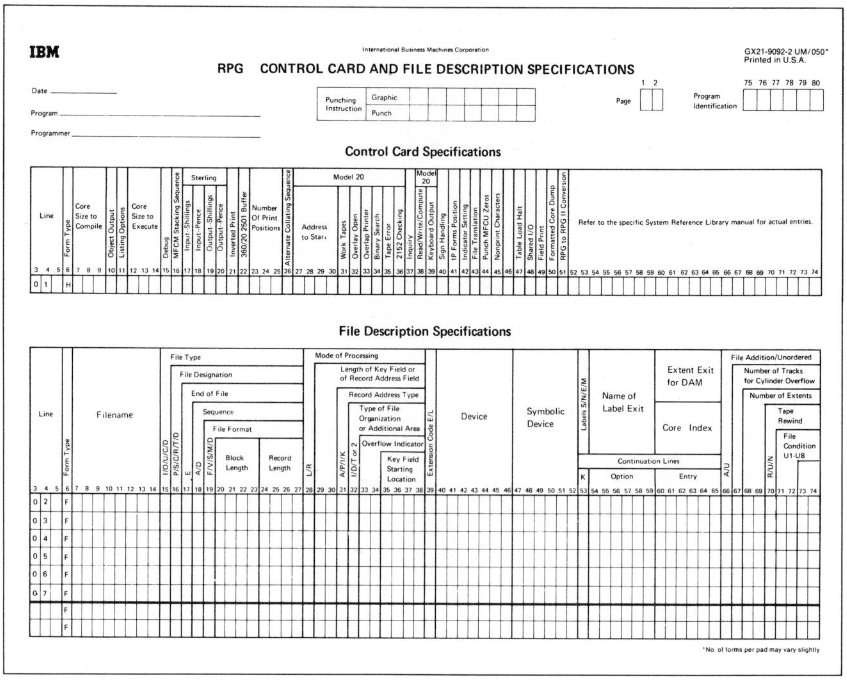
IBM International Business Machines Corporation
GX21-9092-2 UM/050*
Printed in U.S.A.

RPG CONTROL CARD AND FILE DESCRIPTION SPECIFICATIONS

Date
Program
Programmer
Punching Instruction: Graphic / Punch
Page 1 2
Program Identification 75 76 77 78 79 80

Control Card Specifications

Line (3 4 5) | Form Type (6) | Core Size to Compile (7 8 9) | Object Output (10) | Listing Options (11) | Core Size to Execute (12 13 14) | Debug (15) | MFCM Stacking Sequence (16) | Sterling: Input-Shillings (17), Input-Pence (18), Output-Shillings (19), Output-Pence (20) | Inverted Print (21) | 360/20 2501 Buffer (22) | Number Of Print Positions (23 24 25) | Alternate Collating Sequence (26) | Model 20: Address to Start (27 28 29 30), Work Tapes (31), Overlay Open (32), Overlap Printer (33), Binary Search (34), Tape Error (35), 2152 Checking (36) | Inquiry (37) | Model 20: Read/Write/Compute (38), Keyboard Output (39) | Sign Handling (40) | 1P Forms Position (41) | Indicator Setting (42) | File Translation (43) | Punch MFCU Zeros (44) | Nonprint Characters (45) | (46) | Table Load Halt (47) | Shared I/O (48) | Field Print (49) | Formatted Core Dump (50) | RPG to RPG II Conversion (51) | Refer to the specific System Reference Library manual for actual entries. (52–74)

0 1 H

File Description Specifications

Line (3 4 5) | Form Type (6) | Filename (7–14) | File Type: I/O/U/C/D (15) | File Designation: P/S/C/R/T/D (16) | End of File: E (17) | Sequence: A/D (18) | File Format: F/V/S/M/D (19) | Block Length (20–23) | Record Length (24–27) | Mode of Processing: L/R (28) | Length of Key Field or of Record Address Field (29–30) | Record Address Type: A/P/I/K (31) | Type of File Organization or Additional Area: I/D/T or 2 (32) | Overflow Indicator (33–34) | Key Field Starting Location (35–38) | Extension Code E/L (39) | Device (40–46) | Symbolic Device (47–52) | Labels S/N/E/M (53) | Name of Label Exit (54–59) | Extent Exit for DAM (60–65) | Core Index | Continuation Lines: K, Option, Entry | A/U (66) | File Addition/Unordered | Number of Tracks for Cylinder Overflow (68–69) | Number of Extents | Tape Rewind: R/U/N (70) | File Condition U1-U8 (71–72) | (73 74)

0 2 F
0 3 F
0 4 F
0 5 F
0 6 F
0 7 F
F
F

*No. of forms per pad may vary slightly

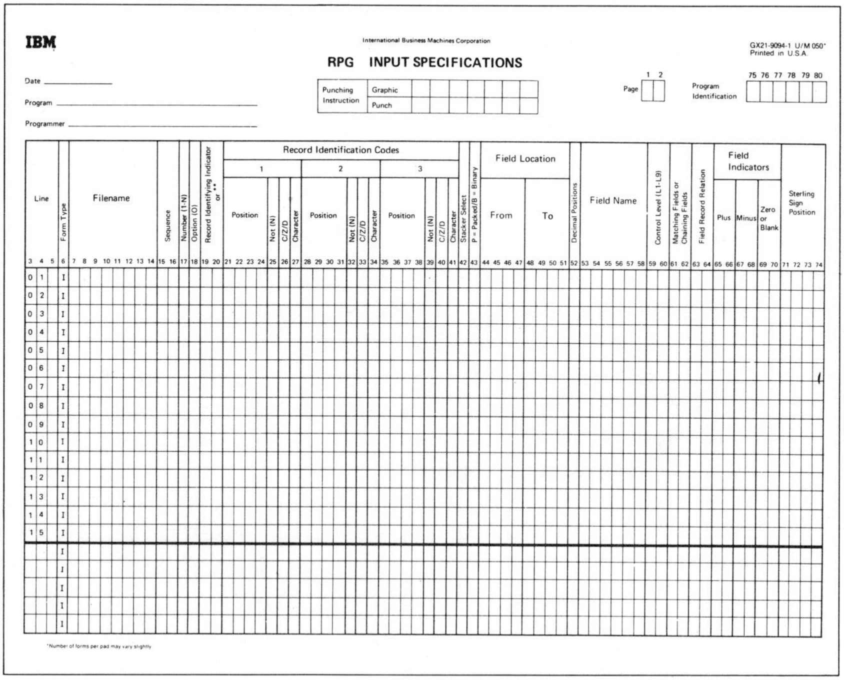
IBM International Business Machines Corporation
GX21-9094-1 U/M 050*
Printed in U.S.A.

RPG INPUT SPECIFICATIONS

Date
Program
Programmer
Punching Instruction: Graphic / Punch
Page 1 2
Program Identification 75 76 77 78 79 80

Line (3 4 5) | Form Type (6) | Filename (7–14) | Sequence (15 16) | Number (1-N) (17) | Option (O) (18) | Record Identifying Indicator or ** (19 20) | Record Identification Codes: 1: Position (21–24), Not (N) (25), C/Z/D (26), Character (27); 2: Position (28–31), Not (N) (32), C/Z/D (33), Character (34); 3: Position (35–38), Not (N) (39), C/Z/D (40), Character (41) | Stacker Select (42) | P = Packed/B = Binary (43) | Field Location: From (44–47), To (48–51) | Decimal Positions (52) | Field Name (53–58) | Control Level (L1-L9) (59 60) | Matching Fields or Chaining Fields (61 62) | Field Record Relation (63 64) | Field Indicators: Plus (65 66), Minus (67 68), Zero or Blank (69 70) | Sterling Sign Position (71–74)

0 1 I
0 2 I
0 3 I
0 4 I
0 5 I
0 6 I
0 7 I
0 8 I
0 9 I
1 0 I
1 1 I
1 2 I
1 3 I
1 4 I
1 5 I
I
I
I
I
I

*Number of forms per pad may vary slightly

IBM

International Business Machines Corporation

RPG   CALCULATION SPECIFICATIONS

GX21-9093-1 U/M 050*
Printed in U.S.A.
*No. of forms per pad may vary slightly

Date _____

Program _____

Programmer _____

Punching Instruction — Graphic / Punch

Page [1 2]   Program Identification [75 76 77 78 79 80]

Line	Form Type	Control Level (L0-L9, LR, SR)	Indicators				Factor 1	Operation	Factor 2	Result Field	Field Length	Decimal Positions	Half Adjust (H)	Resulting Indicators			Comments
			And	Not	And	Not								Arithmetic / Plus Minus Zero; Compare High 1>2 Low 1<2 Equal 1=2; Lookup Table (Factor 2) is High Low Equal			

Lines 0 1 through 1 5 (and 5 additional unnumbered rows), each with Form Type "C"

IBM

International Business Machines Corporation

RPG   OUTPUT FORMAT SPECIFICATIONS

GX21-9090-1 U/M 050
Printed in U.S.A.
Reprinted 3/70

Date _____

Program _____

Programmer _____

Punching Instruction — Graphic / Punch

Page [1 2]   Program Identification [75 76 77 78 79 80]

Line	Form Type	Filename	Type (H/D/T/E)	Stacker Select/Fetch Overflow (F)	Space Before/After	Skip Before/After	Output Indicators			Field Name	Edit Codes	Blank After (B)	End Positon in Output Record	P = Packed/B = Binary	Constant or Edit Word	Sterling Sign Position
							And Not	And Not								

Edit Codes

	Commas	Zero Balances to Print	No Sign	CR	-		
	Yes	Yes	1	A	J	X = Remove Plus Sign
	Yes	No	2	B	K	Y = Date Field Edit
	No	Yes	3	C	L	Z = Zero Suppress
	No	No	4	D	M	

Constant or Edit Word

Lines 0 1 through 1 5 (and 5 additional unnumbered rows), each with Form Type "O"

RPG Coding Sheets

ITEM	MEANING	CARD COLUMNS INTO WHICH DATA IS PUNCHED
Page number (upper right corner)	Used to number coding sheets —optional, with no effect on compiler	1–2 (of each card)
Line number	Prenumbered except for low-order digit	3–5
Form type	Indicates specifications sheet: F — File description I — Input specifications C — Calculation specifications O — Output specifications	6
RPG statements	These columns are coded according to established specifications	7–74
Identification (upper right corner of form)	Identifies the program to the computer. Optional Entry	75–80

The small numbers 3 to 74 above the rectangular boxes represent the corresponding card columns into which the specifications are keypunched.

1. Identification   In the upper right-hand corner, there is a provision for a program identification field, labeled as positions 75 to 80. The identification number provided here will be punched into columns 75 to 80 of *all* cards keypunched from this form. Although this identification field is not required for processing, it should be used in case cards are misplaced or lost. This identification field can be *alphanumeric,* consisting of any combination of characters, or *numeric,* consisting of digits only. Any field that can uniquely identify the program is used.

2. Page and Line Numbers   Columns 1 and 2, representing page number, are the same for an entire sheet, and thus are also coded only once at the top of the form. Page and line numbers, representing columns 1 to 5 of each card in the RPG deck, are not required for processing, but are highly recommended should the deck be dropped or mis-sorted. If a deck is out of sequence, the page and line number information is of great assistance in resorting the cards.

The remaining data recorded on the top of each form is *not* keypunched into cards. It supplies identifying information only, should the coding sheets be misplaced.

3. Form Type If an RPG card is misplaced, a quick glance at column 6 indicates the form from which it was punched. An asterisk (*) in column 7 of any form is used to designate the entire line as a comment, not to be compiled.

C. Illustrative RPG Program

Let us program in RPG the simplified payroll program illustrated in the previous sections in COBOL, FORTRAN and BASIC. The card format is indicated in Figure 9.3.

The output will be a printed report with the format illustrated in the print layout sheet in Figure 9.12. The output, in this case, has been designated as a printed report, rather than as a tape, since RPG is most often used to produce reports. The three input fields will be printed in addition to a WAGES field to be calculated as:

$$\text{WAGES} = \text{HOURS} \times \text{RATE}$$

Figure 9.13 illustrates the specifications sheets required to code the program in RPG.

We will now discuss each of the specification sheets in detail.

1. File Description Specifications This sheet supplies pertinent data on the input and output files utilized. Each file is indicated on a *single* line of this sheet. Since our program consists of two files, an input file and an output file, this File Description Specifications sheet will have *two* lines completed. Notice that there are, however, many programs with more than two files.

7-14: Filename Columns 7 to 14 of each line represent the name assigned by the programmer to each of the files. These same file names will be used on the Input and Output-Format Specifications sheets. In our example, CARDS is the name assigned to the input card file and REPORT is the name assigned to the output print file. The file name field, as all alphanumeric fields in RPG, is left-justified. Names begin in the leftmost positions of the field and nonfilled low-order or rightmost positions remain blank.

15: Filetype: Input or Output Column 15 is simply indicated as an I, for input, or an O for output.

16: File Designation Input files require an entry in column 16; output files do not. For input files, the File Designation in column 16 must be either P, for primary input form, or S, for secondary input. For single input files, this entry is always P. For mul-

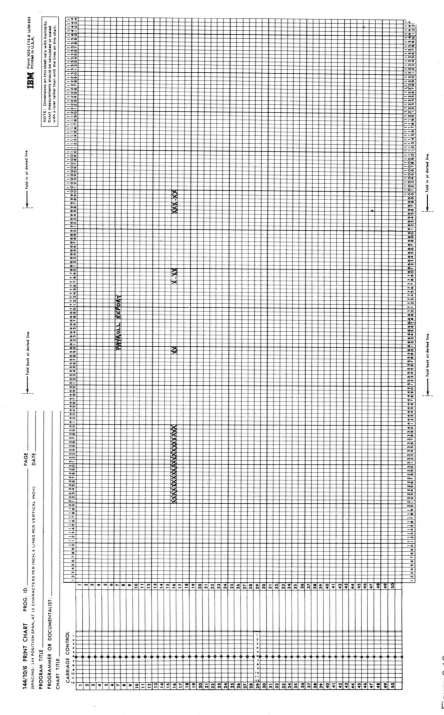

Figure 9.12
Output format for
sample program.

International Business Machines Corporation

RPG CONTROL CARD AND FILE DESCRIPTION SPECIFICATIONS

GX21-9092-2 UM/050*
Printed in U.S.A.

Punching Instruction — Graphic / Punch

Page [ ] [ ]   1 2

Program Identification — 75 76 77 78 79 80

Date _____
Program _____
Programmer _____

Control Card Specifications

Refer to the specific System Reference Library manual for actual entries.

File Description Specifications

Line	Form Type	Filename	File Type	File Designation	End of File	Sequence	File Format	Block Length	Record Length		Mode of Processing	Length of Key Field or of Record Address Field	Record Address Type	Type of File Organization or Additional Area	Overflow Indicator	Key Field Starting Location	Extension Code E/L	Device	Symbolic Device		Labels S/N/E/M	Name of Label Exit	Continuation Lines		Core Index	Extent Exit for DAM		File Addition/Unordered Number of Tracks for Cylinder Overflow Number of Extents Tape Rewind File Condition U1-U8
0 2	F	CARDS	I PE	F				80	80									READ40	SYSRDR									
0 3	F	REPORT	O	F		V	132	132		OF								PRINTER	SYSLST									
0 4	F																											
0 5	F																											
0 6	F																											
0 7	F																											

*No. of forms per pad may vary slightly

Figure 9.13
Coded specification sheets for sample program.

Figure 9.13 continued

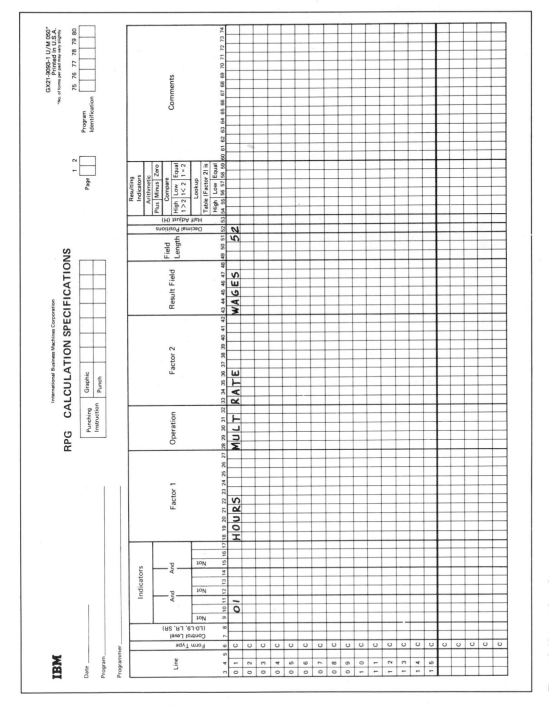

Figure 9.13   continued

332

COMPUTER
PROGRAMMING
FUNDAMENTALS
AND SOFTWARE

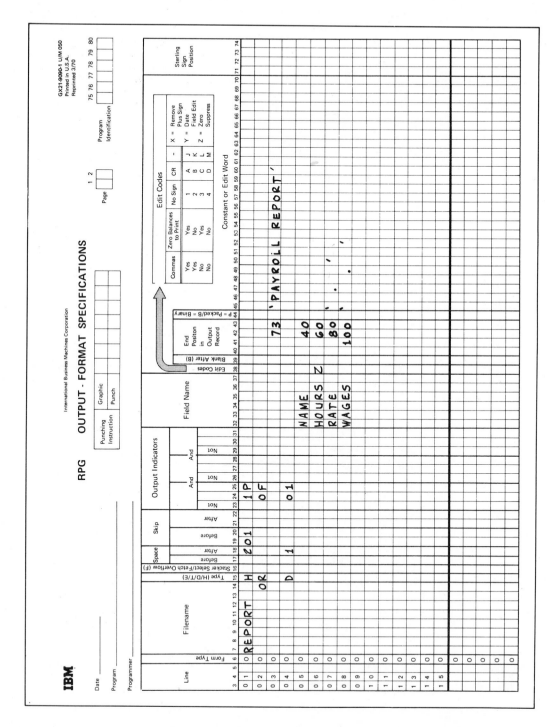

Figure 9.13 continued

tiple input files, one must be designated as P for primary and the other as S, for secondary. An update program, for example, uses a *primary* master input file and a *secondary* detail input file. Output files do *not* have a File Designation.

17: End of File   Column 17, End of File Indicator, contains an E for the input file. This indicates that we want an end-of-file condition to be tested; that is, when there are no more cards in our input file, we want this to denote an end-of-file condition.

18: Sequence   Column 18, Sequence, is an entry that is used for some tape and disk processing.

19: File Format   Column 19 is the File Format field and for card files is always F, denoting fixed format. This indicates that all records within the file are the same size. V, for variable, is in this field when record sizes are not the same within the file. Print files contain a V in Column 19 since print records, in essence, can be any length and require special carriage control characters. We may have 80 position headings and 132 position detail records, for example. Thus card files are coded with an F in Column 19 to denote fixed length, while print files are coded with a V in that column to denote variable length.

20–27: Block and Record Length   Block Length, columns 20 to 23, and Record Length, columns 24 to 27, are typically 80 for cards and 132 for printed reports. Note that these fields, as all numeric fields in RPG, are right-justified; that is, high-order or leftmost nonfilled positions are left blank.

28–32: (omit)   Positions 28–32, representing several fields, are used predominantly for tape and disk processing and will not be discussed here.

33–34: Overflow Indicator   Columns 33 and 34 are required for print files to denote that a page overflow indicator is to be used. That is, if we desire the report to proceed from page to page with the desired headings, we must use an overflow indicator to sense the end of a specified form. Thus print files should have an OF, for overflow, in Columns 33 and 34.

35–39: (omit)   Columns 35 to 39 are not used for simple RPG programs and thus will not be discussed.

40–52: Device and Symbolic Device   The Device and the Symbolic Device names, columns 40 to 46 and 47 to 52, respectively, are assigned specifically at each data processing installation and thus will vary from one computer center to another. In the above illustration, the input device is the READ40 with symbolic name SYSRDR (system reader) and the output device is PRINTER with symbolic name SYSLST (system list device). The programmer must obtain the appropriate entries for these fields from the operations staff at his computer center.

53–74: (omit) The remainder of the File Description Specifications sheet is not used unless tape or disk processing is required.

2. Input Specifications Sheet

7–14: File Name Each input file is described on the Input Specifications sheet. Since our sample RPG program has only one input file, called CARDS, then CARDS is described on this sheet.

15–16: Sequence The sequence AA describes the first card record format within the file. If additional types of records existed within the file they would be coded as AB, AC, and so on.

17–18: (omit) Columns 17 and 18 are not used.

19–20: Resulting Indicator Columns 19 and 20 represent the Resulting Indicator. In our example, indicator 01 is turned on every time a card record is read. This indicator will then be used to determine, for output specifications, when a line is to be printed. If 01 is used in the Output-Format Specifications sheet, then a line will print each time indicator 01 is "turned on," that is, for every card read.

21–41: Record Identification Codes Record Identification Codes (21 to 41) are used to test input positions for specific contents. They are not required in this sample program.

42–43: (omit) Columns 42 and 43 have specialized use and will not be discussed here.

44–58: Field Indicators Field indicators located in the group of columns from 44 to 58 are used to denote fields within the input record. "Field Location From," columns 44 to 47, denotes the high-order or leftmost position of a field and "Field Location To" denotes the low-order or rightmost position of a field. For numeric fields, column 52 must be completed to denote the number of decimal or fractional positions. For alphanumeric fields, it is left blank.

Thus we have for CARDS:

COLUMNS	FIELD NAME	FIELD TYPE
1–20	NAME	Alphanumeric (no entry in 52)
21–22	HOURS	Numeric-integer with no decimal positions (0 in 52)
23–25	RATE	Numeric with two decimal positions (2 in 52) (428 in columns 23–25 of an input card would be treated as 4.28 by the computer)

59–74: (omit) Positions 59 to 74 of this sheet have specialized use and will not be discussed here.

3. Calculation Specifications Sheet Any arithmetic or logic operation is defined on this sheet.

7–8: Control Levels Since no control levels are used here, columns 7 and 8 are blank.

9–17: Indicators Since we wish to perform a multiplication operation (HOURS × RATE) for *all* input cards, we use indicator 01, which is "turned on" for all input cards. This is the only indicator required.

18–48: Operation and Result Field Factor 1, HOURS, is multiplied (MULT) by Factor 2, RATE, to produce a resultant field called WAGES. For other operations we may use:

ADD
SUB
DIV
COMP (compare)
etc.

49–52: Field Length and Decimal Position The field length for the resultant numeric field, WAGES, is 5 (column 51) including 2 decimal positions (2 in column 52).

53: Half Adjust Column 53, Half Adjust, is used for rounding. That is, when we wish the computer to round the results to the nearest position, we use this field.

54–59: Resulting Indicators The Resulting Indicators in Columns 54 to 59 are turned on only for compare (COMP) operations.

60–74: Comments Any comments in columns 60 to 74 may be included. These are printed on the listing, but do not affect processing. We may also include entire lines as comments by utilizing an asterisk (*) in column 7 of *any* sheet.

4. Output-Format Specifications (0 in Form Type) Sheet

7–14: File Name The output file REPORT is described here.

15: Type Three types of records may be included:

Heading (H)
Detail (D)
Total (T)

Since we only have Heading and Detail records, only H and D types (column 15) have been included.

16: Stacker Select This field is appropriate only for punched output, where output data cards can fall into several pockets or stackers.

17–22: Space and Skip These options are appropriate only for printed output. You will recall that a printer can be made to space 1, 2, or 3 lines either *before* or *after* it writes a line. The 2 in Space-After of our illustration indicates that *after* the Heading line is printed, we wish to space the form two lines. Only the digits 1, 2, or 3 may be used in *either* column 17 or 18.

The Skip option for printed output is used to position the form at a specific line. A 01 in either Skip field is a code for skipping to the beginning of a new page. In our illustration, we skip to a new page *before* printing.

Thus the output file REPORT has a heading record (H), which requires the skipping to a new page *before* printing, and the spacing of the form two lines *after* printing.

23–31: Output Indicators The Output Indicator IP (columns 24 and 25) implies that we wish to print the H record (Heading) on the first page (1P). If any other conditions also require the printing of this record, then we code OR on the next line in columns 14 and 15 and the corresponding condition. OF in columns 24 and 25 indicates that we also wish to print a heading on an overflow, or end-of-page condition.

In short, we are indicating that we wish the H or heading type record to print on the first page *or* when the end of a page is reached. In either case, we skip the paper to a new page, print the heading, and then advance the paper two lines.

In most print applications, we want headings to print on the first printed page. Also, when we have reached the end of a page, we want the program to skip to a new page and print new headings.

In this way, each individual page of the continuous form has a heading so that when the report is "burst" into individual sheets, each can be identified.

337 *32–70: Field Delineators* The heading PAYROLL REPORT is to print with the last character in position 73 (Print Layout Sheet, Figure 9.12).

The detail line, D, prints when indicator 01 is on, which is for all cards. Each time a detail line prints, the form is spaced 1 line (after printing). Since each input card turns on indicator 01, a detail line will print for each input card.

Four output fields print:

Printing of Output

FIELD NAME   PRINT POSITIONS (sheet indicates last print position)

NAME	21–40
HOURS	59–60
RATE	77–80 (decimal point prints on output and therefore counts as a position)
WAGES	95–100 (here, too, decimal point appears on output)

The first three fields are directly transmitted from the card record. Note that these input and output fields have the same name. NAME requires no editing. HOURS requires zero suppression (Z in column 38) to eliminate leading zeros and also the standard plus sign generated by the computer. RATE requires a decimal point to print after the first integer position. You will recall that to save space on a card, decimal points are often not coded. They are *implied* or *assumed* in input records. The output document, however, must have these decimal points for readability. Hence the Edit Word, columns 45 to 70, is used. WAGES, obtained from the calculations, requires the printing of a decimal point, after the first three integer positions. Thus, '☐☐☐•☐☐' is the Edit Word.

If, in addition we wish to suppress leading or nonsignificant zeros, we include a zero in the low-order integer position. Thus if WAGES contained an Edit Word of '   0.   ' then 003∧42 would print as 3.42 instead of 003.42. If we also desire a dollar sign to print out, we would include the following Edit Word: '$ 0.   '.

The above four specification sheets will result in a complete RPG program that performs the required operations. Notice that there is no visible step-by-step logic displayed in the specifications. When the sheets are coded so that they conform to the RPG rules, however, then a program is compiled which contains the step-by-step logic. Thus flowcharting is not a required programming tool when RPG coding is employed unless complex calculations are necessary.

Self-Evaluating Quiz

1. RPG is an abbreviation for _____.
2. The coding sheets for an RPG program are called _____ sheets.
3. The usual form of input for an RPG program is _____, and the usual form of output is a _____.
4. (T or F) Small-scale computers that do not have adequate storage to run large COBOL or PL/1 programs often utilize RPG.
5. (T or F) RPG is best suited for programs with complex logic.
6. The four specifications forms that may be used in an RPG program are _____, _____, _____, and _____.
7. Each line for every form is punched into a single _____ which is then part of the _____.

Solutions

1. *Report Program Generator*
2. specifications
3. cards; printed report
4. T
5. F
6. FILE DESCRIPTION; INPUT; CALCULATION; OUTPUT-FORMAT
7. card, RPG program deck

Structured programming is a relatively new term used to describe an efficient programming technique which can facilitate the processing of programs in all languages. It is a technique that attempts to modularize or compartmentalize programs for ease of execution, debugging, and patching where necessary. This technique aims at reducing the number of branch instructions by replacing them with PERFORM statements in COBOL, DO loops in FORTRAN, and FOR-NEXT statements in BASIC. These statements are high-level instructions which execute an entire paragraph or routine and then return to the original point of entry. This technique results in more organized and more understandable programs. In addition, programs that are structured provide a standardized approach to coding. That is, most programs that use this technique have a common shell:

Perform Housekeeping Routines (initializing, clearing, etc.)
Perform Normal Processing Until End of File Is Reached
Perform End of Job Routines
Stop Run

Review Questions

Compare and contrast the programming languages discussed in this chapter with respect to the following (1–6):

1. Englishlike features
2. Applicability to scientific problems
3. Applicability to business problems
4. Format requirements
5. Simplicity
6. Features available
7. Explain the term "structured programming."

Chapter 10
The Operating System: Control and Optimization of Computer Capability

10

10

Since machines can operate on data far more quickly than people can, computer systems are designed to minimize the degree of human intervention. We have already seen how the use of terminals in an online environment can reduce manual procedures involved in the conversion of source documents to computer-readable input. In addition, since the transmittal of data from one location to another is significantly influenced by manpower considerations, terminal processing is an efficient alternative to manual methods of data transmittal.

Another development in computer technology which has minimized the need for operator intervention for computer systems is called the *operating system.* An operating system is a sophisticated control system which enables a computer to automatically handle many tasks that would otherwise require frequent intervention by a computer operator. Such tasks include the following, just to list a few:

Sample Functions of an Operating System

1. Automatic logging in of date, time, cost, and other details of each program.
   Savings: Operator not needed to maintain such information for each program.
2. Automatic access of compilers, assemblers, or other special programs as needed and automatic transmission to CPU.
   Savings: Less Operator time needed to load programs when they are needed, since they are often stored on random-access devices and accessed directly by the system.
3. Automatic termination of each job even if errors have occurred; automatic restart with a new program so that programs can be batched.
   Savings: Operator not needed to watch for programming errors or input errors which might halt the machine; operator not needed to clear out malfunctioning program nor to load in each new program as needed.
4. Automatic communication of computer requirements to operator via a console.

Savings: Operator can determine the status and requirements of each program easily and efficiently.
5.   Automatic operations using multiprogramming, real-time and
time-sharing functions which would otherwise be impossible.

I. Operating System

Definition   The operating system is a series of programs that
controls the functions performed by the computer. Programmers at
any given computer center prepare *user* or *problem programs.*
These are then run on the computer under the general control of
the operating system which supervises all such programs.

Operating System as Part of Software   Each operating system
includes a series of special control programs. In addition, there are
special standard packaged programs which enable the computer to
operate efficiently and which can be readily accessed by the operating system. All these programs are called *software.* Whereas
hardware consists of the physical components of a computer system, software consists of the programming support of a computer
system. Like hardware, software can be acquired from the manufacturer or from specialized companies. Companies that specialize
in software that can be adapted to particular operating systems are
called *software houses* or *facilities management companies.*

A. Library of Programs

Since the entire operating system along with the additional
software cannot all be stored within the computer, it must reside
on some device that the computer can readily access as needed.
The device used depends on the operating system, but is usually a
direct-access device. User programs that are run on a regular basis
such as Payroll or Accounts Receivable programs are also stored
along with the software to be accessed as needed. The collection of
the operating system, additional software, and user programs is
called a *library of programs.*

B. Supervisor

The major program of the operating system which provides it with
much of its capability and flexibility is called a *supervisor.* The
supervisor, sometimes called a *monitor,* is a special program
supplied by the manufacturer, which is stored within the CPU in
third-generation computers. The supervisor resides in storage for
the purpose of controlling the operations of the computer (see Figure 10.1). The supervisor is part of the larger operating system
which is typically stored on a high-speed input/output device such
as a tape or disk. This control system is part of the software
supplied by the manufacturer. The supervisor must be *loaded* into
storage each day prior to any processing unless the computer oper-

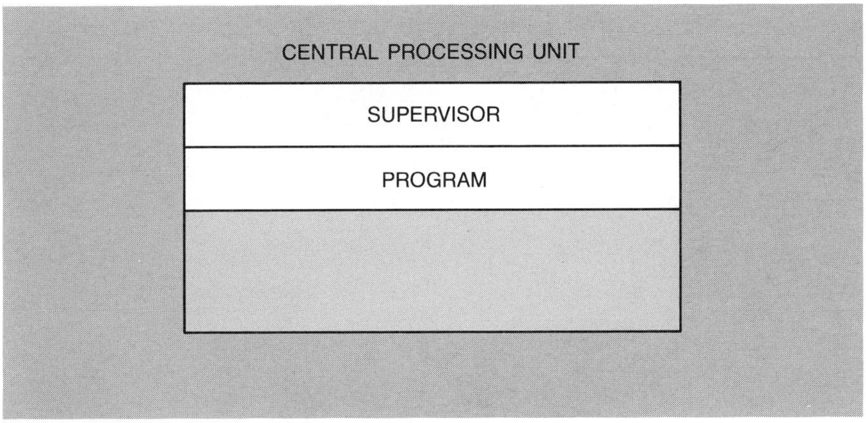

345
THE OPERATING
SYSTEM: CONTROL
AND OPTIMIZATION
OF COMPUTER
CAPABILITY

```
┌──────────────────────────────────────────────┐
│        CENTRAL PROCESSING UNIT                 │
│   ┌────────────────────────────────────┐      │
│   │            SUPERVISOR               │      │
│   ├────────────────────────────────────┤      │
│   │            PROGRAM                  │      │
│   ├────────────────────────────────────┤      │
│   │                                     │      │
│   │                                     │      │
│   │                                     │      │
│   └────────────────────────────────────┘      │
│                                                │
└──────────────────────────────────────────────┘
```

Figure 10.1
The supervisor and a user program in the CPU.

ates on a 24-hour basis. It calls in each user program and extracts items, as needed, from the operating system. That is, if a program needs to be compiled, the supervisor calls in the corresponding compiler. If a complex I/O function is required for the program, the supervisor accesses the operating system and calls the appropriate routines into storage as needed. Thus the supervisor controls the operations of the computer.

While the supervisor resides in storage, other programs of the operating system are stored on a high-speed medium. Additional programs of the operating system will be discussed in detail. But first let us consider some types of operating systems.

C. Types of Operating Systems

The type of operating system employed will depend upon the hardware within the computer system and the degree of sophistication in processing that is required.

The device used to store the operating system again depends on the sophistication desired. Operating systems stored on tape, for example, are not as sophisticated as those stored on disk where random-access capability is a distinct advantage. The device selected for the operating system is called the *resident storage device.* Each day, the *supervisor* is loaded into the CPU from the resident storage device unless, of course, the computer operates on a 24-hour basis.

IBM classifications for their operating systems include the following. They are listed in increasing order of sophistication:

Sample IBM classifications of Operating Systems
Disk Operating System (DOS): control system is on disk

Full Operating System (OS): control system is on disk or magnetic drum, and includes the capability of processing several programs simultaneously.

Operating System/Virtual Storage (OS/VS): control system is also on disk or drum. The major advantage of VS is its efficient use of storage. Through sophisticated overlay techniques, the storage area required by the CPU under VS is far less than it is with other operating systems. (See the following section for a more thorough description.)

1. Virtual Storage The *virtual storage* concept is a recent advance in computer technology which permits a computer system to operate as if it has more primary storage capacity than it actually has. This technique is accomplished by segmenting a program into a series of sections or modules which are stored outside the CPU, typically on a direct-access device such as magnetic disk. Instead of calling the entire program into the CPU at one time to be executed, the control system causes sections of the program to be read in and executed, one at a time. After one section has been executed, another section is brought into the CPU and uses the storage positions occupied by a previous section. In this manner, there is an effective storage capacity far in excess of the actual storage capacity. Several large programs which, individually or collectively, might otherwise occupy too much CPU storage to be executed at the same time can thus be run simultaneously.

2. Other Aspects of an Operating System

Features of an Operating System (see Figure 10.2)
- Supervisor controls operations of computer
- Job control program: provides communication between programmer and supervisor
- Translators: compilers and assemblers
- Utility programs: packaged software which performs common functions such as card-to-print listing, card-to-tape conversion, sorting, merging, and so on
- Input/output control system: maintains proper functioning of tapes and disks by incorporating labeling routines, blocking and deblocking, wrong-length record checks, and so on
- Library of user programs: accessed by supervisor as needed

3. Examples of How Operating System Functions

Example 1: Typical Processing—Translation Phase (Figure 10.3)
1. Supervisor calls in user source program

347

THE OPERATING
SYSTEM: CONTROL
AND OPTIMIZATION
OF COMPUTER
CAPABILITY

2. Supervisor calls in translator program from resident device for assembly or compilation
3. Supervisor stores object program in library for future processing if programmer desires (Figure 10.4)

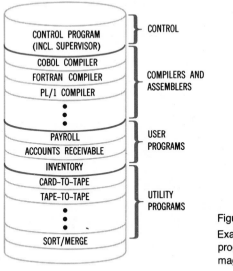

Figure 10.2
Example of typical programs stored on magnetic disk.

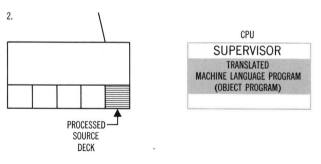

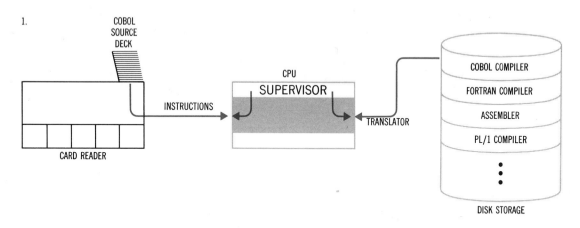

Figure 10.3
The process of obtaining an object (translated) program.

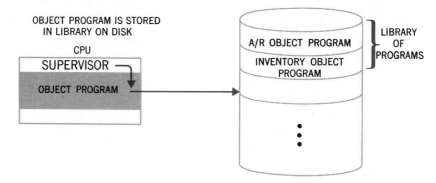

Figure 10.4

Storing an object program in a library.

Example 2: Typical Processing—Execution
1. Supervisor calls in object program from library (Figure 10.5)
2. Supervisor accesses input device
3. Data is processed using input/output control system—labels are checked, record lengths checked, and so on
4. Supervisor accesses output device

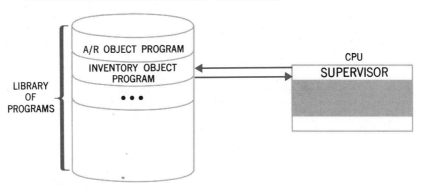

Figure 10.5

Retrieving an object program from the library.

D. Job Control

For a source program processed as above, it is necessary for the programmer to provide the supervisor with information such as:

1. The language of the source program, so that the appropriate translator (compiler or assembler) for that language can be brought into the CPU by the supervisor from the library of programs.

349
THE OPERATING
SYSTEM: CONTROL
AND OPTIMIZATION
OF COMPUTER
CAPABILITY

2. Where the object program should be placed. That is, whether the object program should be stored in the library of programs or on a deck of cards, for example.

3. Identification of the program, so that if it is placed in the library it can be retrieved subsequently by that identification. In addition, if the computer system is operating in a multiprogramming environment, the supervisor can thus maintain control of each program by its specific identification.

One way that the programmer can inform the supervisor of the above type of information is to use certain *job control cards* in conjunction with the source deck, as shown in the diagram in Figure 10.6. These job control cards are read by the supervisor which then determines the precise requirements of the programmer.

Note that the job control cards in Figure 10.6 indicate to the supervisor what operations the programmer wants the computer to perform on the COBOL source deck. The illustrated job control applies to a specific computer (IBM S/370). Note that although job control on all computers can accomplish similar tasks, the specifications may be slightly different.

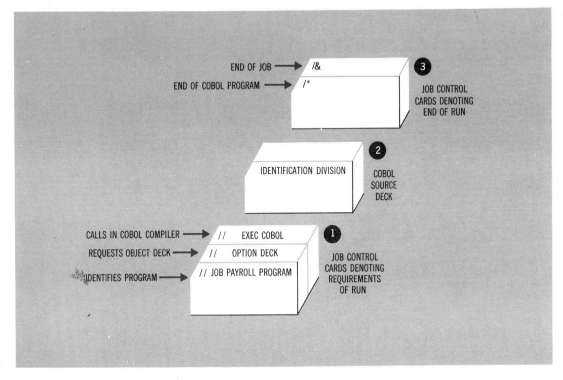

Figure 10.6

Example of job control cards used with a COBOL source deck to produce an object deck.

The illustration in Figure 10.7 indicates how a programmer can direct the supervisor to:

1. Translate a COBOL Accounts Receivable program; and, if the translation is successfully achieved,
2. Execute the resultant object program in the CPU, running it with test data supplied by the programmer.

Similarly, if the programmer wants to direct the computer to use a sort/merge program, a card-to-tape utility program, or a user program that is already in the library, the appropriate job control statements must be read into the computer to direct the supervisor. Thus, any operation that the programmer requires of the computer must be indicated by job control messages to the supervisor.

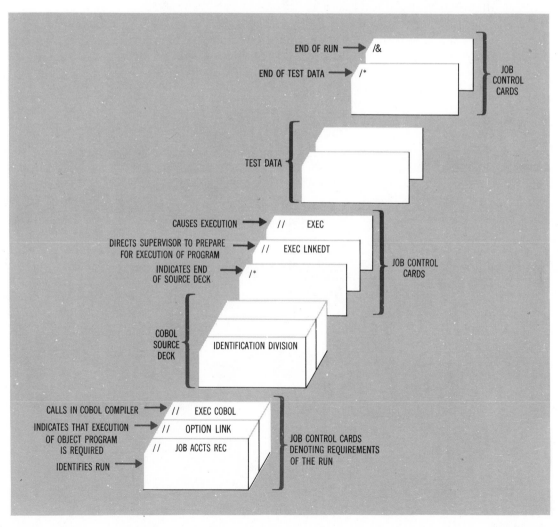

Figure 10.7

Example of job control cards to direct the supervisor to translate and execute a program.

351
THE OPERATING
SYSTEM: CONTROL
AND OPTIMIZATION
OF COMPUTER
CAPABILITY

The various computer manufacturers have their own types of job control statements for communicating with the supervisor. Since there are usually many job control statements to choose from, these statements are commonly thought of as comprising a *job control language* (JCL) by itself. JCL is an integral part of all computer runs.

E. Communicating with the Operating System

There are two ways to communicate with the system:

1. Job control language: programmer provides information concerning the job stream
2. Console

Although third-generation computers are designed to operate with minimal operator intervention, occasions do arise when the supervisor will request the operator to perform certain tasks. Similarly, occasions will arise where the operator needs information from the system. A common way for the supervisor to communicate with the operator is for it to print out its requests on a *console typewriter,* such as the one shown in Figure 10.8.

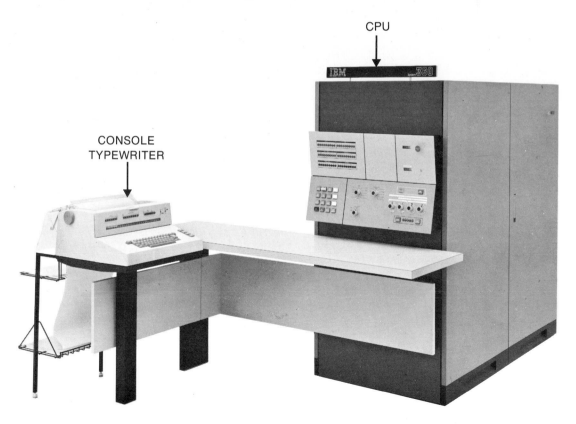

Figure 10.8
Console typewriter and CPU. Courtesy IBM.

The supervisor may direct the operator to perform various tasks, such as typing in the current date on the console typewriter in the morning, so that the date of the run can appear on listings produced on the printer that day. Likewise, the operator may, for example, be requested to mount a specific tape file required for the processing of a specific program.

In addition, various errors may occur during the control or processing of a program which may require operator intervention. The supervisor will then request the operator to key in, on the console typewriter, what action should be taken. Suppose, for example, that a tape has an invalid label; the operator can type in "ignore" if the error is not considered serious, or "cancel" if the job is to be aborted.

Frequently the operator will direct the supervisor to perform various jobs either through the use of job control instructions, as indicated previously, or through the use of messages typed on the console typewriter.

II. Sort/Merge and Other Utility Programs

Certain commonly used programs, called *utility programs*, are usually supplied by the computer manufacturer to facilitate the efficient processing of operations. These operations include such things as the sorting of data and the transferring of data from one I/O device to another. Since the programs to perform these standard operations have already been supplied, they can be accessed immediately. In many cases, what may seem to a businessman to require complex programming effort is, in reality, a simple process because of the existence of the types of software mentioned above. The programmer need only supply a set of specifications indicating the type of processing required, and the utility program will then perform the operations.

A. The Sort/Merge Program

Typically, a sort/merge program is available that will, for example, take an input file of records and rearrange or sort them in a different sequence. This program also provides for the merging of two separate files into one file. The input files that can thus be processed can usually be on such devices as tape or disk.

The sort/merge program is typically stored in the library of programs that can be accessed by the supervisor and brought into the CPU. The supervisor must usually be supplied with certain specifications to inform the sort/merge program as to (a) the device on which the input is located; (b) the device where the resultant file should be placed; (c) the control field that will be used for sorting or merging the records; (d) the type of sort involved (numeric, alphanumeric), as required; (e) any special modifications to records, such as the rearrangement of fields, the addition or deletion of records, and so on.

353

THE OPERATING
SYSTEM: CONTROL
AND OPTIMIZATION
OF COMPUTER
CAPABILITY

B. Other Utility Programs

Frequently, data must be transferred from one I/O device to another. As an example, in many companies, data is first key-punched on cards and then fed into the computer where it is stored on magnetic tape or a direct-access medium such as disk for future high-speed processing. Likewise, it is often necessary to transfer a file for backup purposes. For example, an Accounts Receivable file on disk may be duplicated on tape, just in case the disk file should be inadvertently lost or damaged. Many times, a file will be transferred from a particular I/O device to the printer, so that a businessman can see what information is stored in that file. These types of operations are so common that the manufacturer usually supplies programs, called utility programs, that will transfer a file from one I/O device to another.

As with the sort/merge program, utility programs are usually stored in the library of programs and can thus be accessed by the supervisor and brought into the CPU.

III. Input/Output Control: Multiprogramming and Overlapped Processing

The illustrations throughout this chapter have shown only the supervisor and *one* program in the CPU at any given time. A third-generation computer, however, usually has the control capability of allowing the simultaneous processing of more than one program at a given time in the same CPU. This is referred to as *multiprogramming*, which is an essential and integral feature necessary for time-sharing and data communication applications. The I/O control program of the operating system provides the computer with this capability.

We will examine the situation where there are two programs in the CPU to be processed, as shown in Figure 10.9.

A computer typically performs I/O operations much more slowly than processing operations. Thus, in previous generation computers, the CPU was basically idle while it waited for read or write commands to be executed. Multiprogramming enables a computer with a sophisticated operating system to interleave programs in such a way that when an I/O operation is being performed for one program the CPU can perform the arithmetic or logic operations of another. Note, however, that the control process must be very complex and high level to permit the computer to effectively switch from one program to another.

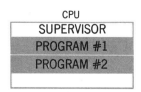

Figure 10.9

Two programs in the CPU.

Suppose at some particular point in program 1, there is an instruction to read in a punched card. Let us assume that the reader in this system can read at the rate of approximately 1000 cards per minute. This means that it will take at least 0.001 min (or 0.06 sec) to read one card. In this same time period required to perform *one* I/O function, a typical commercial computer could, for example, perform more than 300 additions of six-digit numbers. Suppose, at the time program 1 is reading a card, arithmetic operations of program 2 can be performed. Then both programs can operate simultaneously without loss of time since, they will, in essence be utilizing different circuits within the CPU. After program 1 has finished its I/O operation, the next instruction might be an arithmetic one. It may be that, at this point, program 2 is ready to perform an I/O operation, such as read a tape. Assuming that the system has only one card reader, it might appear that an I/O operation in program 2 could not include the card reader as an input device, since this device is currently being used by program 1. However, this is not a problem, since card input data for program 2 might first be converted to another medium by the computer, thus enabling data to be processed in a multiprogramming environment.

The illustration in Figure 10.10 will help dramatize the major advantage of multiprogramming.

In essence, then, a program is not necessarily run continuously by itself from beginning to end in a computer capable of handling multiprogramming. If it were, then while a particular I/O operation were being performed, the rest of the computer would be idle. It is common to hear of computer systems being *I/O bound;* that is, the operations of the computer are hampered because of the extremely slow I/O processing that inhibits the rapid processing of non-I/O functions, such as arithmetic operations.

The student should be aware that many computer systems can operate in a multiprogramming environment. This results in the overall completion of programs in far less time than if they were stacked, where one program is executed completely, then another.

Thus there is great advantage to computers with a multiprogramming capability. Note, also that time-sharing and data communication systems, where programs and their corresponding input are entered from terminals at remote locations, *must* be used in conjunction with computers that have the ability to handle multiprogramming. In this way, several programs keyed in by terminals can be interleaved and processed quickly enough to provide each user with the required output in a relatively short time.

Figure 10.10 illustrates how it is possible on many business computers to have numerous programs in the CPU being processed at essentially the same time.

It should be noted that the supervisor has an important function in scheduling programs that are run in a multiprogramming

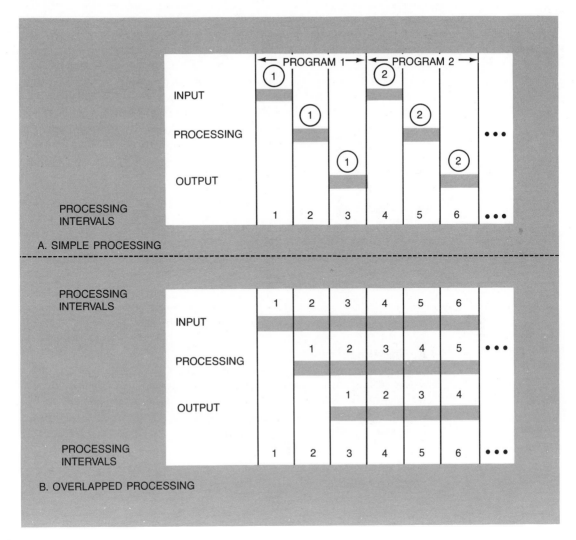

Figure 10.10
Simple processing compared to overlapped processing.

system. For example, suppose two programs are brought into the CPU at essentially the same time and both happen to have arithmetic instructions at the beginning. If one program is for Payroll, and the other is for Accounts Receivable, for example, which one should have priority? The supervisor can be directed to assign different priorities to different programs. In the above example, it might be that, based on the businessman's requirements, priority numbers have been assigned to programs, as follows: Payroll—9; Accounts Receivable—8; Sales Forecasting—7; and so on, where programs with the largest numbers have the highest priorities. Thus Payroll programs are of higher priority than Accounts Receivable programs. Therefore, whenever there is a situation in a multiprogramming environment where two or more programs require the same circuits in the CPU, the supervisor will process them in priority order, according to their preestablished priority ratings.

Priorities can also be assigned in some computer systems in such a manner that more important programs, when read by the computer, can interrupt other processing and thus receive the first order of preference. Thus an Inventory program with priority of 9 will be run before any programs with lower priority.

In summary, computer systems consist of three main aspects:

Elements of Computer System
1. CPU: Central Processing Unit
2. Hardware: physical devices linked by cable to CPU
3. Software: programming support which maximizes efficiency of the system

---

IV. Additional Features of an Operating System

A. The Timer

One of the features of an operating system is a *timer*, or clock, within the CPU that can be used to supply data on computer usage. With this timer, the control program can provide figures that will show, for example, the distribution of computer use by each department within the company. That is, each application and the time it takes to process it is logged for reference purposes. This can be of particular interest to the businessman, since, in many companies, computer usage is "charged" to each department that requires it for processing. In such an environment, the businessman might want to carefully review data processing needs before arbitrarily requesting various outputs from the computer.

The timer is also of use to the programmer, since it provides an indication of the efficiency of each program. The programmer frequently analyzes the time it takes to run a program, and if such time is excessive, he or she can attempt to simplify the logic in order to reduce processing time.

It is thus possible to employ the results of the timer to achieve a more efficient utilization of the computer.

B. Storage Protection

We have seen that it is common for more than one program to be in the computer at one time. Without any storage protection, the possibility exists that one program, if incorrectly coded, could inadvertently destroy or modify parts of another program and its corresponding data that are in the computer at the same time. This danger might arise especially when a new program is being tested.

To avoid this potential problem, a storage protection feature is generally available for third-generation computers which is managed by the operating system.

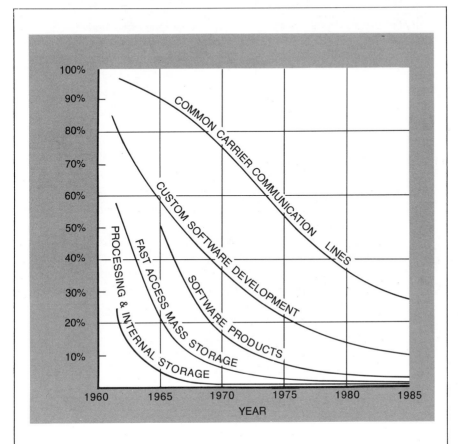

Data is synthesized from at least 20 different sources to show the cost to the user for different elements of a computing system relative to their cost in 1960. The major difficulty encountered is that changes are so rapid that one cannot buy a directly comparable item at the end of a decade that he could at the beginning. Much better CPU's in 1975, for example, cost 0.5% of what they cost in 1960. Costs for more powerful, fast access mass storage in 1975 are about 2% of what they were in 1960. These costs will continue to decline considerably by 1985. The decreases in communications and software are less than decreases in other elements, but are still considerable.

Important Terms Used in this Chapter

Console
Disk Operating System (DOS)
Hardware
Input/Output Control System
I/O Bound
Job Control Language (JCL)
Library
Monitor
Multiprogramming
Operating System (OS)

Overlapped Processing
Resident Storage Device
Software
Storage Protection
Supervisor
Timer
User Programs
Utility Programs
Virtual Storage

Self-Evaluating Quiz

1. The term _____ denotes those programs usually supplied by the computer manufacturer that are designed to achieve maximum utilization of the computer.

2. _____ are those organizations that develop packaged applications which are sold to computer users.

3. The _____ is another name for the control program.

4. (T or F) The supervisor always resides in the CPU for the purpose of controlling computer operations.

5. The control system is also referred to as a(n) _____.

6. The purpose of a supervisor is to _____.

7. The compilers and assemblers used with a computer are typically located on high-speed devices such as a _____ and are accessed by the _____.

8. Working object programs are usually placed on a _____ for access by the supervisor.

9. The control program also enables more than one program to be run simultaneously within the computer, a concept referred to as _____.

10. The Sort/Merge program is called a(n) _____.

11. The typical operating system is usually stored on a _____.

12. The programmer communicates with the supervisor with the use of _____ cards.

13. The computer operator communicates with the supervisor and accesses a program by using the _____.

14. A(n) _____ within the CPU can be used to supply statistics on how long it takes to run programs.

15. Storage Protection is a term used to prevent _____.

Solutions

1. software
2. Software houses or facilities management companies

359

THE OPERATING
SYSTEM: CONTROL
AND OPTIMIZATION
OF COMPUTER
CAPABILITY

3. supervisor
4. T
5. operating system
6. control the operations of the computer
7. direct-access device; supervisor
8. library
9. multiprogramming
10. utility program
11. direct-access device
12. job control
13. console typewriter
14. timer
15. accidental access by the programmer of a critical or reserved area of storage

Review Questions:

I. Answer True or False

1. (T or F) The terms *hardware* and *software* refer to the computer devices within a computer system.
2. (T or F) Software can be obtained from the computer manufacturer or from "software houses."
3. (T or F) The control program within a computer system can minimize programmer and operator effort, if utilized properly.
4. (T or F) The supervisor is called into the computer by each program.
5. (T or F) The supervisor is usually supplied by the manufacturer.
6. (T or F) Each computer system is supplied with its own supervisor.
7. (T or F) The supervisor is part of a larger control system that is typically stored on a high-speed input/output device such as a tape or disk.
8. (T or F) One of the purposes of a supervisor is to minimize operator intervention.
9. (T or F) When a source program requires translation prior to execution, the supervisor must call in the compiler or translator.
10. (T or F) It is possible for a supervisor to retrieve specific programs from a library of programs stored on a high-speed input/output device.
11. (T or F) On most third-generation computers, it is possible to run several programs simultaneously.
12. (T or F) Multiprogramming is made possible by a sophisticated control system.
13. (T or F) For most commercial computers, it is the calculations that require the most computer time.
14. (T or F) The sort/merge program is part of software.
15. (T or F) Utility programs are usually written by programmers in a user company.
16. (T or F) The Job Control Language enables the programmer to communicate with the supervisor.
17. (T or F) The Job Control Language is the same for all computers.

18. (T or F) When the supervisor cannot perform a specified operation, for some reason, it usually prints a message on the console typewriter.
19. (T or F) During the execution of any program, the supervisor is always maintained in the Central Processing Unit.

II. Fill in the Blanks

1. The devices within a computer system that can be used to accept input or produce output are referred to as _____.
2. The program support that is designed to achieve maximum utilization of the computer is called _____.
3. This program support can be supplied by _____ or by _____.
4. The _____ is a special control program usually supplied by the manufacturer which must be in the CPU in order for programs to be run.
5. If a program needs to be compiled, the _____ calls in the required compiler.
6. The control system that is typically stored on a high-speed device, such as disk, is sometimes referred to as a(n) _____.
7. Once a source program has been completely debugged, its object program equivalent is usually stored _____.
8. Two major functions of a supervisor are to _____ and to _____.
9. A third-generation computer that has the control capability of allowing the simultaneous processing of more than one program at a time in the same CPU is said to have _____ ability.
10. A computer generally performs _____ operations much slower than processing operations; because of this, it is said to be _____ bound.
11. Specially supplied programs, referred to as _____, are supplied to the user to handle commonly used routines and procedures.
12. Two examples of the above programs are _____ and _____.
13. The Job Control Language is used to facilitate communication between the _____ and also between the _____.
14. When the supervisor communicates with the operator, it prints messages on the _____.
15. JCL is the abbreviation for _____.

Unit Two: Selected Bibliography

Flowcharting

1. "Experimental Investigations of the Utility of Detailed Flowcharts in Programming," Ben Schneiderman, Richard Mayer, Dore McKay, and Peter Heller, *Communications of the ACM*, vol. 20, June 1977, p. 373.

361

THE OPERATING
SYSTEM: CONTROL
AND OPTIMIZATION
OF COMPUTER
CAPABILITY

(a)   Tests the commonly held belief in the utility of detailed flowcharts as an aid to programming.

(b)   Provides students with a perspective on the issue which significantly differs from that presented in the text.

2.   *Flowcharting*, Mario Farina (Englewood Cliffs, N.J.: 1970).

3.   *Flowcharting: A Tool for Understanding Computer Logic*, Nancy Stern (New York: 1975).

Both works provide a step-by-step approach to flowcharting techniques with numerous examples.

Programming—General: Texts

1.   *The Art of Computer Programming*, Donald E. Knuth (Reading, Mass.: 1968).

2.   *Programming Languages: History and Fundamentals*, Jean E. Sammet (Englewood Cliffs, N.J.: 1969).

Operating Systems

1.   "The IBM System/370 Model 3033," Angeline Pantages and Michael Cashman, *Datamation*, vol. 23, May 1977, p. 235.

(a)   Focusses on the operating system features of a large-scale computer system.

(b)   Provides the student with information on how computer systems can be compared and evaluated.

2.   "Software Cuts Waste in Operations," Frank L. Harvey, *Computer Decisions*, June, 1977.

3.   "Package Goods," Staff Report, *Computer Decisions*, June 1977.

Unit Three
Programming in COBOL

The Fundamentals of COBOL

11

11

I. Review

In Chapter 9 you learned the following about COBOL programs:

Review of COBOL
1. Nature
   a. Business-Oriented
   b. Standard for Most Machines
   c. Englishlike
   d. Relatively Easy to Code
2. Structure
   a. One Line in Coding Sheet = One Card in Source Deck
   b. 1–6 = Page and Line Number—optional
   c. 7–72 = COBOL Statement
   d. 73–80 = Identification Code
3. Divisions of a COBOL Program: All four must appear in following sequence:
   a. IDENTIFICATION DIVISION—identifies program to computer
   b. ENVIRONMENT DIVISION—indicates equipment to be used
   c. DATA DIVISION—describes files and work areas
   d. PROCEDURE DIVISION—contains all instructions

11

You were also provided with a sample program and explanation so that you could learn to read a relatively simple COBOL program. In this chapter, we will provide the fundamentals necessary for writing simplified COBOL programs in their entirety.

II. Coding Requirements

A. IDENTIFICATION DIVISION

The IDENTIFICATION DIVISION is the smallest, simplest, and least significant division of a COBOL program. As the name indicates, it supplies identifying data about the program.

The IDENTIFICATION DIVISION has no effect on the execution of the program but is, nevertheless, required as a means of identifying the job to the computer.

The IDENTIFICATION DIVISION may consist of the following paragraphs:

Paragraphs in IDENTIFICATION DIVISION

PROGRAM-ID.

AUTHOR.

INSTALLATION.

DATE-WRITTEN.

DATE-COMPILED.

SECURITY.

REMARKS.

Margin Rules in COBOL—(Figure 11.1) You will note that on the COBOL Coding Sheet, Column 8 is labeled A, and Column 12 is labeled B. These are margins. Certain entries must begin in Margin A and others must begin in Margin B.

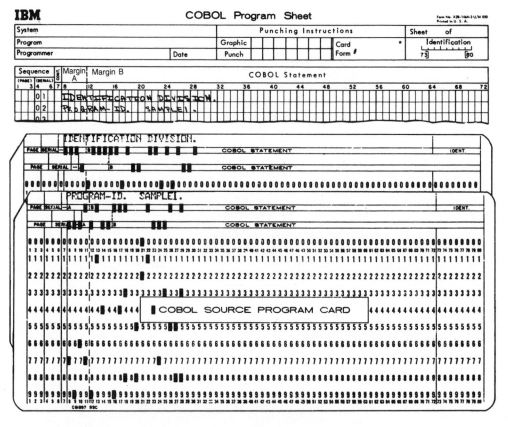

Figure 11.1

The conversion of COBOL coding sheets to punched cards.

If an entry is to be coded in Margin A, it begins in position 8. If an entry is to be coded in Margin B, it may begin anywhere after position 11. That is, it may begin in position 12, 13, 14, and so on. Note that margin rules specify the beginning point of entries. A word that must begin in Margin A may extend into Margin B.

IDENTIFICATION DIVISION—Margin Rules
1. Division and paragraph names coded in Margin A and followed by a period.
2. All periods followed by at least one blank.
3. All other entries begin in Margin B.

The only required entry in the IDENTIFICATION DIVISION is the PROGRAM-ID. That is, all programs must be identified by a name. Rules for forming such a name vary from computer to computer. We will use the convention of an eight-character program name, letters and digits only.

Thus the first two entries of a program must be IDENTIFICATION DIVISION and PROGRAM-ID:

```
IDENTIFICATION DIVISION.
PROGRAM-ID. SAMPLE1.
```

PROGRAM-ID is followed by a period and then a space. The program name is coded in Margin B and must conform to the rules specified above. Note that the two entries may also be coded as:

```
IDENTIFICATION DIVISION.
PROGRAM-ID.
    SAMPLE1.
```

In either case, the name must be followed by a period.

The other paragraph names listed above are optional. They are useful items which provide significant facts about the nature of the program, but are not required.

For ANS COBOL[1] users, the DATE-COMPILED paragraph can be coded simply as:

```
DATE-COMPILED.
```

The computer-generated source listing will be provided with the actual date of run.

---

[1]ANS is an abbreviation for American National Standard and is a standard form of COBOL used by many companies. It is the form of COBOL which will be presented here.

The following is a brief summary of the IDENTIFICATION DIVISION:

Features of IDENTIFICATION DIVISION
1. Paragraphs are for information only—no effect on compilation.
2. IDENTIFICATION DIVISION entry and PROGRAM-ID are the first two program entries and are required.
3. PROGRAM-ID is followed by a period, a space, and program name.
4. All other paragraphs optional.

Self-Evaluating Quiz

1. The first two entries of a COBOL program must always be _____ and _____ .
2. Each of these entries must be followed by a _____ , which, in turn, must be followed by a _____ .
3. They are both coded in Margin _____ .
4. The name that follows PROGRAM-ID is the _____ name.
5. Code the IDENTIFICATION DIVISION for a program called EXPENSES for a corporation, Dynamic Data Devices, Inc., written July 15, 1980. This program has a security classification and is available to authorized personnel only. It produces a weekly listing by department of all operating expenses.

Solutions

1. IDENTIFICATION DIVISION
   PROGRAM-ID
2. period
   space or blank
3. A
4. program (rules for forming such names are computer dependent)
5. The following is a suggested solution:

```
IDENTIFICATION DIVISION.
PROGRAM-ID. EXPENSES.
AUTHOR. N. B. STERN.
INSTALLATION. DYNAMIC DATA DEVICES. INC.
DATE-WRITTEN. 7/15/80.
SECURITY. AUTHORIZED PERSONNEL ONLY.
REMARKS. THIS PROGRAM PRODUCES A WEEKLY LIST BY DEPARTMENT OF
    ALL OPERATING EXPENSES.
```

B. ENVIRONMENT DIVISION

The ENVIRONMENT DIVISION of a COBOL program supplies information concerning the equipment to be used in the program. The ENVIRON-MENT DIVISION entries are machine-dependent. Unlike the other divisions of a COBOL program, the entries in this division will be dependent upon (1) the computer, and (2) the specific devices used in the program.

The ENVIRONMENT DIVISION is composed of two sections: the CONFIGURATION SECTION and the INPUT-OUTPUT SECTION. The CONFIGURA-TION SECTION supplies data concerning the computer on which the COBOL program will be compiled and executed. It has no effect on execution, is not required, and hence will be omitted here. The INPUT-OUTPUT SECTION supplies information concerning the specific devices used in the program. The card reader, printer, card punch, tape drives, and mass storage units are devices that may be referred to in the INPUT-OUTPUT SECTION of the ENVIRONMENT DIVISION.

The ENVIRONMENT DIVISION is the only division of a COBOL program that will change significantly if the program is to be run on different computers. The entries required in the ENVIRONMENT DIVI-SION are generally supplied to the programmer by the installation. Throughout this discussion, we will use some sample statements, keeping in mind that such entries are dependent upon the actual computer used, and the devices available with that computer.

INPUT-OUTPUT SECTION   The INPUT-OUTPUT SECTION of the ENVI-RONMENT DIVISION supplies information concerning the devices used in the program. In FILE-CONTROL, a paragraph in the INPUT-OUTPUT SEC-TION, a file name will be assigned to each device used.

Hence, thus far we have the following entries:

```
ENVIRONMENT DIVISION.
INPUT-OUTPUT SECTION.
FILE-CONTROL.
```

The FILE-CONTROL paragraph consists of SELECT clauses. Each SELECT clause defines a file name and assigns an input or output device to that file. The format may be as follows:

```
SELECT (file name) ASSIGN TO (device specification)
```

The device specifications vary among computer manufacturers. Consider the following format of a SELECT clause, required for most ANS compilers.

$$\text{SELECT} \begin{pmatrix} \text{file} \\ \text{name} \end{pmatrix} \text{ASSIGN TO} \begin{pmatrix} \text{system} \\ \text{number} \end{pmatrix} - \begin{bmatrix} \text{UR} \\ \text{UT} \\ \text{DA} \end{bmatrix} - \begin{pmatrix} \text{device} \\ \text{number} \end{pmatrix} - \begin{bmatrix} \text{S} \\ \text{D} \\ \text{I} \end{bmatrix}$$

Examples

SELECT CARD-IN ASSIGN TO SYS001-UR-2540R-S.

SELECT TAPE-OUT ASSIGN TO SYS002-UT-2400-S.

The FILE-CONTROL paragraph may seem unnecessarily complex at this point. The entries, however, are standard for a particular installation. The only programmer-supplied term is the file name.

The file name assigned to each device must conform to the general rules for forming programmer-supplied names:

Rules for Forming File Names
1. 1 to 30 characters.
2. No special characters except a dash.
3. No embedded blanks.
4. At least one alphabetic character.

In addition to conforming to these rules, the file name must be *unique:* that is, the name may not be assigned to any other data element in the program.

For each device used in the program, a SELECT clause must be specified. If a program requires cards as input and produces a printed report as output, two SELECT clauses will be specified. One file name will be assigned to the card file, and another to the print file.

In the second format noted above, each device has a specification in the SELECT clause. The SELECT clause will assign a file to a:

1. System number: supplied by computer installation
2. Classification:
   UR for unit-record—files produced on card reader, punch or printer
   UT for utility—tape files
   DA for direct access—files produced on disk, drum, data cells
3. Device number: supplied by computer manufacturer; for IBM, for example, we have
   Tape—2400
   Reader—2540R
   Punch—2540P
   Printer—1403

4.   Access mode:
      S for sequential—card, tape, or print files
      D or I for disk files[2]

All SELECT clauses are coded in Margin B. The order in which the files are specified is not significant.

Example 1
A card file, consisting of transaction data, may be assigned as follows:

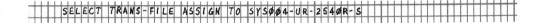

The name, TRANS-FILE, is supplied by the programmer. The remaining data in the statement is necessary when utilizing the reader. The reader is a UNIT-RECORD device with number 2540R, and assigned to SYS004, for this installation.
      Note that SELECT clauses are coded in Margin B.

Example 2
A tape file, consisting of employee data, may be assigned as follows:

EMPLOYEE-FILE is the name assigned to the tape file. All entries after the words ASSIGN TO are supplied by the installation to indicate a specific tape drive.

Self-Evaluating Quiz

1.   Code the IDENTIFICATION and ENVIRONMENT DIVISION entries for the system corresponding to the flowchart at the top of p. 374.

2.   Code the IDENTIFICATION and ENVIRONMENT DIVISION entries for a program that edits input cards, creates an error listing for all erroneous cards, and puts valid card data onto a tape.

---

[2]In general, references to disk processing, because of its complexity, will be omitted.

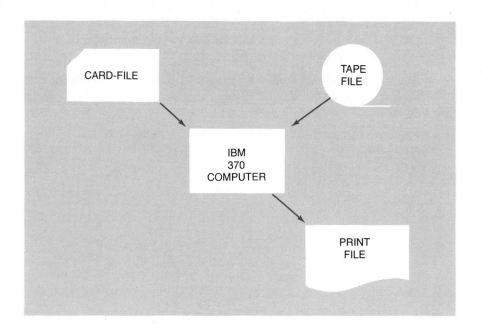

Solutions

1.

```
IDENTIFICATION DIVISION.
PROGRAM-ID. SAMPLE2.
AUTHOR. R. A. STERN.
REMARKS. THE PROGRAM PRODUCES A PRINTED REPORT FROM A MASTER
    FILE AND SELECTED DETAIL CARDS.
ENVIRONMENT DIVISION.
INPUT-OUTPUT SECTION.
FILE-CONTROL.   SELECT CARDIN ASSIGN TO SYS002-UR-2540R-S.
                SELECT TAPE-IN ASSIGN TO SYS008-UT-2400-S.
                SELECT PRINT-FILE ASSIGN TO SYS003-UR-1403-S.
```

2.

```
IDENTIFICATION DIVISION.
PROGRAM-ID. EDIT1.
AUTHOR. N. B. STERN.
REMARKS. THIS PROGRAM EDITS INPUT CARDS, CREATES A TAPE AND
    AN ERROR LISTING.
ENVIRONMENT DIVISION.
INPUT-OUTPUT SECTION.
FILE-CONTROL.
    SELECT CARD-FILE ASSIGN TO SYS001-UR-2540R-S.
    SELECT ERROR-FILE ASSIGN TO SYS002-UR-1403-S.
    SELECT TAPE-FILE ASSIGN TO SYS003-UR-2400-S.
```

Review Questions

1. Indicate which entries are coded in Margin A:
   a. ENVIRONMENT DIVISION.
   b. CONFIGURATION SECTION.
   c. SOURCE-COMPUTER.
   d. FILE-CONTROL.
   e. SELECT clause.
2. (T or F) The ENVIRONMENT DIVISION of a COBOL program, like the other three divisions, is generally the same regardless of the computer on which it is run.
3. (T or F) The INPUT-OUTPUT SECTION of the ENVIRONMENT DIVISION assigns the file names.
4. Make the necessary corrections to each of the following and assume that device specification, where noted, is correct:
   a. INPUT OUTPUT SECTION
   b. SELECT FILE A ASSIGN TO SYS002-UR-2540R-S.

Problems

1. Code the IDENTIFICATION DIVISION and the ENVIRONMENT DIVISION for a COBOL update program which uses a card file and an inventory tape file to create a current master inventory tape file.
2. Code the IDENTIFICATION DIVISION and the ENVIRONMENT DIVISION for a COBOL program which will use a master billing tape to punch gas-bill cards and electric-bill cards.
   Note: Code these programs for the computer used at your installation. Obtain SELECT clause specifications from the data processing manager.

C. DATA DIVISION

The DATA DIVISION is that part of a COBOL program which defines and describes data fields in storage. Any area of storage that is required for the processing of data must be established in the DATA DIVISION.

The DATA DIVISION consists of three sections:

DATA DIVISION Sections

1. FILE SECTION: defines all data areas that are part of the input and output files
2. WORKING-STORAGE SECTION: sets aside storage for fields of data not part of input or output but nonetheless necessary for processing
3. REPORT SECTION: describes specific formats of reports that are generated by the report writer feature. This section is not necessary in a COBOL program and will not be discussed.

---

1. FILE SECTION

a. The File Description, or FD Any program that reads data as input or produces output data requires a FILE SECTION to describe the input and output files. Such files have already been defined in the ENVIRONMENT DIVISION, in a SELECT clause, where the file name is designated and an input-output device is assigned.

For every SELECT clause written in the ENVIRONMENT DIVISION, a file name is assigned. Thus, for every SELECT clause, we will have one *File Description* or FD in the FILE SECTION:

Example:

```
ENVIRONMENT DIVISION.
INPUT-OUTPUT SECTION.
FILE-CONTROL.
    SELECT FILE-1 ASSIGN TO SYS005-UR-2540R-S.
    SELECT FILE-2 ASSIGN TO SYS007-UR-2540P-S.
    SELECT FILE-3 ASSIGN TO SYS006-UR-1403-S.
DATA DIVISION.
FILE SECTION.
FD FILE-1
    •
    •
    •
    •
FD FILE-2
    •
    •
    •
FD FILE-3
    •
    •
    •
```

Each FD entry will be followed by a file name, as it appears in a SELECT statement, and specified clauses, to be discussed. Thus for every SELECT statement there will be one file to be described.

b. Margin Rules The two entries, DATA DIVISION and FILE SECTION, are coded in Margin A. FD is also coded in Margin A. The file name, however, is coded in Margin B. *No period* follows the file name since further description will be necessary:

Format for FD Entries

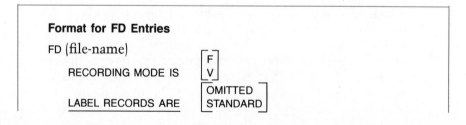

```
┌─────────────────────────────────────┐
│ DATA RECORD IS (record-name)         │
│ DATA RECORDS ARE (record-names)      │
└─────────────────────────────────────┘
```

First, let us consider the meaning of items in the format statement itself:

FORMAT Statement—Rules

[ ]: denotes choice of items

( ): denotes programmer-supplied word(s) required

Capitalized word: COBOL RESERVED WORD with special meaning to the compiler

Underlines: word(s) required within the format; all others optional

---

Note that these are the fundamental entries of an FD; others are available. Check your manual's specifications for additional entries, if desired.

Let us consider each of the clauses of the File Description independently:

ENTRY	MEANING	USE
RECORDING MODE IS F	Fixed length records	Cards, print, tapes, disk
	[v is optional for variable length records] (not used here)	
LABEL RECORDS ARE STANDARD	Standard identifying labels on file	Tape or disk
OMITTED	No labels	Always used for cards or print, sometimes for tape and disk, too
RECORD CONTAINS (no.) CHARACTERS	How many characters per record	Optional
BLOCK CONTAINS (no.) RECORDS	How many records per block	Only used for tape or disk, otherwise omitted
DATA RECORD IS DATA RECORDS ARE	Name of record format	Always used

Example 1

Description of a card file that contains employee records:

```
FD  CARD-FILE
    LABEL RECORDS ARE OMITTED
    RECORD CONTAINS 80 CHARACTERS
    DATA RECORD IS EMPLOYEE-REC.
```

Example 2

Description of a tape file containing transaction credit records and transaction debit records. Record size is 50, block size is 20:

```
FD  TAPE-FILE
    RECORDING MODE IS F
    LABEL RECORDS ARE STANDARD
    RECORD CONTAINS 50 CHARACTERS
    BLOCK CONTAINS 20 RECORDS
    DATA RECORDS ARE TRANS-DEBIT, TRANS-CREDIT.
```

Self-Evaluating Quiz

1. The DATA DIVISION is that part of a COBOL program which _____ .

2. The two sections of a DATA DIVISION to be considered in this chapter are the _____ and the _____ .

3. The FILE SECTION defines _____ .

4. The first time a file name appears in a COBOL program is in a _____ clause of the _____ DIVISION.

5. File names must be 1 to _____ characters in length, contain at least one _____ , and have no _____ .

6. FILE 1 is not a valid file name because it _____ .

7. File names (must, need not) be unique.

8. For every file defined in a SELECT clause, there will be one _____ entry in the FILE SECTION.

9. Fill in the Matrix

	CLAUSE	OPTIONAL OR REQUIRED	PURPOSE	OPTIONS
a.	RECORDING MODE			
b.	LABEL RECORDS			
c.	RECORD CONTAINS			
d.	BLOCK CONTAINS			
e.	DATA RECORD(S)			

10. Unit-record files always have _____-length records.
11. When LABEL RECORDS ARE STANDARD is specified, header and trailer labels will be _____ on input files and _____ on output files.
12. Write an FD entry for a tape file blocked 20 with 100 position records and standard labels; one record format exists.
13. Write an FD entry for a print file with header and detail records.
14. Make any necessary corrections to the following DATA DIVISION entries (14–15):

        DATA DIVISION
        FILE-SECTION
        FD   CARD-FILE.
                RECORDING MODE F
                LABELS ARE OMITTED
                DATA RECORD IS REC-IN.

15. FD   PRINT-FILE
                LABEL RECORDS ARE OMITTED,
                RECORD CONTAINS 132 CHARACTERS,
                DATA RECORD IS PRINT-REC

Solutions

1. defines and describes data fields in storage
2. FILE SECTION
   WORKING-STORAGE SECTION
3. all data areas that are part of input or output
4. SELECT
   ENVIRONMENT
5. 30
   alphabetic character
   special characters (except a dash) or embedded blanks
6. contains an embedded blank
7. must
8. FD
9.

	CLAUSE	OPTIONAL OR REQUIRED	PURPOSE	OPTIONS
a.	RECORDING MODE	Optional	Indicates fixed or variable length records	IS F or V
b.	LABEL RECORDS	Required	Indicates whether labels are included and if so, whether they are standard	ARE STANDARD or OMITTED
c.	RECORD CONTAINS	Optional	Indicates how many characters per record	(no.) CHARACTERS

| d. | BLOCK CONTAINS | Optional | Indicates how many records per block | (no.) RECORDS |
| e. | DATA RECORD(S) | Required | Indicates names of records | IS (record-name) ARE (record-names) |

10. fixed
11. checked
    created
12. FD   TAPE-FILE RECORDING MODE IS F, LABEL RECORDS ARE STANDARD, RECORD CONTAINS 100 CHARACTERS, BLOCK CONTAINS 20 RECORDS, DATA RECORD IS REC-1.
13. FD   PRINT-FILE
            LABEL RECORDS ARE OMITTED,
            RECORDING MODE IS F,
            RECORD CONTAINS 132 CHARACTERS,
            DATA RECORDS ARE HEADER, DETAIL.

     Note: FD entries may be coded in paragraph form, as in the solution to Question 12 or as above, in Question 13. Note, too, that commas are optional between clauses.

14. Period after DATA DIVISION.
    No dash between FILE and SECTION; period after all SECTION names.
    No period after FD CARD-FILE
    LABEL clause should read LABEL RECORDS ARE OMITTED (assuming it is a card file).

    Corrected entry:

    DATA DIVISION.
    FILE SECTION.
    FD   CARD-FILE
            RECORDING MODE F
            LABEL RECORDS ARE OMITTED
            DATA RECORDS IS REC-IN.

    (The COBOL reserved word IS is optional.)
15. File Description entries must end with period.
    Corrected entry:

    FD   PRINT-FILE
            LABEL RECORDS ARE OMITTED
            RECORD CONTAINS 132 CHARACTERS
            DATA RECORD IS PRINT-REC.

c. Record Description Entries After a file has been described by an FD, the structure of records within the file must be denoted by record description entries. For every record named in the DATA RECORD clause, one series of record description entries defining that record is required.

Just as the file description entries begin with the FD level, record description entries begin with the 01 level. Thus, if there is one record within a file, we have:

Example 1

```
FD  CARD-FILE
    RECORDING MODE IS F
    LABEL RECORDS ARE OMITTED
    RECORD CONTAINS 80 CHARACTERS
    DATA RECORD IS CARD-REC.
01  CARD-REC.
        (Entries to be discussed)
```

Each FD must be followed by record description entries for the file. We have observed that records are defined on the 01 level. Now we must indicate just what is contained in each record of the file and how the items are organized.

Data is grouped in COBOL around the *level* concept. Records are considered the *highest level of data* and thus are coded on the 01 level. Any field of data within the record is coded on a level *subordinate to* 01, that is, 02, 03, etc. Any level number between 02 and 49 may be used to describe data fields within a record.

Let us examine the following card layout:

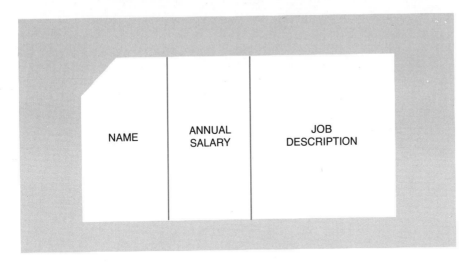

| NAME | ANNUAL SALARY | JOB DESCRIPTION |

The record description entries within the FD are as follows:

Example 2

```
01  EMPLOYEE-REC.
    02  NAME
    02  ANN-SALARY
    02  JOB-DESCRIPTION
```

Field names, as record names and file-names, must conform to the rules for forming data-names:

Rules for Forming Data-Names
1–30 characters
No special characters, except a hyphen (-)
No embedded blanks
At least one alphabetic character
No COBOL reserved words

The name of the above record, EMPLOYEE-REC, is coded on the 01 level in Margin A. All fields within the record are coded on any level between 02 and 49, anywhere in Margin B. By specifying the above fields on the 02 level, two facts are established:

1. All fields on an 02 level are subordinate to, or part of, the 01 level entry.
2. All fields that are coded on the same level are independent items.

Thus NAME, ANN-SALARY and JOB-DESCRIPTION are fields within EMPLOYEE-REC, and each is independent of the other.

Let us redefine the above input:

NAME			ANNUAL SALARY	JOB DESCRIPTION		
				TITLE		
INITIAL 1	INITIAL 2	LAST NAME		LEVEL	POSITION	DUTIES

A field may be subordinate to, or contained in, another field within a record. MONTH and YEAR, for example, may be fields within DATE which is itself contained within a record. MONTH and YEAR, then, would be coded on a level subordinate to DATE. If DATE were specified on level 02, then MONTH and YEAR could each be specified on level 03.

Thus, for the above card format, we may have:

```
01  EMPLOYEE-REC.
    02  NAME
        03  INITIAL1
        03  INITIAL2
        03  LAST-NAME
    02  ANN-SALARY
    02  JOB-DESCRIPTION
        03  JOB-TITLE
            04  LEVEL
            04  POSITION
        03  DUTIES
```

Note that 03 and 04 level items can be indented in Margin B for ease of reading.

An item within record description entries that is *not* further subdivided is called an *elementary item*. An item that is further subdivided is called a *group item*.

Where a NAME field is subdivided into LAST-NAME and FIRST-NAME, for example, we say that the latter two are elementary items and NAME is a group item. Records, themselves, when they are subdivided into fields are called group items since they contain further subdivision.

Elementary items are followed by PICTURE clauses to indicate size and type of the field. Group items merely end with a period.

Self-Evaluating Quiz

1. All records are coded on the _____ level.
2. Levels _____ to _____may be used to represent fields within a record.
3. An 03 level item may be subordinate to an _____ level item if it exists.
4. What, if anything, is wrong with the following data-names:
   a. CUSTOMER NAME
   b. TAX%
   c. DATA
5. An elementary item is defined as _____, and a group item is defined as _____.
6. 01 level is coded in Margin _____, 02 to 49 levels are coded in Margin _____.
7. Write record description entries for the following:

TRANSACTION RECORD

INVOICE NUMBER	LOCATION			PRODUCT DESCRIPTION		
	WARE-HOUSE	CITY	JOB LOT	NO. OF ITEM		ITEM NAME
				SIZE	MODEL	

Solutions

1. 01
2. 02
    49
3. 02
4. No embedded blanks allowed.
    No special characters (%).
    DATA is a COBOL reserved word.
5. one that is not further subdivided
    one that is further subdivided
6. A
    B
7.

```
01  TRANSACTION-REC.
    02  INVOICE-NO
    02  LOCATION.
        03  WAREHOUSE
        03  CITY
        03  JOB-LOT
    02  PRODUCT-DESCRIPTION.
        03  NO-OF-ITEM
            04  SIZE
            04  MODEL
        03  ITEM-NAME
```

Note: Periods follow group items only.

d. PICTURE Clauses Group items are defined by a level indicator. Elementary items are those fields that are not further subdivided, and they must be described in detail. We must specify:

1. The *type* of data contained within an elementary item.
2. The *size* of the field.

---

1. Type of data is denoted in a PICTURE clause with:

X	for alphanumeric
9	for numeric
A	for alphabetic (letters and blanks only)

2. Size of data is denoted by the respective number of X's, 9's or A's.

The elementary item:

        02   AMT   PICTURE 9(5).

is a five-position numeric field. Note that this may be written as:

        02   AMT   PICTURE 99999.

A period must follow the PICTURE clause for all elementary items.

Margins and Spacing for PICTURE Clauses The PICTURE clause, as all COBOL clauses, may appear anywhere in the B Margin, as long as one space is left after the data name defining the item. If parentheses are used to denote size of a field in a PICTURE clause, it must be specified as:

        A(15).

with no spaces on *either* side of the parentheses. A period must *directly* follow.

In place of the word PICTURE, we may use the abbreviation PIC. Thus, the following is a valid entry:

        02   AMT   PIC 9(5).

Additional Requirements for PICTURE Clauses All items must be defined in the *order* in which they appear on the record. The PICTURE clauses in a record description entry must, in total, yield the number of characters in a record. Thus, if a card record is described, all PICTURE clauses on the elementary level must produce 80 characters, even if some of them will not be used. The word FILLER, a COBOL reserved word, along with an appropriate PICTURE clause is used to define an area of a record not required in the program.

Consider the following card record:

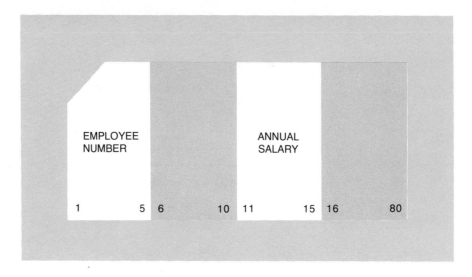

Write the record description entries required:

```
01   CARD-REC.
     02  EMP-NO         PICTURE 9(5).
     02  FILLER         PICTURE X(5).
     02  ANN-SAL        PICTURE 9(5).
     02  FILLER         PICTURE X(65).
```

Note that the word FILLER may be used in more than one place in the DATA DIVISION since it will *not* be used to process data later in the PROCEDURE DIVISION. Note, too, that FILLER fields are usually defined as alphanumeric since it is not always known what the specifications of these fields are.

Implied Decimal Points in PICTURE Clauses   You will recall that most computer files, except for print files, are designed to conserve space. Thus, decimal points are often omitted from numeric fields. We can, however, direct the computer to *assume* the existence of a decimal point so that arithmetic operations can be properly performed even though the decimal point is not part of the field.

Suppose a five-position amount field, with contents 10000, should be interpreted as 100.00. We use the PICTURE clause:

```
02   AMT     PICTURE 999V99.
```

The *V* is used to indicate an *assumed* or *implied* decimal position. The field is still five positions, but the computer assumes the existence of a decimal point after the first three positions for all arithmetic operations.

2. WORKING-STORAGE SECTION The DATA DIVISION, as a whole, contains all defined storage areas to be used for the processing of data. It is divided into first the FILE SECTION, where input and output storage areas are defined, and then the WORKING-STORAGE SECTION which contains all fields *not* part of input or output but necessary for the processing of data. That is, any constants, intermediate totals, or work areas are established in the WORKING-STORAGE SECTION.

a. Independent Items Independent items in the WORKING-STORAGE SECTION are coded on the 77-level in Margin A. Any dataname may be used to define fields. Each such field *must* contain a PICTURE clause.

b. Group Items Group items may be stored in the WORKING-STORAGE SECTION on the 01 level with subordinate fields as in the FILE SECTION. All 01 level items must *follow* all 77 level items.

c. Value Clauses Unlike items in the FILE SECTION of a COBOL program, WORKING-STORAGE items may be assigned values. These values are used to initialize the fields. The corresponding values remain in the fields until COBOL instructions alter the contents.

Examples

```
77      CTR       PICTURE 999       VALUE 000.
77      TAX       PICTURE V99       VALUE .05.
77      NAME      PICTURE AAAA      VALUE 'ABCD'.
```

Note that the VALUE clause must contain a literal that conforms to the mode of the PICTURE clause. Thus, if a 77 level item has a nonnumeric PICTURE clause (either alphabetic or alphanumeric) then the VALUE clause should contain a nonnumeric literal of the same size. Similarly, if a 77 level item has a numeric PICTURE clause then the VALUE clause must contain a numeric literal of similar specifications.

Numeric literals may not exceed 18 digits. Thus the VALUE of a numeric item in the WORKING-STORAGE SECTION may not exceed 18 digits. A nonnumeric VALUE clause, however, may contain up to 120 characters. A nonnumeric VALUE clause is enclosed in quotes.

Since the VALUE clause for an alphabetic or alphanumeric field may contain 120 characters, it is sometimes necessary to continue a VALUE clause from one line of the coding sheet to another. The continuation of nonnumeric literals to two or more lines conforms to the following rules:

Rules for Continuation of Nonnumeric Literals

1. Begin the literal with a quotation mark.
2. Continue the literal until the end of the line is reached (*do not* close with quote mark).

3. Place a dash (-) in the position marked CONT. (continuation) of the next line (position 7).
4. Continue the literal in Margin B of the next line, beginning with a quote mark.
5. End literal with a quotation mark and then a period.

Example

```
CONT.
  8   12                                                                            72
 77  HEADING    PICTURE X(36) VALUE 'MONTHLY TRANSACTIONS FOR APRI
-       'L, 1980'.
```

Self-Evaluating Quiz

1. A PICTURE clause must be used in conjunction with each _____ in a record description.
2. A PICTURE clause specifies the _____ and the _____ of a data field.
3. The three types of data fields are _____, _____, and _____.
4. The characters that may be included in an alphabetic field are _____.
5. The characters that may be included in an alphanumeric field are _____.
6. The characters that may be included in a numeric data field are _____.
7. An alphanumeric PICTURE clause contains _____; an alphabetic PICTURE clause contains _____; a numeric PICTURE clause contains _____.
8. What, if anything, is wrong with the following entries (8-10):

   01 CARD-REC.
      02 DATE1 PICTURE 9999.
         03 MONTH PICTURE 99.
         03 YEAR PICTURE 99.

9. 03 FIELDA PICTURE X9.
10. 04 FIELDB PICTURE X (22).
11. The PICTURE clauses in a record description must, in total, indicate _____.
12. The word _____ is used to denote an area of a record that will not be used for processing.
13. The symbol _____ is used to denote an implied decimal point in an arithmetic field.
14. A PICTURE clause of 9V9 indicates a _____-position data field.
15. If a three-position tax field is to be interpreted as .xxx its PICTURE clause should be _____.

1. elementary item
2. size
   type
3. alphabetic
   numeric
   alphanumeric
4. letters and blanks
5. any character in the COBOL character set
6. digits and plus or minus sign
7. X's
   A's
   9's
8. Group items, such as DATE1, should not have PICTURE clauses.
9. OK
10. Should be:04 FIELDB PICTURE X(22). There is no space between X and (.
11. the number of positions in the record
12. FILLER
13. V
14. two
15. V999.

Review Questions

1. Which of the following entries are coded in Margin A?
   a. FD
   b. FILE SECTION
   c. 01
   d. 03
   e. LABEL RECORDS ARE OMITTED
   f. 77
2. Name the clauses that are required within an FD.
3. Name the clauses that are optional within an FD.
4. How many FD entries are required in a COBOL program?
5. Under what conditions is the BLOCK CONTAINS clause required?
6. State exactly what is meant by the PICTURE clause 9999V9999.
7. (T or F) There may be only one 01 level for a specific file.
8. (T or F) The order in which fields are specified in a record description is not significant.
9. (T or F) Group items must not have PICTURE clauses.
10. (T or F) Elementary items may or may not have PICTURE clauses.
11. (T or F) FILLER is a COBOL reserved word that may be used in the DATA and PROCEDURE DIVISIONS.
12. (T or F) A record name is assigned in the ENVIRONMENT DIVISION.
13. (T or F) Two files may be assigned the same names.
14. (T or F) Levels 03, 08, 75 may be subordinate to a record level.
15. What are the rules for forming data-names?

16. How many characters must be included in the PICTURE clauses used to describe a card record?

17. Correct the following DATA DIVISION:

```
DATA DIVISION
FILE-SECTION.
FD    TAPE FILE.
      RECORDING MODE F.
      DATA RECORD IS INPUT.
01    INPUT.
      02 TRANS. NO                    PICTURE 9999.
      02 TRANSACTION-NAME             PICTURE 20X.
      02 ADDRESS
         03 NUMBER                    PICTURE XXXX.
         03 STREET                    PICTURE A(15).
         03 CITY                      PICTURE AAA.
      02 CREDIT-RATING                PICTURE XX.
         03 CREDIT-CODE               PICTURE X.
         03 LIMIT OF PURCHASE         PICTURE X.
      02 UNIT-PRICE                   PICTURE 99.9.
      02 QTY-PURCHASED                PICTURE 9(5).
      02 DISCOUNT-%                   PICTURE V99.
```

Problems

1. Write the FD and record description entries necessary for an inventory file with the record format specified on the adjacent page.

   The inventory file will be on magnetic tape with standard labels and blocked 20.

2. Write the FD and record description entries for the following purchase record:

ITEM DESCRIPTION	FIELD TYPE	FIELD SIZE	POSITIONS TO RIGHT OF DECIMAL POINT
Name of item	Alphabetic	20	—
Date of order (month, day, year)	Numeric	6	0
Purchase order number	Numeric	5	0
Inventory group	Alphanumeric	10	—
Number of units	Numeric	5	0
Cost/unit	Numeric	4	0
Freight charge	Numeric	4	0
Tax percent	Numeric	2	2

D. The PROCEDURE DIVISION—An Overview

In this section you will learn to:

- Access input and output files
- Read and write information

Record Layout

LOCATION				PART NO.	PART NAME	REORDER LEVEL	UNIT COST	TOTAL SALES 2 MOS. AGO	TOTAL SALES LAST MO.
STATE (alphabetic)	WAREHOUSE		CITY (alphabetic)		alphanumeric		XXX.XX	XXX.XX	XXX.XX
	FLOOR	BIN							

Column positions: 1 — 3 4 — 5 6 — 7 8 — 11 12 — 16 17 — 25 26 — 29 30 — 34 35 — 39 40 — 44

BALANCE ON HAND	QTY. SOLD	TOTAL COST	BIN CAPACITY	DESCRIPTION OF PART
		XXXXX.XX		alphanumeric

Column positions: 45 — 50 51 — 55 56 — 62 63 — 67 68 — 100

(UNLESS OTHERWISE NOTED, FIELDS ARE NUMERIC)
XXX.XX denotes a PICTURE clause of 999V99

- Perform simple move and branch operations
- Perform specific end-of-job operations

An understanding of these types of instructions will be sufficient for writing elementary COBOL programs in their entirety.

1. Structure of the PROCEDURE DIVISION The PROCEDURE DIVISION, as all divisions, is coded in Margin A and ends with a period. It is subdivided into paragraphs, each paragraph defining an independent routine or series of instructions designed to perform a specific function. Paragraphs are coded in Margin A and basically conform to the rules for forming data names.

Each paragraph is further subdivided into sentences, consisting of one or more COBOL statements.

Statements are coded in Margin B. Several statements may be written on one line of a COBOL coding sheet, but words may not be subdivided when the end of a line is reached.

All statements are executed in the order written unless a branch instruction transfers control to some other part of the program.

2. OPEN Statement Before an input or output file can be read or written, we must first OPEN the file. The OPEN statement accesses the file.

An OPEN statement has the following format:

OPEN INPUT (file name(s))   OUTPUT (file name(s))

All files defined in the SELECT statements must be opened as either input or output.

Format Statements:
1. All capitalized words are COBOL reserved words.
2. All lower case words are programmer supplied.

The major function of an OPEN statement is to designate which files are input and which are output. It also makes files available for processing. That is, it tests to see if the device is ready, checks headers if applicable, and so forth.

The order in which files are opened is *not* significant. The only restriction is that a file must be opened *before* it may be read or written; a file must be accessed before it may be processed. Since the OPEN statement accesses the files, it is generally the first instruction issued to the computer in the PROCEDURE DIVISION.

Example

OPEN INPUT CARD-FILE, OUTPUT TAPE-FILE.

3. READ Statement After an input file has been opened, it may be read. A READ statement transmits data from the input de-

vice, assigned in the ENVIRONMENT DIVISION, to the input storage area
defined in the FILE SECTION of the DATA DIVISION.

The format for a READ statement is:

> READ (file name) AT END (statement(s)).

The AT END clause, which determines if there is no more input,
usually indicates a branch to an end-of-job routine:

Example

> READ FILE-X AT END GO TO EOJ.

The GO TO EOJ is a branch instruction which transfers control
to the paragraph called EOJ only when there is no more data. The
routine at EOJ performs an *End-Of-Job* function. All sequential files
require the AT END clause with the READ statement. For many computers, a /* card at the end of the input data cards causes an AT END
condition.

4. Simplified MOVE Statement Now that we are able to OPEN
files and READ input files, we must learn how to manipulate input
data to produce output. The simplest method for obtaining data in
the output area is to MOVE it there.

A MOVE statement has the following format:

> MOVE (data-name-1) TO (data-name-2)

Any field in storage may be moved to another field by the
MOVE instruction. MOVE instructions do not transfer data from one
area to another but *duplicate* data from one field in the other.

Example

Consider the input and output records in Figure 11.2 and the corresponding COBOL program for the first three divisions in Figure
11.3. The first five statements of the PROCEDURE DIVISION are:

```
PROCEDURE DIVISION.
     OPEN INPUT CARD-FILE, OUTPUT TAPE-FILE.
     READ CARD-FILE AT END GO TO EOJ.
     MOVE NAME-IN TO NAME-OUT.
     MOVE AMT-OF-CREDIT-IN TO AMT-OF-CREDIT-OUT.
     MOVE AMT-OF-DEBIT-IN TO AMT-OF-DEBIT-OUT.
```

5. WRITE Statement The WRITE instruction takes data accumulated in the output area of the DATA DIVISION and transmits it
to the device specified in the ENVIRONMENT DIVISION.

The WRITE statement has the following format:

> WRITE (record name)

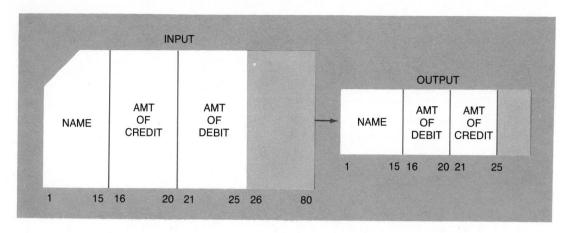

Figure 11.2
Input and output formats for sample program.

One important point must be noted. While *files* are *read*, we *write records.*

6. GO TO Statement   Most COBOL programs operate on more than one input record. We may assume that programs are written only if there is a reasonable amount of input data to be processed. Thus we must learn how to repeat the series of steps given. After we WRITE, we wish to *branch* to the READ instruction to begin the series of steps again. A branch is coded by a GO TO instruction.

GO TO (paragraph name)

The GO TO statement transfers control to the *paragraph name* indicated. Thus to branch, we insert a paragraph name, followed by a period, *prior* to the branch point and then code a GO TO instruction after we have completed processing a single record.

The rules for forming paragraph names conform to programmer-supplied name formats with one exception. A programmer-supplied name must have at least one alphabetic character; a paragraph name can contain all digits. It is best, however, to use Englishlike paragraph names such as ADD-ROUTINE, END-OF-JOB, START1, etc.

Such paragraph names must be unique. That is, EOJ as a paragraph, may not appear as a date name or as another paragraph name.

Paragraph names may be coded on separate lines:

```
START1.
    READ CARD-FILE AT END GO TO EOJ
```

```
IDENTIFICATION DIVISION.
PROGRAM-ID. SAMPLE.
ENVIRONMENT DIVISION.
INPUT-OUTPUT SECTION.
FILE-CONTROL.
    SELECT CARD-FILE ASSIGN TO SYS005-UR-2540R-S.
    SELECT TAPE-FILE ASSIGN TO SYS008-UT-2400-S.
DATA DIVISION.
FILE SECTION.
FD  CARD-FILE RECORDING MODE IS F, LABEL RECORDS ARE OMITTED,
    RECORD CONTAINS 80 CHARACTERS, DATA RECORD IS CARD-REC.
01  CARD-REC.
    02  NAME-IN             PIC X(15).
    02  AMT-OF-CREDIT-IN    PIC 9(5).
    02  AMT-OF-DEBIT-IN     PIC 9(5).
    02  FILLER             PIC X(55).
FD  TAPE-FILE RECORDING MODE IS F, LABEL RECORDS ARE OMITTED,
    RECORD CONTAINS 25 CHARACTERS, DATA RECORD IS TAPE-REC.
01  TAPE-REC.
    02  NAME-OUT            PIC X(15).
    02  AMT-OF-DEBIT-OUT    PIC 9(5).
    02  AMT-OF-CREDIT-OUT   PIC 9(5).
```

Figure 11.3
Coding of first three divisions of sample COBOL program.

or on the same line as the corresponding instruction:

```
START1.    READ CARD-FILE AT END GO TO EOJ.
```

Make certain, however, that there is at least one space after the period that follows the paragraph name. The READ statement may begin anywhere within Margin B.

For the problem in Figures 11.2 and 11.3, the PROCEDURE DIVISION entries can be coded so that the steps are properly repeated:

```
PROCEDURE DIVISION.
      OPEN INPUT CARD-FILE, OUTPUT TAPE-FILE.
START1.
      READ CARD-FILE AT END GO TO EOJ.
      MOVE AMT-OF-CREDIT-IN TO AMT-OF-CREDIT-OUT.
      MOVE AMT-OF-DEBIT-IN TO AMT-OF-DEBIT-OUT.
      WRITE TAPE-REC.
      GO TO START1.
```

7. End-of-Job Functions   We are practically ready to write *complete* COBOL programs. We must learn, however, how to end or terminate a program.

You will recall that a program that has a READ instruction for a sequential input file must have an AT END clause indicating what should be done when there is no more input:

```
READ CARD-FILE AT END GO TO EOJ.
```

For the above, we wish to branch to a paragraph called EOJ when there are no more cards. At an end-of-job paragraph, called EOJ above, the files must be deactivated and the run terminated. In addition, any final or total routines may be performed if required.

There are two statements that *must* be coded before the program is complete. Files are deactivated by a CLOSE statement:

```
CLOSE (file name(s))
```

All files that have been opened must be closed at the end of a job. The files must not be categorized as input or output in a CLOSE statement.

The run must be terminated with a

```
STOP   RUN
```

instruction. This statement returns control to the supervisor or control program which in turn, reads in the next program.

As indicated these two statements are required before a program can be considered complete. An end-of-job routine can, however, contain any totalling or printing required.

1. Code the OPEN and READ statements for a program that reads tape data and prints an output report.

2. Consider the following:

```
PROCEDURE DIVISION.
    OPEN INPUT TAPE-FILE OUTPUT PRINT-FILE.
START1.
    READ TAPE-FILE AT END GO TO FINISH.
    MOVE TAPE-IN TO PRINT-REC.
    WRITE PRINT-REC.
    GO TO START1.
```

The above program excerpt will proceed from the READ statement to _____, unless _____, at which time a branch to _____ will occur.

3. Is the following a valid COBOL statement?

READ CARD-FILE.

4. The READ statement is coded in Margin _____.

5. Is the following a valid COBOL statement?

READ TAPE-FILE AT END MOVE ZERO TO CTR
GO TO PART-2.

6. Indicate what, if anything, is wrong with the following:

```
PROCEDURE DIVISION.
    OPEN INPUT FILE-1, OUTPUT FILE-2.
BEGIN.
    READ REC-1 AT END GO TO EOJ.
    MOVE REC-1 TO REC-2.
    WRITE FILE-2.
    GO TO BEGIN.
```

7. Indicate what, if anything, is wrong with the following:

WRITE REC-2 AT END GO TO EOJ.

8. The two statements required to terminate a COBOL program are _____ and _____.

9. The purpose of the CLOSE statement is to _____.

10. What, if anything, is wrong with the following:

STOP THE RUN.

11. (T or F) If any total routines are required in the program, they should be performed after the CLOSE statement.

Solutions

1. OPEN INPUT TAPE-1 OUTPUT PRINT-1.
   READ TAPE-1 AT END GO TO EOJ.

2. the next sequential step (MOVE)

there are no cards to be read

FINISH

3. No (it must contain an AT END clause)

4. B

5. Yes

6. READ statement should be: READ FILE-1 AT END GO TO EOJ.
   WRITE statement should be: WRITE REC-2.

7. The WRITE statement must not contain an AT END clause

8. CLOSE
   STOP RUN

9. deactivate the files and devices used in the program.

10. The word "THE" is incorrect. It should read: STOP RUN.

11. False—they should be performed *before* the files are deactivated.

Review Questions

1. When the computer encounters a READ command in the PROCEDURE DIVISION, how does it know which of its input units to activate?

2. Give two functions of the OPEN statement.

3. When are paragraph names assigned in the PROCEDURE DIVISION?

4. State which of the following, if any, are invalid paragraph-names:
   a. INPUT-RTN
   b. MOVE
   c. 123
   d. %-RTN

5. If a READ statement is used for a sequential file, what clause is required? Why?

   Make necessary corrections to each of the following (6–10). Assume that spacing and margin use are correct:

6. OPEN MASTER-IN, MASTER-OUT.

7. PROCEDURE DIVISION
   START 1.
       OPEN INPUT OLD-FILE, OUTPUT NEW-FILE
   UPDATE-RTN
       READ OLD-REC AT END GO TO EOJ.
       MOVE OLD-REC TO NEW-REC.
       WRITE NEW-REC.

8. CLOSE INPUT FILE-A, OUTPUT FILE-B.

9. WRITE REC-A AT END GO TO EOJ.

10. START1.
       OPEN INPUT X, OUTPUT Y.
       READ X AT END GO TO EOJ.
       MOVE FLDA TO FLDB.
       WRITE X-REC.
       GO TO START1.

Problems

1. Write a program to create a master tape file from input sales records. The input is on punched cards in the following format:

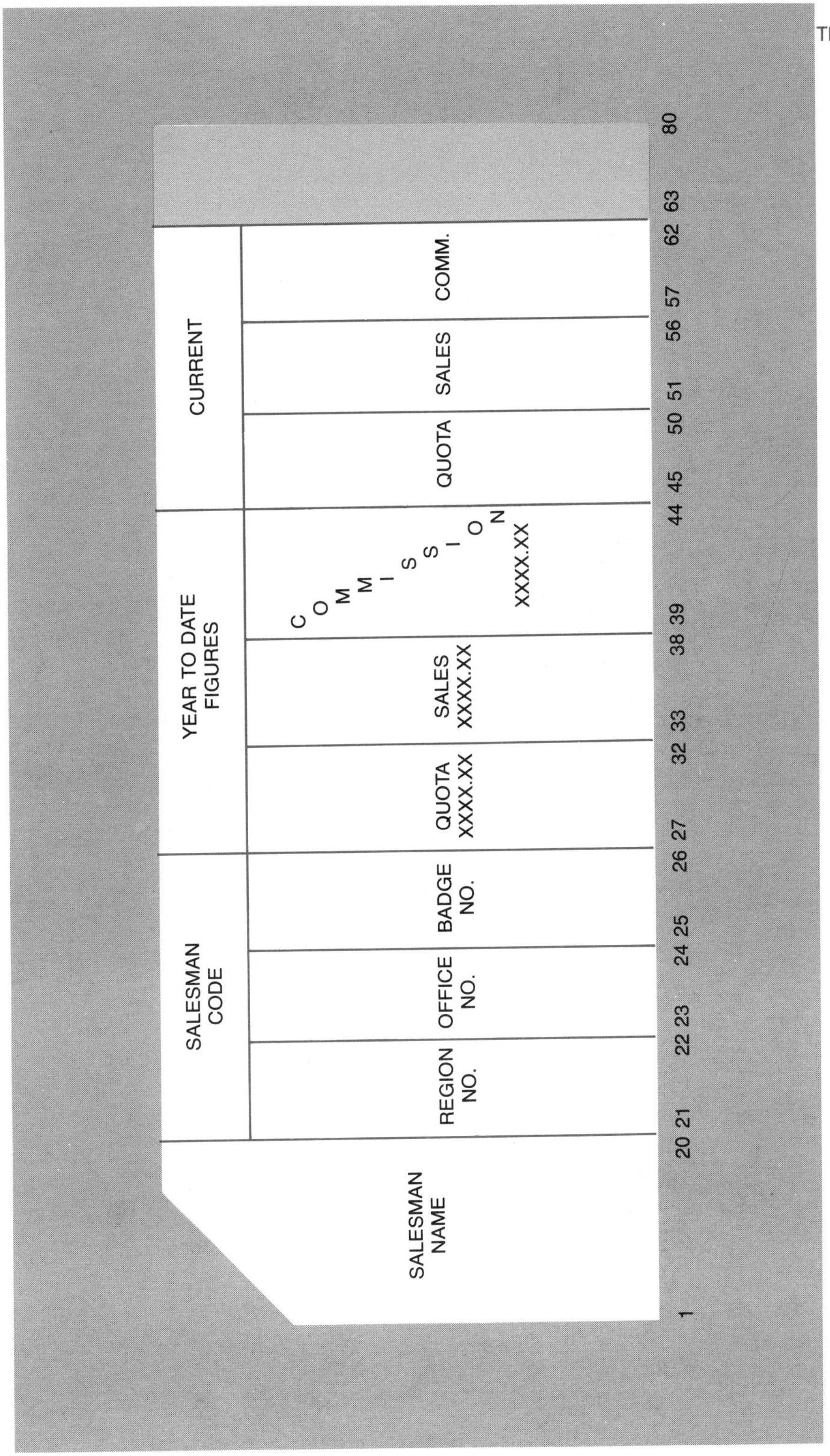

SALESMAN NAME

SALESMAN CODE
- REGION NO.
- OFFICE NO.
- BADGE NO.

YEAR TO DATE FIGURES
- QUOTA XXXX.XX
- SALES XXXX.XX
- COMMISSION XXXX.XX

CURRENT
- QUOTA
- SALES
- COMM.

Column positions: 1 20 21 22 23 24 25 26 27 32 33 38 39 44 45 50 51 56 57 62 63 80

The output is on magnetic tape which contains standard labels and is blocked 20. The output format is exactly the same as the input.

2. Write a program to punch output salary cards from the following input employee record card format:

cc		
	1–20	Employee name
	21–25	Salary
	26	Number of dependents
	27–31	F.I.C.A. (xxx.xx)
	32–36	State tax (xxx.xx)
	37–41	Federal tax (xxx.xx)
	42–80	Unused

The output contains only employee name and salary as its first two fields. The remainder of the output card should be blank.

(*Hint:* You must move SPACES to output record to ensure that the FILLER in the last 55 positions is blank.)

8. MOVE Statement

a. Numeric MOVE

MOVE $\begin{pmatrix} \text{numeric literal} \\ \text{data-name} \end{pmatrix}$ TO (data-name)

Numeric Literal: All numbers, + or − sign to left of number, decimal point if appropriate

Examples

```
MOVE    12.5    TO    FLD1.
MOVE    FLDA    TO    FLDB.
```

Rules for Numeric Move
1. Integer portions are moved right to left
2. High-order (leftmost) nonfilled integer positions are zero-filled
3. Fractional portions are moved left to right
4. Low-order (rightmost) nonfilled fractional positions are zero-filled

Examples

```
MOVE    TAX    TO    TOTAL
```

	TAX		TOTAL	
	PICTURE	CONTENTS	PICTURE	CONTENTS AFTER MOVE
1.	99V99	10$_\wedge$35	999V999	010$_\wedge$350

2. 99V9   37$_\wedge$2   999   037
3. 9(4)   1234   999   234
4. V99   12   V9 $_\wedge$1
5. 99V99   02$_\wedge$34   9V9   2$_\wedge$3
6. 9V9   1$_\wedge$2   V99 $_\wedge$20

Examples

MOVE   12.35   TO   AREA-1

                    AREA-1
             PICTURE   CONTENTS

1.   999V99   012$_\wedge$35
2.   999V9   012$_\wedge$3
3.   999V999   012$_\wedge$350
4.   9V9   2$_\wedge$3
5.   V999 $_\wedge$350

b. Nonnumeric MOVE

MOVE (nonnumeric literal / data-name) TO [data-name]

Nonnumeric literal: Any group of characters enclosed in quotes

Examples:

'ABC'
'12.6CD'

Rules for Nonnumeric MOVE
1. Movement is from left to right
2. Low-order nonfilled positions are filled with blanks

Examples

MOVE   CODE   TO   FLD1.

	CODE		FLD1	
	PICTURE	CONTENTS	PICTURE	CONTENTS AFTER MOVE[3]
1.	XXX	ABC	X(4)	ABCb̸
2.	XXX	ABC	X(2)	AB
3.	XXX	ABC	X(3)	ABC

[3] A blank is denoted by a b with a slash through it (b̸).

c. Moving figurative constants

> MOVE (figurative constant)   TO   (data-name)

Figurative Constant: ZEROS and SPACES (reserved words with special meaning)

Examples
1.   MOVE ZEROS TO (data-name)
     Result: moves zeros to entire field
2.   MOVE SPACES TO (data-name)
     Result: moves blanks to entire field

9. Compute Statement

a. Introduction   In COBOL, the following verbs can be used to perform arithmetic operations:

ADD
SUBTRACT
MULTIPLY
DIVIDE

Rather than learning the rules for each arithmetic statement, you will be provided with rules governing the COMPUTE statement, a "short-cut" method for performing one or more arithmetic operations.

The COMPUTE statement uses arithmetic symbols rather than arithmetic verbs. The following symbols may be utilized in a COMPUTE statement:

    + corresponds to ADD
    − corresponds to SUBTRACT
    * corresponds to MULTIPLY
    / corresponds to DIVIDE
        denotes EXPONENTIATION
    (no corresponding COBOL verb
    exists)

The following examples illustrate the use of the COMPUTE verb.

Examples
1.   COMPUTE TAX   =   .05 * AMT
2.   COMPUTE A   =   B * C/D
3.   COMPUTE NET   =   AMT − .05 * AMT

Note that the COMPUTE statement has a data-name to the left of, or preceding, the equal sign. The value computed from the arithmetic expression to the right of the equal sign is made equal to the data field.

Thus, if AMT = 200 in Example 1, TAX will equal 200 × .05, or 10, at the end of the operation. The original contents of TAX before the COMPUTE is executed is not part of the operation. The fields specified to the right of the equal sign remain unchanged.

COBOL rules for spacing are crucial when using the COMPUTE statement. All arithmetic symbols must be preceded and followed by a space.

In place of the COMPUTE statement, the arithmetic verbs ADD, SUBTRACT, MULTIPLY, DIVIDE may be used. Indeed, for some compilers, the COMPUTE verb is unacceptable and these four arithmetic verbs *must* be used. Table 11.1 indicates how these four statements are utilized.

Use of Arithmetic Verbs in COBOL

Table 11.1

Arithmetic Statement	Value After Execution of the Statement			
	A	B	C	D
ADD A TO B	A	A + B		
ADD A, B, C TO D	A	B	C	A + B + C + D
ADD A, B, C, GIVING D	A	B	C	A + B + C
SUBTRACT A FROM B	A	(B–A)		
SUBTRACT A, B FROM C	A	B	[C–(A + B)]	
SUBTRACT A, B FROM C GIVING D	A	B	C	C–(A + B)
MULTIPLY A BY B	A	(A × B)		
MULTIPLY A BY B GIVING C	A	B	A × B	
DIVIDE A INTO B	A	(B/A)		
DIVIDE A INTO B GIVING C	A	B	(B/A)	
DIVIDE A BY B GIVING C	A	B	(A/B)	

b. ROUNDED Option Consider the following example:

COMPUTE C = A + B

A		B		C	
PICTURE	CONTENTS	PICTURE	CONTENTS	PICTURE	CONTENTS AFTER ADD
99V999	12$\wedge$857	99V999	25$\wedge$142	99V99	37$\wedge$99

This situation is not uncommon in programming. Two fields, each with three decimal positions, are added together, and the answer desired is only valid to two decimal places. In the above example, the computer adds the two fields A and B, and obtains the sum $37 \wedge 999$ in an accumulator. It attempts to place this result into C, a field with two decimal positions. The effect is the same as performing the following MOVE operation: MOVE 37.999 TO C. The low-order decimal position is truncated. Thus C obtains the sum of $37 \wedge 99$.

It should be clear that a more desirable result would be $38 \wedge 00$. Generally, we consider results more accurate if answers are ROUNDED to the nearest decimal position.

To obtain rounding of results, the ROUNDED option may be specified with any arithmetic statement or with the COMPUTE statement:

Examples

1. COMPUTE C ROUNDED = A + B
2. COMPUTE E ROUNDED = T * 1.6

c. ON SIZE ERROR Option   Let us suppose that the following operation were performed:

COMPUTE D = A + B + C

The fields before the operation look like this:

A		B		C		D	
PICTURE	CONTENTS	PICTURE	CONTENTS	PICTURE	CONTENTS	PICTURE	CONTENTS
999	800	999	150	999	050	999	000

The computer will add 800, 150, 050 in an accumulator. It will attempt to place the sum, 1000, into a three-position field. The effect would be the same as an internal MOVE operation: MOVE 1000 TO D. Since numeric MOVE operations move integer data from right to left, 000 will be placed in D. In such a case, where the resultant field is not large enough to store the accumulated sum, we say that an overflow or *size error* condition has occurred. It is important to note that the computer will not stop or "hang up" because of a size error condition. It will merely truncate high-order positions of the field. In our example, 000 will be placed in D.

The best way to avoid a size error condition is to be absolutely certain that the receiving field is large enough to accommodate any possible result. Sometimes, however, the programmer, who must be concerned with many details, forgets to account for the rare occasion when an overflow might occur. COBOL has a built-in solution. Each time any arithmetic operation is performed, use an ON SIZE ERROR option as follows:

COMPUTE   D = A + B + C ON SIZE ERROR
           GO TO ERROR-RTN

In addition to the above, a size error condition will occur whenever an attempt is made to divide by zero.

The full format for the COMPUTE statement is:

$$\text{COMPUTE (data name)} \quad \underline{\text{ROUNDED}} = \begin{bmatrix} \text{literal} \\ \text{arithmetic expression} \\ \text{data name} \end{bmatrix}$$

$$\underline{\text{ON SIZE ERROR}} \text{ (imperative statement)}$$

Self-Evaluating Quiz

1. Are the following two statements equivalent?
   a. ADD 1 TO A.
   b. COMPUTE A = A + 1.
2. What, if anything, is wrong with the following COMPUTE statements?
   a. COMPUTE A = B + C ROUNDED
   b. COMPUTE A = 10.5
   c. COMPUTE E = A * B / * C + D
   d. COMPUTE X = (4 / 3) * PI * (R * * 3)
   e. COMPUTE X + Y = A
   f. COMPUTE 3.14 = PI
3. Do the following pairs of operations perform the same function?
   a. COMPUTE SUM = 0
      MOVE ZEROS TO SUM
   b. COMPUTE A = A − 2
      SUBTRACT 2 FROM A.
   c. COMPUTE X = A * B − C * D
      COMPUTE X = (A * B) − (C * D)
   d. COMPUTE Y = A − B * C − D
      COMPUTE Y = (A − B) * (C − D)

Solutions

1. Yes
2. a. ROUNDED follows the receiving field: COMPUTE A ROUNDED = B + C
   b. Okay
   c. /* may not appear together; each symbol must be preceded by and followed by a data field or a numeric literal.
   d. Okay.
   e. Arithmetic expressions must follow the equal sign, not precede it: COMPUTE A = X + Y.
   f. Data-names, not literals, must follow the word COMPUTE: COMPUTE PI = 3.14.

3. a. Same
    b. Same
    c. Same
    d. First = A − (B × C) − D
        Second = (A − B) × (C − D)
        Not equivalent; see discussion below

d. Hierarchy of operations Let us now examine the following COMPUTE statement:

$$\text{COMPUTE } D = A + B / C$$

Depending upon the order of evaluation of arithmetic operations, one of the following is the mathematical equivalent of the above:

(a) $D = \dfrac{A + B}{C}$ (b) $D = A + \dfrac{B}{C}$

Note that (a) and (b) are not identical. If A = 3, B = 6, and C = 3, the result of the COMPUTE statement evaluated according to the formula in (a) is 3 and, according to the formula in (b), is 5.

The hierarchy of arithmetic operations is as follows:

1. **
2. * or /
3. + or −

Exponentiation operations are evaluated, or performed, first. Multiplication and division operations follow any exponentiation and precede addition or subtraction operations. If there is more than one multiplication or division operation, they are evaluated from left to right. Addition and subtraction are evaluated last, also reading from left to right.

Thus, COMPUTE A = C + D ** 2 results in the following order of evaluation.

1. D ** 2   Exponentiation
2. C + (D ** 2)   Addition

The formula, then, is $A = C + D^2$, not $A = (C + D)^2$.

COMPUTE S = T * D + E/F results in the following order of evaluation:

1. T * D   Multiplication
2. E/F   Division
3. (T * D) + (E/F)   Addition

The formula, then, is $A = T \times D + \dfrac{E}{F}$

THE FUNDAMENTALS
OF COBOL

Thus in the statement COMPUTE D = A + B/C the calculation is as follows:

1. B/C
2. A + B/C

The formula, then, is $D = A + \dfrac{B}{C}$ or formula (b).

To alter the order of evaluation in a COMPUTE statement, parentheses are used. Parentheses supersede all hierarchy rules.

10. Conditional Statements

a. Simple Condition We will define a conditional statement as any sentence that performs an operation dependent upon the occurrence of some condition. Such statements, in COBOL, generally begin with the word IF and as such are performing a specific test.

The basic format for all conditional statements is as follows:

$$\text{IF (condition)} \quad \begin{pmatrix} \text{imperative} \\ \text{statement(s)} \end{pmatrix} \left\{ \begin{bmatrix} \underline{\text{ELSE}} \\ \underline{\text{OTHERWISE}} \end{bmatrix} \begin{pmatrix} \text{imperative} \\ \text{statement(s)} \end{pmatrix} \right\}$$

An imperative statement, as opposed to a conditional statement, is any COBOL expression that issues a direct command to the computer regardless of any existing conditions. ADD A TO B, MOVE C TO D, OPEN INPUT MASTER-TAPE are examples of imperative statements that do not test for values but perform direct operations. Hence we say that COBOL statements are divided into two basic categories: imperative and conditional.

A condition as indicated in the format above tests for a specific relation. A *simple condition,* which is the topic discussed in this section, is a single relation test of the following form:

1.	IF A IS EQUAL TO B	or	IF A = B
2.	IF A IS LESS THAN B	or	IF A < B
3.	IF A IS GREATER THAN B	or	IF A > B

If the simple condition is met, then the imperative statement or statements following it are executed, the entire ELSE clause is ignored, and the program continues execution with the very next sentence. If the simple condition is *not* met, the entire ELSE clause is executed and the program continues with the next sentence.

Keep in mind that conditional statements, for proper execution, must utilize data fields that have the same modes. In the statement, IF A = '123' MOVE C TO D, it is assumed that A is an alphanumeric field, since it is compared to a nonnumeric literal. As in MOVE operations, the literal should be in the same form as the data name. If B is a numeric field, with a PICTURE clause of 9's, the following conditional would be appropriate: IF B = 123 MOVE E TO F.

In the case where data fields are compared to one another, both fields should be numeric, alphabetic, or alphanumeric. In the statement, IF A = B GO TO RTN1, both A and B are either numeric, alphabetic, or alphanumeric.

Regarding the comparisons of numeric fields, the following are considered equal:

    012
     12.00
     12
    + 12

This implies that comparisons are performed logically. Although 12.00 does not have the same configuration as 012, their numeric values are known to be equal.

Similarly, when comparing alphanumeric or alphabetic fields, the following are considered equivalent:

    ABC
    ABC⌷ (⌷ denotes a blank space)

Blanks, or spaces, will not upset the balance of equivalence. Only significant positions are compared.

When performing an alphanumeric comparison, the hierarchy is as follows:

$$\text{⌷ABC} \ldots \text{Z0123} \ldots 9$$

Thus A is less than B which is less than C, etc. Any letter is considered less than any digit. The comparisons are performed from left to right.

Note that several imperative statements may appear within one conditional. Thus the following is valid:

```
IF A < B COMPUTE A = B + C GO TO RTN5
OTHERWISE COMPUTE E = F + G GO TO RTN6.
```

The above statement may be flowcharted as shown in Figure 11.4.

The full range of conditionals include the following:

Sign Test We can test a data field to determine its value relative to zero:

Figure 11.4

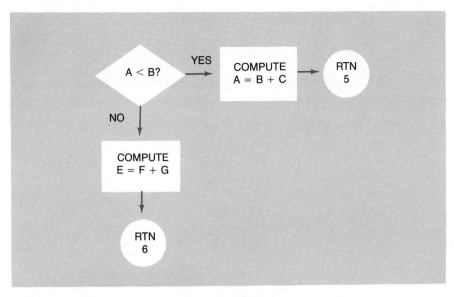

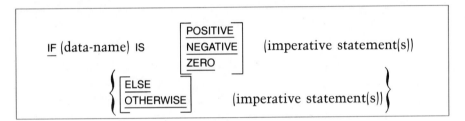

Note that saying IF A = ZERO is the same as saying IF A IS ZERO. If a numeric field contains an amount less than zero, it is considered negative. If it has an amount greater than zero, it is considered positive:

$$
\begin{array}{rl}
- \ 387 & \text{is negative} \\
382 & \text{is positive} \\
+ \ 382 & \text{is positive} \\
0 & \text{is neither negative nor positive}
\end{array}
$$

Class Test   We can test the *format* of a field as shown below:

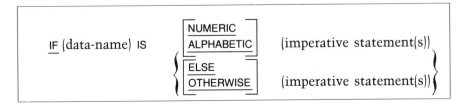

In the NUMERIC class test, the IF clause is executed when the data field contains strictly numeric data; the ELSE or OTHERWISE option is executed when the data field is either alphabetic or al-phanumeric. In the ALPHABETIC class test, the IF clause is exe-cuted when the data field contains letters and/or blanks only.

Negated Conditionals All simple relations, class or sign tests may be formed using a negated conditional:

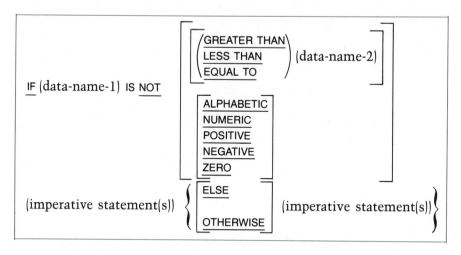

b. Compound Conditionals To be an efficient program-mer, it is not enough simply to learn the rules of a programming language. We must be able to apply these rules to difficult logic problems. The conditional statement, as illustrated is of prime im-portance in solving these logic problems. The *compound condi-tional* greatly extends the significance of IF statements. It enables the programmer to test for several conditions within one state-ment, and thus eases the difficulties in logic.

To perform an operation or a series of operations if any one of several conditions exists, the compound conditional may be utilized. Each condition within the statement may be separated by the COBOL word OR, to imply that any one of the conditions so stated will cause execution of the imperative statement:

IF (condition-1) OR (condition-2) . . . (imperative statement(s))

$$\left\{ \begin{array}{c} \text{ELSE} \\ \text{OTHERWISE} \end{array} \right. \qquad \text{(imperative statement(s))} \left. \right\}$$

Examples
1. IF A = B OR B > C GO TO RTN5.
2. IF A < 3 OR A = 5 MOVE A TO B ELSE GO TO ERR-RTN.
3. IF A = 5 OR 7 GO TO RTN1.

The number of conditions that may be specified in one statement is relatively limitless depending only upon the physical limitations of the computer.

Note that in Example 3 there is an *implied* operand. That is, we implied the data name A in the second condition (A = 7). This is permitted in ANS COBOL only.

By using OR in a compound conditional, any of the conditions specified will cause execution of the first imperative statement. If none of the conditions is met, either the ELSE option, if used, or the next sentence will be performed.

If a statement is to be executed only when all of several conditions are met, then the COBOL word AND may be used in the compound conditional.

IF (condition-1) AND (condition-2) . . . (imperative statement(s))

{ [ELSE / OTHERWISE] } (imperative statement(s))

Note that the ELSE or OTHERWISE condition will be performed if any *one* of the stated conditions is not met.

Hierarchy Rule
1. Conditions surrounding the word AND are evaluated first.
2. Conditions surrounding the word OR are evaluated last.
3. When there are several AND connectors or OR connectors, the AND conditions are evaluated first, as they appear in the statement, from left to right. Then the OR conditions are evaluated, also from left to right.
4. Parentheses supersede all hierarchy rules.

Examples
Indicate whether the following statement tests to determine if A is between 10 and 100:

IF A < 100 or A = 100 AND A = 10 or A > 10 GO TO PRINTOUT-RTN.
*****

No. Using the hierarchy rule for evaluating compound conditionals, the first conditions to be considered are those surrounding the word AND.

Then, from left to right, those surrounding the OR groupings are evaluated. Thus, we have:

        1.   IF A = 100 AND A = 10

OR 2.   A < 100

OR 3.   A > 10

We see that the compound expression in (1) is an impossibility: A can never equal 10 and, at the same time, be equal to 100. Since the first expression will never cause a branch, it can be eliminated from the statement, which reduces to:

IF A < 100 OR A > 10 GO TO PRINT-RTN.

This, obviously, is not the solution to the original problem. In addition to the above two conditions, we want to branch to PRINT-RTN if the field is equal to either of the two endpoints, 10 or 100.

The original statement would have been correct if we could change the order of evaluation. If the following order of evaluation were utilized, the statement would be correct:

        1.   IF A < 100 or A = 100

AND 2.   A = 10 OR A > 10

To change the normal order of evaluation, place parentheses around the conditions to be evaluated together. Parentheses supersede the hierarchy rule. All conditions within parentheses are evaluated together. Thus the following statement is correct:

IF (A < 100 OR A = 100) AND (A = 10 OR A > 10) GO TO PRINT-RTN.

When in doubt about the normal sequence of evaluation, make use of the parentheses.

Important Terms Used in this Chapter

DATA DIVISION	IDENTIFICATION DIVISION
ENVIRONMENT DIVISION	PROCEDURE DIVISION
FILE SECTION	WORKING-STORAGE SECTION

Review Questions

Code the following flowchart exercises with a single statement (1–3).

1.

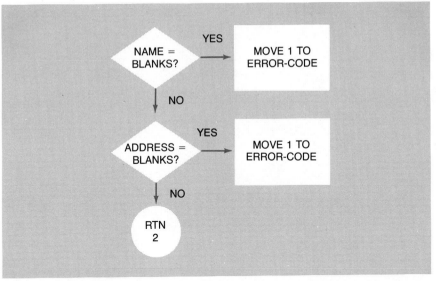

2.

3.

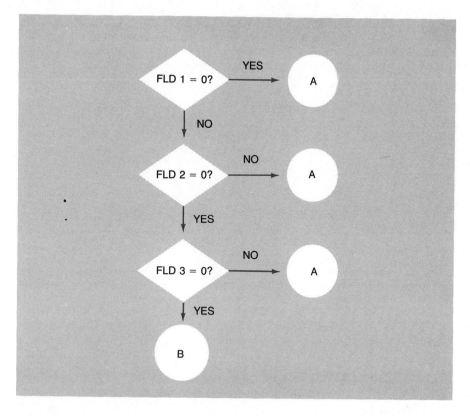

State whether FIELDA is equal to, greater than, or less than FIELDB (4–8):

	FIELDA	FIELDB
	FIELDA	FIELDB
4.	012	12
5.	12.0	12
6.	−89.0	89.0
7.	ABC	ABC∅
8.	43	+43

9. Write a routine for determining FICA where a field called SALARY is given. FICA is equal to 5.85% of SALARY up to $16,500.00. Salary in excess of $16,500.00 is not taxed.

10. Find the largest of four numbers A, B, C, and D and place it in the field called HOLD.

Are the following groups of statements equivalent (11–14)?

11. (a) IF A = B COMPUTE D = C + D ELSE COMPUTE F = E + F. GO TO RTN-1.
    (b) IF A = B COMPUTE D = C + D GO TO RTN-1 ELSE COMPUTE F = E + F.
12. (a) IF A IS POSITIVE GO TO RTN-X ELSE GO TO RTN-Y.
    (b) IF A IS NOT NEGATIVE GO TO RTN-X ELSE GO TO RTN-Y.
13. (a) IF DISCOUNT IS GREATER THAN TOTAL GO TO ERR-RTN ELSE SUBTRACT DISCOUNT FROM TOTAL.

(b)   IF TOTAL IS GREATER THAN DISCOUNT OR TOTAL = DISCOUNT NEXT SEN-
TENCE ELSE GO TO ERR-RTN. SUBTRACT DISCOUNT FROM TOTAL.

14.   (a)   IF A = B ADD C TO D GO TO RTN-5 ELSE GO TO RTN-5.

    (b)   IF A = B ADD C TO D. GO TO RTN-5.

What, if anything, is wrong with the following statements (15–20)?

15.   IF A IS GREATER THAN OR EQUAL TO B GO TO RTN-3.

16.   IF A IS NOT EQUAL TO B OR A IS NOT EQUAL TO C GO TO RTN-4.

17.   IF A DOES NOT EQUAL 5 GO TO STEP-3.

18.   IF A = 3 OR IF A = 4 GO TO RTN-2.

19.   IF A = '123' GO TO BEGIN.

20.   IF B = '23' or B = 21 GO TO END1.

21.   Write a routine to branch to a paragraph called NO-TEMP if C is between
98.6 and 100.2, inclusive.

Problems

1.   Write a program to create output tape records from the following input
tape:

      1–34   Identifying data
    35–39   Sales amount xxx.xx
       40   Not used

The output record format is as follows:

      1–34   Same as input
    35–39   Sales amount xxx.xx
    40–41   Discount % .xx
    42–46   Discount amount xxx.xx
    47–51   Net xxx.xx
    52–75   Not used

NOTES

(a)   Both files have standard labels and are blocked 10.

(b)   If sales exceed $100.00, allow 3% discount.
If sales are $100.00 or less, allow 2% discount.

(c)   Discount amount = Sales × Discount %.

(d)   Net = Sales − Discount amount.

2.   Write a program to print out patient name and diagnosis for each of the
following input medical cards:

1–20	Patient name	
21	Lung infection	1–if found
		0–if not found
22	Temperature	1–high
		0–normal
23	Sniffles	1–present
		0–absent

24 Sore throat

1–present
0–absent

25–80 Not used

NOTES

(a) Output is a printed report with heading:
     DIAGNOSIS REPORT

(b) If patient has lung infection and temperature, diagnosis is
     PNEUMONIA.

(c) If the patient has a combination of two or more symptoms
     (except the combination of lung infection and temperature),
     the diagnosis is COLD.

(d) If the patient has any single symptom, or no symptoms, the
     diagnosis is PHONY.

3. Write a program for a dating service that uses the following format for
    its input data:

    1–20   Name
    21–23   Weight (in lbs.)
    24–25   Height (in inches)
    26   Color of eyes: 1–Blue, 2–Brown, 3–Other
    27   Color of hair: 1–Blonde, 2–Brown, 3–Other
    28–79   Not used
    80   Sex   M–male, F–Female

Output is punched cards with the names of all:

(1) Blonde hair, blue-eyed males over 6 feet tall and weighing
     between 185 and 200 lbs.

(2) Brown eyed, brown hair females between 5 feet 2 inches
     and 5 feet 6 inches and weighing less than 120 lbs. All
     other combinations should not be printed.

4. Write a program to generate, in effect, a compiler program. Input shall
    be punched cards with the following format:

    ccs   1–2   Operation code
           3–12   First operand (field to be operated upon)
           13–22   Second operand
           23–80   Not used

Operation Codes

    10   corresponds to ADD
    20   corresponds to SUBTRACT
    30   corresponds to MULTIPLY
    40   corresponds to DIVIDE
    50   corresponds to STOP RUN

Program should read in each input card, perform the required operation, and print the result. For example, an input card with 20 0000080000 0000010000 as its first 22 positions should result in the printing of 0000070000 (80000−10000)

(*Hint:* Make sure that the output field is large enough to accommodate the answer.)

5. Write a program to accept, as input, cards that have a date in Columns 1–6 in the form of month/day/year, i.e., 022579 refers to Feb. 25, 1979. If the date is valid, convert it to Julian date (year/day of year). (In the above example, the Julian date would be 79056.) Punch an output card with the resultant Julian date.

(*Hint:* Leap years have 29 days in FEB. All others have 28 days in FEB.)

6. Write a program to read a detail Bank Transaction Tape with the following format:

    1–19 Name of depositor
      20 Type 1–Previous balance, 2–Deposit, 3–Withdrawal
    21–25 Account number
    26–30 Amount xxxxx
    31–50 Not used

The tape records are blocked 50 and have standard labels. The tape is in sequence by account number. Type 1 records exist for each account number followed by Types 2 and 3, if they exist. Types 2 and 3 may be present for a given account number and may appear in any sequence.

Print out the name of the depositor and his current balance (Previous Balance + Deposits − Withdrawals). Also print the heading BANK REPORT.

7. Write a program to print an inventory reorder form for each specified card input. Information on the inventory reorder form is obtained from the card record and its corresponding tape record. Input, then, consists of a detail card record and a master inventory tape record:

    CARD INPUT   MASTER TAPE INPUT

    1–10   Product name   1–5   Product number
    11–15 Product number   6–15 Product name
    16–80 Not used   16–20 Unit price xxx.xx
                                   21–35 Name of vendor

                                   block size is 10; standard labels

If an input card for a specific product exists, find the corresponding tape record and print PRODUCT NUMBER, PRODUCT NAME, and NAME OF VENDOR. When there are no more cards, stop the run. Cards and tape are in product number sequence. Print the heading: INVENTORY REORDER FORM. (*Hint:* A flowchart may be helpful before attempting to code the program.)

Unit Three: Selected Bibliography

Programming—COBOL
1. *COBOL Programming*, Nancy and Robert Stern, 2nd edition (New York: 1975).
2. *Standard COBOL*, Mike Murach, (Chicago: 1971).
3. *A Simplified Guide to Structured COBOL Programming*, Daniel D. McCracken, (New York: 1976).

Unit Four
Programming in a Time-Sharing Environment

Chapter 12
A Guide to
Terminals and Time-Sharing

12

12

I. Why Terminals

We have seen that a major objective of commercial computers is the processing of vast amounts of data in a relatively short period of time.

One bottleneck that frequently occurs, however, is in the time required to physically transport input to the computer room and then transport the required output to the proper department or business area.

Using traditional data processing methods there are several steps necessary to ensure proper control of input and output (see Figure 12.1). These steps are usually performed by a Control Unit Staff within a data processing center.

Figure 12.1
Conventional data processing methods.

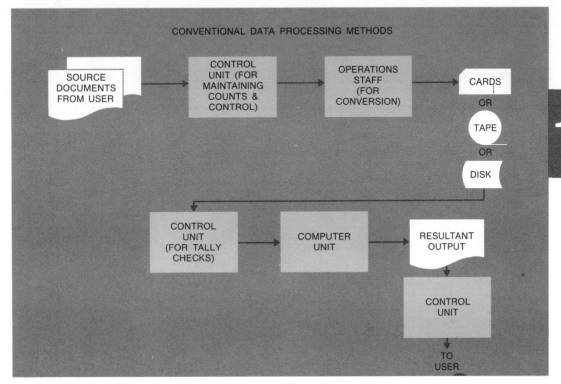

CONVENTIONAL DATA PROCESSING METHODS

SOURCE DOCUMENTS FROM USER → CONTROL UNIT (FOR MAINTAINING COUNTS & CONTROL) → OPERATIONS STAFF (FOR CONVERSION) → CARDS OR TAPE OR DISK

CONTROL UNIT (FOR TALLY CHECKS) → COMPUTER UNIT → RESULTANT OUTPUT → CONTROL UNIT → TO USER

12

Manual Procedures that Reduce Computer Efficiency

1. Incoming source documents must be logged in: to ensure that no source documents are lost in transit, a Control Unit Staff must maintain a count and check to see if the number of records received is the same as the number sent. Documents are then usually transmitted to an Operations Staff for conversion to a machine-readable form such as card, tape, or disk.

2. Tally checks on source documents and the resulting input records must be performed to ensure proper conversion: when source document counts match the number of input records, then input is sent to the computer room for processing and source documents are returned to originating department.

3. Resulting output from computer run must be logged out and sent to originating department.

Each of the above procedures relies, in large part, on manual operations which can result in inefficiencies or which can produce delays. Thus while it may only require 30 minutes to process data,

an entire job may take three or four days to complete, including the transmittal of the input to the data processing center, conversion to a machine-readable form, use of various control procedures, and transmittal back again from the data processing center.

Many jobs require methods that will reduce this overall time. We have thus far discussed some systems that use MICR and OCR equipment to eliminate the conversion process (see Chapter 6). But even with these systems, there are still transmittal problems.

Terminal equipment is used by an increasing number of companies to reduce delays caused both by transmittal of data and by conversion. See Figure 12.2 for illustrative terminal equipment.

A. Use of Terminals in a Teleprocessing Environment

Teleprocessing, sometimes called *data communications*, is a concept in data processing that uses terminals to facilitate the flow of data both into and out of a computer center.

Teleprocessing systems usually make use of the following:

Features of Teleprocessing
1. Remote Terminals: these are devices, usually with typewriter-like keyboards for entering data, which are placed in remote locations. That is, such terminals do not appear in a computer room with a CPU as do traditional input/output devices but are placed at the point of data entry. Hence, these devices might be in a different department, a different building or even a different geographic location from the main frame or CPU.
2. Communication Link: these remote terminals must be linked in some manner, to the CPU. Usually leased or public telephone lines provide the communication link from a remote terminal to a CPU.
3. Computer System: standard medium- and large-scale computer systems in use today are capable of accepting input from remote terminals. Special programming is, however, required.

Figure 12.3 provides an illustration of a sample teleprocessing system.

B. Advantages of Teleprocessing: An Overview

We have thus far suggested a major advantage of teleprocessing, the saving of time in the transmittal of data. In addition, data entered at remote terminals can be checked for validity and tallied where necessary, thereby eliminating the need for additional manual checks and procedures.

Another major reason for using teleprocessing equipment is for immediate or online processing in preference to batch process-

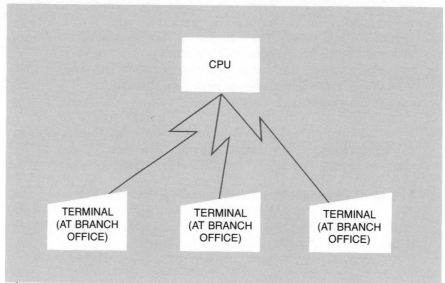

Figure 12.3

Sample
teleprocessing
system.

ing. Terminals can be linked to a CPU so that they have direct access to files or so that data entered can be immediately processed. Immediate accessing and immediate processing are two main objectives of many teleprocessing systems. An airline reservation system is a prime example of a teleprocessing system with these two objectives.

Lastly, teleprocessing systems often eliminate the conversion process. That is, frequently purchase orders, payroll changes, and customer inquiries are keyed directly onto the terminal eliminating the need to prepare a source document which later must be converted to a machine-readable form.

In short, the advantages of teleprocessing can be summarized as follows:

Advantages of Teleprocessing

1. CONTROL UNIT STAFF NEED NOT MAINTAIN TALLIES: incoming data is automatically transmitted and hence there is no need for controls.
2. MESSENGERS NOT NEEDED TO TRANSPORT DATA BETWEEN DEPARTMENTS AND COMPUTER ROOM
3. CONVERSION PROCESS IS MINIMIZED: input data can be keyed directly into the terminal.
4. COMPUTER CAN BE PROGRAMMED TO OPERATE ON DATA ONLINE, THAT IS, IMMEDIATELY, AS IT IS ENTERED: this provides a more responsive alternative to batch processing.

A central computer can have numerous terminals hooked up to it. These terminals may be utilized by separate *departments* employing a central computer, or by separate *companies* employing a central computer. These terminals may be located in the same building, to be used by various departments, or they may be spread out across the country if the user departments or businesses are not centrally located. (See Figure 12.4.)

The recent rise in the use of terminals in businesses today signals a major advance in computer technology. With the use of terminals in many departments throughout companies, the communication gap between data processing personnel and businessmen is minimized. The *direct* transmittal of data from departments to the Data Processing Center increases the contact between data processing and management while it minimizes inefficiencies and communication errors. Thus, it is imperative for business and data processing students to be cognizant of how these devices can enhance operations within specific business areas.

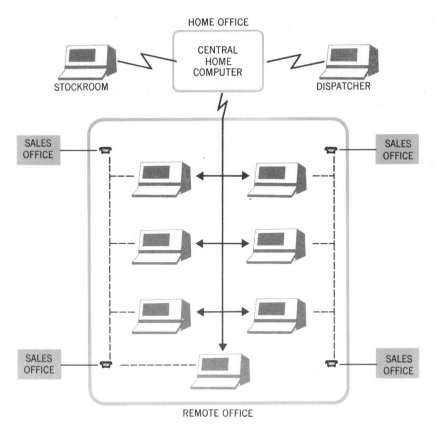

Figure 12.4

Illustration of terminals remotely linked to a central computer. Courtesy UNIVAC.

This chapter will attempt to enlighten students as to the potential of terminals in business, and will indicate how to effectively utilize and understand terminal processing.

Self-Evaluating Quiz

1. Computers can process data in a relatively short time. Timing problems in data processing do occur, however, in _____.
2. Thus, while computer operations generally present no timing difficulties, _____ operations do.
3. _____ is the term applied to an area of data processing that facilitates the flow of information both into and out of a computer center with the utilization of terminal equipment.
4. Remote terminals are _____.
5. (T or F) Remote terminals are usually in the same physical room as the Central Processing Unit.
6. Remote terminals sometimes use _____ to connect them to the CPU.
7. (T or F) Data entered into a terminal must be converted to a machine-readable form.
8. (T or F) The input unit of a terminal usually resembles a typewriter keyboard.
9. Terminal processing eliminates much of the _____ necessary in other forms of processing data.
10. (T or F) A central computer can have only one terminal hooked up to it.
11. The direct transmittal of data from departments to the Data Processing Center minimizes _____.

Solutions

1. getting the data *to* the computer and transmitting the output *from* the computer to the business area
2. manual
3. Data communications or teleprocessing
4. devices that are hooked up to a central computer but are physically located in different areas or business departments so that these departments can have access to a computer.
5. F
6. leased or public telephone lines
7. F
8. T
9. manual intervention or control
10. F
11. manual inefficiencies or communication gaps

II. Data Communications Concepts

There are four major areas in which terminal technology is most often employed. Let us discuss each in detail.

A. Remote Data Entry

As we have noted, numerous terminals, spaced remotely in key locations, may have access to a central computer for the purpose of entering input. These terminals may be placed in different departments, such as Payroll, Accounts Receivable, Inventory, Accounts Payable. In this way, the Accounts Receivable Department, for example, can enter billing data into the computer via its terminal and the Payroll Department can similarly enter salary changes via its terminal. Both departments, then, have direct access to one central computer that is capable of processing all the data.

Several terminals may also be used within a *single* department. Suppose, for example, that the Inventory Department has several warehouses throughout the United States. To computerize inventory procedures *without* the use of terminals, these warehouses would be required to prepare inventory statements and send them to the Data Processing Center where they would be logged in and then converted to a machine-acceptable form, prior to computer processing. The transmittal of this data would be performed manually and could, therefore, become very inefficient. With the use of remote data entry, however, terminals can be placed at each of these warehouses. The inventory data can then be transmitted speedily and *directly* to the computer via the terminal without conversion or rigid manual controls. The computer can accumulate all warehouse data efficiently and effectively by minimizing manual intervention (see Figure 12.5).

In short, terminals may be used in many different business areas for the remote accumulation of data. Let us consider the two main techniques that can be used for processing data entered remotely.

1. Immediate Processing When input data is entered from a terminal for the purpose of *immediately* altering the contents of records on a file, an *online* operation is required. That is, the computer processes the input data as it is entered and alters or *updates* the required files immediately. Terminals are utilized to enter data for online operations, since they provide immediate and direct input to the data processing flow, eliminating the need for manual transmittal and for batch processing. Magnetic disks are most often utilized for storing files when data is to be updated online, since they provide the ability to access records via terminals directly and rapidly.

An Inventory disk file, for example, may be altered or updated by an online operation at the precise time that changes in stock items are keyed into the computer by a terminal. In this way, all inventory data on the disk is current and may be used to answer inquiries or to produce printouts at any time. Without the use of online processing, data files would only be current immediately after a periodic (weekly, semimonthly, monthly) update procedure.

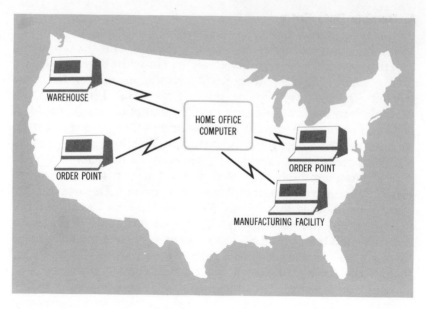

Figure 12.5

Remote data entry inventory system.
(a) Four branch offices throughout country
(b) Request for an item made directly at either
ORDER POINT
(c) If item is in stock, WAREHOUSE is notified by computer and item is shipped
(d) If on-hand stock of item is depleted, MANUFACTURING FACILITY is notified by
computer to produce more.   Courtesy UNIVAC.

At all other times, these files would not contain changes that have
occurred during the current period or cycle.

In short, terminals are often used for online operations where
immediate updating of files is considered a necessity.

Point-of-Sale (POS) systems are the most re-
cent advance in teleprocessing and are a form of remote data entry.
In these systems, the remote terminals are specially designed cash
registers. The clerk, who serves as a terminal operator, keys in item
number, amount of purchase, units purchased and, in department
stores, charge account number for purchases to be charged. In addition to a sales receipt, this system produces marketing and inventory information which is then processed by the CPU. In such a
system, the computer keeps an account of items to be reordered,
departments with the best sales records, and so on. In addition to
its widespread use in major department stores, point-of-sale systems are becoming increasingly popular in supermarkets as well
for electronic check-out systems.[1] Figure 12.6 provides an illustration of a typical point-of-sale system.

---

[1]The reasons for consumer opposition to electronic check-out systems will
be explored in Chapter 17.

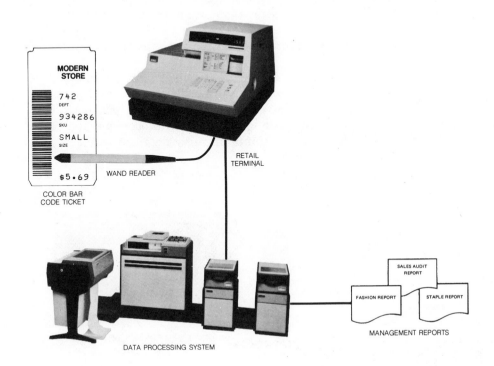

MODERN
STORE

742
DEPT

934286
SKU

SMALL
SIZE

$5.69

COLOR BAR
CODE TICKET

WAND READER

RETAIL
TERMINAL

SALES AUDIT
REPORT

FASHION REPORT

STAPLE REPORT

MANAGEMENT REPORTS

DATA PROCESSING SYSTEM

Figure 12.6
Example of a typical point-of-sale system. Courtesy National Cash Register.

2. Offline Processing

a. Description of Offline Operations While terminals are frequently used when immediate access to a CPU is desired, it is also possible to use terminals for batch-processing. In this case, data is entered on a terminal and is then converted to high-speed media such as punched paper tape, magnetic tape, or magnetic disk. This operation is performed directly at a remote location. Since the conversion is *not under the control of the CPU*, it is called an *offline* procedure.

b. Batch Processing Using Terminals When all the data has been entered and stored in an offline operation, the entire file created can be transmitted to the CPU in *batch-processing mode*. This is a more efficient method of processing for two main reasons:

Advantages of Using Terminals for Offline Entry (To Be Processed Later in Batch-Processing Mode)

1. Amount of communication time is significantly reduced: transmission of high-speed data (tape or disk) over communication lines is much faster than when an operator keys in data. Since the actual keying in of data by an operator is performed offline, no communication cost is associated with the conversion.

2. Communication lines may be used when rates are cheaper, that is, after working hours or during the night: since the use of telephone lines during working hours is very expensive, offline operations which allow for (1) batch processing, and (2) more suitable hours for communicating data can result in a significant cost savings.

Figure 12.7

C.O.D.E. (Computer Oriented Data Entry) scanner. This is a terminal device which reads data from embossed plastic cards utilizing an optical scanning unit and converts the data, offline, to either a punched paper tape or a magnetic tape. This paper tape or magnetic tape then serves as input, using communication lines, to a computer system. Courtesy Addressograph Multigraph Corp.

c. Illustration of Offline Operation for Remote Data Entry Suppose a department store chain, with several branches, wishes to computerize its Accounts Receivable system so that customers' charges can be automatically credited to their accounts. When immediate updating of accounts is desired, point-of-sale systems are utilized. When, however, charged data can be stored at the location where the purchase was made for some fixed period of time, then an offline operation can be used for entering the data. After working hours, all such data can be processed, in a batch-processing mode, and used to update the main files (see Figure 12.7).

In summary, when a terminal is used for converting data to a more efficient medium using specialized equipment *not directly under the control of the computer,* we call this an offline operation. Offline conversions followed by batch processing of data from high-speed devices can result in substantial savings of computer time, where online processing is not required.

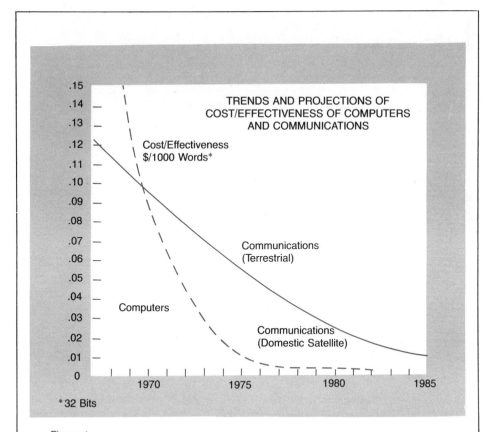

Figure 1

The most significant development in the near future of communications will be the drop in the cost of transferring a bit of information. The carrier component of the costs is falling at about 15% annually, the computer component even more rapidly. Here the measurement is in $/1000 32-bit words. Source: The Diebold Research Program.

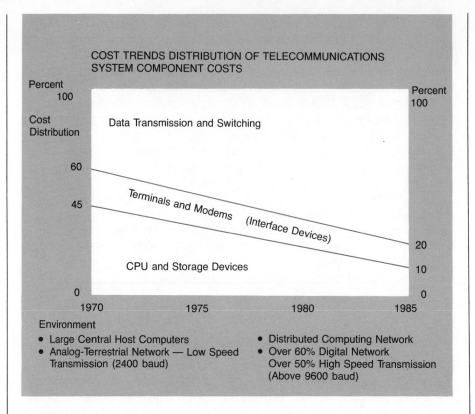

COST TRENDS DISTRIBUTION OF TELECOMMUNICATIONS SYSTEM COMPONENT COSTS

Percent 100

Cost Distribution

Data Transmission and Switching

60

Terminals and Modems (Interface Devices)

45

CPU and Storage Devices

0

Percent 100

20

10

0

1970   1975   1980   1985

Environment

* Large Central Host Computers
* Analog-Terrestrial Network — Low Speed Transmission (2400 baud)

* Distributed Computing Network
* Over 60% Digital Network Over 50% High Speed Transmission (Above 9600 baud)

Figure 2

Terminal and modem costs are expected to drop very little, and processing costs to drop rapidly, making transmission costs an ever larger percentage of the total communications cost. Source: The Diebold Research Program.

B. Inquiry

A central computer with files of data stored on a medium such as a disk may be accessed by remote terminals for the purpose of requesting information. That is, the terminal at a remote location is *not* used to update or alter a file, but to make inquiries concerning the data on that file.

Various businesses require terminal devices for inquiry purposes. Brokerage firms, for example, rely on such devices for quoting stock prices to their customers. A central, direct-access file is maintained with stock prices which are updated online as new prices become available. This file can be accessed by a wide variety of stock brokers with terminals at their desks. To obtain a price, the stock code is keyed in. The computer receives this code immediately, accesses the price from the file, and transmits the information back to the terminal. In this way, any stock price may be quoted within seconds. The computer itself must be preprogrammed to accept the inquiry, seek the appropriate information, and transmit it to the user.

Insurance firms also use inquiry terminals to quote insurance rates to their customers. Such terminals are *not* used to alter central files but only to access them.

The terminal is a beneficial method of access or inquiry only when information must be extracted from a file *immediately*. When a request can be delayed, or answered at a later date, then the expense of utilizing terminals is generally not justified.

Terminals are generally used for inquiry purposes where:

Terminals for Inquiry

1. Customers need immediate replies to inquiries.
2. Business representatives or managers need information for decision-making purposes.

C. Real-Time Systems

Figure 12.8 illustrates the use of terminals for *both* remote data entry *and* for inquiries. The stockroom, for example, has a terminal for accumulation of data, while the executive offices use a terminal for inquiry on stock levels, about which companywide decisions are made. This combination is called a real-time system.

A *real-time* system is one that has the capability of accessing *and* updating computer files using terminal equipment quickly enough to affect decision-making. A typical example of such a system is an airlines reservation system. This is a real-time application, where customers can request airline information and receive responses quickly enough to make a decision concerning the reservation of an airplane seat.

1. Description of Airlines Reservation System   A customer can inquire about a specific flight or about flights leaving for a specific location on a given day. The airline representative keys the inquiry into a terminal. The terminal is hooked up to a central computer, which immediately accesses the data and prints the requested information on the terminal. This information can include flight number, date of departure, time, destination, arrival time, number of seats available, and so on. If the customer wishes to make a reservation, the airline representative can enter the appropriate data into the terminal. The data will be used to immediately *update* the main file, which would then indicate one less space on the specific flight. Similarly, cancellations can be keyed into the terminal to update the file so that it reflects one more space. These terminals may be placed in hundreds of airline offices throughout the country.

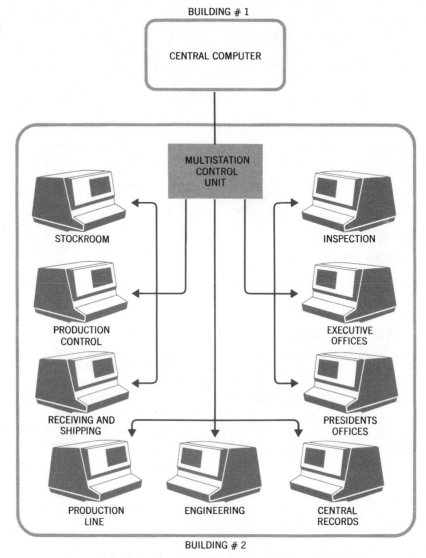

BUILDING # 1

CENTRAL COMPUTER

MULTISTATION
CONTROL
UNIT

STOCKROOM

INSPECTION

PRODUCTION
CONTROL

EXECUTIVE
OFFICES

RECEIVING AND
SHIPPING

PRESIDENTS
OFFICES

PRODUCTION
LINE

ENGINEERING

CENTRAL
RECORDS

BUILDING # 2

Figure 12.8
The use of terminals for both the remote accumulation of data and for inquiries.
Courtesy UNIVAC.

2. Other Examples of Real-Time Systems   Thus real-time systems are *online* systems with the facility of *accessing and updating* files using terminal equipment, *quickly enough to affect decision-making*. This is also referred to as an *interactive data communications system*. This type of processing is utilized by hotel reservation systems, as well as airlines. Banks frequently use real-time systems to update accounts and to answer inquiries concerning specific transactions. Betting establishments use terminals in a real-time environment to key in statistics. The computer can then instantaneously print the existing odds.

Real-time systems may also be employed for the internal operations of a company, in an integrated manner. In this way, management can make quick and effective decisions based on inquiries made to the computer via terminal equipment. That is, profits and losses, assets and liabilities, profit ratios, and so on may be maintained accurately and precisely through real-time processing, and may be accessed, at any time, by management for the purpose of making executive-level decisions.

Real-time systems utilize the most sophisticated programming and systems techniques in data processing today. They can generally be employed only in large-scale companies that can afford the vast equipment required. Real-time systems require large expenditures both for sophisticated equipment and for high-level programming effort. Although they do not initially result in savings to a company because of their great expense, the intangible benefits (to the customers served, or to management, which can employ real-time systems for its decision-making) can produce high profits in the long run.

D. Remote Job Entry (RJE)

1. Definition of RJE When a large-scale computer system is implemented, it is possible for the system to run several jobs at the same time. To maximize the efficient use of these systems, terminals may be set up, at remote locations, to be used for entering small programs and the necessary data.

Remote Job Entry is the term used to describe the process of entering input along with a program on a terminal. RJE terminals process input and receive output as well.

2. Uses of RJE Terminals, then, may be used for *time-sharing* operations. A large company has a central computer; it permits users to share the computer's time via terminals for the purpose of entering programs and/or data to be processed. This is quite advantageous for small companies which find the cost of acquiring and maintaining their own systems prohibitive.

Note that in the previous three applications of terminal equipment, the terminal devices were used either for input or input/output. The program to accept and transmit this data was already stored in the computer. That is, an airlines reservation clerk who keys an inquiry into the computer will not receive a reply unless the computer has been previously programmed to accept the input. Similarly, the terminals at warehouses throughout the country may not be used to key in inventory data in an online environment unless the central computer has a stored program that instructs it to *accept* the data. With terminals used for RJE, however, these devices can be used to key in *programs* first. These programs are generally simple ones, since the terminal, as a manual device, is not a very efficient method for entering large-scale programs. Most often, these simplified programs are coded in BASIC, a programming language specifically suited for terminal processing. Once the program has been transmitted to the CPU via the terminal, any required data can be entered.

Prediction

"The market for remote job entry services (RJE) will grow from 25,000 clients and $360 million in gross revenues in 1975 to 115,000 clients and $1.3 billion by 1984.

Revenue from health care applications, to grow the most rapidly, will increase five-fold over the decade, while revenues from banking and finance will quadruple. Scientific applications, which currently account for more than 25% of the remote job entry market, will decline in importance to a 2% market share by 1984."

Computer Digest, May 1977. Reprinted with permission.

---

3. RJE as a Teaching Tool   RJE, using terminals linked to a CPU, has recently become highly effective in educational institutions for teaching programming. A school may have several terminals linked to its CPU. Students are taught the BASIC language and can then write programs and enter data on the terminal to be transmitted to the CPU. The results and/or any programming errors are immediately indicated.

4. RJE as a Scientific Tool   Many companies find great benefit in using a central computer with terminals in various engineering offices or technical locations. Engineers or scientists with equations to solve can utilize a terminal in conjunction with a computer to obtain a solution. The scientists are spared tedious hours necessary for manually solving mathematical problems that the computer can do accurately and efficiently in seconds. Here, again, most programs are usually written in BASIC.

5. Summary   From the above, we can see that teleprocessing, or Data Communications, is an exceedingly useful and efficient method of processing data. The following is a summary of Teleprocessing uses:

Teleprocessing Systems
1.   Remote Data Entry
     a.   IMMEDIATE: Example—Point-of-Sale System
     b.   OFFLINE: not directly under the control of CPU; data

processed in batch-processing mode; results in considerable savings in communications (telephone) cost

2. Inquiry: immediate access to CPU and central computer files
3. Real-Time: combines features of Remote Data Entry (immediate) and inquiry
4. Remote Job Entry: program and input entered on terminal at remote locations

Self-Evaluating Quiz

1. Name the four major areas in which terminals are most often used.
2. A(n) _____ operation is the entering of data from terminals so that it may be transcribed or converted to another medium for future batch processing.
3. (T or F) Offline operations result only in computer transmittal of data from the terminal to another device, such as a tape or disk drive, for future processing.
4. (T or F) Offline operations may be performed when immediate processing by the computer is not required.
5. (T or F) A stock exchange would be likely to store incoming stock quotations on an offline device for future processing rather than immediately updating the master file.
6. (T or F) A bank that performs its updating once a day would be likely to store incoming transactions on an offline device for future processing rather than immediately updating the master file.
7. When input data is entered from a terminal for the purpose of immediately altering the contents of a file, a(n) _____ operation is required.
8. One example of an online operation is a(n) _____.
9. Data communications systems for inquiry purposes most often utilize _____ files, since they have the advantage of increasing the _____.
10. Terminals are most often used for inquiry purposes when _____ and _____.
11. A(n) _____ system is one that has the capability of accessing and updating computer files in an online environment, using terminal equipment, for decision-making purposes.
12. (T or F) Real-time systems utilize offline operations to immediately update files.
13. (T or F) Real-time systems are generally used only by large companies since they are very costly.
14. Entering both a program and input from terminals at remote locations is called _____.
15. _____ and _____ are examples of remote job entry users.

Solutions

1. remote data entry; inquiry; real-time systems; remote job entry
2. offline
3. T
4. T
5. F—Stock exchanges require the data immediately.
6. T
7. online
8. reservation system
9. direct-access or disk; speed of access
10. customers require information; managers require company data
11. real-time
12. F—online
13. T
14. remote job entry
15. Educational institutions; engineering firms

III. Equipment

There are three major facets of a data communications system:

Facets of Data Communications Systems
1. Terminal Devices
2. Communication Lines
3. Computer System

A. Terminal Devices

As we have indicated, terminal devices are located wherever large amounts of input data are anticipated. That is, it is important to space remote terminals at strategic points where the data flow is the greatest.

1. Commonly Used Terminals   Most terminals have the capability of both transmitting and receiving computer messages. Even for remote data entry where transmitting data to a CPU is the main requirement, some facility for receiving computer messages is usually necessary (control messages, error messages, and so on, from computer to operator).

a. Terminal typewriter or keyboard (figure 12.9)   This is the most widely used terminal. It can receive messages and send them.

Figure 12.9
Keyboard terminal.
Courtesy IBM.

The device is like a typewriter. When input is entered, an operator keys the data by depressing the various keys in much the same way as data is typed on a typewriter. It generally has a standard alphanumeric keyboard, where all characters are included. There is a typed *hard-copy* printout of all data entered. A *hard-copy* printout is one that may be maintained for future reference, as opposed to data displayed on a screen, which is not available in tangible form after it is viewed. When the computer communicates with the user, the typewriter is activated by the CPU, and the required information is printed on the typed sheet.

As indicated, this is the most widely used I/O terminal. Operators may key in input consisting of stock receipts, purchase orders, payroll changes, and so on. In addition, these operators can make requests of the computer via the terminal and receive immediate responses (see Figure 12.10).

b. Cathode ray tube with keyboard or light pen The keyboard is the standard input medium. An operator keys in data or makes inquiries using this typewriterlike unit.

The cathode ray tube (CRT) is a visual display device similar to a television screen (see Figure 12.11). This output unit instantaneously displays information from the computer on the screen. This is a high-speed device, since data is *not* transmitted to a typed page using a relatively slow print device. Instead, large amounts of information can be displayed instantly.

As indicated, the keyboard is the standard transmittal unit for the CRT. A light pen can also serve as an input tool, to be used for making graphic corrections or additions to the visual display on the cathode ray tube. An operator simply uses the pen to modify data on the screen. These modifications are then transmitted to the CPU. (See Figure 12.12.)

Figure 12.10

Traveling computer terminal. This IBM communication terminal, mounted on a four-wheeled cart and connected to an IBM computer by cable, lets an industrial engineer quickly spot any recurring problems on an assembly line. After singling out a car for computer review, the engineer uses his traveling computer terminal to tell a centrally located IBM computer everything that has been listed on the car's inspection log as it is indexed along the assembly line. Any recurring problems are quickly spotted, and immediate action may be taken to alleviate the condition. Courtesy IBM.

CRT devices are extremely beneficial where output from a computer is desired at remote locations very quickly. Airline terminals, for example, use cathode ray tubes to display flight information. Changes to the data displayed on the screen are made instantaneously. Similarly, stock brokerage firms use CRTs in conjunction with a keyboard for requesting the latest stock quotations. The computer responses are displayed on the screen (see Figure 12.13). Such CRT output provides *soft copy,* a visual display with no permanent record.

For high-speed output, CRT devices are extremely beneficial. They are, however, more costly than other terminals. If hard-copy versions of the output are necessary, then CRT devices must be equipped with additional features such as a printer or a display copier (see Figure 12.12).

c. Graph plotter and CRT with graphics capability A graph plotter is often used with a keyboard for I/O teleprocessing. The keyboard is used for making inquiries. The plotter produces an

Figure 12.11
Display terminal. Courtesy DatagraphiX, Inc.

Figure 12.12

Cathode ray tube terminal with keyboard. Operator can make modifications to the displayed data using a light pen. Drawings, diagrams, charts, etc. can be modified with the use of this electronic light pen. The display copier can produce a hard copy version of information which is visually displayed on the CRT. Courtesy IBM.

output graph that is transmitted from the CPU. This is a very useful terminal for management, to be used for decision-making, and for engineers and mathematicians, who require charts and graphs that display specific activities (see Figure 12.14). New CRT's with graphics capability are now available which can perform the functions of a graph plotter, as well as the traditional terminal functions.

d. Audio response unit The input unit may be a keyboard, where requests are typed. Or, the input unit may be telephone equipment, where the dialing of appropriate digits or codes or the depressing of keys with touchtone equipment, results in a computer inquiry. The computer-generated output or response is a verbal one instead of a printed one. The computer is equipped with various prerecorded key phrases or words that are extracted, as required, for the purpose of answering a specific request, and are transmitted via an audio response unit.

Many banking establishments use telephone equipment as audio response units. A customer wishes to cash a check at a branch office. The touchtone digits are used to key in the customer's account number and the amount of his or her check. The

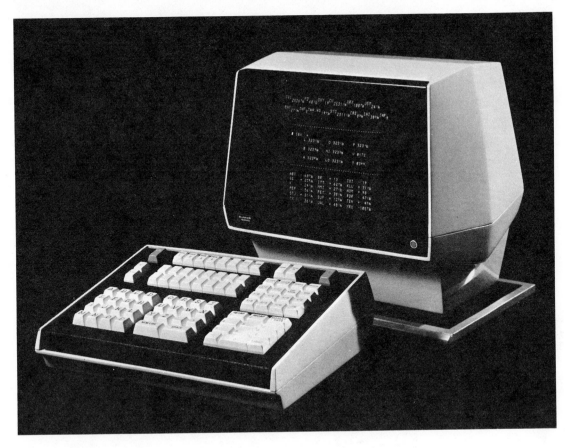

Figure 12.13
Teleprocessing system which provides stock brokers with simultaneous display of data from tickers, newswires, and stock market data bases. System can also be used to transmit buy and sell orders. Courtesy Bunker Ramo Corp.

computer then determines if the account has sufficient funds on hand. The appropriate response is then transmitted to the teller via the telephone (an audio response unit). The teller will then either cash the check or politely refuse, depending on the computer's response. (See Figure 12.15.)

Rapid On-Line Order Entry
RAPIDVOICE, an on-line order entry service of Rapidata, Inc., Fairfield, NJ, has replaced a segment of the manual order taking operation at Hoechst-Roussell Pharmaceuticals, Inc., a subsidiary of American Hoechst, Somerville, NJ. The on-line service allows Hoechst-Roussel customers or salesmen to input product codes directly by push-button phone (or dial) and receive simulated voice responses to instantly verify inventory status, pricing and other information.

According to Joseph Macaluso, manager, information systems, errors in ordering have been reduced because there are no transcription steps between the person doing the ordering and the computer. Orders are transmitted to American Hoechst's IBM 370/158 under OS/VSI and CICS using a special program called RAPID-LINK. "RAPIDLINK effectively bridges the Rapidata network to our CPU," says project leader George Fear, senior programmer/analyst, American-Hoechst. He states that system installation was relatively easy. Major portions of the development and implementation of the first testing phase were completed in about a month.

e. Traditional input/output devices modified for teleprocessing It is not unusual for remote data entry or remote job entry to use the following forms of equipment.

Figure 12.14

Graph plotter.
Tektronix, Inc.

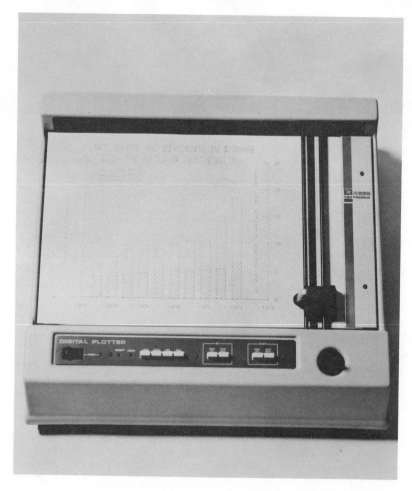

Figure 12.15
Touch-Tone telephone used in teleprocessing system.
(a) Touch-Tone telephones can be used to transmit billing information to a central billing and service organization to automatically control inventories, purchasing, shipping, etc.
(b) Here, a bank teller uses a Touch-Tone telephone to call a remote computer and request the status of an account. After keying the account number and a code for the information desired, the teller receives a voice response. Courtesy Bell System Data Communications Service.

Transmittal
1. Punched Card Reader
2. Paper Tape Reader
3. Magnetic Tape
4. Magnetic Disk
5. Optical Character Reader

When offline operations are used, some high-speed medium is frequently employed to take the place of the slower, keyboard entry.

Receive
1. Card Punch
2. Printer
3. Paper Tape Punch

2. Factors To be Considered When Selecting Terminal Equipment   There are several factors that must be considered in determining the most suitable terminal equipment for a given application. The following represents a partial list:

a.   *Computer and communication lines* (to be discussed in the next sections)

The computer and the communication lines must be compatible with the terminals under consideration. You will see that some terminals require high-speed lines and highly complex computer equipment.

b.   *Functions to be performed by the terminal*

It is obviously inefficient to select an input/output terminal if a strict output one would serve the purpose. That is, an input/output device should only be selected if computer response to the remote station is a requirement or if the businessman and computer specialist think that it may be a requirement in the future.

c.   *Cost*

d.   *Speed*

The speed of transmission will normally vary directly with the cost of the device. Slow-speed terminals transmit approximately 20 characters per second, while high-speed devices can transmit as many as several thousand characters per second. There are numerous speeds available between these limits. A device must be selected that is fast enough to serve the needs of the company within budgetary limitations.

e.   *Human adaptability*

In most cases, input to the terminal is provided by an operator who keys in the appropriate data. Unless the device selected is easy to operate, training time may prove to be excessive. One reason for the popularity of the keyboard device is that it is very similar to a typewriter, and special training is therefore unnecessary. When establishing the type of data to be entered as input to the terminal, human adaptability must be considered. A *conversational code*, for example, is generally easier for an operator to transmit than, perhaps, a digital code. The former consists of words and phrases that are more meaningful to an operator than a series of digits. In most cases, there is less error when transmitting conversational codes.

f.   *Size and type of display*

If large amounts of data are required as output on a single printed line, then the size of the output display must be considered. That is, if 100 characters must be displayed on a single line, then some typewriter terminals are not appropriate, since only a maximum of 72 characters can be displayed on some devices. Since the various output units differ widely in their characteristics, we will not list them all. Notice, however, that size is a key factor when determining the terminal device to employ. For some applications a hard copy or permanent-record output is required and for others a soft copy or visual display is more appropriate.

B. Communication Lines

The actual grade of telephone lines used in a data communication system may be classified as follows:

Communication Lines

TYPE	CHARACTERISTICS
Teletype Lines	Least costly, slowest
Voice Grade Telephone Lines	Most common, some noise on lines interferes with transmission
Leased Private Telephone Lines	Most expensive, eliminates noise

---

In order to convert terminal data to an electronic form which can be transmitted over communication lines, a special interface device is required. Similarly, the unit must be able to convert messages transmitted from the computer across communication lines back into a form acceptable by the terminal. Two such devices are:

Interfaces

Hard-wired modem (modulator-demodulator): device providing a permanent connection between a terminal and a CPU (Figure 12.16)

Acoustic coupler: device connected to terminal which enables the terminal to access a CPU, using any standard telephone

---

Figure 12.17 illustrates typical types of data transmission in a remote job entry system.

C. Computer Requirements

A computer used in conjunction with teleprocessing equipment generally requires the following:

Figure 12.16
A modem. Courtesy
Burroughs Corp.

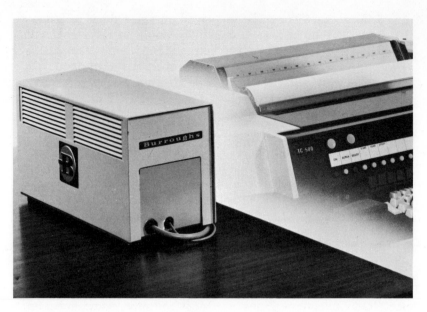

Computer Requirements for Teleprocessing

1. A Large CPU Storage Capacity: this is necessary so that the computer can hold incoming and outgoing messages in case of busy lines. That is, when queues occur, the computer must possess enough *buffer* areas to store messages. In addition, a large CPU is needed to hold the operating system programs.

2. Complex Control: a highly sophisticated control system is required to effectively process data with numerous entry points.

3. Interrupt ability: because of priority schedules, the computer is often required to interrupt a given task so that it may execute a more urgent one. It must possess the ability to then complete the previous job. This condition is often compounded by several operations that may require the use of a given device at the same time. In such cases, the interrupts must proceed from job to job.

4. Multiprogramming Facility: the ability to partition primary storage so that several programs may be executed at the same time is called multiprogramming.

Chapter 10 includes a more extensive discussion of these concepts.

IV. Advantages and Disadvantages of Data Communications

The following will serve as a summary of the features of data communications:

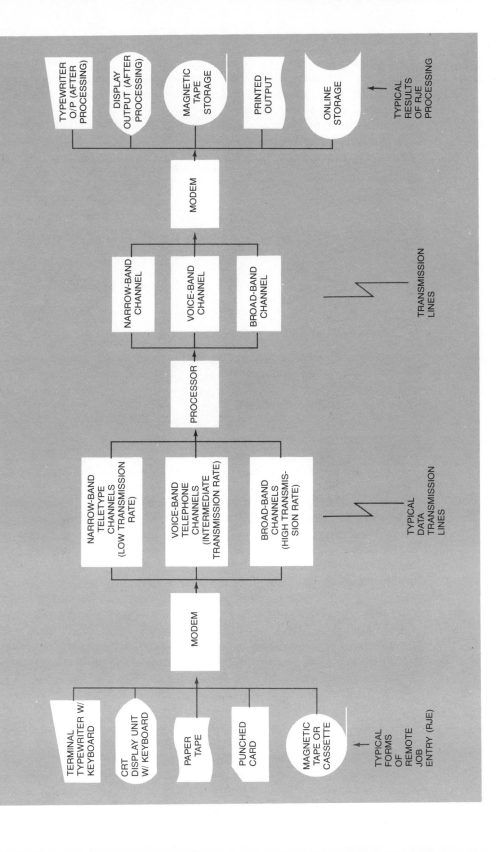

Figure 12.17

Typical types of data transmission in a remote job entry (RJE) system.

Advantages
1. Remote entry of data at point where input is entered
2. Eliminate excessive manual transmission to and from data processing installation
3. Immediate access, processing, and inquiry capability
4. Many users can share a system

Disadvantages
1. Cost of communication lines
2. Need for additional equipment and complex programming
3. Noise on lines results in high error rate
4. Security risk is very high

See Chapter 17 for a formal discussion of security problems in data processing systems.

A Data Communications Primer
by Sheila Owen

For those who would like a better understanding of data communications terminology, but are afraid to ask, we offer the following.

First, let's look at the world of data communications. Data communications is just one machine talking to another machine in their own language . . . which is data. A terminal is a machine that talks to a computer, another machine. Some terminals look like typewriters, others like TV sets.

Terminals talk to computers through computer ports. A port is simply an opening on a computer through which data goes in and out.

Now if all of these machines were in the same room or building, it would be easy and cheap to connect them all to each other and let them talk (or data communicate) all day. But many of the terminals would like to talk with their computer in the home office which is in another city. And so we wind up with terminals all over the place wanting to talk (exchange data) with other terminals or computers.

The problem of having these machines talk to each other is pretty easily solved. You know there are telephone lines all over the world which were designed for voice traffic. Some genius found that these lines can carry data (the language of the machines), too. Now I understand that when voice is sent over a telephone line, it looks something like a wavy line. Data coming out of a terminal or computer looks much more square. Our friends, the engineers, designed a little box which will take the square wave of data information and turn it into a wavy line so it can fool the telephone line by looking like voice. At the other end, this wavy line goes through another little box and is made square again so it may talk with the machine it was sending the data to. Now this marvelous box is called a modem, which stands for MOdulator-DEModulator and simply means the box has the ability to turn the square data waves from machines into wavy voice waves for the trip over the phone lines . . . and vice-versa when destination is reached.

If companies are using the phone lines a great deal for their data communications, they sometimes reserve their very own leased lines which are exclusively theirs. The largest companies or those very heavily involved in data communications may lease many lines between two cities. And that is where a multiplexer can help. A multiplexer is about the size of a small apartment refrigerator. It eliminates the need for multiple leased lines between cities.

It can shuffle the data from many phone lines into just one. Instead of each terminal having its own phone line, a multiplexer at one end accepts information from several terminals and shuffles it all into one phone line for the long-distance expensive trip. At the other end, another multiplexer unshuffles it all properly, and you wouldn't even know it had come in over one "multiplexed" phone line. It is a transparent device, meaning it doesn't change the data or information at all.

A time division multiplexer (TDM) does the "shuffling-in" of information on a time divided basis. There are clocks which keep an eye on all the information being shuffled in at one end to make sure it is all shuffled out of the phone line to exactly the right place. The clocks keep in touch and keep the whole operation flowing smoothly.

Multiplexers are divided into channels. A channel is similar to a port on a computer. The data (information) from each terminal or computer has its own channel to flow in and out of the multiplexer. There are different kinds of channels to match the different kinds of terminals.

I hope I've helped a little.

Reprinted from *Infosystems*, March 1977, p. 37. By Permission of the Publisher. ©
1978 Hitchcock Publishing Company. All Rights Reserved.

V. Recent Advances in Terminal Processing

The applications of terminal equipment have been increasing almost daily. Two recent innovations in this area include:

A. Intelligent Terminals

These are terminal devices that contain a built-in facility for performing simple data processing operations on incoming data *even before* the data is transmitted to the computer. Because they can edit information and perform simple manipulations on the data, they are referred to as *intelligent* terminals. This term is used in contrast to standard terminals which are simply used as vehicles for entering and/or receiving data. Intelligent terminals contain microprocessors.

B. Word Processing

This is a type of data processing which attempts to automate specific clerical functions performed in most offices. Instead of typing documents, reports, and letters using standard typewriters, for example, a secretary may use a word processing terminal system which stores and displays the information. Any changes that need to be made can simply be keyed in. A new report with the alterations is then automatically stored or produced. Word processing systems have already saved office workers in many organizations considerable time and energy in the preparation of documents.

Important Terms Used in this Chapter

Acoustic Coupler	Offline
Audio Response Unit	Online
Batch-Processing	Point-of-Sale (POS) System
Communication Lines	Real-Time System
Conversion	Remote Data Entry
CRT	Remote Job Entry
Data Communications	Soft Copy
Graph Plotter	Telecommunications
Hard Copy	Teleprocessing
Hard-Wired Modem	Terminal
Inquiry	Time-Sharing
Intelligent Terminal	Update
Light Pen	Word Processing

Self-Evaluating Quiz

1. The three major facets to a data communications system are _____, _____, and _____.
2. Most teleprocessing applications utilize (type) _____ terminals.
3. The most widely used input/output terminal uses a(n) _____.
4. A hard-copy printout is one that _____.
5. CRT is an abbreviation for _____ which displays data on a(n) _____-like screen.
6. (T or F) A CRT is considered a high-speed device.

7. A device called a _____ may be used with a CRT as an input tool for making graphic corrections or additions to the visual display.
8. A common use of CRTs is by _____.
9. An input/output terminal that has an output unit which gives verbal answers to inquiries is called a(n) _____.
10. The device referred to in Question 9 is usually used in conjunction with a(n) _____.
11. The factors that must be considered when determining the most suitable terminal equipment to employ at a given installation include

_____ , _____ , _____ , _____ ,

_____ , and _____.
12. Most data communication systems utilize _____ or _____ lines for the transmission of data.
13. Voice-grade telephone lines provide fast transmission but the error rate due to _____ is frequently unacceptable.
14. _____ telephone lines, while expensive, eliminate noise and interference.
15. A computer utilized with teleprocessing equipment generally requires a large _____ and a highly sophisticated _____ system.
16. _____ is the term used to describe the execution of several programs simultaneously in a single computer.
17. The two types of devices that provide interface between terminal and communication lines are called a _____ and an

_____.
18. A major added cost incurred in the use of a teleprocessing system is the _____.
19. The difference between remote data entry and remote job entry is

_____.
20. (T or F) Teleprocessing systems reduce security risks.

Solutions

1. terminal devices; communication lines; computer system
2. input/output (receive and transmit)
3. typewriter-like keyboard
4. can be maintained for future reference
5. cathode ray tube; television
6. T
7. light pen or keyboard
8. airline reservation systems; brokerage houses
9. audio response unit
10. telephone
11. cost; speed; human adaptability; computer and communication lines; functions to be performed by the terminal; size and type of display
12. telephone; teletype
13. noise on the line
14. Leased private

15. CPU storage capacity; control
16. Multiprogramming
17. modem; acoustic coupler
18. cost of telecommunication lines
19. remote data entry—program resides in computer, data is read in from terminal;

remote job entry—both program and data read in from terminal
20. F

Review Questions

I. Answer True or False

1. (T or F) Data communication equipment is used to reduce computer processing time.
2. (T or F) Data communication equipment may only be used with large-scale computer systems.
3. (T or F) The use of data communication equipment decreases the work load of the control staff of a data processing center.
4. (T or F) The use of data communication equipment eliminates the need for source document conversion.
5. (T or F) The use of data communication equipment reduces the need for manual tally checks which could be performed by computer.
6. (T or F) A major benefit of data communications is to facilitate the flow of data both into and out from a computer center.
7. (T or F) Remote terminals can be placed strategically at different locations, but must be in the same building as the computer.
8. (T or F) The use of terminals enables businessmen to have direct contact with data processing equipment.
9. (T or F) Businessmen should know how to program data communication systems.
10. (T or F) Warehouses throughout the United States can key in data to a central computer, but cannot receive data from the computer.
11. (T or F) If warehouses were not linked to a computer through the use of terminals, the time needed to transmit input to the computer center would be greatly increased.
12. (T or F) Terminals can only be used for online processing.
13. (T or F) A terminal may be used for entering input that will be transmitted to the computer in order to immediately alter a master file.
14. (T or F) The use of terminals in an online environment enables files of data to be as current as possible.
15. (T or F) Offline processing is usually employed when data is to be processed in groups or batches, at some later date.
16. (T or F) An Accounts Receivable system that utilizes a daily update procedure to make the file current could use an offline device to process charge slips once a day rather than immediately process the charges as they are made.

17. (T or F) A stock exchange could normally process changes in stock quotations offline and then transmit these changes, once a day, in a batch-processing mode.
18. (T or F) Educational institutions are apt to use a terminal for time-sharing since it is likely to be more economical than acquiring a computer system.
19. (T or F) All third-generation computers can process data received from data communication equipment.
20. (T or F) All terminals can both transmit and receive data.
21. (T or F) A disadvantage of Cathode Ray Tubes is that data, once displayed, is not available in hard-copy form, unless a special adapter is installed along with the CRT.
22. (T or F) Airlines use Cathode Ray Tubes to display flight information.
23. (T or F) With the use of an Audio Response Unit, the computer can be programmed to transmit verbal messages.
24. (T or F) Leased private telephone lines, while generally expensive, reduce noise and interference for data communication systems.

II. Fill in the Blanks

1. Data communication systems utilize _____ placed strategically at key locations which are used to enter input.
2. Data is transmitted to the CPU from terminals via _____ lines.
3. With the use of terminals in businesses, the communications gap between _____ and _____ is greatly reduced.
4. When input data is entered from a terminal for the purpose of immediately altering the contents of records on a file this is called a(n) _____ operation.
5. A(n) _____ procedure is the process of making a file of data current.
6. _____ is most often the file type used for storing data when online processing is performed, since it provides _____ ability.
7. When terminal data is first converted to a separate medium, such as cards, tape, or disk, then _____ processing is usually utilized.
8. If an Accounts Receivable System utilizes terminals to enter all sales information for charge customers and the system has the ability to provide up-to-the-minute charge information for customer inquiries, then _____ processing is required.
9. If, in the above system, customer inquiries are answered with data that is current only through the previous day's sales, then _____ processing is being used.
10. A _____ system is one that has the capability of accessing and updating computer files using terminal equipment quickly enough to affect decision-making.
11. Small-scale companies that have need of data processing equipment but find the cost of acquisition and maintenance prohibitive could benefit from renting terminals with access to a central processing unit. This concept is referred to as _____.

12. If a company utilizes a terminal for answering inquiries then a(n) _____ terminal would be required.

13. If a company utilizes a terminal exclusively as a method of remotely entering data to a CPU then a(n) _____ terminal would be the least costly type that could be employed.

14. Where time cards are used as input to a data communication system, then the specific terminal device utilized is a(n) _____.

15. Where source documents are not converted into another medium or keyed into the terminal, but are entered as input themselves, then the terminal device utilized is a(n) _____.

16. The most widely used terminal that can both receive and transmit data is the _____.

17. The terminal device that can use a light pen as an input or transmission tool is called a(n) _____.

18. Where output from a computer must be displayed with maximum speed, a(n) _____ device is usually used.

19. A terminal device that can produce an output graph is called a(n) _____.

20. Where computer-generated output or responses are verbal, instead of printed, then the terminal device must contain a(n) _____.

21. The telephone lines used with some terminal equipment but which are not designed for the degree of noise-free transmission and reliability required are called _____.

22. _____ telephone lines are more expensive than those above, but they eliminate noise and interference.

Chapter 13
Fundamentals of BASIC

13

* Optional topic

I. Terminal Processing with the Use of BASIC

BASIC is a programming language that has been especially developed for use in a time-sharing environment. That is, a program in BASIC is usually typed on a terminal and transmitted directly to the computer along with the required input. The resultant output is then immediately transmitted back to the terminal. A BASIC program may similarly be stored by the computer and then run periodically with data that has been typed on the terminal.

BASIC is an abbreviation for *B*eginner's *A*ll-purpose *S*ymbolic *I*nstruction *C*ode. It is a relatively simple language that enables the beginner to program the computer by following some elementary rules.

Terminals with keyboards require keying effort to communicate with the computer. Since such effort is relatively time-consuming for the professional, BASIC was designed to require minimum coding or keying. Instructions and data formats are simple and require less programming effort than in most other languages. Thus, this language may be learned in a relatively short time. Its instruction set is very similar to that of a simplified FORTRAN instruction set.

Note that while BASIC is most often used in conjunction with terminal processing, it can be used as a standard programming language, compiled and executed in a batch-processing environment. While this chapter assumes that the student is using BASIC with a terminal, the fundamental rules apply to all uses of the language. Those students not using BASIC on a terminal may skip the rest of this section.

A. Interaction Between the Programmer and the Terminal

Because most students who program in BASIC will be using the terminal, we will begin our discussion with procedures that must be followed to access the terminal.

Note that the precise method of access varies from one system to another but that the general procedures are the same. One system, for example, may type "HELLO" to indicate that contact was made, another might type "YOU ARE NOW ONLINE." Both, however, and all similar messages mean the same thing. While there may be slight variations for the system you are using, the following discussion will help you to understand the concepts of terminal processing.

1. Establishing Contact with the Computer Via a Terminal Typically, most terminals are electronically linked to a computer by telephone lines, although some are hard-wired or connected by direct cable. Where a telephone connection is used, a regular telephone can be used to establish communication between the terminal and the computer. Thus, when a user wishes to run a program on a terminal these simple steps must be followed in order to "log on":

Steps to Log On
1. If there is no hard-wired cable, dial a specified telephone number obtained from the data processing manager.
2. Wait for the computer to type a message on the terminal. This message may merely indicate that the computer is ready or it may be a request for an *authorization code.* An authorization or user code is required by many computer centers to ensure that only authorized personnel utilize the terminal and the computer. These authorized users are billed periodically for the computer time they have used in this time-sharing environment.
3. If an authorization code is required, the user must type in such a code and wait for the computer to determine if it is valid.
4. If an authorization code has been transmitted via the terminal, the computer will typically respond by indicating either (a) that the code has been accepted and the user can proceed with the program or (b) that it is not valid and a proper code must be retransmitted.
5. Type in a message that tells the computer:
   a. The name of the program to be entered and/or run; and
   b. That BASIC is the language that will be used.

The following example illustrates a typical set of entries to be typed on a terminal in order to gain access to a computer:

LOGON USERID	(typed by user)
READY	(computer response)
EDIT PROGRAM1 BASIC	(typed by user)

For the particular computer system illustrated, the user must type the word LOGON followed by his or her user code. In this example, the user code is USERID. The computer then checks the list of valid authorization codes that it has stored in its memory. Once the code is verified, the computer responds with the word READY on the terminal. The user then enters the name of the program (PROGRAM1) to be entered and/or run, and indicates that BASIC is the language to be used. The word EDIT is simply required by the particular system being illustrated here as part of the entry.

2. Operating a Terminal

a. Basic Elements Most terminals have a standard typewriterlike keyboard for typing instructions. The printing of these instructions and the computer's responses vary; in some cases it is a visual display, in other cases it is a typewritten printout.

The programmer types the BASIC instruction or any other message and then depresses a control key to indicate the end of the line; usually this is a RETURN key. On some systems, the user must hold down both the CONTROL key and the letter s, for example, to indicate the end of the line.

b. Simple Program—An illustration The following is a sample BASIC program, typed by a programmer on a terminal. The program computes the square root of 18.

```
EDIT SQR BASIC
10 PRINT SQR(18)
20 END
RUN
4.24264
```

B. Correcting Errors

1. Backspacing This enables the programmer to delete previous characters. Depending upon the terminal, this is accomplished by a backwards arrow key (←), an "at" (@) key, or some other special character. Suppose, for example, that we begin our program by typing

EDIT SQR BASII

instead of

EDIT SQR BASIC

and we recognize the error right after we type the second I and before we signal the end of the line. We press the backwards arrow key (or a corresponding key on your terminal) to denote a "backspace" of one position, then type the correct letter and signal the end of the line. The following is what would appear on the terminal:

EDIT SQR BASII ← C

The computer now recognizes this line as containing only the correct spelling of BASIC.

It should be noted that in many systems every time a backspace is made, each position that is backspaced over is automatically erased. Thus, if we have typed the following:

EDIT SQR BBSIC

we can correct it by backspacing four positions. Note, however, that the *remainder* of the line must be retyped from that point on:

EDIT SQR BBSIC ←←←← ASIC

2. Correcting a Typographical Error After the Line Has Been Typed In summary, if an error on a line is discovered prior to signaling the end of the line, we can backspace to the error and then type in the necessary correction(s).

Suppose, however, that the error is not detected until *after* the next line has been reached. That is, we discover the error after we have signaled the end of the line. Consider the following:

EDIT SQR BASIC
10 PRRNT SQR(18)

We have just typed the last line shown and signaled the end of the line before realizing that PRINT was spelled incorrectly. It is possible to correct this statement by retyping the entire line with the *same* line number and the necessary corrections

10 PRRNT SQR(18)
10 PRINT SQR(18)

The computer substitutes the new statement number 10 for the previously typed one.

3. Deleting a Line It often happens that it is necessary to delete an entire line from a program. This can occur, for example, when you decide to modify the logic. The specific way of deleting a line will depend on your particular system. There are, however, two common techniques:

1. On a new line, simply type the line number of the line to be deleted and then signal the end of the line. Since nothing follows the line number, the computer knows that it is to be deleted.
2. On a new line, type the instruction DELETE, followed by the line number of the line to be deleted. Note that a line number does not precede the word DELETE.

We might therefore use either of the following lines to delete line 60 from a program:

```
                60
  or
        DELETE 60
```

4. Typing Instructions Out of Sequence Sometimes a user inadvertently omits an entire line while typing a program. Suppose that while entering a program, line 20 is typed first instead of line 10:

```
20 LET D = A + B − C
```

The omitted line (line 10) can be typed directly after line 20, but it must contain its appropriate line number indicating where it belongs in the sequence of instructions. Thus, the following sequence is valid:

```
20 LET D = A + B − C
10 READ A, B, C
```

The computer automatically executes BASIC statements *in sequence* by their line numbers, regardless of the order in which they are typed.

5. Listing a Program It often becomes difficult to "proofread" a program before entering RUN if there have been many errors that have been corrected as the instructions have been entered. Consequently, before we type RUN, we often type LIST first to have the computer print out a "clean" copy of the program with all typing errors omitted. It should be noted that LIST has no line number since it is a system command. It is thus easier to check the program before having it executed. For example, we might have the following sequence:

```
EDIT SQR BASIC
10 PRRN←←INT SQR(18)
20 NND←←←END
LIST
10 PRINT SQR(18)
20 END
RUN
4.24264
```

It should be noted that there is also another use for LIST. If a BASIC program has been stored in the computer and a user wants to run it, he may want it to be listed out first. With this listing, the user can refresh his memory as to the logic involved. He can then make any modifications that may be deemed necessary. If, as an example, the above program has been previously stored and a listing is now required, the following entries would be used:

```
EDIT SQR BASIC
LIST
```

At this point, we have seen some of the common ways of correcting errors on a terminal. Note, again, that different computer and terminal configurations may cause minor variations in some of the techniques we have discussed. The purpose of the above discussion has been to familiarize you with some basic techniques of terminal processing. Given some familiarity with data communications equipment it is hoped that you can approach a terminal with relative ease.

Self-Evaluating Quiz

1. The first step generally required to establish contact with a computer via a terminal is to _____.
2. A user must usually enter a(n) _____ to identify himself/herself.
3. Once a line has been typed, a(n) _____ must be keyed as well.
4. After the program has been typed, the user must request the computer to _____ the program.
5. To correct a typographical error while typing a line, you can _____ and then _____.
6. One use of LIST is to instruct the computer to _____ so that _____.
7. To correct a line after the end of the line has been signaled, simply _____.

Solutions

1. dial the computer's telephone number
2. authorization code
3. end-of-line indicator such as RETURN
4. execute or run—usually achieved by typing RUN
5. backspace to the error by use of the ←, @, or special symbol used by your system; type the rest of the line from that point on
6. print a "clean" listing of the program with all typographical errors corrected; sloppy typographical corrections do not make the listing easy to read by the user
7. retype the line with the same statement number

II. Essential Elements of a BASIC Program

Let us review a few simple fundamentals:

> 1. Every line in BASIC must begin with a line number
> 2. Statements are executed in line number sequence
> 3. The END statement must be the last entry and must contain the highest line number

A. Line Numbers

Any line numbers from 1 to 99999 may be used. We will adopt the convention of using line numbers in multiples of 10; that is, 10, 20, 30, ... This allows us to make as many as nine insertions between original entries should this be necessary. Suppose for example, we discover that a statement was inadvertently omitted between lines 10 and 20. We can simply assign the new entry a line number from 11 to 19 at the end of the program and it will be properly sequenced by the computer.

B. Representation of Data in BASIC

1. Fields—Areas Reserved for Variable Data Variable data is that data which changes within the program. The contents of data fields in the input record, for example, change each time data is read. The contents of storage fields change each time arithmetic operations are performed using them.

a. Numeric Variables The term "variable" in BASIC refers to a field that contains *numeric* data. Since BASIC programs are usually typed on terminal keyboards, the rule for forming variable names has been devised to minimize typing effort. The rule is as follows:

A variable is represented by any single letter, or by any letter followed by one digit.

The following are thus valid variables in BASIC: A, A1, and T. Conversely, AMT1, TOTAL, and NUMBER are *not* valid in this language.

One way to read in a variable is to simply code an INPUT statement with the variable name. Hence, to alter our original example, so that the square root of *any variable* is calculated we code:

```
10    INPUT  N
20    LET X = SQR (N)
25    PRINT X
30    GO TO 10
40    END
RUN
```

X and N are variable names; N refers to an input field and X to an output field. The INPUT statement indicates to the computer that the user will be typing in values for N when the program is actually run or executed. Once the program has been read into the computer, a signal will be transmitted to the user at the terminal requesting a value for N. The signal requesting input consists of a question mark. The user types in a number and the answer, calculated by the computer, is then printed. Statement 30, GO TO 10, is a *branch* statement which causes the computer to branch or transfer to line 10 to repeat the process for other values of N that may be supplied. A listing of this program with sample data is shown below:

```
10 INPUT N
20 LET X = SQR(N)
25 PRINT X
30 GO TO 10
40 END
RUN
DATE: 79-284; TIME: 13:01:56.7; PROG: RAS.VSBASIC
?
10
 3.162277
?
23.5
 4.847679
?
567.5
 23.82225
?
234.0
 15.29706
```

b. String Variables (Nonnumeric Fields) We have seen up to this point that a BASIC program can utilize variables, or numeric fields. In addition, the program might utilize alphanumeric or non-numeric fields, such as name, address, and job description. Alphanumeric fields are called *string variables* in BASIC. We cannot simply use a letter to designate such a field, since this would indicate to the computer that the field is to hold only numeric data. The rule for forming names for string variables is simple:

A string variable is represented by any letter followed by a *dollar sign.*

The following names are therefore valid for string variables: A$, J$, and N$. A$ might represent an address field, J$ a job description field, and N$ a name field. It should be noted that, typically, the maximum size of an alphanumeric field is 15 characters. Fields of greater length may have to be subdivided into several fields of smaller length in order to be used in a BASIC program. A name field, for example, might be subdivided into last name, first name, and middle initial so that each does not exceed 15 characters.

C. Constants

1. Numeric Constants Numbers in a BASIC program can be expressed in many ways. The positive number 1800, for example, can be represented in any of the following ways: 1800, 1800.0, +1800, or +1800.0. Notice that the comma is *always* omitted from a number. The number 12,000,000 would therefore be represented as 12000000. Negative numbers can be expressed with a minus sign; −18.6, for example, is a valid constant.

E Form of Numbers There may, however, be a problem in reading certain numbers printed out by the computer. The computer usually prints out numbers that have more than a specified number of digits in an exponential, or E form. The number 12,000,000 will therefore be printed out as $1.200000E+07$ by some systems. These systems, for example, do not print numbers in the ordinary way if they contain more than seven digits.

The E form of a number can be broken up into three parts for analysis:

1. A number preceding the letter E
2. The letter E
3. A number following the E

The number then can be interpreted in the following manner. The number before the E is multiplied by 10 to the power, or exponent after the E. Thus when the computer prints out $1.200000E+07$, we know that it is equivalent to 1.200000 times 10^7, or 12,000,000. Similarly, the number $1.234560E-02$ is equal to 1.234560 times 10^{-2}, or .0123456. Notice that multiplication of a number by 10 to a *positive* power moves the decimal point to the *right* by the number of places indicated by the power; for example, $1.000000E+02$ equals 100.0000. When multiplication is by 10 to a *negative* power, the decimal point is moved to the *left* by the number of places indicated by the power.

2. Nonnumeric Constants These are coded with the use of quotation marks. The following are valid nonnumeric constants:

"THE TOTAL IS"

"ERROR MESSAGE 101"

The following routine to print square roots of input data has been modified to print a nonnumeric constant as well:

```
10 INPUT N
20 LET X = SQR(N)
30 PRINT "THE SQUARE ROOT OF",N,"IS",X
40 GO TO 10
50 END
RUN

?
100
THE SQUARE ROOT OF 100   IS 10
?
25
THE SQUARE ROOT OF 25   IS 5
?
.5
THE SQUARE ROOT OF .5   IS .7071068
?
3.5
THE SQUARE ROOT OF 3.5   IS 1.870829
```

Since the purpose of most BASIC programs is to perform calculations, we will now discuss the rules for coding formulas.

D. Arithmetic Operations

1. **Symbols** Five arithmetic operations can be included in BASIC formulas. The symbols for these operations are shown in the following table.

OPERATION	SYMBOL
Exponentiation	↑ or **, depending on the system
Multiplication	*
Division	/
Addition	+
Subtraction	−

Exponentiation indicates the number of times a value is to be multiplied by itself. Mathematically, the formula $X = B^3$, for example, means that X is equal to B times B times B, or $B \times B \times B$. Therefore, if B were equal to 2, X would be equal to 8 ($2 \times 2 \times 2$).

Note that only variables, or numeric fields, are used in arithmetic operations. That is, we cannot perform a calculation on an alphanumeric field, or string variable.

The following statements illustrate the use of the various symbols for arithmetic operations.

```
10   LET X = A * B * C
20   LET R = (A ** 2) + (B ** 2)
30   LET B = (40 * R) + 100
```

Statement 10 tells the computer to multiply A by B by C and store the answer in X. Statement 20 indicates that A² is to be added to B², and the answer stored in R. The last statement tells the computer to multiply 40 times R and add that to 100.

Notice that the following rules apply in the statements above:

1. Each statement begins with a line number.
2. The "LET" in each statement tells the computer to evaluate the formula or expression to the right of the equal sign, and then place the answer in the field designated to the left of the equal sign.
3. Parentheses can be used for clarification.

The following points should be noted about the LET statement:

1. The statement 10 LET N = 0 is valid, and instructs the computer to take the value on the right side of the equal sign and store it in N. The result is to *initialize* the variable N. We will see later that this is necessary when we want the computer to accumulate a total. Fields must be cleared before data is added to them.
2. The statement 25 LET N$ = B$ is a valid statement which takes the value of the string variable B$ and stores it in the string variable N$. Similarly, we might have a statement such as 85 LET C$ = "CREDIT". The value between the quotes is a string or nonnumeric literal. The instruction will result in the literal CREDIT being stored in C$. It should be noted that the maximum length of a string is generally 15 characters.
3. The statement 20 LET X = X + 1 is valid in BASIC, although it is not a valid algebraic equation. It increments X by 1. That is, we set X equal to one more than the original X. Thus, if X = 1 and the statement LET X = X + 1 is executed, X is set equal to 2. The statement does not make the two items (X and X + 1) equal; it sets the field on the left side of the equal sign equal to the result calculated on the right side. Similarly, the statement 60 LET T = T + A is also valid and is used for accumulating a total for all the values of A.
4. The word LET is optional on some systems. Thus, the following statement would be valid for such a system:
    ```
    10  N = A * B * C
    ```

2. Hierarchy Now that we have an idea of the symbols used in formulas, we will discuss the importance, or *hierarchy*, that the computer attaches to each of them. Consider the following statement:

What formula are we asking the computer to evaluate? It might be either (1) a = (b–c)d or (2) a = b – cd.

Suppose, for example, that b = 10, c = 5, and d = 2. If the computer interprets statement 10 according to formula (1), then a = (10 – 5) 2 = 10. If it interprets the statement according to formula (2), then a = 10 – 5 × 2 = 0. Thus you can see that the hierarchy of arithmetic operations is extremely important, since it significantly affects the results.

The computer operates on fields according to the following sequence:

Hierarchy—Order of Operations
1. Exponentiation
2. Multiplication and division
3. Addition and subtraction

When two or more operations on the same level occur, they are executed in sequence from left to right.

In statement 10, above, we therefore have the following:

1. C * D
    Since the highest level of priority in this problem is the multiplication operation, C is multiplied by D first.
2. B – (C * D)
    After C is multiplied by D, the product is subtracted from B, since subtraction has a lower level of priority than multiplication.
3. A = B – C* D
    A is set equal to the quantity calculated since there are no more computations to be performed.

Note that in the case where we have several operations of the same priority level or hierarchy, they are evaluated in order from left to right. Thus in the statement

15   LET X = B * C * D

the computer first multiplies B by C and then multiplies the answer by D.

Suppose, in the above that we really want the computer to evaluate the formula as a = (b–c)d. We have just seen that we cannot write the statement 10 LET A = B – C * D, because that is evaluated as a = b – cd. Parentheses may be used to override standard priority rules. Thus, we can write our desired formula as:

E. Comparisons

1. Relation Symbols   It is usually necessary, in most programs, to make comparisons between fields or to perform a logical test. The IF statement, as we shall see, is of prime importance in solving logic problems. There are six symbols which can be used for comparison purposes:

SYMBOL	EXPLANATION
<	Less than
=	Equal to
>	Greater than
<=	Less than or equal to
>=	Greater than or equal to
<>	Not equal (less than or greater than)

2. IF-THEN Statement   Suppose we have a statement such as the following one, where A is a field representing age:

    10   IF A <= 30 THEN 80

This instruction tells the computer that if, in fact, A is less than or equal to 30, it should proceed to line 80; otherwise, the computer will *automatically* go to the *next* line directly following the IF statement.

Note that the IF statement takes the following form:

IF (condition is true) THEN (go to this statement number)

The following examples show how the logic in the flowchart excerpts can be programmed in BASIC.

Example 1

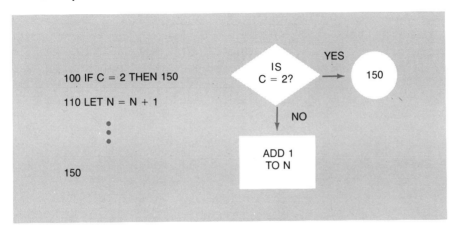

Example 2

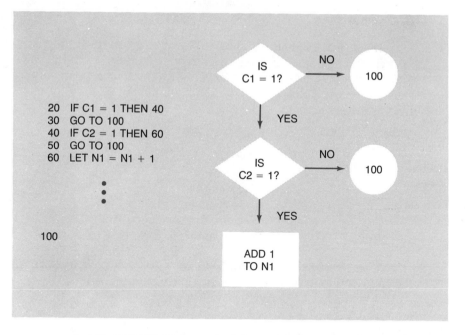

```
20   IF C1 = 1 THEN 40
30   GO TO 100
40   IF C2 = 1 THEN 60
50   GO TO 100
60   LET N1 = N1 + 1
       ⋮

100
```

3. ON—GO TO Statement   Many BASIC compilers allow the programmer to use the ON—GO TO statement, which is also known as the *computed* GO TO. The computed GO TO can be used to replace several IF statements. Consider the following program excerpt:

```
10   INPUT A, C, F
20   IF A = 1 THEN 110
30   IF A = 2 THEN 145
40   IF A = 3 THEN 65
       •
       •
       •
```

Lines 20 through 40 could be replaced with an ON—GO TO statement:

```
20   ON A GO TO 110, 145, 65
```

If A is equal to *1*, then a branch or transfer is made to the *first* line number indicated (110). If A is equal to *2*, then a branch is made to the *second* line number (145). If A is equal to *3*, then a branch is made to the *third* line number (65). It should be noted that if A is not equal to 1, 2, or 3, the program will ordinarily stop.
The general form of the ON—GO TO statement is:

ON (expression) GO TO (line number) . . . , (line number)

It should be noted that if the value of the expression is not an integer, it will automatically be truncated to an integer. Thus, if we have the statement

ON A + B GO TO 115, 117, 23

and A equals 1.3 and B equals .8, a branch to line 117 will be made, since A plus B equals 2.1, which is truncated to 2.

4. Looping A *loop* is a sequence of instructions in a program that is to be repeated a fixed number of times. To illustrate the use of a loop, let us find the sum of the odd numbers from 1 to 99.

```
10   LET T = 0
20   LET N = 1
30   LET T = T + N
40   LET N = N + 2
50   IF N < 99 THEN 30
60   PRINT "THE SUM OF THE ODD NOS. FROM 1 TO 99 IS", T
70   END
```

Notice the following about the program:

1. We have seen that the statement 40 LET N = N + 2 is used to increment N by 2.
2. We have also seen that the statement 30 LET T = T + N is used to accumulate the values of N in the field called T.
3. The technique of looping just shown involves the following elements:
   a. *Initializing* a field which will be used for controlling the number of times the loop is repeated:

   20 LET N = 1

   b. *Testing* the value of that field to see whether or not the loop should be repeated:

   50   IF N < 99 THEN 30

   c. *Modifying* that field to obtain a new value each time the loop is executed:

   30   LET N = N + 2

Self-Evaluating Quiz

1   (T or F) The following statement is valid: 100 LET X = SQR (15,000)
2   Indicate which of the following are valid variable names:

    a.   A1

    b.   AMT

    c.   AMOUNT

    d.   D

    e.   Z53

    f.   AB

3. A field name N would represent a(n) _____ field, whereas N$ would represent a(n) _____.

4. Indicate the results if the following is executed:

$$30 \text{ LET } X = V + W/S - E + C * D$$

where V = 30, W = 10, S = 5, E = 20, C = 3, and D = 6.

5. Indicate the results if the following is executed:

$$20 \quad \text{LET } V = W + C ** 2 - E + F/S$$

where W = 20, C = 10, E = 50, F = 20, and S = 5.

6. Write a program to calculate F, a Fahrenheit temperature, when C, a Centigrade temperature, is read in as INPUT. Note that the Fahrenheit temperature is equivalent to 9/5 of the Centigrade temperature + 32.

7. Write a series of statements to proceed to line 90 if A is between 98.2 and 100.6 including the end points. If A is not between these two points, proceed to line 190.

8. Write a series of statements to find the largest of three numbers A, B, C, place the result in H, and proceed to line 200.

Solutions

1. False—numbers cannot contain commas

2. a, d—only a single letter, or a letter followed by a digit can be used for a variable name.

3. variable or numeric
   string variable or alphanumeric field

4. 30

5. 74

6.
```
10   INPUT C
20   LET F = 9/5 * C + 32
30   PRINT F
35   GO TO 10
40   END
```

7.
```
10   IF A > 100.6 THEN 190
20   IF A < 98.2 THEN 190
30   GO TO 90
```

   or

```
10   IF A <= 100.6 THEN 30
20   GO TO 190
```

```
          30    IF A >= 98.2 THEN 90
          40    GO TO 190
8.        10    LET H = A
          20    IF B > H THEN 50
          30    IF C > H THEN 70
          40    GO TO 200
          50    LET H = B
          60    GO TO 30
          70    LET H = C
          80    GO TO 200
```

Review Questions

1. Write and run a program to read in five amounts from a terminal, calculate and print their average, and then repeat the process.

2. Write a program to read in a Sales Amount on a terminal. If the Sales Amount is greater than $500.00, the Commission is computed as 5% of the Sales Amount. If the Sales Amount is not greater than $500.00 but is greater than $200.00, then the Commission is 3% of the Sales Amount. If the Sales Amount is $200.00 or less, then the Commission is zero. Print the Commission.

3. Write a program to calculate and print F.I.C.A. tax on salary to be read in on a terminal.
    F.I.C.A. = 5.85% of the salary up to $16,500.
    (No tax is computed beyond the first $16,500.)

4. Write a program to calculate and print salary from an input hourly-rate figure and an input hours-worked figure. Salary is computed as:

    $$\text{salary} = \text{rate} \times \text{hours, for hours} \leq 40$$
    $$\text{salary} = \text{rate} \times (40) + \text{rate} \times 1.5 \times (\text{hours} - 40) \text{ for hours} > 40$$

III. Input/Output Statements

BASIC programs are usually entered into the computer via a terminal. These programs may be used just once, or they may be stored in the computer and run on a repetitive basis. If the program is to be stored and used on subsequent occasions, then we can allow for input data to be accepted from the terminal whenever the program is run. The INPUT statement can be used for this purpose. If, however, we are dealing with a "one-shot" program, or one that is to be used only once, we may decide instead to include the data as *part of the program.* In this case, the READ and DATA statements are used in place of the INPUT statement.

A. INPUT Statements
As we have seen, the INPUT statement can be used to accept data from the terminal as the program is being run. An INPUT statement

to accept a person's name and salary, for example, would have the following format:

15   INPUT N$,S

When an INPUT instruction is encountered while a program is running, the computer will cause a question mark to appear on the terminal. This signals the terminal user that data must be typed in, in response to an INPUT statement.

The following program excerpt calculates the square root of $X^2 + Y^2$ for each set of values for X and Y.

```
10    INPUT X, Y
20    LET A = SQR(X ** 2 + Y ** 2)
30    PRINT A
40    GO TO 10
50    END
```

When this program is run, the computer will first print a question mark on the terminal, and then wait for two numeric values for X and Y to be entered. The computer knows that the values must be numeric, since X and Y are numeric field names.

The following output would appear on the terminal for the first set of values for X and Y:

```
? 3,4
  5
?
```

The question mark tells the user that data must now be typed in. Notice that only *one* question mark is printed even though data must be supplied for two variables. The data is then typed in and the computer proceeds to line 20, where A is calculated as the square root of $X^2 + Y^2$ ($3^2 + 4^2$). The answer is then printed on the next line. Line 40 instructs the computer to return to line 10 and repeat the process for additional values of X and Y, as required.

If we are dealing with a BASIC compiler that requires quotes around nonnumeric data, then the user must include these quotes in the input. That is, when an INPUT calls for nonnumeric data the quotes must be included on some systems. Thus, if a program has the statement 10 INPUT N$,S then the following shows how input data might appear on the terminal.

```
? "JAMES PARKS",10250
```

If we are using a program that has previously been stored, it may not be clear what data is to be supplied when a question mark appears on the terminal. It is possible, however, for the programmer to have the computer print out directions before the question mark so that the user knows exactly what to enter. One way this can be accomplished is by having a PRINT statement with directions placed immediately prior to the INPUT statement:

```
5   PRINT "WHAT ARE THE VALUES FOR X AND Y"
10  INPUT X, Y
```

These instructions will result in the following being printed out:

```
WHAT ARE THE VALUES FOR X AND Y
?
```

B. READ and DATA Statements

When data is included as part of a program, we use the READ statement in conjunction with one or more DATA statements. The READ statement lists the input fields we are dealing with, and instructs the computer to get the corresponding values of these fields from the appropriate DATA statement(s) *within the program.*

Example

Suppose that for every set of values of X and Y, we would like to calculate the square root of $X^2 + Y^2$. Consider the following program:

```
10   READ X, Y
20   LET A = SQR(X ** 2 + Y ** 2)
30   PRINT A
40   GO TO 10
50   DATA 3, 4
60   DATA 5, 7
70   END
```

The READ statement directs the computer to get a value for X and a value for Y from a DATA statement. The first time the READ instruction is executed, the computer will get the values from the *first* DATA statement (3 and 4). After the desired calculations are performed and the answer is printed out, the computer goes back to statement 10 again. The computer is told to get *another* set of values—one for X and one for Y. Since the values in the first DATA statement have already been used, the computer knows automatically that it must get the data from statement 60, the next DATA statement. When the computer goes back to statement 10 for the third time, it finds no data to read in. A message, such as "OUT OF DATA" will then usually be printed by the computer.

It would have been equally valid to have DATA statements such as the following:

Alternative

50   DATA 3, 4, 5, 7

Here, only *one* DATA statement is used. The first READ causes only the first two values in statement 50 to be used since only two variables are to be read. The second time the READ is executed, the next two values in the DATA statement are used. As many items of data as can fit on one line may be used in this form of the DATA statement.

It should be noted that DATA statements are typically located at the end of a program just before the END statement. However, since DATA statements are not instructions as such, but merely serve to provide data for the READ statements, they can be located anywhere within a BASIC program. This is true because of the fact that they do not affect the logic of the program at all. The following sequence of instructions is therefore valid:

```
10    READ X, Y
20    DATA 3, 4
30    DATA 5, 7
40    LET A = SQR(X ** 2 + Y ** 2)
50    PRINT A
60    GO TO 10
70    END
```

Thus we see that DATA statements can appear anywhere throughout the program and that they can have any one of a number of formats.

The examples just discussed illustrate how *numeric* data can be included within a program. Alphanumeric data can also be included in DATA statements, although the rules vary slightly, depending on the computer on which the program is run. Some BASIC compilers require alphanumeric data to be enclosed in quotes, as illustrated in the following program excerpt:

```
10    READ N$, S
         •
         •
         •
180    DATA "JAMES PARKS",10250
190    DATA "ANNE STONE",13175
200    END
```

Statement 10 instructs the computer to get the values from a DATA statement for two fields—N$, a string variable representing name, and S, a numeric field representing salary. You will recall that when forming a string variable name we use a letter followed by a dollar sign. The rule for forming numeric field names or variables is to use a letter or a letter followed by a digit.

The same program run on a computer where the BASIC compiler does *not* ordinarily require quotes around string variable data would appear as follows:

```
10    READ N$, S
        •
        •
        •
180   DATA JAMES PARKS,10250
190   DATA ANNE STONE,13175
200   END
```

Notice that the comma in a DATA statement is only used to separate fields of data. It may *not* be included within numeric data. That is, the number 10,250 must be entered as 10250. The following DATA statement is therefore interpreted by the computer as having four numeric values:

```
145    DATA 723,12735,123,128.17
```

The four values in this statement are (1) 723 (2) 12735 (3) 123 (4) 128.17.

C. Testing for the End of Data

In the programs illustrated up to this point, when there was no more input data our logic was completed. In many programs, however, once the end of the data is detected, we may want to continue our logic in order to calculate an average, determine a percentage, print out final results, and so on. Thus, we need a convenient way of determining when there is no more data to be processed. In BASIC, we often use a "fictitious" or "dummy" set of data, as illustrated in the following program.

Example

A teacher would like to have the computer determine the average grade for each student in the class at the end of the semester. In addition, he or she would like to know the overall class average. Each student has taken four exams, which have the following weights associated with them:

EXAM	VALUE, IN TERMS OF FINAL GRADE
EXAM 1	10%
EXAM 2	30%
EXAM 3	20%
FINAL	40%
	100%

The input will consist of each student's name and the four grades. The output will consist of the average for each student and, at the

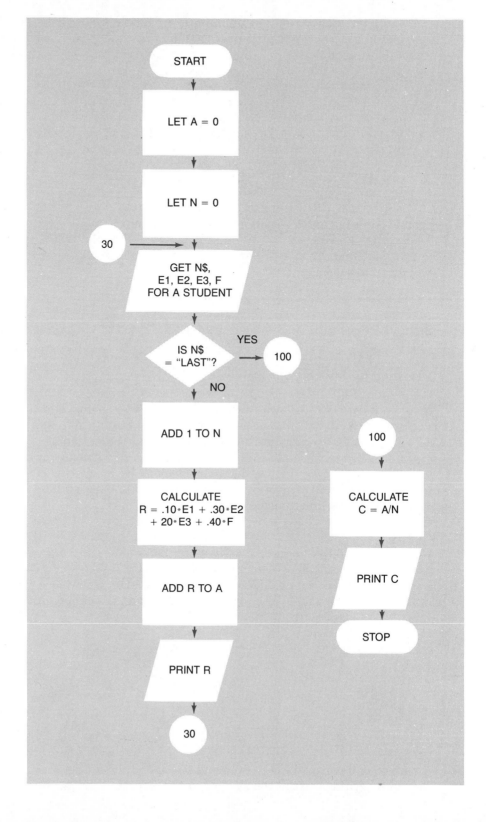

Figure 13.1
Flowchart for
sample problem.

START

LET A = 0

LET N = 0

30

GET N$,
E1, E2, E3, F
FOR A STUDENT

IS N$
= "LAST"?   YES → 100

NO

ADD 1 TO N

100

CALCULATE
R = .10*E1 + .30*E2
+ 20*E3 + .40*F

CALCULATE
C = A/N

ADD R TO A

PRINT C

PRINT R

STOP

30

end of the list, the overall class average. The flowchart in Figure 13.1 will clarify the logic involved.

Note that after each input record is read, we test the name field, N$, to determine if it equals "LAST." If it does, we proceed to an end-of-job routine. Thus "LAST" is a fictitious or dummy name used to "force" an end-of-job condition. Without such an end-of-job condition, we could not calculate a class average because we would have no way of determining when there was no more input.

The program in Figure 13.2 incorporates the logic shown in the flowchart, and shows the results for four students.

Several items should be noted concerning the logic of this program.

1. In this program, it is essential that the computer recognize specifically when the last set of input data has been processed. This is necessary so that the overall class average can then be determined and printed out.

```
10 LET A = 0
20 LET N = 0
30 INPUT N$,E1,E2,E3,F
40 IF N$ = "LAST" THEN 100
50 LET N = N + 1
60 LET R = .10*E1 + .30*E2 + .20*E3 + .40*F
70 LET A = A + R
80 PRINT R
90 GO TO 30
100 LET C = A/N
110 PRINT C
120 END
RUN
```

Figure 13.2

Program for sample problem.

```
?
"JOAN ABRAMS",85,90,75,88
 85.69998
?
"JOHN BARTON",88,88,65,78
 79.39996
?
"ROBERT EARLING",74,60,95,97
 83.19997
?
"JOAN FOUNTAINE",60,85,88,72
 77.89998
?
"LAST",999,999,999,999
 81.54993
```

2. Line 40 could have been replaced with any *one* of the following, based on the last record used to signal an end-of-job condition:

```
40  IF  E1  =  999 THEN 100
40  IF  E2  =  999 THEN 100
40  IF  E3  =  999 THEN 100
40  IF  F   =  999 THEN 100
```

It should be noted that the user of this program must be given specific instructions to enter a fictitious name of "LAST" with fictitious grades on all exams of 999 as the last set of input data. The question might arise as to why it is necessary to enter fictitious grades in addition to "LAST". The reason is that the INPUT statement (30 INPUT N$, E1, E2, E3, F) indicates that *every* set of input data will consist of one string variable (N$) and four variables (E1, E2, E3, and F). If only "LAST" were entered, the computer would indicate that there is insufficient data, and would not proceed with the program as desired.

3. Note that a count of the number of students processed is accomplished with line 50, which adds 1 to N each time student data is entered as input. Notice also the use of line 70 to keep a running total or accumulation of averages.

4. Line 100 could have been eliminated by changing line 110 to PRINT C = A/N. Where the calculation is long and complicated it may be more readable to use separate LET and PRINT statements. A PRINT statement can, however, incorporate arithmetic computations as we have seen.

D. The Print Statement and Its Options

We have thus far utilized the PRINT statement to print values for specified fields. A statement such as 90 PRINT N$,S,B is used to print values for N$,S and B. A statement such as 110 PRINT C = A/N is used to compute A/N, place the result in C, and print C.

Although the above types of PRINT statements have been adequate for their specific purposes, we will see that sometimes modifications are required to obtain results in the precise format desired. When printed output is to be retained for future reference, it is imperative that the output form be neat and clear.

Consider the report in Figure 13.3.

Notice, for example, that the report lacks proper identification, such as a title and column headings. It would be very difficult for someone to examine the report at a later date and understand its purpose. The report in Figure 13.4, then, is more appropriate.

Thus a printed report should contain data neatly spaced across the form. It should also contain identifying information, especially

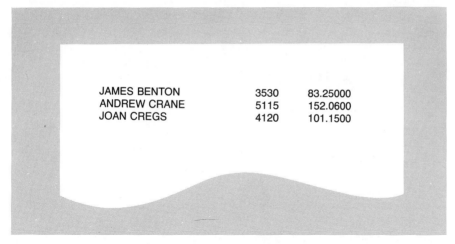

Figure 13.3

JAMES BENTON	3530	83.25000
ANDREW CRANE	5115	152.0600
JOAN CREGS	4120	101.1500

Figure 13.4

		10/10-80
COMMISSION REPORT		
SALESMAN	SALES	COMMISSION
JAMES BENTON	3530	83.25000
ANDREW CRANE	5115	152.0600
JOAN CREGS	4120	101.1500

if the user of the terminal intends to save the results for future reference. Such identifying information might include:

Identifying Information
A. A title or heading for the report.
B. Appropriate column headings, sometimes called field headings or field delineators.
C. Identification of summary information, such as subtotals, totals, and grand totals.
D. The date the report was produced.

The purpose of this section is to indicate how the PRINT statement can be modified to achieve a more complete printed report format. When printed output is to be retained for future reference, it is imperative that such reports be clear, neat, and "readable."

1. Spacing of Output

a. Use of the Comma A typical terminal usually allows for an output line of 72 or 75 characters. To enhance the appearance of the form, it is necessary to space the required data across these 72 or 75 characters per line.

These positions on one line of the terminal display are divided into *zones*. Some BASIC compilers provide for four zones, each 18 positions long. Others provide five zones, each 15 positions long. The number of zones and the size of each is dependent upon the system being used. The purpose of these zones is to give the user an easy means of spacing data across a line instead of having it cramped into adjacent positions.

The use of a comma in a PRINT statement causes the computer to print the next specified item *in the next zone*. For example, the statement 125 PRINT N$,A,B will cause the value of N$ to be printed at the left side of the line *(in the first zone)*, A to be printed in the second zone, and B in the third zone. The results are thus spaced as shown in the following printout.

1st Zone	2nd Zone	3rd Zone
JOAN CREGS	4120	101.1500

For a BASIC compiler allowing for four print zones, the PRINT statement 125 PRINT A, B, C, D, E will cause values for A, B, C, and D to be evenly spaced on one line, one value in each zone. The value of E will automatically be printed in the next zone; that is, E will print in the first zone of the *next line*.

b. Use of the Semicolon We have thus far seen how the use of commas in a PRINT statement causes output to be spaced into zones across the terminal line. Using commas, we can obtain either four or five values per line, depending upon whether the specific system provides four or five zones per line.

Suppose, however, that we require more than four or five values to print on a single line but we still need adequate spacing. A semicolon, in place of a comma, results in smaller subdivisions per line and thus more values for each line. Examine the following program which illustrates the distinctions between the comma and the semicolon in a PRINT statement.

```
10 READ A,B,C,D
20 PRINT A,B,C,D
30 PRINT A;B;C;D
40 DATA 1,2,3,4
50 END
RUN
```

1			2	3	4
1	2	3	4		

Note that we can accommodate many more values per line with the use of the semicolon in place of the comma. Where many values per line are required, use the semicolon in a PRINT statement; where only a few values per line are required, use the comma in a PRINT statement.

c. Use of the TAB Option The TAB option, available with some BASIC compilers, enables the user to indicate precisely where on the line he or she wishes to print data. That is, specific positions on a report may be specified with the TAB option in a PRINT statement.

Consider the following statement:

35 PRINT TAB (5); A; TAB (10); B; TAB (15); C

Upon executing the above statement, the computer will print A beginning in print position 5; B will print beginning in print position 10; and C will print beginning in print position 15.

The program in Figure 13.5 demonstrates the use of the TAB option.

Note that it is necessary, when using this option, to be cognizant of the size of the terminal display (usually 72 or 75 positions).

d. Spacing Between Lines After each PRINT statement is executed, the next line on the terminal is ordinarily made available for processing. If the statement:

10 PRINT A

Figure 13.5

```
10 READ A,B,C
35 PRINT TAB(5);A;TAB(10);B;TAB(15);C
45 DATA 1,2,3
50 END
RUN
    1    2    3
```

is executed, each value for A will print on a separate line. That is, the above PRINT instruction produces the necessary output and then advances the terminal to the next line. Thus, if the following instructions appear in a program, the terminal will print the values of A and B on one line, and the values of C and D on the *next* line. The result is single spacing.

```
25 PRINT A, B
30 PRINT C, D
```

It is possible, however, to have results double spaced by including a PRINT statement which indicates that nothing is to be printed; that is, a blank line is to be created on the terminal. Consider the following program excerpt:

```
10    READ A, B, C, D
20    LET X = A + B + C + D
30    PRINT
40    PRINT X
50    GO TO 10
         .
         .
         .
```

Every time a set of values is obtained for A, B, C, and D, they are added together and the sum is placed in X. Line 30 causes a blank line to print. Line 40 causes the value of X to be printed. All values of X that are printed will thus be preceded by a blank line.

2. Including Identifying Information on Reports

a. Titles and Column Headings   When the results of a BASIC program are printed out on paper at the terminal, rather than simply appearing on a CRT screen, it is important to include appropriate identification for future reference.

A title for the report should be supplied as a primary means of identifying the document. This can be accomplished by using a PRINT statement which includes the heading in quotation marks.

The following statement

```
10 PRINT "          SALES ANALYSIS BY DISTRICT"
```

results in the printing of a heading: SALES ANALYSIS BY DISTRICT. The computer will print the heading starting in print position 11, since there are 10 spaces between the quote mark and the s of SALES. If there were no spaces indicated, then the title would start at the left end margin.

Suppose we wanted the heading to be evenly spaced or centered on the form. Assuming that the terminal allows for 72 print positions, we can center the heading by the following procedure:

1. Count the number of characters to be printed. There are 26 characters in the title SALES ANALYSIS BY DISTRICT, including spaces.

2. Subtract 26 from 72, giving 46 positions, which are to be divided equally between the left and right sides of the heading.

3. Divide 46 by 2, giving 23 spaces that are to appear at the left of the title and 23 spaces that are to appear at the right of the title.

The PRINT statement will now appear as shown below, with 23 spaces before the s of SALES.

```
10 PRINT "                        SALES ANALYSIS BY DISTRICT"
```

Note that rather than provide the exact number of spaces required preceding the heading, we can use the TAB option, if available:

```
10 PRINT TAB (24); "SALES ANALYSIS BY DISTRICT"
```

In addition to a title, it is useful to have column headings or field delineators to identify the specific results that are going to be printed out. Consider the report in Figure 13.6.

The following program excerpt will indicate one way of producing the title and column headings:

```
10 PRINT "          COMMISSION REPORT"
20 PRINT
30 PRINT "SALESMAN          SALES          COMMISSION"
```

Notice that the line with the column headings has simply been treated as a title. Note, also, that it is imperative that the user

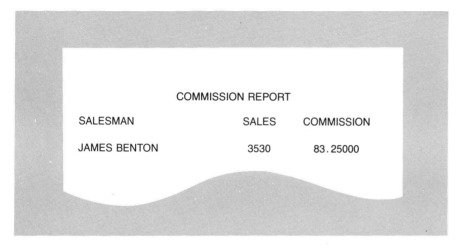

Figure 13.6

```
10  PRINT "NAME","SØC.SEC.NØ.","TEL.NØ."
20  READ N$,S$,T$
30  PRINT N$,S$,T$
40  GØ TØ 20
50  DATA "JØHN DARKS","123-45-6789","(516)127-3521"
60  DATA "JANE DRYSDALE","745-45-2378","(516)325-5678"
70  END
RUN

NAME                SØC.SEC.NØ.         TEL.NØ.
JØHN DARKS          123-45-6789         (516)127-3521
JANE DRYSDALE       745-45-2378         (516)325-5678
```

Figure 13.7

be precise in determining the number of spaces between each column heading when using this technique. The main purpose of this heading is to identify the data that appears directly below it. If headings are not aligned properly, the report will appear sloppy.

To avoid the problem with spacing that we have just encountered, we might subdivide the column headings into individual items within a PRINT statement, as shown in Figure 13.7.

It should be noted that line 10 causes each heading to be placed into a different zone of the print line. Line 30 causes each item of information (N$, S$, T$) to be printed out in a different zone. Thus, this represents a method for ensuring that headings are properly aligned with the data. In addition, the user need not be concerned with the exact spacing in between. The spacing was handled automatically as a result of the zone breakdown of the print line.

b. Identification of Summary Information   When summary information, such as final totals, appears at the end of a report, it is often useful to have specific messages or identifying comments appear on the same line as the actual results.

Consider the following illustration.

THE NUMBER OF STUDENTS PROCESSED WAS 37
THE OVERALL CLASS AVERAGE WAS 85.7

We see in the above examples the need for incorporating *both* messages and total fields in a PRINT statement. The following PRINT statements will indicate how this might be accomplished.

180   PRINT "THE NUMBER OF STUDENTS PROCESSED WAS"; N
190   PRINT "THE OVERALL CLASS AVERAGE WAS"; M

c. Date of the Report   When a given program is to be run at different times, each resultant report can be made more useful for future reference by including the date that it was produced. The following illustration shows how the date might appear at the top of the report.

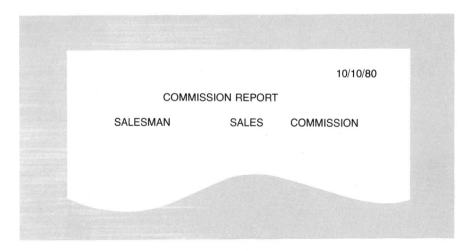

The date can be incorporated in one of several ways. The user might type a statement such as the following at the beginning of the program.

```
5 PRINT "                              10/10/80"
```

If the TAB option is available, we might use the following instead:

```
5 PRINT TAB (50); "10/10/80"
```

In either case, every time the program is used, line 5 will have to be typed to change the date before the program is run.

Another method would require the user to simply supply the date in response to an INPUT instruction:

```
10   PRINT "ENTER DATE AS MM/DD/YY"
20   INPUT D$
30   PRINT
35   PRINT
40   PRINT TAB(50); D$
```

Notice that line 10 causes directions to the user to be typed. The next item to be printed will be the question mark, as a result of line 20. After the date is supplied *on the same line*, the terminal will skip two lines (because of lines 30 and 35) and then proceed with the program by printing out the date at the top of the report.

Important Terms Used in this Section

Authorization Code	LIST
DATA Statement	LOG ON
Dummy Data	Print Zones
E Form of Numbers	READ Statement
Hierarchy of Operations	RUN
INPUT	String Variable
Line Number	Variable

Self-Evaluating Quiz

1. An INPUT statement is used when _____.

2. To include data as part of a program, we use _____ and _____ statements.

3. How many values for D will print out in the following program:

```
10  READ A, B, C
20  LET D = A*B–C
30  PRINT D
40  GO TO 10
50  DATA 10,5,20,30,8,50,60,20,100
60  DATA 30,40,50,20,10,100,40,60
70  END
```

4. Write a program, using READ and DATA statements, to read in a code field and an amount. If the code is "A", calculate and print T, tax, as 4.5% of the amount. If code is "B", calculate and print T, tax, as 3.7% of the amount. If code is "C", calculate and print T, tax, as 2.2% of the amount. Use this procedure for the following values:

CODE	AMOUNT
C	5200
A	463
B	8211
B	3372
A	495
B	625
C	42

5. Code a program to read the names and weights for each of several individuals and print only the names of those people who weigh less than 120 pounds or more than 250 pounds. Use READ and DATA statements.

6. Revise the above program to read in for each person his or her weight and height (in inches). Print the name of any person whose weight is less than 120 pounds *and* height is less than 64 inches or whose

weight is greater than 250 pounds *and* height is greater than 74 inches. Print the total number of names on the report at the end.

7. Code a program to read in amount fields and to print the *average* amount after all input has been read. Assume that an amount of 999.99 signals an end-of-job condition. Use an INPUT statement.

Solutions

1. the input entered is *not* actually part of the program.
2. READ
   DATA
3. five—We will get an "OUT OF DATA" message when the computer goes through the READ statement the sixth time. There is no value for C.
4.
```
10   READ C$, A
20   IF C$ = "A" THEN 70
30   IF C$ = "B" THEN 100
40   LET T = .022 * A
50   PRINT T
60   GO TO 10
70   LET T = .045 * A
80   PRINT T
90   GO TO 10
100  LET T = .037 * A
110  PRINT T
120  GO TO 10
130  DATA "C",5200,"A",463,"B",8211
140  DATA "B",3372,"A",495,"B",625,"C",42
150  END
```
5.
```
10   READ N$, W
20   IF W < 120 THEN 50
30   IF W > 250 THEN 50
40   GO TO 10
50   PRINT N$
60   GO TO 10
70   DATA "JOAN CONNORS",125,"MARK DORBS",275
80   DATA "KATHY FRANKS",118,"ROBERT PETERS",185
90   END
```
6.
```
10   LET T = 0
20   READ N$, W, H
30   IF W = 999 THEN 140
40   IF W < 120 THEN 70
50   IF W > 250 THEN 90
60   GO TO 20
70   IF H < 64 THEN 110
80   GO TO 20
90   IF H > 74 THEN 110
```

```
100  GO TO 20
110  LET T = T + 1
120  PRINT N$
130  GO TO 20
140  PRINT T
150  DATA "JOAN CONNORS",125,59
160  DATA "MARK DORBS",275,65
170  DATA "KATHY FRANKS",118,62
180  DATA "ROBERT PETERS," 185,64
190  DATA "LAST",999,999
200  END
```

7.
```
10  LET T = 0
20  LET N = 0
30  INPUT A
40  IF A = 999.99 THEN 80
50  LET T = T + A
60  LET N = N +1
70  GO TO 30
80  PRINT T/N
90  END
```

Review Questions

1. Write and run a program to read in accident data as indicated below and produce a report with the information shown. Use READ and DATA statements for the input. Supply appropriate identification on the report. *INPUT:* Information for each driver involved in an accident in past year:

    1. Driver's name
    2. State code (1 for New York)
    3. Sex (M for Male, F for Female)

    OUTPUT: A report that shows the following results:

    1. The percentage of drivers who were female.
    2. The percentage of drivers from New York.

2. Change the output in the above problem as follows. Produce a report that lists the names of all females from New York who were involved in an accident. Indicate the total number of New York drivers involved in accidents at the end of the report. Assume a fourth field is added with a 1 for accident, and a 0 for no accident.

3. Write and run a program to determine the most economical quantity of each product for a manufacturing company to produce. The economic order quantity Q may be determined from the formula

$$Q = \sqrt{\frac{2RS}{I}}$$

The input for each product will consist of:

1. Product name
2. Total yearly production requirement (R)
3. Inventory carrying cost per unit (I)
4. Setup cost per order (S)

The output should be a report that lists the above data for each product along with the value of Q that has been determined. Include appropriate identifying information.

*IV. Loops and Arrays

A. Loops

You will recall that a loop is a sequence of instructions that is to be repeated a certain number of times. Let us consider a problem that will illustrate how a loop is performed. Suppose we wish to compute the amount of money we will accumulate at the end of one, two, and three years if we bank a specified amount at a given rate of interest. Assume all money (principal and interest) remains in the bank. The following general formula is useful for solving problems involving compound interest:

$$P_n = P_o (1 + r)^n$$

P_n is equal to the total amount of money after n years of investment of an initial amount (P_o) at a given rate of interest (r).

We will now write a program to evaluate the above formula, where values of P (principal) and R (rate of interest) are to be entered as input. We are interested in the results when n equals 1, 2, and 3.

1. Method 1—Without Loops

```
 10  INPUT P, R
 20  PRINT "              COMPOUND INTEREST RESULTS"
 30  PRINT
 40  PRINT "RATE OF INTEREST ="; R; "INITIAL AMOUNT ="; P
 50  PRINT
 60  LET A = P * (1 + R) ** 1
 70  PRINT "AMOUNT AFTER YEAR 1 EQUALS"; A
 80  LET B = P * (1 + R) ** 2
 90  PRINT "AMOUNT AFTER YEAR 2 EQUALS"; B
100  LET C = P * (1 + R) ** 3
110  PRINT "AMOUNT AFTER YEAR 3 EQUALS"; C
120  END
```

Notice that lines 60 through 110 have many similarities. Lines 60, 80, and 100 utilize the same basic formula with only one modification each time the calculation is performed—the value of the exponent is either 1, 2, or 3. Lines 70, 90, and 110 which print the output are likewise very similar, except that each message indicates a different year—either 1, 2, or 3.

Notice that one routine could be established, instead of three separate routines, to compute the three values. This one routine could establish a variable exponent N, for example, which begins as one and is incremented by one each time until it exceeds three. That is, a *loop* can be established to be executed three times, varying N from 1 to 3.

2. Method 2—Using a Loop

```
10   INPUT P, R
20   PRINT "                COMPOUND INTEREST RESULTS"
30   PRINT
40   PRINT "RATE OF INTEREST ="; R; "INITIAL AMOUNT =";P
50   PRINT
60   LET N = 1
70   LET A = P * (1 + R) ** N
80   PRINT "AMOUNT AFTER YEAR"; N; "EQUALS"; A
90   IF N = 3 THEN 120
100  LET N = N + 1
110  GO TO 70
120  END
```

Notice that this program utilizes a loop. The sequence of instructions that is to be repeated begins with line 70. Lines 70 and 80 are executed for the *first* time with a value of N equal to 1. At line 90, the computer performs a test to see if the sequence should be repeated. Since N is not equal to 3 the first time the statement is executed, the computer proceeds automatically to the next line, where 1 is added to N, so that it now equals 2. With N equal to 2, the computer is then instructed at line 110 to go back to line 70 and process the sequence of instructions again.

3. Method 3—Using the FOR and NEXT Instructions

We have seen from the previous solutions that we wish to perform a series of operations using a variable N which begins as 1 and is incremented until it reaches 3. The FOR and NEXT statements provide some flexibility in dealing with this type of problem.

The FOR statement establishes a variable and specifies the range in which it is to vary. Thus for our problem we would have:

$$FOR\ N = 1\ TO\ 3$$

with an appropriate line number.

The statements to follow will be executed, for the first time, with N = 1. The NEXT statement essentially instructs the computer to repeat these steps with N at the next value (N = 2). Our NEXT statement would read as:

NEXT N

with an appropriate line number.

This procedure would be repeated until N were equal to 3 and all the instructions performed for that value. Then the program would continue with the statement directly *following* the NEXT statement.

Let us now consider this most effective method for handling loops:

```
10   INPUT P, R
20   PRINT "                    COMPOUND INTEREST RESULTS"
30   PRINT
40   PRINT "RATE OF INTEREST ="; R; "INITIAL AMOUNT ="; P
50   PRINT
60   FOR N = 1 TO 3
70   LET A = P * (1 + R) ** N
80   PRINT "AMOUNT AFTER YEAR"; N; "EQUALS"; A
90   NEXT N
100  END
```

The FOR statement in line 60 indicates that the sequence of instructions *up to the NEXT statement* (line 90) is to be repeated three times, with N = 1 the first time, N = 2 the second time, and N = 3 the last time through the statements.

The NEXT statement (line 90) causes the field N, specified in the FOR statement (line 60), to be automatically incremented to the next value each time the sequence has been executed.

The FOR statement used in the above program will initialize N at 1 and result in N being incremented by 1 until it equals 3.

Suppose, however, that we wish to initialize N at 10 and increment N by 10 each time rather than by 1. That is, we wish N to assume the values 10, 20, 30, and so on, until N equals 100. The FOR statement is specified as:

FOR N = 10 TO 100 STEP 10

The omission of the STEP option in the FOR statement implies that the variable is to be incremented by 1. In the above, we initialize N at 10 and "step" it or increment it by 10 each time the succeeding operations are performed until N is equal to 100.

B. Arrays

There are many types of problems where it is convenient, and sometimes necessary, to store all the input data with *subscripted variables* before further processing is performed. A subscripted variable refers to either a list or a table of data stored in the computer. A *subscript* or number is necessary to indicate the position of a particular value in the list or table. Consider the following program, where each student in a particular course has taken six exams which are to be averaged by the computer.

```
10   INPUT E1, E2, E3, E4, E5, E6
20   LET A = (E1+E2+E3+E4+E5+E6)/6
30   PRINT A
40   GO TO 10
50   END
```

This oversimplified program allows the instructor to sit at the terminal, enter one student's grades at a time, and then get the average printed out before proceeding to the next student.

Notice that six different variable names were used in lines 10 and 20: E1, E2, E3, E4, E5, and E6. Suppose the instructor had given 12 exams. We may run into several problems when writing the program. First, we cannot use variable names such as E10, E11, and E12, since a variable name can only consist of a letter, or a letter and *one* digit after it. Even if we can choose meaningful variable names, the instructions become rather cumbersome to type:

```
10   INPUT E1, E2, E3, E4, E5, E6, E7, E8, E9, T1, T2, T3
20   LET A = (E1+E2+E3+E4+E5+E6+E7+E8+E9+T1+T2+T3)/12
```

One way around such a problem is to use a subscripted variable for the exam scores. Consider again the problem where six exam scores are to be entered for each student. Suppose we want the computer to set up a *list*, or *one-dimensional array*.[1] The term one-dimensional array simply means that the data can be visualized as being stored in *one* column within the computer. The name of the list will be E. It will have six slots or cells into which the numbers can be placed. After the data is stored in the list, we can refer to any specific item by indicating the appropriate *position* in the list with the use of a subscript. The values in the list can then be referred to as $E(1)$, $E(2)$, $E(3)$, $E(4)$, $E(5)$, and $E(6)$. $E(1)$ refers to the first number in the list called E, $E(2)$ refers to the second number, and so on. Figure 13.8 illustrates how the list just described can be visualized inside the computer.

Our instructions to read in the scores and average them *might* then be as follows:

```
10   INPUT E(1), E(2), E(3), E(4), E(5), E(6)
20   LET A = (E(1)+E(2)+E(3)+E(4)+E(5)+E(6))/6
```

[1] A table, or two-dimensional array, refers to data that is stored in columns and rows within the computer.

Figure 13.8

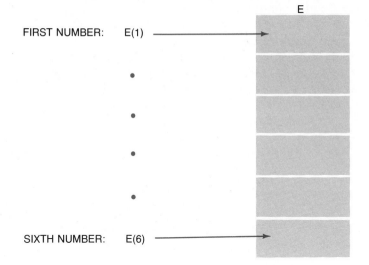

FIRST NUMBER: E(1)

SIXTH NUMBER: E(6)

Although these instructions illustrate the use of a subscripted variable, we have not saved anything by doing it this way. However, it may have occurred to you that we might use the FOR and NEXT statements to facilitate our programming. The following instructions simplify the coding:

```
 5  LET T = 0
10  FOR I = 1 TO 6
20  INPUT E(I)
30  LET T = T + E(I)
40  NEXT I
50  PRINT T/6
60  GO TO 5
70  END
```

Line 5 sets up a variable T to accumulate the total of each student's grades. Line 10 indicates that the following lines (20 and 30) are to be repeated six times, with I varying from 1 to 6, in increments of 1. Lines 20 and 30 process the Ith value of E; that is, the first time through the loop, the first value of E, or the first exam grade, is entered as input and stored in the first slot of the list—E(1). This value is then added to the current value of T, which is zero. Line 40 increments I by 1 and the loop is repeated. The second time through, the second exam grade is entered and stored as E(2), and so on. After all six grades have been entered and accumulated, the computer goes to line 50 automatically, where the accumulated total for the student just processed is divided by 6, and the answer is printed out. The process is then repeated for the other students.

It should now be apparent why subscripted variables are so useful. Regardless of how many values are to be read into a particular list, essentially the same simple instructions can be used. There is one additional instruction, however, that is necessary *if the subscript will exceed 10.* The instruction that is required is the *dimension statement* (DIM). Its purpose is to explicitly tell the computer how much room to reserve for a subscripted variable when it is known that there will be subscripts greater than 10. The BASIC compiler automatically reserves enough room to allow for a subscript up to 10 whenever a subscripted variable is encountered during compilation. If we know, for example, that there will be 12 grades entered for each student, we will need a dimension statement such as

10 DIM E(12)

at the beginning of the program. This statement explicitly tells the computer to reserve enough room for a list called E to allow for a subscript up to 12.

Self-Evaluating Quiz

1. Write a FOR statement varying X so that it assumes all the odd number values to 99.
2. Write a routine, using one INPUT statement and the FOR and NEXT statements, to read in 20 class grades and to then determine and print a class average.
3. Indicate how many times the loop will be executed with the following statement and what values X will assume.

10 FOR X = –5 TO 8 STEP 3

4. The purpose of a dimension (DIM) statement is to _____.
5. A subscript is used to indicate _____ in a list or one-dimensional array.
6. Write a program using FOR-NEXT statements to read in the weights of 11 students and print the average. The weights will be supplied in one DATA statement. Store all the data in a list before proceeding with the calculations.

Solutions

1. FOR X = 1 TO 99 STEP 2
2.
```
10  LET F = 0
20  FOR N = 1 TO 20
30  INPUT E
40  LET F = F + E
50  NEXT N
```

```
60  PRINT "AVERAGE GRADE IS"; F/20
70  END
```

3. five times: X = –5, X = –2, X = 1, X = 4, X = 7
4. tell the computer exactly how much room to reserve for a subscripted variable
5. the position of a particular value

6.
```
10   DIM W(11)
20   LET T = 0
30   FOR I = 1 TO 11
40   READ W(I)
50   NEXT I
60   FOR I = 1 TO 11
70   LET T = T + W(I)
80   NEXT I
90   PRINT T/11
100  DATA  123,175,186,110,137,142,147,189,184,122,201
120  END
```

Unit Four: Selected Bibliography

Teleprocessing: General Discussion

1. "Hardware/Data Entry, Intelligent Terminals and OCR," excerpted from a Datapro 70 report, *Computer Decisions,* February 1977.
2. "Five-Year Planning for Data Communications," Joseph Ferreira and Jack M. Nilles, *Datamation,* November 1976.
   (a) Focusses on the recent trends in data communications
   (b) Provides the student with information on available equipment and the distribution of telecommunication costs
3. "Voice Recognition Comes of Age," Edward K. Yasaki, Sr. *Datamation,* August 1976.
   (a) Focusses on the ability of some systems to recognize speech patterns and to accept verbal input
   (b) Provides student with information on new methods of remote data entry
4. "IBM versus Bell in Telecommunications," Howard Anderson, *Datamation,* vol. 23, May 1977, p. 91.
   (a) Focusses on the competition between IBM and ATT in the communications field.
   (b) Will provide students with information on types of communication services which currently exist and will also shed light on the competitive aspects of the data processing field.

BASIC

1. *Business Programming with BASIC,* George Diehr, (New York, 1972).
2. "Structured Programming in BASIC," Peter B. Worland, *Datamation,* vol. 23, June 1977, p. 149.
   (a) Focusses on structured programming, a new concept in programming technique
   (b) Provides the student with an advanced approach to the BASIC language

Chapter 14

Business Organization and the Role of the Data Processing Department

14

14

Thus far, we have provided the student with a basic understanding of computer equipment, how it operates, and what it can realistically be made to do. In this and the next unit we will discuss the various applications of computer systems.

The main orientation of this text has been on an understanding of computers for the business and data processing student. In this unit, the emphasis will be on the use of computers for business applications.

I. Business Organization

Before considering the ways in which computers are used in business organizations, the student should have some idea of the ways in which businesses are themselves organized.

Each company has its own individual organization, but general statements can be applied to all of them.

Business functions in all companies can be described with regard to their flow of information. That is, each department operates on information and alters it in some way. The relationship between the Data Processing Department and the various business departments lies in this information flow. The primary objective of data processing in any business is to *optimize information flow.*

Businessmen, as well as data processing personnel, must understand both the organizational structure and the flow of information within their specific company. Both groups must realize that a department, whether it be the Accounting Department or the Marketing Department, does not function independently. Each facet of a company must be considered in relation to the business as a whole. The businessman who is a manager of the Sales Department must understand the relation of that department to the Inventory and Accounts Receivable departments, for example. He or she must be aware that decisions that are made for one department could affect other departments. Similarly, the EDP staff cannot attempt to automate procedures for a given department without being cognizant of how such changes will affect other departments. For example, no competent computer specialist would redesign an input document without considering the effects of those changes on other departments.

14

A. Typical Department Functions

In an effort to provide a general frame of reference for the reader, we will discuss the *fundamental* objectives of typical departments within a company. In this way, the reader will obtain a general understanding of the functions of each department. It will then be easier to relate the data processing functions subsequently discussed to each department's needs.

In each of these departments the computer may be used for one or more of the following:

1. To automate procedures in individual departments in order to achieve increased efficiency and productivity. For example:
   a. Prepare payroll checks from time cards.
   b. Prepare accounting ledgers from ticket transactions.
   c. Maintain records on stock for inventory.
2. To assist each department's management in its decision-making role.

   A computer may be used to prepare forecasts or projection statistics, for example, that will assist management in its decision-making functions. Often these operations are not currently performed, even manually, but with the use of a computer, they could prove extremely beneficial to management. For example:
   a. Economic Order Quantities may be computed so that management can determine what items to buy and in what quantity.
   b. Sales forecasts may be prepared so that management can be made aware of expected profits in the near future.
   c. Personnel turnover studies may be performed so that management can determine how many new employees to hire.
3. To integrate departmental information so that a network of information processing can be achieved.

   This can result in the creation of a Management Information System (MIS) which involves the sophisticated, high-level computerization of *all* pertinent facets within a company's organization to assist top-level management in making key decisions about the company as a whole. MIS can utilize a computer in determining, for example, the company's financial position for a given period. Similarly, MIS can be used to predict growth factors, project production growths, and so on. The concept of MIS will be more fully explored in Chapter 16.

Regardless of the data processing function for which a computer is used, it is important for business people and computer specialists to recognize that departments do not function independently.

Functions that are performed by one department affect others. Although each department must fulfill its specific objective, as stated in Figure 14.1, the overall objective of every company, as a whole, is to increase profits while minimizing costs. It is the responsibility of each department to work toward this ultimate end. That is, although a specific procedure employed by the Inventory Department to meet its objectives may result in increased efficiency, if it is excessively costly or is not responsive to the needs of the other departments, it will not result in increased profits or minimized costs. Thus it is an unsound procedure. Similarly, an EDP department which, in the narrow view, usually results in increased cost expenditures for the company, must, in the broader or long-range view, result in increased profits, or it should be eliminated from the organization.

B. Organizational Structure

The organization of a business indicates how each element, or department, relates to the company as a whole. The last section considered the fundamental operations of some departments. We must

509

BUSINESS
ORGANIZATION
AND THE ROLE
OF THE DATA
PROCESSING
DEPARTMENT

Figure 14.1

Review of
typical business
departments
and their functions.

PRODUCTION (where applicable)
Produces Items to be Sold

INVENTORY
Controls stock in warehouse and on sales floor

SHIPPING & RECEIVING
Receives goods from vendors, inspects them, ships to customers; receives returned merchandise

PAYROLL
Maintains employee pay records and produces payroll checks

PERSONNEL
Hires personnel needed to maintain company operations; maintains employee records for statistical personnel reports

ACCOUNTING
Maintains and processes records on company transactions—money owed by company (accounts payable) and money owed to company (accounts receivable); processes financial dealings with customers and vendors

MARKETING & SALES
Determines best combination of products to merchandise in order to maximize profits, and advertises accordingly; maintains sales force; performs sales forecast

now discuss the integration of departments to determine how the proper flow of information between them is achieved.

Organization Chart An *organization chart,* which is a pictorial representation of the organizational hierarchy within a company, is a document that is useful for evaluating structural organization.

Figure 14.2 illustrates a sample organization chart for a retail firm. Figure 14.3 illustrates a sample organization chart for a manufacturing firm.

Note that from an organization chart we can determine the relation of each department to the company as a whole. Also note that the executive-level management personnel, the president and

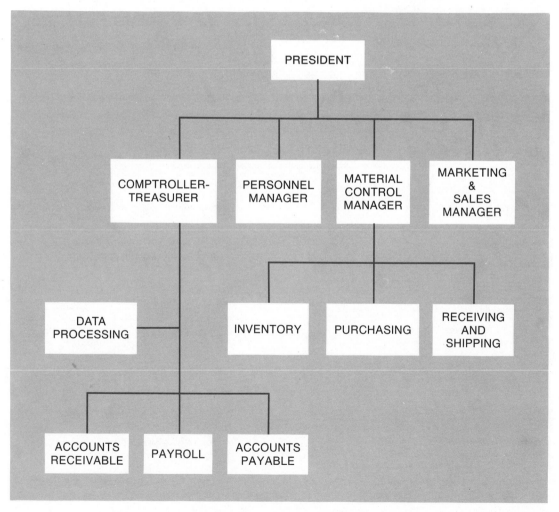

Figure 14.2

Sample organization chart for a retail firm.

vice presidents, are ultimately responsible for making major policy decisions for the company as a whole. Although management generally has top-level personnel managing each individual depart-

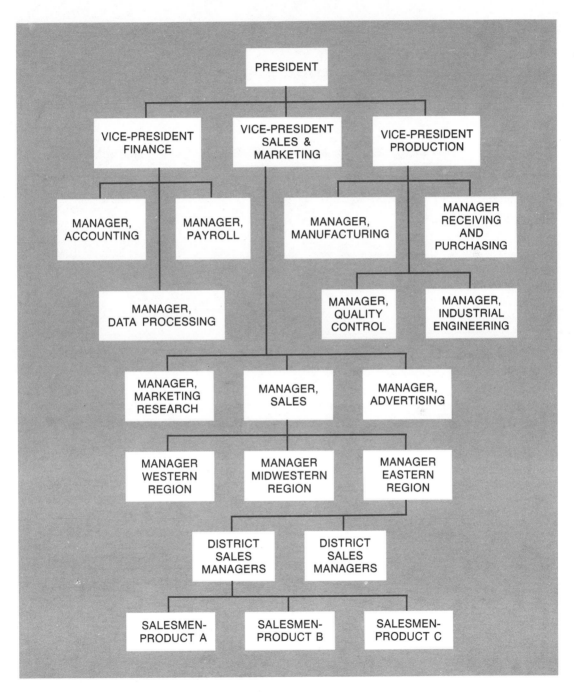

Figure 14.3

Sample organization chart for a manufacturing firm.

ment, it is the task of the top executives to integrate departments so that a meaningful, productive, and profitable organization results.

C. Data Processing Function

Keep in mind that a data processing center is often employed to achieve this end. While extremely useful in automating manual procedures, a computer, if used properly, can also contribute to the overall decision-making function. Table 14.1 indicates the percentage of a company's total operating budget that is spent on data processing.

Table 14.1

Percentage of a Company's Total Operating Budget that is Spent on Data Processing

Percentage of Budget	Percentage of Companies
1% or less	33.6%
1.0 – 1.9%	24.3
2.0 – 4.9%	18.2
5.0 – 7.9%	7.7
8.0% or higher	16.2[a]

[a]This figure includes DP service bureaus.

Reprinted from *Infosystems*, June 1977, p. 53. By Permission of the Publisher. © 1978 Hitchcock Publishing Company. All Rights Reserved.

1. Line and Staff Operations A company's departmental structure generally focusses on two separate functions: line and staff.

Line and Staff Operations
Line functions: *direct* responsibility for achieving company goals
Staff functions: advisory or service groups which *indirectly* enhance company profits

---

In a typical business, sales is a line function since its direct and primary goal is the sale of goods that results in increased profits. Production is also a line function, since it directly affects company profits. The resulting sales records and productivity levels are used directly in producing profit statements.

Typical staff departments within a company include Personnel and Accounting. The Personnel Department is responsible for hiring employees. There is no concrete measure of its productivity. How well the staff of this department performs its function cannot be measured directly against company profits. That is, Personnel is a service department that only *indirectly* enhances profits.

Similarly, the Accounting Department maintains financial records. If the employees perform their record-keeping poorly, the company will certainly lose customers. But we can only measure the department's effectiveness or productivity indirectly.

513
BUSINESS
ORGANIZATION
AND THE ROLE
OF THE DATA
PROCESSING
DEPARTMENT

2. Data Processing as a Staff Function   In general, the Data Processing (DP) Department also performs a *staff* function. This department is maintained generally as a service to other departments. Let us now consider the various ways in which the Data Processing Department relates to other departments.

a. DP as a Service Department.   In this case, DP is a *separate* entity that serves other departments. Its primary function is to computerize company operations and, by so doing, make them more efficient. The staff within a Data Processing Center is called upon by managers to analyze operations for each department. The DP staff must then become familiar with each department's operations and how they relate to the company as a whole.

b. DP as a subdivision of the most important user department   Here, computer specialists become well versed in the procedures of that one department and, thus, they require less time to analyze each job for that department. When the data processing installation reports to a specific department, other departments that require computerized functions must wait until the needs of this "priority" group are met.

A typical case is when the Data Processing Center reports directly to the company controller, who supervises all accounting operations. During the early stages of computer development, when the potential of computers was being tested, it was logical to assume that these electronic "brains" would be utilized mostly by the Accounting Department. Thus, the newly organized Data Processing unit initially became a subdivision of the Accounting Department. Even though many other departments currently utilize the computer center as a service organization, such companies simply have not found it necessary to reorganize their data processing installations.

c. DP as a decentralized unit within each major department   In the above cases, the DP function was performed by a *single* center within the company. This is called *centralized data processing.* Sometimes it is financially expedient to establish, instead, numerous centers each reporting to a specific department. In this way, each department's needs are met by a staff that is specifically trained by the user department. Second, the costs associated with each data processing application are more easily assessed. That is, in decentralized systems, each user is held accountable for its own data processing costs. This is sometimes referred to as *distributed data processing.*

d. DP on a Time-Sharing basis using another company's computer system and staff It is possible for some companies to utilize computerized operations with no data processing installation. They employ outside consultants to perform the necessary programming and they utilize computers and operators on a time-sharing basis. For companies that cannot afford a computer staff or that cannot maintain one on a full-time basis, there are *service bureaus* or *facilities management* organizations which, for a given fee, will computerize any company's operations. If a firm wishes to computerize just a few procedures, it is usually not feasible to hire a full data processing staff. Instead, a service bureau can be hired to analyze and design these new procedures.

Keep in mind, however, that both the use of time-sharing and service bureaus can be very costly if employed to excess. That is, such outside contracting is economical only if used on a limited basis.

Before deciding to employ outside firms, a company should consider its own growth factor and future potential. It may be that the expense of a computer center could be offset by increased efficiency and decreased expenditure in other areas. Similarly, if the company's growth will necessitate a data processing facility in future years, it might be more economical, in the end, to acquire one initially rather than to utilize outside assistance.

Table 14.2 provides some indication of the percentage of firms that use the services of outside organizations. The use of accounting firms to audit DP activities has become of major importance.

Table 14.2

Percentage of Firms that use Data Processing Services of Outside Organizations

Service	Percentage of Firms
Systems design	11.4%
Programming	22.1
Facilities management	1.1
Additional data processing (including service bureaus)	22.6
Timesharing services	11.5
Software packages	25.8
DP training	23.4
Installation security	3.6

Self-Evaluating Quiz

515
BUSINESS
ORGANIZATION
AND THE ROLE
OF THE DATA
PROCESSING
DEPARTMENT

1. (T or F) Some businesses do not have Production Departments.
2. (T or F) A banking organization would have a Production Department.
3. (T or F) All business organizations have the same structure.
4. (T or F) The role of data processing in any business is to optimize information flow.
5. A(n) _____ is a pictorial representation of the organizational hierarchy within a company.
6. Name six typical departments within a business.
7. (T or F) The function of the Payroll Department, generally, is to hire employees.
8. (T or F) The Data Processing Department performs a line function.
9. (T or F) It is possible for a company to perform computerized operations without having its own computer.
10. The term _____ is used to indicate that data flows through a company and can have resounding effects on more than one organizational element or department.

Solutions

1. T
2. F
3. F
4. T
5. organization chart
6. Production; Payroll; Personnel; Accounts Receivable; Accounts Payable; Marketing; Sales; Shipping; Receiving; Inventory
7. F
8. F—staff
9. T—through the use of time-sharing or service bureaus
10. information flow

II. The Data Processing Department

For proper analysis and successful computerization of business operations, businessmen and data processing personnel must be fully cognizant of each other's functional responsibilities and capabilities. Improper communications between these two departmental representatives is a major cause for inadequately automated procedures.

The businessman who requires the assistance of the EDP department to computerize some functions must specify requirements in the utmost detail. Data processing personnel must extract from the businessman *all* relevant data so that the computer output is exactly what is required. Unfortunately, however, the transfer of all pertinent data from the businessman to data processing personnel is no simple task. Information is sometimes omitted by the businessman and/or misunderstood by the computer specialist. Errors in computer output are often the result of these omissions and misconceptions.

Most of us are familiar with the results of poor communications between these two departments, having been victims of inadequate or erroneous computerization. Some of us have witnessed computerized registration procedures that have caused gross scheduling errors. Similarly, many of us have been billed for goods not purchased, because of computer problems in an Accounts Receivable Department. More dramatically, there are those who have had to wait for outstanding checks that are long overdue, because of computer foul-ups. The computer, which is often not responsible, is usually blamed for these problems.

Be advised, however, that in the great majority of cases the errors or inadequacies are caused by poor communications between the major business representatives and the appropriate data processing personnel. In such cases, both must share the blame. The data processing personnel were not adequately familiar with the requirements of the job, and the businessmen failed to communicate their needs properly.

This chapter (indeed, this entire text) is aimed at familiarizing the business and data processing students with the requirements of data processing personnel so that business functions can be properly computerized.

With an understanding of computer concepts and basic terminology the businessman can thus actively interact with data processing personnel. Note that the businessman is not required to fully understand the intricacies of computer operations. He or she should, however, know enough of computer processing to effectively communicate his or her needs to the data processing staff. Similarly, the computer specialist is not required to be expert in business areas, although he or she should be cognizant of how data processing is most effectively utilized by various departments.

Consider the organization chart in Figure 14.4, which represents the relationships within a typical Data Processing Center or installation. Note that there are four major groups for which the data processing manager is responsible: systems, programming, operations, and control.

A. The Systems and Programming Staff

1. The Systems Staff

a. Performs a systems study to determine the feasibility of computerizing a specific system A system, in the business sense, is an organized method of accomplishing a business function.

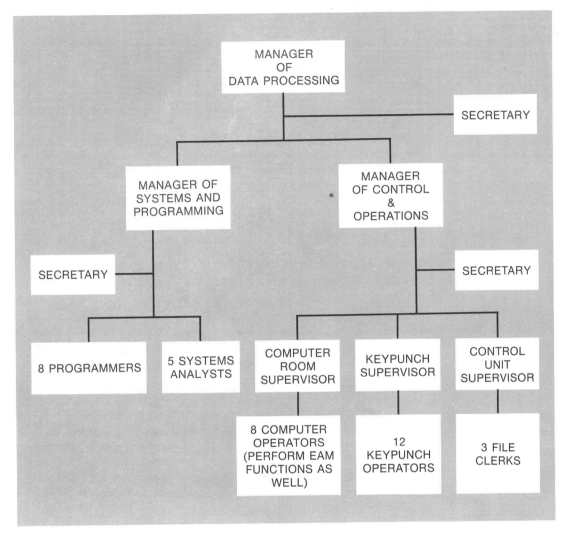

Figure 14.4
Organization chart for a typical data processing department.

The systems analyst analyzes the elements of the present system, determines the requirements of the job, and decides if a computerized set of procedures is economically justifiable.

If computerized operations can save the company money, then they are considered feasible. If they are, the systems analyst then:

b. Designs a more efficient, computerized system This design includes *all* elements, operations, and procedures to be utilized in the new system. It is the analyst, therefore, who has initial contact with the businessman. In order for the analyst to fully understand the latter's job requirements, he or she must be aware of *all* facets of the present system. Similarly, the businessman must be fully cognizant of the analyst's requirements and the computer's capabilities in order to provide a smooth transition from the old system to the new one.

This unit will be devoted to a study of the systems function.

2. Programming Staff   Once a system has been designed, the programming staff is then called on to write the set of computer instructions (programs) that are required within the system. Again, the programmer must be fully cognizant of each program's requirements to ensure proper conversion. Communication with both the analyst and the business manager is necessary to clarify all details.

Once the programs are written, they must be tested to make certain that no errors or "bugs" exist. After the programs have been tested and are executing properly, the businessman in conjunction with the analyst and programmer is responsible for ensuring a smooth conversion to the new system.

Supervision of Programming Staff   In some installations, the programming staff reports directly to the systems staff. In this way, the analysts can assign programs to their subordinates, according to the strengths of each programmer. Similarly, the analyst can ensure that proper priorities are placed on all assignments.

In other installations, the programming staff is a separate division. In this way, programmers are not constrained in their discussions; that is, they are free to question analysts without being conscious of a supervisor-subordinate relationship.

In still other installations, the systems and programming functions are performed by programmer-analysts who do *both* jobs. This further reduces the communication problem, since a single programmer-analyst can perform all aspects of the job.

Table 14.3 is a tabulation of the number of programmers in the United States from 1955 until the present and projected into the future. It will provide the reader with some idea of the huge growth in this profession over the last two decades.

B. Operations Staff

When design and programming efforts have been completed, the system is ready for conversion. During this phase, the systems and programming staff turn the job over to the operations staff, which is responsible for implementing it. The operations staff consists of keypunch operators, EAM operators, and computer operators.

1. Key Operators—Keypunch, Key-to-Tape, Key-to-Disk   Operators are usually required to convert incoming or source documents to a machine-readable form such as punched cards, magnetic tape or magnetic disk.

Number of Programmers in the United States [a]   Table 14.3

Year	Number of Programmers
1955	10,000
1960	30,000
1965	80,000
1970	165,000
1975	220,000
1980	275,000
1985	330,000

[a]*Data Processing in 1980–1985: A Study of Potential Limitations to Progress*, T. A. Dolotta et al., (New York: 1976), p. 173. Reprinted with permission.

2. Electrical Accounting Machine Operators EAM operators are required to prepare card input for computer processing. For example, they sort, merge, and reproduce cards when necessary.

3. Computer Operators Computer operators must then feed input into the computer, communicate with the computer via the console-typewriter, and transmit the output produced, according to specifications supplied by the systems and programming staff. Ordinarily, the programming and systems staff give directions to the computer operators. Operators are given schedules indicating when they can expect input to arrive, and when output is required. They are also given a set of procedures that they must follow. Note that the analyst is usually responsible for preparing the above schedules and instructions for the operations staff.

C. Control Unit Staff

Once implementation is complete, the Control Unit Staff ensures that all steps are followed systematically. This group is responsible for maintaining control of data as it is processed through the data processing installation. The staff maintains various totals to ensure that data is not lost.

You will note that the businessman maintains contact primarily with the systems analyst and the programmer. These are the two professional positions requiring extensive training and expertise. Because of its complexity, the analyst's job generally requires even more background than that of the programmer.

D. Training of Computer Specialists

An individual can become a programmer or programmer trainee usually in one of four ways:

Programmers
1. Graduate from a four-year college as a computer science or business major.
2. Graduate from a two-year or junior college with a major in data processing or computer science: although these individuals do not have a four-year degree, their expertise in the data processing field is a distinct asset. Many junior colleges have extensive data processing courses that prepare the student for advanced work in systems analysis and programming.
3. Graduate from a certified data processing institute: this offers the individual, for a fixed fee, a concentrated course in data processing. This course does not, however, receive college credit.
4. Possess experience in the operations phase of data processing: individuals in the computer operations field are sometimes promoted to the programming staff. Note that this would not constitute an actual promotion, since these two groups are on separate organizational levels.

Positions in systems analysis, because of their complexity, require more training. Typically, a systems analyst will have had the following background.

Systems Analysts
1. Possess several years of business experience and have completed computer course work on the undergraduate and graduate level.
2. Possess several years of business and data processing experience.
3. Possess thorough knowledge of programming and computer operations.
4. Possess some management experience.

Table 14.4 provides a breakdown of average reported weekly salaries by job description within a data processing department.

Important Terms Used in this Chapter

Centralized Data Processing	Production
Computer Operator	Programmer
Control Unit Staff	Service Bureau
Decentralized Data Processing	Staff Function
Line Function	Systems Analyst
Management Information System (MIS)	Time-Sharing
Organization Chart	

Average Reported Weekly Salaries for Data Processing Personnel By Job Description (Dollars)

National Average Salary Comparison 1977-1976	Manager of Data Processing	Asst. Mgr of Data Processing	Project/ Team Leader	Mgr or Supv. of Comp. Sys. Anal. and Programming	Lead Computer Systems Analyst and Programmer	Senior Computer Systems Analyst and Programmer	Junior Computer Systems Analyst and Programmer	Mgr or Supervisor of Computer Systems Analysis	Lead Computer Systems Analyst	Senior Computer Systems Analyst	Junior Computer Systems Analyst	Mgr or Supervisor of Programming
'77	444	405	415	416	375	337	286	435	385	358	309	379
'76	436	381	**	399	360	326	274	433	384	339	276	378
% of increase (decrease)	1.8	6.3	—	4.3	4.2	3.4	4.4	0.5	0.3	5.6	12.0	0.3

	Lead Programmer	Senior Programmer	Junior Programmer	Programmer Trainee	Data Comm. Manager	Data Comm. Operator	Mgr or Sup of Comp. Oper.	Lead Computer Operator	Senior Computer Operator	Junior Computer Operator	Computer I/O Control Manager	Tape Librarian	Key Entry Supervisor	Lead Key Entry Operator	Senior Key Entry Operator	Junior Key Entry Operator
'77	325	304	251	199	385	203	320	235	214	179	218	178	206	174	160	145
'76	321	282	231	192	380	196	333	230	206	175	215	170	201	169	154	139
%	1.2	7.8	8.7	3.6	1.3	3.6	(–3.9)	2.2	3.9	2.3	1.4	4.7	2.5	3.0	3.9	4.3

**Not included in 1976 study.

Table 14.4

Self-Evaluating Quiz

1. More data processing jobs are deemed inadequate because of poor _____ than for any other reason.
2. Communications between _____ and _____ must be adequate to ensure proper computerization.
3. (T or F) The responsibility for failures in computerization of jobs generally rests with the businessman and the data processing staff rather than with the computer.
4. Name the three basic elements within a Data Processing Center.
5. Who is in charge of a Data Processing Center?
6. Name two major functions of the programming staff.
7. Name two major functions of the systems staff.
8. How are the systems and programming staff related?
9. Name the types of operators within the operations staff.
10. Who is usually responsible for writing the procedures to be followed by the operations staff?
11. State what is meant by a conversion procedure.
12. What is the purpose of the control unit staff?
13. Who is responsible for writing the set of procedures to be followed by the control staff?

Solutions

1. communications
2. businessmen; data processing personnel
3. T
4. operations staff; systems and programming staff; control staff
5. Data Processing Manager
6. write programs and debug programs.
7. study present system to determine problem areas; design new, more efficient systems.
8. they are under the supervision of a single manager—they may be separate entities, or a systems analyst may supervise several programmers, or the entire unit may consist of programmer-analysts who handle both tasks.
9. keypunch operators; EAM operators; computer operators
10. programming and systems personnel
11. a conversion procedure is the process of transferring from the old system to a new one.
12. the purpose of the control unit is to maintain control over the data entered into a data processing department and the output that is sent to the requesting departments.
13. the systems staff, in conjunction with the businessman.

Review Questions

I. Answer True or False

1. (T or F) Electronic Data Processing, often abbreviated EDP, is defined as the use of automated procedures to enter data, to operate upon it, and to produce desired results.
2. (T or F) Regardless of whether business or scientific functions are to be computerized, the procedures, processing, and total EDP approach are the same.
3. (T or F) It is important for data processing specialists to have a general understanding of business organization.
4. (T or F) Similar types of businesses may have very different structures.
5. (T or F) Large companies usually have only one accounting department.
6. (T or F) It is possible for some companies to utilize computerized operations without having a Data Processing Staff.
7. (T or F) The businessman who requires the assistance of the EDP department to computerize certain functions need only specify the requirements broadly with no necessity to become detailed.
8. (T or F) Once a system has been designed, the Programming Staff is then called upon to write the set of computer instructions that are required within the system.
9. (T or F) The Programming Staff always reports directly to the Data Processing Manager.

10. (T or F) The Control Unit Staff is responsible for maintaining control of data as it proceeds through the data processing installation.

523
BUSINESS
ORGANIZATION
AND THE ROLE
OF THE DATA
PROCESSING
DEPARTMENT

II. Fill in the Blanks

11. The organization and structure of typical businesses vary because of _____.

12. Departments within a company do not function independently because of _____.

13. A company which produces a product usually has a _____ Department.

14. A computer is generally used for each department within a company to _____ procedures and to assist management in their _____.

15. MIS is an abbreviation for _____.

16. The term _____ is used to indicate that data, or information, flows through a company and can have resounding effects on more than one organizational element or department.

17. The ultimate objective of each department within a company is to _____.

18. A pictorial representation most often used to evaluate structural organization is called a(n) _____.

19. From an organization chart, we can determine the relationship of each _____ to the company as a whole.

20. A company's departmental structure can generally be divided into the two separate functions of _____ and _____.

21. A data processing organization usually has a _____ staff, a _____ staff, and a _____ staff.

22. Once programs have been tested and are executing properly, the businessman in conjunction with the analyst and programmer is responsible for ensuring a smooth _____ from the old system to the new system.

23. The _____ analyzes the elements of the present system, determines the requirements of the job, and decides if a computerized set of procedures is economically justifiable.

Chapter 15
Systems Analysis and Design

15

I. Systems Analysis

A. Collection of Data
B. Basic Systems Elements
C. Analysis of Current System Costs
D. Formal Analysis
E. Management OK
   Self-Evaluating Quiz

II. Systems Design

A. Design of Systems Elements
B. Cost Analysis
C. Documentation
D. Conversion and Implementation
   Self-Evaluating Quiz

III. Feasibility Study

A. Analyze Current Company Operations
B. Determine Justification for Computer
C. Derive a List of Requirements and Criteria for the Prospective Computer
D. Analyze Bids from Computer Manufacturers
E. Devise a Plan to Prepare for the Computer

Important Terms Used in this Chapter

Self-Evaluating Quiz

Review Questions

15

What is a System We have seen that a business system is an organized method for accomplishing a business function. A business system requires an efficient *flow of information* in order to operate effectively. More and more business systems are being computerized in an effort to improve this flow of information and, in the end, to increase the profits of the company.

You will recall that a *systems analyst* is a computer specialist who is responsible for analyzing current procedures and designing the most efficient and economical systems or procedures to better accomplish given tasks within a company. The analyst must work closely with the businessman in order to achieve this basic objective.

Purpose of Chapter This chapter will consider the basic concepts of systems analysis and design. The purpose here is simply to familiarize the student with the subject, not to treat it in its entirety. Most colleges offer full semester courses in systems analysis and design and there are textbooks devoted completely to the subject.

Systems Analysis: Overview A systems analyst studies two types of systems:

Types of System Studies
- Where a current set of procedures exists, but a new or revised one is considered desirable
- Where a current set of procedures does not exist but is necessary

---

In both cases, there are two phases to the analyst's job. The first is to *analyze* the current requirements and the current system, if one exists. Systems analysis focusses on the following:

Analysis
- Collection of data on current system and requirements
- Understanding of current requirements and procedures:

15

1. Objectives
2. Constraints
3. Output
4. Processing
5. Input
6. Controls
7. Feedback
- Analysis of current system costs
- Preparation of a formal document called the *problem definition* which describes the system in its entirety and outlines the major flaws or problem areas which must be eliminated

Each of these will be described in detail later on in the chapter.

Systems Design: Overview   After the present system and the requirements for a new system have been thoroughly analyzed and the formal document called the problem definition has been prepared, the management of the company must decide whether a new design is necessary or economically justifiable. It may be, for example, that minor revisions to an existing system would eliminate many of its problems; or, it may be that a new system would simply be too expensive. In such a case, the design phase is not implemented.

In most cases, however, management gives its "OK" to the analyst to proceed with the design phase. The analyst must then design a new set of procedures which will perform the basic operations more efficiently and effectively than current operations permit.

The design phase focusses on the same elements as the analysis phase, where redesign is substituted for analysis:

Design
- Design of new requirements and procedures:
  1. Objectives
  2. Constraints
  3. Output
  4. Processing
  5. Input
  6. Controls
  7. Feedback
- Preparation of new cost estimates
- Preparation of a formal report called *documentation* which describes the new system in its entirety

See Figure 15.1 for a description of systems analysis and design as they will be discussed in this chapter.

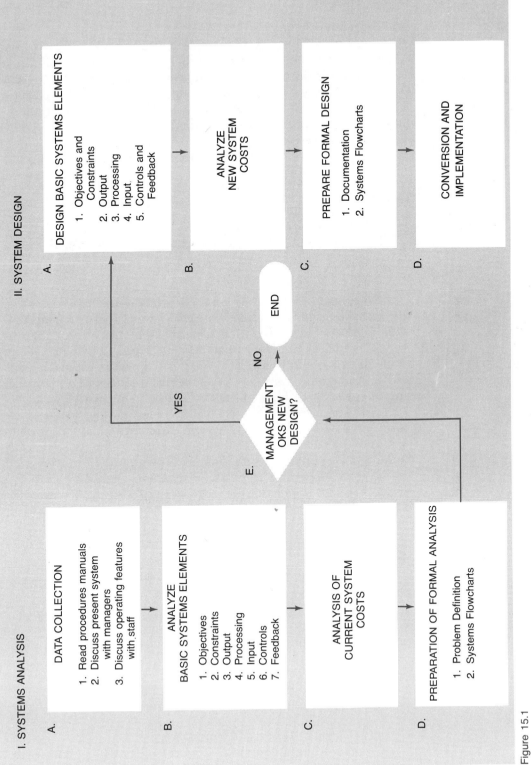

Figure 15.1
Flowchart of the steps involved in systems analysis and design.

I. Systems Analysis

A. Collection of Data

The collection of accurate, complete, and updated data by the analyst is an essential part of the job. The careless omission of a single factor or the acceptance of an idealized version of the present procedure obtained from an overzealous businessman could drastically alter the analyst's interpretation of the present system. Similarly, the smallest fact, misunderstood, could change the interpretation of the system.

Data can be collected by the following means:

Data Collection
1. Study of procedures manuals
2. Evaluation of forms
3. Interviews with the businessman and other personnel who work on the current system

---

Most companies have formalized written manuals containing the procedures and operations for each system. These manuals provide a general idea of how a system *should* function. Unfortunately, they are often out of date and the procedures indicated are sometimes not followed. The analyst can, however, utilize them to obtain background information about the system without expending valuable time of the businessman to obtain this information.

Similarly, the analyst should become familiar with all the forms used within the current system, thus minimizing the need to ask the businessman superfluous questions. The analyst must know the exact nature of the data presented on the forms, as well as the *distribution* of forms. The analyst will often draw form distribution charts which will then be reviewed with the businessman to ascertain that a clear understanding of current distribution of forms exists.

In analyzing forms, the analyst will be evaluating such things as:

Typical Elements to Look for
1. Are there any unnecessary items of information on particular forms?
2. Is there any unnecessary distribution of forms?
3. Are there manually prepared forms that could be more efficiently prepared by computer?
4. Are there some forms that could be combined into a single, comprehensive report?

The most important tool for the collection of data is the *interview* with the businessman. The analyst can learn all the details about the system from the interview. What has been learned from procedures manuals is how the system, if functioning as originally constituted, would operate; what is learned from the interview is how the system *actually* operates. In addition, the analyst will be asking the businessman questions, such as those in the checklist below, to assist in evaluating existing forms and their distribution.

Checklist: Requirements of Forms
1. Who uses the report or form?
2. How often is it used?
3. How much of the information on it is used?
4. Is the data on this report necessary for:
   a. Making decisions on some form of action?
   b. Keeping the department informed of current conditions?
   c. Checking the accuracy of other matters?
   d. Establishing control of other matters?
5. What would be the effect on each employee's job if he or she:
   a. Did not receive the report at all?
   b. Received less information than at present?
   c. Received more information than at present?
6. What other reports or records are prepared from data on this report?
7. Can the data on this report be obtained from any other source?
8. Is this report easy to read and use?
9. How long is each copy maintained?
10. How and where is it filed?
11. How often is it referred to after its original use?

The following is a checklist of *general* items that represent the type of information that the analyst will be seeking from interviews with the businessman.

Checklist: Items to be Analyzed
1. Can a monetary savings possibly be realized with new or revised operations?
2. Do the present procedures and operations utilize too much time and effort of the employees?
3. Does inaccurate reporting result in duplication of effort? Similarly, is the output data reliable enough for decision-making purposes?
4. Is the present system so rigid and inflexible that minor changes require major revamping?
5. Can the present system handle larger volumes which would result from normal growth?

Note that the businessman working within a current system is in the best position to evaluate its problem areas and to make recommendations on revisions that will result in more efficient processing. The businessman with knowledge of data processing requirements and capabilities is the single greatest asset in assisting computer specialists to realize the most effective designs possible.

B. Basic Systems Elements

Analysis of a system is performed according to a set of procedures that are designed to be as scientific and objective as possible. Figure 15.2 illustrates the basic elements used to analyze a system and how they relate to one another. We will discuss each of these in depth.

1. Objectives   The systems analyst must be aware of exactly what the businessman requires from a specific system. That is, management's goals or objectives must be fully known and understood. For example, one of a company's objectives for a new design might be to establish a computerized Accounts Receivable system so that a customer can walk into any branch store and have a clerk immediately determine the customer's balance at that time, based on computer records.

After reviewing the objectives of a current system with the businessman, it is quite possible that the systems analyst will recommend a modification to those objectives. The analyst has specialized expertise in data processing. Consequently, he or she may be aware of computer capabilities that can be utilized to give outstanding performance or to attain broader objectives for some systems.

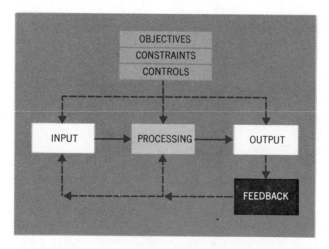

Figure 15.2

Basic structure of a business system.

2. Constraints The analyst *and* the businessman must both recognize any limitations or constraints that may be imposed when the analyst is designing a computerized system. There are several common constraints that usually affect most systems being computerized. These are legal constraints, budgetary constraints, and equipment constraints, as discussed below.

a. Legal Depending on the specific system, there are certain legal requirements to which the system must adhere. For example, in a Payroll system, the company must withhold various taxes such as federal, state, social security, and local. In addition, a W-2 withholding form must be sent to each employee at the end of the year. The analyst may feel, for example, that the design of the W-2 form is inefficient. There may, in fact, be a better design. However, there is little that the analyst can do. In this instance, the federal and local governments have dictated what the form should look like, how many copies there should be, and when they must be sent to employees. The businessman must thus make the analyst aware of all legal constraints under which the system is to operate.

b. Budgetary Often the management of a company imposes a budgetary constraint on the analyst, limiting the time, and hence money that can be expended in analyzing and designing a new system. Management may say, for example, that the new computerized Accounts Receivable system must be operational within one year. The analyst must therefore work with the businessman to achieve a functional system within the allotted time. However, because of the budgetary constraint, the result may be a system that is not as sophisticated as that which the analyst and/or the businessman might have ideally desired, but it is still one that satisfies the basic needs.

c. Equipment Computer equipment or hardware devices that are employed within the company represent another type of constraint. Systems analysts generally attempt to utilize the computer configuration that is currently available at the company. Additional equipment not currently utilized in the company which the analyst considers an asset to the system must be justified from a cost standpoint. In this case, the analyst must perform a *feasibility study* to determine the economic feasibility of acquiring such equipment.

3. Output The analyst must ascertain from the businessman just exactly what is currently produced as output under the present system. In a Payroll system, for example, some of the common outputs are paychecks and W-2 withholding statements. However, there are other outputs, such as Internal Revenue Service Form

941—Employer's Quarterly Federal Tax Return. This form is a detailed breakdown by employee of wages earned during a specific quarter and federal income taxes and social security taxes withheld. This form accompanies the check issued by the company to the government for taxes withheld.

It is the businessman's job to be cognizant of *all* output forms so that they can be described to the analyst.

Based on experience and on a complete comprehension of how the particular system functions, the analyst should be able to recommend to the businessman new or revised reports, for example, that can be readily obtained from a computerized system.

Output, however, constitutes more than just reports. For example, it is usually necessary to save information in the form of updated files that can be used for producing reports in the future. The businessman must therefore make the analyst aware of how output information is currently stored for future processing.

4. Processing Now that the analyst is aware of the output that is produced under the current system, he or she must recognize what processing, or types of operations, are currently performed in order to achieve the desired results. All procedures that are followed and the way in which various computations are made must be understood. For example, in an Accounts Receivable system, the company may include a finance charge for late payment. The computation may be as follows: 1½% charge on the first $500 overdue, and 1% charge on the excess over $500, with a minimum charge of $0.50. It is imperative that the businessman relay *all* processing steps, in detail, to the analyst. Any omission or misunderstanding can result in expensive redesign and reprogramming effort once the new system has been implemented.

5. Input The businessman must make the analyst aware of all input data that serves as the basis for desired outputs. The analyst will typically seek answers to questions such as the following, to ensure that the desired information about inputs is obtained:

Checklist
1. Where does all data used for processing originate?
2. How often is each type of input generated?
3. If there are codes or abbreviations used for input, does the analyst have *complete* lists of these?
4. What happens to input documents after they have been processed?

In a Payroll system, for example, we might expect to find time cards as an input form. In addition, we must consider, as input, various forms filled out by a new employee. These would include such items as a W-4 form (Internal Revenue Service)—Employee's Withholding Exemption Certificate. On this form, the number of exemptions for tax purposes is indicated.

6. Controls The businessman must familiarize the analyst with the ways in which errors are minimized under the current system. That is, the methods used to control or check errors must be specified. With knowledge of these controls, the analyst can then incorporate them in the computerized system, and perhaps suggest some controls with which the businessman may not be familiar. The following is a brief sample of some of the common controls that have been utilized in many business systems.

a. Batch Total If a group of inputs is to be batch-processed, a total figure is taken of a specific input field prior to processing. After processing, this *batch* total is compared to the input total to confirm that all input was, in fact, processed. For example, suppose that in a department store at the end of each day, each sales clerk takes all of the charge slips from one department and adds up the total of charge sales for that day. The clerk then sends the slips to the Accounts Receivable department, where posting is made to each customer's account and various reports are prepared. After all posting is done for that day, a report is prepared that shows the total of the charge sales that were posted from each department. If one of these totals disagrees with the batch total obtained by a particular sales clerk, then data has been incorrectly processed. Appropriate measures must then be taken to ascertain the reason for the discrepancy and to take corrective action (see Figure 15.3).

b. Item Count In addition to using a batch total, another control is to count the number of items both before and after processing. In this manner, if any items are lost during processing, an error in the item count will occur.

c. Limit Check A limit check is a test that is performed to make certain that figures being processed are reasonable. If a

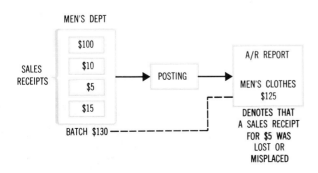

Figure 15.3
The use of a batch total.

particular figure is found to be unreasonable, then the specific item must be investigated. For example, in a particular Payroll system, a reasonable limit check for weekly payroll checks might be $2000. If any check that is processed exceeds a gross of $2000, then we must ascertain if an error has occurred. In this case, we might not issue the check until it has been verified.

  d. Trial Balances   A trial balance is a report that is prepared to ensure the accuracy of all posting to account ledgers. If the transactions for the specific time period are properly posted, the total debits will equal the total credits (see Figure 15.4.)

  7. Feedback   It is essential that the analyst be made aware of how errors in the current system are handled once they are discovered.

  Even with the use of many controls, it is still possible for errors to occur. The businessman must therefore explain all current procedures for adjustments and corrections when feedback procedures indicate that errors have occurred.

  For example, in a Payroll system, what happens when a paycheck is issued for an incorrect amount? Suppose, for example, that the check is in excess of the correct amount. The procedure may call for the check to be voided and a new one issued. In addition, however, appropriate adjustments must be made to the employee's year-to-date figures for earnings, federal tax withheld, social security tax deducted, etc. Similarly, in an Accounts Receiv-

Figure 15.4
Trial balance.

ACCOUNTS RECEIVABLE TRIAL BALANCE		
AS OF 9-30-80		
ACCOUNT NO.	DEBITS	CREDITS
01025	50.25	
01026	27.65	
01030	35.10	
01035		27.15
01037	26.07	
01038		
TOTALS	557,233.10	385,957.15
DEBITS–CREDITS	171,275.95	

able system suppose that a customer complains that a charged item has incorrectly appeared on a monthly statement. The procedures might call for the Accounts Receivable department to investigate the claim, and if it proves valid, to issue a credit to the customer's account. In addition, appropriate adjustments to various sales figures must be made.

C. Analysis of Current System Costs

While the analyst is studying a particular system, he or she will be collecting data on the cost of operating the system. This information will be useful later for comparing present costs to costs of a revised design. Management often will not approve a proposed system unless it can show a savings in operating costs over the current way of doing things. Another reason for analyzing current costs is that many systems have subsystems, or specific facets, that are disproportionately expensive. The analyst must determine when these costly operations are inefficient and when they should be maintained.

The analyst will probably want to compare the system costs to expenditures in previous years. In this way, he can determine how well growth factors have been accommodated in the system.

The businessman may thus be called on to supply appropriate cost data to the analyst. The major costs that must be considered are labor, equipment, material, supplies, and overhead associated with the current system.

D. Formal Analysis

1. Problem Definition The *problem definition* is the formal document prepared by the analyst, which defines in the utmost detail all aspects of the current system (including cost) and its basic inadequacies. It ferrets out the fundamental flaws in the system that impede the achievement of its stated objectives. In essence, it highlights those areas that the analyst will improve in a new design for the system.

Generally, the analyst will show the completed problem definition to the businessman who has responsibility for the specific system and who has worked closely with the analyst to provide all relevant information.

The businessman might have some pertinent suggestions or comments on items overlooked or misrepresented in the document. It is possible that the analyst has misunderstood various facets of the current system.

Thus the problem definition contains the analysis of the present system. This document is used to provide management and the businessman in a specific department with the analyst's understanding of the system and its basic problem areas. All data obtained in this problem definition represents a joint effort of both the analyst and the businessman.

INPUT/OUTPUT SYMBOLS		
SYMBOL	MEANING	DESCRIPTION
	INPUT/OUTPUT (I/O)	This is a generalized I/O symbol used to denote data entering the system or information that is generated as output. It is most often used when the medium of input or output is not specifically designated. i.e.  INVENTORY ERROR CORRECTIONS where such corrections may enter the system by cards, slips of paper or even telephone messages.
	PUNCHED CARD	This symbol is used when the data entered into the system or coming out of the system is in the form of a punched card.
	MAGNETIC TAPE	Magnetic tape is either the input or output medium.
	DOCUMENT	The input or output is a printed document or report.
	ONLINE STORAGE	Data is stored on all online or direct-access device such as a magnetic disk or drum.

Figure 15.5

Systems flowchart symbols.

2. Systems Flowchart A common tool used by the analyst for communicating ideas on analysis and also design is the *systems flowchart*. The systems flowchart, like its more detailed counterpart, the program flowchart, depicts the relationships between inputs, processing, and outputs, in terms of the system as a whole. It is a general representation of the information flow within the total system.

The businessman who is familiar with the organization of a systems flowchart can understand the analyst's new design far more quickly and completely than if he or she had to wade through numerous pages of narrative describing the system.

Figure 15.5 illustrates the symbols used in a systems flow-chart. The representation of a systems flowchart is very similar to that of a program flowchart.

	INPUT/OUTPUT SYMBOLS	
SYMBOL	MEANING	DESCRIPTION
	DISPLAY	*Output* information is displayed on console typewriters, displays, online terminals, plotters, etc.
	MANUAL INPUT	*Input* Information is supplied manually at the time of processing from an online device such as a console typewriter.
	COMMUNICATION LINK	Information is transmitted automatically from one location to another via communication lines.
	OFFLINE STORAGE	Data is stored on an offline medium; that is, data stored is not immediately accessible by the computer. An online device, such as a magnetic disk may always be available for immediate processing. A magnetic tape, however, is generally stored offline in a tape library and cannot be accessed immediately.
	PUNCHED TAPE	Data is stored on a punched paper tape as either input or output. This medium is often used as the initial data form, before conversion to magnetic tape. i.e. 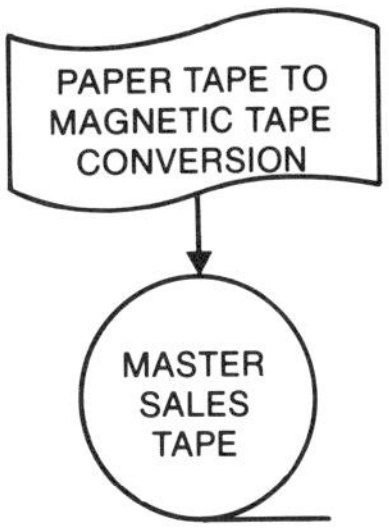

Figure 15.5 (cont'd) Systems flowchart symbols.

PROCESSING SYMBOLS

SYMBOL	MEANING	DESCRIPTION
	PROCESSING	This symbol represents the performing of an operation or a group of operations, generally by a computer or accounting machine, where the processing is a major function of the system. i.e. 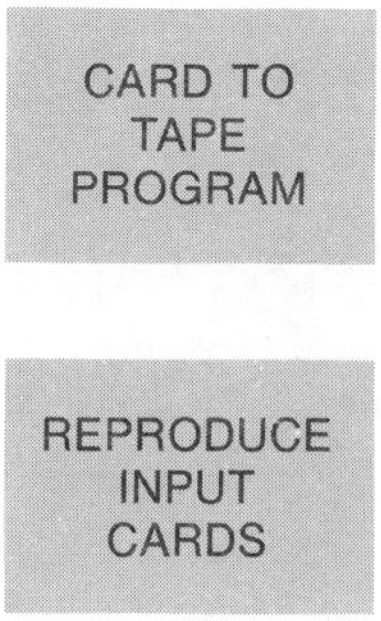 CARD TO TAPE PROGRAM REPRODUCE INPUT CARDS
	MANUAL OPERATION	This symbol represents a manual operation or one which requires an operator. Keypunching and verifying are examples of manual operations.
	ANNOTATION	This symbol is used when explanatory notes are required to clarify another symbol. This symbol is not in the main flow of the diagram. i.e. 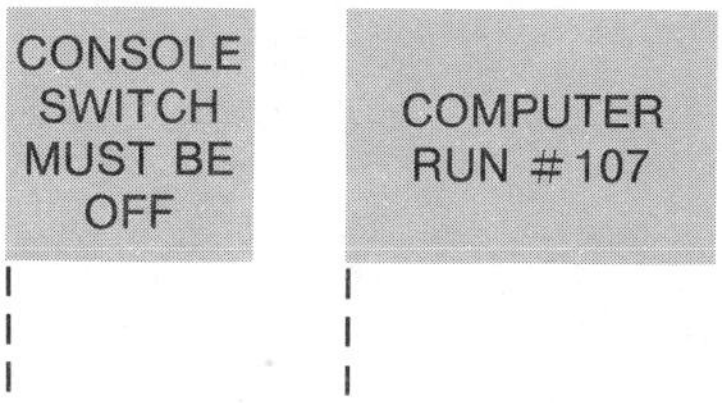 CONSOLE SWITCH MUST BE OFF COMPUTER RUN #107
	AUXILIARY OPERATION	Offline equipment is used to perform such functions as sorting, merging, collating, etc.
	CONNECTOR	This symbol is used to alter or terminate the flow of data. i.e.  2-B Go to page 2, symbol labelled B

Figure 15.5 (cont'd) Systems flowchart symbols.

Elements of Systems Flowchart
1. Each symbol indicates a type of function.
2. A notation appears inside each symbol, indicating the specific operations.
3. The flowchart is normally read from top to bottom.

Example 1

Figure 15.6 illustrates a sample systems flowchart for a Payroll system. Payroll forms indicating new employees and changes in position are punched into cards, sorted, and used to update a master payroll tape. In addition to the updated payroll tape, the payroll checks and a payroll report are generated by the computer.

Figure 15.6
Sample systems
flowchart for
payroll application.

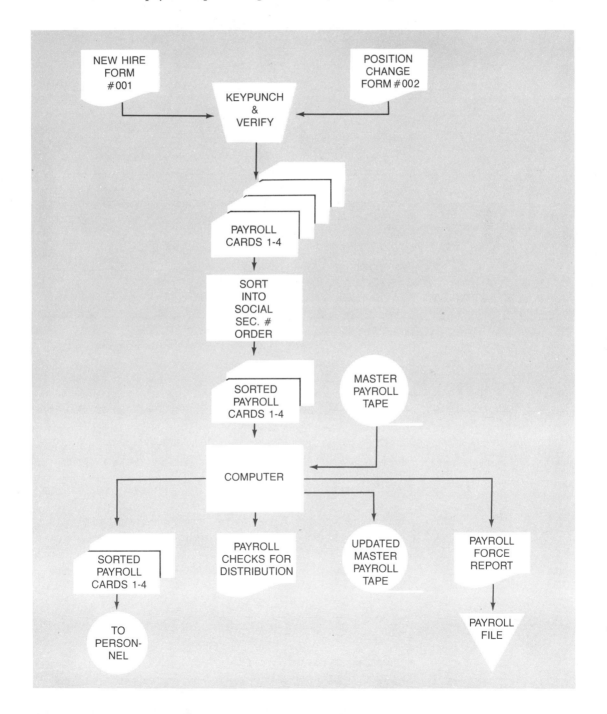

Note that it is relatively easy for trained businessmen to understand the processing involved by reading a systems flowchart.

E. Management OK

After a system has been analyzed and the formal problem definition and system flowcharts prepared, the analyst presents his or her analysis and ideas for a new design to management for its approval. Once approved, the analyst can begin the formal design work for the new system.

Self-Evaluating Quiz

1. Before an analyst can design a new system that will alleviate system flaws, he or she must _____.

2. The seven basic elements of any system are _____, _____, _____ _____, _____, _____, and _____.

3. (T or F) After analyzing a system's objectives, it is quite possible that these objectives could be more efficiently met with the use of computers.

4. A constraint is a(n) _____ imposed on a system.

5. Two common types of constraints are _____ and _____.

6. To determine the economic possibility of acquiring new equipment to handle business tasks, a(n) _____ study must be performed by the analyst.

7. (T or F) Control procedures are built into systems to minimize errors.

8. A batch total is _____.

9. A(n) _____ is a test that is performed to make certain that figures being processed are reasonable.

10. A(n) _____ is a report that is prepared to ensure the accuracy of all posting to account ledgers.

11. The three basic methods for collecting data are _____, _____, and _____.

12. Procedures manuals generally indicate how a system _____.

13. The single most effective method of collecting data is the _____.

14. (T or F) When an analyst attempts to determine current system costs, the businessman should favorably impress him by minimizing these figures.

15. The _____ is the formal document prepared by the analyst which defines in the utmost detail all aspects of the current system.

Solutions

1. study the present system in depth
2. objectives; constraints; outputs; processing; input; control; feedback

3. T
4. limitation or restriction
5. legal; budgetary; equipment
6. feasibility
7. T
8. a total figure of specific input fields to be used for comparison purposes to confirm that all input has been processed
9. limit check
10. trial balance
11. study of procedures manuals; evaluation of forms; interview
12. *should* function
13. interview
14. F
15. problem definition

II. Systems Design

A. Design of Systems Elements

The same basic elements that are examined in the analysis phase must be restructured in the design phase. See Figure 15.2 for a review of these elements. We will discuss here those that most frequently require redesign.

1. Objectives and Constraints   These are modified only when necessary.

2. Input and Output   In redesigning input and output, new file types must be selected, new formatting provided, and new information added, when necessary. A major portion of the analyst's task is devoted to redesigning input and output.

   a. Selection of file type   Cards, tape, or disk are traditional file types that are selected by the analyst as input. The selection of file type is based on:

Factors in Selecting File Type
1. Cost
2. Speed of device
3. Volume
4. Projected future growth
5. Current hardware
6. Type of processing

The relative merits of each file type have been outlined in Chapters 2 and 5. The businessman should be aware of the file types selected by the analyst for the input files and should be advised as to the reasons why the analyst chose the specific types. In this way, the businessman who possesses some familiarity with data processing equipment can perhaps make suggestions for alternative file types based on his expertise in the business area.

b. Design of the files Once the file type has been chosen, the analyst must structure, organize, and design the file as efficiently as possible.

Generally, the analyst will illustrate file design with the use of a Card Layout Sheet (Figure 15.7) for card files, or a Tape or Disk Layout Sheet (called a Storage Layout Sheet; Figure 15.8) for tape or disk files.

These sheets serve the same purpose as Print Layout Sheets. They indicate the positioning of data within a record so that the record format can be exhibited.

The businessman who must work with the analyst should pay particular attention to the following file design items that will directly affect processing:

Figure 15.7

Card layout form.

1. Field Size: each field must be long enough to accommodate the largest data item. A NAME field, in a Payroll file

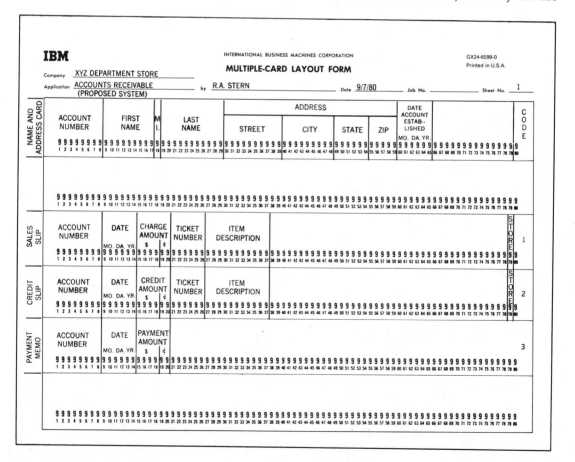

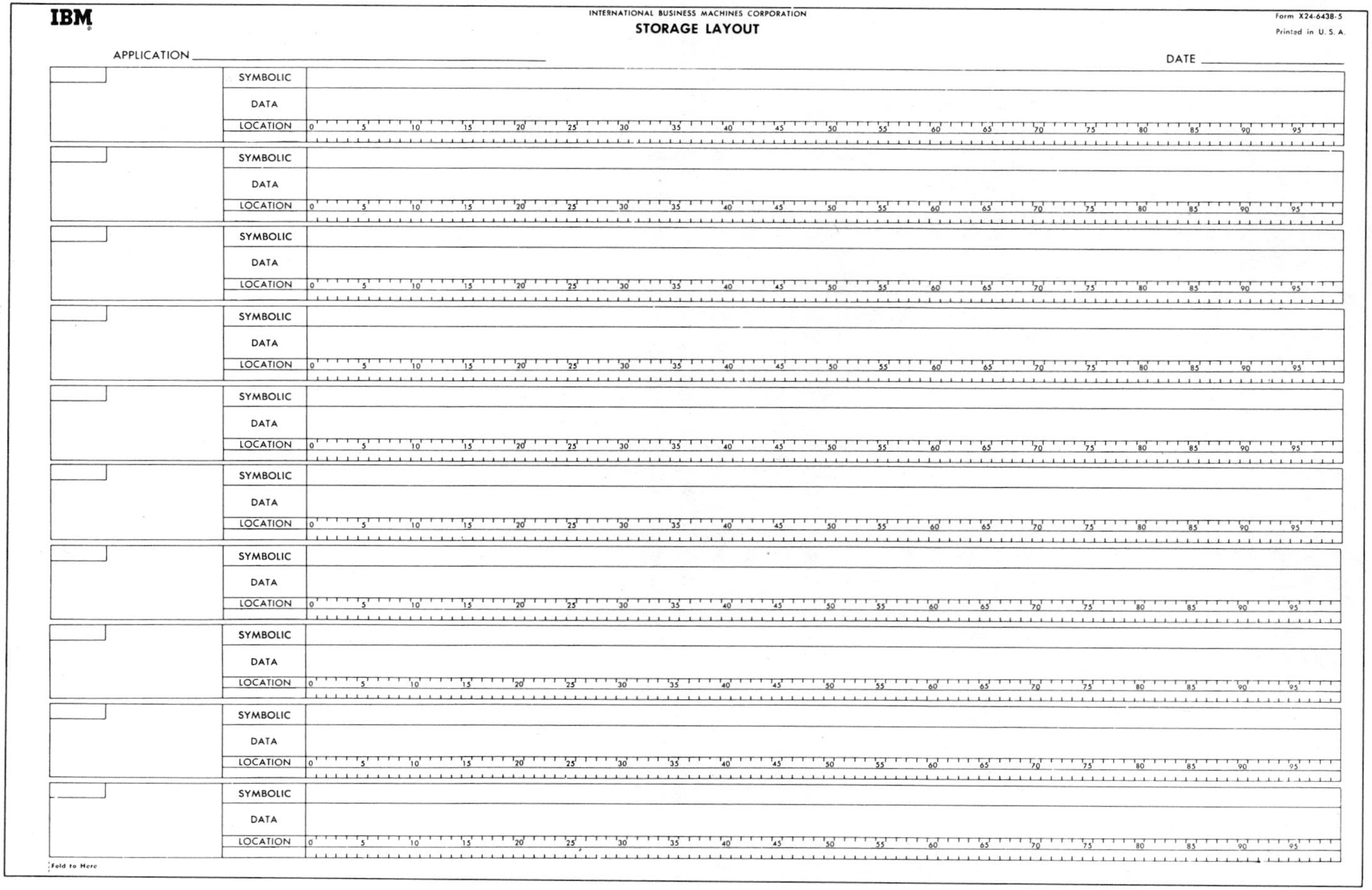

Figure 15.8
Storage layout sheet.

for example, must generally be large enough to accommodate the employee with the longest name.

The analyst determines the field size, but the businessman must ascertain that it is adequate.

2. Coded Fields: to conserve space on a file and to facilitate the processing of data, the analyst often uses coded fields of information. ACCOUNT NUMBER, for example, in place of CUSTOMER NAME, may become a new design item in a file. It is more appropriate for computer processing to use integer fields (ACCOUNT NUMBERS), as key items rather than alphanumeric fields (CUSTOMER NAME). Similarly, it is easier to sort on such numeric fields.

If coded fields are employed by the analyst in the file design, the businessman must make certain that they are adequate and will be used effectively. It should be ascertained that the length of the coded field is adequate enough to handle all items—both for the present and in the future. For example, an Accounts Receivable Department which currently has 986 customers should use an ACCOUNT NUMBER field of at least four positions (0001–9999) to ensure that it is large enough to allow for future growth.

3. Positioning of Data Within a Record: generally, the analyst arranges a record format so that the encoding operations are facilitated. For tape or disk files, it matters little to the business staff how fields are arranged. If, however, card files are to be used by the business staff, then data should be arranged in a meaningful way so that any manual operations which use the cards are simplified. Key fields such as ACCOUNT NUMBER, SOCIAL SECURITY NUMBER, and INVENTORY NUMBER should be easily identifiable at the *beginning* of the record.

3. Processing Once the outputs for the new system have been prepared, the analyst designs the processing steps that will be needed to produce them. At this point he or she has a *general* idea of the types of inputs that will be employed in the new system, based on familiarity with current inputs. These will provide a general frame of reference for processing requirements even though the inputs may be modified later on in the new design.

An experienced and thorough analyst designs a *total* system, utilizing computer equipment, that does not necessarily follow the present way of performing operations. The use of a computer affords the analyst a greater degree of flexibility than is feasible in a manual system.

Thus it is possible that the analyst may recommend *online* (or immediate-update) processing to replace *batch* (or group) processing in a particular system, if such online capabilities will enhance productivity or increase profits.

For example, a small department store may currently utilize an Accounts Receivable system that manually updates customer records once a week. That is, weekly, all charge slips are *batch* processed to update the file. The analyst may suggest a new design that utilizes terminals at sales counters within the store. These devices are keyed with customer charge account data, at the time of purchase, to immediately update the specific record.

Here, again, the businessman is far more informed on the department's needs and operations than the analyst. Thus the businessman must work closely with the analyst so that the processing adequately serves the department.

4. Controls and Feedback These are modified as necessary.

B. Cost Analysis

1. Justification of the New Design from a Cost Standpoint Note that the new design must be approved by management and the business leaders of the related department before it can be implemented. In most companies management will study the cost figures on the proposed system for justification of the new design.

The chief reason, in most cases, for converting to a new design is that it *eventually* will save the company money. Thus a proposed system, in such cases, must clearly indicate a monetary savings. In other cases, a proposed system, while not resulting in a monetary savings, may mean increased productivity or profits for the company as a whole. Initially, we will limit our discussion to those proposed systems that are designed to result in a monetary savings over present operations.

Costs of the present system cannot, however, be compared *directly* to the costs of a proposed system without some economic analysis. Initially, costs of the proposed system will include programming and implementation expenses. Often it takes many years to assimilate these expenses. Thus the new system cannot usually show a savings before several years have passed.

The analyst often prepares a cost analysis which indicates the break-even point, that is, the point at which revenue equals costs or where profits are no longer negative or indicating a loss.

In summary, many new designs are approved by management mainly because they will eventually save the company money. Often, however, business leaders seek new systems because of intangible cost factors. A new system may not directly result in a monetary savings but may result in the following intangible benefits, which will improve a company's profits:

Intangible Benefits of New Systems

1. Better service: a new system may attract more customers. This is often justification for utilizing terminals at key locations in an online or real-time environment to answer customer inquiries and to update customer files.
2. Improved production planning: the businessman may have tighter control over production scheduling and material requirements.
3. Reduction in work loads of clerical staffs: with the use of computers, a new system may stabilize manpower requirements and reduce extensive overtime.
4. Provision for future growth with the use of computer processing: a new system needs fewer revisions and fewer increases in labor and equipment.

Thus, the monetary factors associated with a new design must be outlined and justified before management or business supervisors, in the respective departments, will give approval. These factors may mean a monetary savings to the company within a few years after initial design and programming expenditures have been assimilated. Or they may mean an intangible benefit or savings to the company. In either case, the analyst must justify, from a cost standpoint, the new design to help "sell" it to those businessmen who will be required to work within it.

2. Basic Cost Factors The costs of the proposed system fall into two basic categories:

DESIGN COSTS

Systems Design
Programming
Training of Data Processing and Business Staff to Effectively
    Work with the System
Conversion and Testing

RECURRING COSTS

Personnel
Equipment Rentals
Supplies
Overhead

Cost figures for a proposed system should be projected at least three years into the future to adequately allow for projected growth. After three years, cost estimates tend to become inaccurate due to alterations within the system and changes in the economy.

C. Documentation

Once a system has been designed by integrating all of the above elements, the analyst must prepare a formalized, detailed record called the *documentation* package which describes that design. This documentation serves many functions.

Purpose of Documentation

1. It is a businessman's tool for evaluating the design: the documentation is utilized by business representatives within a department, and management. Together they determine if the new design satisfies the objectives of the company within the established constraints and if it is justifiable from a cost standpoint. That is, the documentation provides a record that is used by management to assess the new design.

2. It provides a frame of reference on the new system: the department in which the new system will function needs formalized procedures by which the staff can be guided. Similarly, the programming and operations personnel assigned to implement the new design will need a standard from which an understanding of the system as a whole can be derived and from which a detailed picture of the program specifications can be obtained.

Basically, the documentation contains the following:

Documentation Format

1. Cover Letter
   This defines the objectives and constraints of the new system and indicates briefly how the new design will meet these. It is an introduction to the revised system and is an attempt to "sell" it or to convince management of its feasibility and advantages. Keep in mind that unless business leaders approve the new design effort, then a new system cannot be implemented.

2. Narrative
   This is a brief outline, in narrative form, of the workings of the new system.

3. Systems Flowcharts
   These show the flow of information in the new system.

4. File Specifications
   In addition to the required layout sheets, each file must be described with respect to:
   a. Purpose
   b. Programs that will utilize the file
   c. Volume

    d.   Frequency of use
    e.   Source from which file is obtained
    f.   Description of fields
    g.   Layout and samples
5. Specifications of Each Program Necessary Within the System
6. Costs of the Proposed System and Economic Justification of the New Design

D. Conversion and Implementation

The analyst must prepare a conversion procedure to ensure a smooth transition from the old system to the new, once the new design has been approved and programming effort has been completed.

Typically, the new system is used in a *parallel run*, together with the old, to ascertain that the same results are achieved. If output data is not the same, then the causes of the inaccuracies must be found and eliminated before the new system can be implemented. Once the new design has been proven error-free, all procedures and operations can be systematically transferred.

The steps involved in most system conversions that must be prepared by the analyst include the need to:

System Conversion
1. Establish schedules for the transfer of operations to the computer. An estimate must be included indicating the time required to completely convert or cut over to the new system.
2. Assist in the creation of master files that will be required for most operations. The data for these master files must be amassed from manual files, edited, and converted to a machine-readable form.
3. Supervise a pilot operation.
4. Train and reorient clerical and business staffs.

Clerical staffs will often be given new assignments after conversion has been completed. They must receive proper training from the analyst on their new tasks. Similarly, businessmen who receive the output must be advised of all changes in forms or forms distribution.

After a system has been cut over, the analyst still has the responsibility to follow up and ensure that it is functioning properly. Approximately three months after the new system is fully operational, the analyst should check back to see if the system is working properly. It may happen, for example, that some employees are no longer following the procedure exactly. They may have found a better way of performing some aspect, or new personnel may have been misinformed on some procedure. The analyst might also discover some flaws in the design during the follow-up. Note that it is much easier to correct a flaw after a short time has elapsed than to wait and attempt to patch it after a considerable duration.

In summary, the systems analyst's design tasks involve many major responsibilities. In each phase, however, he or she must work closely with the businessman to ensure a proper understanding of the system's requirements. Similarly, the businessmen must become familiar with aspects of the new design so that successful implementation can be achieved.

Guidelines for a Documentation Library
Quick access to DP documentation requires a simple, easily understood classification scheme.
    by K. Clark Davis

Over the past few years, the trade literature in data processing has been replete with articles and reports concerning documentation standards; but very little has been written about the acquisition, classification and circulation of documentation. Even the most complete and best written documentation is of little value without an efficient method of retrieval. It is as important to be able to quickly access documentation as it is to be able to access other types of data in a DP environment.

In my capacity as documentation administrator, I have designed, implemented and managed two documentation libraries: one for the data processing department of a medium-size commercial bank; the other for a bank service organization owned by a large bank holding company where I am currently employed.

Delimit and specify
The first and probably most important step in setting up a documentation library is to delimit and specify its exact contents and to devise a simple, easily understood classification scheme. Our library's holdings are divided into two broad categories: typewritten documentation and source language listings. One file is maintained for current source language listings for every production program; and another file is used to store the previous compile of these same program listings. This practice provides us with a valuable backup tool when changes to production programs do not work as they should. A quick review of the previous source language listing has helped both analysts and programmers locate and correct program bugs on numerous occasions.

The other major category of data processing documentation, typewritten documents, consists of flowcharts, system descriptions, program specifications and so on. In our library, each of these is assigned a two digit numeric identifier. The listing that follows illustrates this scheme:

01   Systems Documentation
    systems flowchart
    systems narrative
    file narrative for each file
    file cross reference
    file/record descriptions
    report cross reference
    example reports

02   Program Documentation
    program flowchart
    program abstract
    input/output identification
    processing logic narrative
    file/record description

03   Input Forms/Print Layouts
    sample input forms
    completion instructions for input forms
    print layouts

04   Operator's Guide/Keypunching Instructions
    run inventory
    run instructions
    output distribution
    error and recovery procedures
    card layout and keypunch specifications

05   User Documentation
    systems narrative
    input specifications and instructions
    output descriptions and disposition

06   Ready reference
    master file layouts for all systems
    transaction codes for all systems
    listing of printed output for all systems
    preprinted forms and instructions for completion

07   Technical Reference
    hardware specifications
    systems software specifications
    other vendor supplied documentation

Self-Evaluating Quiz

1.   Business leaders and the _____ must work together to create
    a new systems design.

2. First, the _____ and the _____ must be revised so that they provide realistic requirements of the new system within appropriate limitations.

3. Next the _____ of the system are revised to provide business leaders with more meaningful reports.

4. The processing steps involved in a new design are best illustrated by a _____.

5. The revised inputs must be redesigned with respect to _____.

6. The new files are best illustrated by _____ sheets.

7. Once all the elements for a new design have been prepared and integrated, the analyst must prepare a _____ of the proposed system.

8. The chief reason for converting to a new design, in most cases, is that it eventually will _____.

9. Initially, costs of the proposed system will include _____, _____, and _____ expenses that must be assimilated before a comparison between present and proposed system costs can be evaluated.

10. In addition to saving the company money, a new design may have _____ cost benefits.

11. An example of an intangible cost benefit is _____.

12. Elements included with *design costs* are _____, _____, _____, and _____.

13. Elements included within *recurring costs* are _____, _____, _____, and _____.

14. Once the analyst has fully designed a system by integrating all of the above elements, he must prepare a formalized, detailed record called _____ describing that design.

15. After the system has been designed and approved, and programming effort has been completed, the analyst must have a _____ procedure to ensure a smooth transition from the old system to the new.

16. A parallel run is _____.

17. The follow-up is a procedure where _____.

Solutions

1. systems analyst
2. objectives; constraints
3. outputs
4. systems flowchart
5. file type used and design of the file
6. layout
7. cost analysis
8. save the company money
9. design; programming; conversion
10. intangible
11. improved production planning; better customer service

12. systems design costs; programming costs; training costs; conversion costs
13. personnel costs; overhead costs; equipment costs; supply costs
14. the documentation
15. conversion
16. a procedure where the current and the new system are run together, in parallel, to ensure that the new system operates properly
17. the analyst checks the system, after a three-month interval, for example, to ensure that it is functioning properly

III. Feasibility Study

Many companies do not have their own computer facility. They process data in one of the following ways:

Data Processing Without an In-House Computer
1. Manual processing
2. Electronic Accounting Machines: usually used in conjunction with manual operations
3. Service Bureaus: companies that provide systems analysis and design, programming, and operations for businesses for a fixed fee
4. Time-Sharing: rental of computer time from a central organization

---

When company processing expands greatly, the management will generally request that a study be conducted to determine if a data processing facility could be justified; that is, a group is appointed to determine if it is feasible to acquire, maintain, and profit from a computer system. This type of study is called a *feasibility study.*

A special committee within the company is generally formed with the authority to conduct the feasibility study. The typical committee consists of the following employees.

Members of Feasibility Committee
1. One member of each department in the company, who can best convey the department's need for a computer.
2. A member of the executive committee of the company, who is most concerned with the company's policies and monetary limitations.
3. A senior systems analyst who is best suited, because of training and background, to determine a company's need for a computer.
4. An outside consultant, who is considered an expert in designing alternative computer systems.

The importance of each of these members is discussed below.

Departmental Member   It is important to have each department represented on the committee for several reasons. Each representative is aware of the particular needs within his or her area and can often indicate any special requirements that could be handled by a computer system. In addition, once management decides to obtain a computer, it needs the operational support of all departments within the company. Since each department takes part in computer selection through its representative on the feasibility committee, the possibility of resistance to the computer from independent areas is reduced.

Executive   A member of the executive committee of the company is needed on the feasibility committee to act as chairman. Since a feasibility study involves much time and effort and extensive paperwork, a chairman is required to coordinate the committee's efforts. In addition to serving as chairman, this member's high position in the management echelon lends great prestige and support to the committee. It is always advantageous for a committee of this kind to have management's explicit support so that any barriers to its endeavors can be easily handled. For example, the committee generally spends much time in collecting information, interviewing employees, and in meeting in conferences. These disruptions in normal daily activities are more readily tolerated by department managers, when a committee has the explicit endorsement of the management. An executive is an added advantage on this committee because of his or her familiarity with company policies and monetary limitations. This can save the committee much time and effort by channeling its proposals to insure their future acceptance.

Senior Systems Analyst   The senior systems analyst is needed on the committee because of his or her expertise in computer hardware and software. By synthesizing and analyzing the requirements of all departments in the company, the analyst can determine the size and specifications of the computer system that should be installed. He or she can also determine the type of system that would be most suitable. For example, a suggestion might be made that a computer system incorporating data communications through a terminal network be adopted. Or, one might recommend a much smaller system that would be adequate. The analyst, then, must possess specific knowledge of various computer configurations in order to assist management in determining the most practical one for the company.

Outside Consultant   An outside consultant is often needed to act as a kind of catalyst on this committee. Note that, like the senior systems analysts, the consultant has specialized knowledge of computer hardware and software. Unlike the analysts, however, he or she can be completely objective, since his or her responsibilities are independent of any company or department ties. An analyst who reports to the Comptroller of the company may recommend computer systems that are most conducive to handling accounting procedures, since this is the area with which he or she is most familiar. A consultant, however, can maintain objectivity and can often make valid recommendations.

The basic functions of the feasibility committee can be segmented into several phases:

Functions of Feasibility Committee

1. Analyze the current operations of the company.
2. Determine if the implementation of a computer system can be justified. It is possible that an overhaul of the current operations might eliminate the need for a computer installation. If not, a further investigation would be required.
3. Assuming that a computer system is still feasible, it would now be necessary to devise a list of requirements and criteria to be fulfilled by the prospective computer. This list of specifications would then be submitted to several computer manufacturers. They would evaluate the data and make bids to supply specific computer configurations to fulfill the requirements.
4. Evaluate carefully the bids received by the feasibility committee. The computer manufacturer that can best meet the company's needs is then recommended to management.
5. Devise a plan for the company to prepare for the installation of the computer system, if management gives its approval.

The above steps are not unlike the systems analyst's tasks in analysis and design. All areas must be scrutinized carefully, a design recommended and, if approved, a plan must be indicated for implementing the system.

It is important to examine each of the above functions in more depth so that the scope of a feasibility study can be fully appreciated.

A. Analyze Current Company Operations

This is generally regarded as a major systems analysis, where the company itself is evaluated in depth. Each department must be individually considered, as well as its relation to the others. Documents must be evaluated and costs must be compiled. Each department is *not* evaluated with regard to its flaws but, instead, with regard to how a computer system could improve its productivity.

B. Determine Justification for Computer

Conceivably, analysis of the company's operations may indicate that a computer installation is not justifiable from a cost standpoint. Perhaps a redesign effort of various forms and procedures can lead to a more efficient utilization of the company's manpower. Even with this type of redesign effort, the feasibility committee may feel that a computer is still warranted.

Notice, however, that a computer installation must pay for itself in the end in order to be considered profitable. This implies that the cost of acquiring and of maintaining a computer system must be approximated at this time to determine if further investigation should be conducted. These costs would include the following items.

Cost Factors
1. Cost of designing computerized systems.
2. Cost of programming effort.
3. Rental and/or purchase costs of computer hardware and software.
4. Cost of training company personnel to use computer inputs and outputs.
5. Cost of supplies.
6. Costs of operating a computer facility.
7. Cost associated with "housing" the computer, that is, the construction of an air-conditioned room for the computer.

The current cost of processing data must be compiled and then compared to the projected computer costs. Note that often it is necessary to project present costs into the future to determine what the costs would be under the present system, but with normal growth trends. Very often, an existing system, if continued indefinitely, would require extensive revision anyway. These revision costs should be included in present system costs so that a fair comparison to a computerized system can be made.

If, after cost comparison is completed, there appears to be a savings in the end by installing a computer, then the company can proceed to derive a list of requirements and criteria to be fulfilled by a computer system. Observe that the savings need not be in the near future. Sometimes, the savings obtained by installing a computer system takes many years to be realized.

If a computer system cannot be justified, the committee may recommend a redesign of forms or procedures. Or, a service bureau that can perform company operations on a computer for a fee could be investigated. The distinct advantage of contracting a service bureau is that the initial cost is greatly reduced. Note, however, that the company would have no computer systems of its own; everything is owned and operated by the service bureau. If the company decides to install a computer at a future date, it must buy or rent the programs and procedures from the service bureau, or must develop them on its own.

C. Derive a List of Requirements and Criteria for the Prospective Computer

This represents the set of specifications of what is desired from the computer. The various computer manufacturers will use this as a basis for preparing bids to supply specific computer configurations. The type of information required would be as follows.

1. A review of the company's objectives and goals.
2. The sample input and output forms currently used and the frequency with which they are generated.
3. The descriptions of the type of processing done, including types of arithmetic operations performed.
4. The statements of the major controls currently used.
5. The description of the information that is on file, including the length of time it is maintained.
6. A list of any special capabilities desired under a computer system, such as terminal inputs, specific processing requirements, and so on.
7. The description of the company's physical structure, including locations of branch offices, warehouses, and so on.

D. Analyze Bids from Computer Manufacturers or Leasing Firms

Once the bids are received from the manufacturers or leasing organizations, they must be carefully evaluated by the feasibility committee. The cost of operating each computer system proposed is the most important factor in rating competitive bids. However, intangible benefits must be considered as well. The following items must be considered prior to rendering any decision:

1. The cost of renting the computer system.
2. The programming languages available with the system.
3. The multiprogramming and data communications capability.
4. The ability to expand storage as required at a later date.
5. The specifications of input-output devices included in the configuration.
6. The availability of educational materials and their corresponding charges.
7. The availability and cost of service in case of computer malfunction.
8. The compatibility with larger models in case a future conversion is deemed necessary.

Once the committee has reviewed all the bids, it should make its recommendations to management in writing. The recommendation should highlight the reasons that this particular system was chosen over the others considered.

E. Devise a Plan to Prepare for the Computer

When a company finally signs a contract with a computer manufacturer, it may have to wait a year or longer before delivery is made. The feasibility committee should map out a plan to ensure a smooth transition from current operations to a computer system. A typical plan includes these items:

1. Establish a Data Processing Department. This necessitates the hiring of computer and keypunch operators, programmers, systems analysts, and managers. Some members may be transferred from other departments and may be trained for new positions in the Data Processing Department.
2. Design systems for the new computer.
3. Program the new systems. Even though the computer has not yet arrived, it is possible to write programs and have them tested. Often a computer manufacturer has test centers available for running programs for a company that has not yet received its computer. If this is not available, programs can usually be tested by renting computer time from other companies. If systems work and programming efforts for specified systems are completed when a new computer arrives, there need be no delay before the implementation occurs. Often, these phases are not even begun until the computer is delivered and, as a result, the equipment is rarely used for many months.
4. Test the new system. It is possible to have people simulate their projected tasks until the computer comes by using sample forms and data. In this manner, "bugs" in the system can often be detected. In addition, the personnel who are required to use the system will become familiar with its operations and procedures.

From the foregoing discussion, one can easily realize why feasibility studies sometime take two or more man-years to complete. These studies are the foundation for tremendous change within a company.

Important Terms Used in this Chapter

Collection of Data	Design costs
Constraints	Documentation
Controls	Feasibility Study
Conversion—System	Feedback
Cost Analysis	Implementation

Problem Definition
Recurring Costs
System
Systems Analysis

Systems Analyst
Systems Design
Systems Flowchart

Self-Evaluating Quiz

1. The typical feasibility committee consists of a _____ , _____ , _____ , and _____ .
2. (T or F) The tasks involved in a feasibility study are similar to those in system analysis and design.
3. (T or F) Analysis of current company operations is required for a feasibility study.
4. (T or F) Cost evaluations are not required in a feasibility study.
5. Bids from _____ must be compared during a feasibility study.
6. (T or F) A feasibility study may indicate that it is cheaper, in the long run, to use a service bureau than to establish a computer center.

Solutions

1. businessman; executive; systems analyst; consultant
2. T
3. T
4. F
5. computer manufacturers
6. T

Review Questions

I. Answer True or False

1. (T or F) An experienced systems analyst can generally computerize a system in less than a week.
2. (T or F) The businessman must work closely with the systems analyst to achieve an effectively computerized business system.
3. (T or F) Once a computerized system is operational, it is relatively easy to make modifications to it.
4. (T or F) Before a new system can be designed, the current system must be completely analyzed.
5. (T or F) The major reasons for the analyst analyzing the current system are to understand the operations required and to find the current problem areas.
6. (T or F) An objective of most Personnel Systems is to provide salary checks for employees.
7. (T or F) The way in which objectives are met constitutes the system for carrying out a business application or function.

8. (T or F) Once goals or objectives for a system are known, it is possible that the analyst can suggest more far-reaching goals that are possible with a computerized system.

9. (T or F) The procedures involved in systems design follow a step-by-step approach.

10. (T or F) A new design must be based on current systems objectives which cannot be altered in the revised system.

11. (T or F) It is possible that current constraints are unrealistic and severely limiting with respect to the objectives of the system.

12. (T or F) Legal constraints can generally be revised in the new system.

13. (T or F) A systems design will generally include revisions in output so that more meaningful reports are produced.

14. (T or F) If a systems analyst suggests a new output form in the design, then the businessman should accept it since the analyst is more qualified to decide what is best for the system as a whole.

15. (T or F) An analyst can revise reports, but should not alter the distribution of forms.

16. (T or F) The design of output is usually the single most important element of systems design.

17. (T or F) A systems analyst should design a total system, utilizing computer equipment where applicable, and not necessarily following the current method for performing operations.

18. (T or F) A systems analyst should always design his system utilizing computer equipment to replace all manual operations.

19. (T or F) A systems flowchart depicts the relationships between inputs, processing, and outputs for the system, as a whole.

20. (T or F) Businessmen who can read a systems flowchart are better able to understand the intricate details of the new design.

21. (T or F) If the department manager is in accord, the systems analyst is free to redesign all inputs to a system.

22. (T or F) To conserve space on a file and to facilitate the processing of data, the analyst often uses coded fields of information.

23. (T or F) Systems design should eventually cost less to operate than the current set of procedures.

24. (T or F) A new systems design may not directly result in a monetary savings but, when implemented, it may result in intangible benefits.

25. (T or F) Cost figures for a proposed system should be projected at least ten years into the future to indicate how growth factors are accommodated.

26. (T or F) The documentation supplied by the businessman describes the new systems design in detail.

27. (T or F) The documentation can be the businessman's tool for evaluating the new design.

28. (T or F) The systems analyst must supply a conversion procedure to ensure a smooth transition from the old system to the new one.

II. Fill in the Blanks

1. An analyst must evaluate the manner in which a current system meets its _____.

2. The most common type of constraint imposed on the analyst is a(n) _____ one.

3. The way in which errors are minimized is through the use of _____ procedures.

4. If a procedure is performed to check if an amount field does not exceed $150.00, we call this control a(n) _____.

5. Suppose, in the current system, a payroll check is incorrectly computed. The procedures used to correct the error are part of _____.

6. The methods for collecting data on the present system are _____, _____ and _____.

7. The analyst learns from the _____ how a specific system *should* function.

8. The analyst learns from the _____ how a specific system actually functions.

9. Often, management will not approve the design of a new system unless it can show a _____ of operating costs.

10. Before the analyst can design a new system, he must _____.

11. The basic inadequacies of the present system are formalized in the _____.

12. Generally, the fields that are positioned at the beginning of a record are _____.

13. _____ and _____ procedures must be integrated in a new design to ensure that the proposed system will function properly and to spot any minor flaws so that they may be corrected before they become major ones.

14. Once all elements for the new design have been prepared and integrated, the analyst must prepare a _____ analysis of the proposed system.

15. It is usually necessary for the systems analyst to justify his new design from a _____ basis.

16. Projected cost figures for a new design must usually be compared to _____ cost figures.

17. The first few years in which a new design has been implemented are usually very costly because _____.

18. Once the analyst has fully designed a system by integrating all of its basic elements, he must prepare a formalized detailed record called the _____ which describes that design.

19. The analyst must prepare a _____ procedure to ensure a smooth transition from the old system to the new, once the new design has been completed and approved.

Chapter 16

Management Information Systems

16

I. Definition of MIS

    A.   Requirements

    B.   Limitations of MIS

II. Advanced Techniques Used in MIS and Other Systems

    A.   Simulation

    B.   Management Games

    C.   Linear Programming

Important Terms Used in this Chapter

Self-Evaluating Quiz

Review Questions

Unit Five: Selected Bibliography

16

I. Definition of MIS

Our discussion of data processing systems has thus far focussed on the techniques commonly used in analyzing and designing individual systems. The systems approach which treats business departments as independent entities has been found, in recent years, to be frequently inefficient and sometimes even inadequate.

Management Information Systems (MIS), sometimes called Information Systems or Information Management Systems (IMS), aim to treat business departments as integrated parts of one total system, rather than as separate entities.

Objectives The major objectives of Management Information Systems are:

Objectives of MIS
1. To eliminate duplication of effort: treating the entire organization as one major system eliminates the need to establish separate files and reports for payroll and personnel, accounts receivable and payable, inventory and production, and so on
2. To provide management with integrated computerized reports that can be used by many different departments: with one common system, management can obtain up-to-the minute reports on profit/loss ratios, sales forecasts, and any aspect of the company's operations

---

In short, the major goal of MIS is to provide management with a tool for facilitating the decision-making process.

For business data processing applications, MIS represents the zenith in computerized systems. Yet the success of such systems depends, in large part, on the one factor that has been emphasized throughout this text: proper communication between the businessman and the computer specialist. Effective and efficient Management Information Systems require businessmen with a firm understanding of the capabilities and limitations of computers, and computer specialists with a similar understanding of how business organizations function.

16

A. Requirements

When MIS is used in a company, each department has computerized *subsystems* that are subordinate to an overall companywide
system. That is, we no longer refer to departmental systems that
function autonomously, but, rather, we consider that each *subsystem* will interact to result in a more efficient total company
system.

1. Common Data Base One of the prominent features of the
MIS concept revolves around a *common data base.* In lieu of each
subsystem within the company having its own unique file, all subsystems can access data from the same vast storage medium
through a computer system. This storage medium contains data
required by *all* subsystems. In this manner data does not have to be
duplicated by each system requiring it. It can be retained in one
place, and then accessed by each subsystem that utilizes it. Figure
16.1 presents a comparison that shows how data is conventionally
stored on a system-by-system basis and then how it can be stored
utilizing a common data base. For the purpose of demonstrating

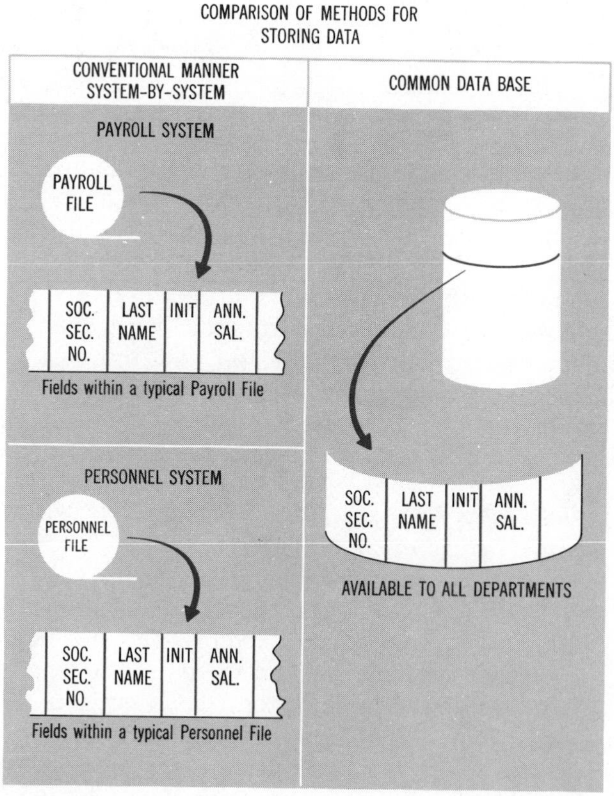

COMPARISON OF METHODS FOR
STORING DATA

Figure 16.1

Comparison of a common data base to conventional system-by-system files.

the fundamental concept, two systems, Payroll and Personnel, are used for illustrative purposes.

In this illustration we can see immediately one of the many features of a Management Information System—the saving of storage space. Suppose this illustration pertains to an automobile manufacturer that employs approximately 100,000 people. With the conventional manner of designing systems (the system-by-system approach), 100,000 records would be required in the Payroll File. Similarly, 100,000 records would be required in a Personnel File. A common data base incorporating all Personnel and Payroll information in a *single* employee record would save much storage space.

Another obvious advantage of the common data base is the elimination of duplication of effort. For example, it is not necessary to update two separate files with the same data, since all data is maintained in one massive file. In short, MIS can effectively increase profits by optimizing customer service and can decrease the production and distribution time of individual items. In addition, MIS projects help to standardize the decision-making process. The computer is used to produce results that are obtained by integrating all the systems.

2. Online Real-Time Capability Data must not only be current but also immediately accessible in order to provide management with reliable and timely information needed for planning and for decision-making purposes. As a result of this requirement, an *online system with real-time capability* is an essential feature.

3. Data Communications Equipment In order to employ the online real-time feature, it is essential that data communications equipment be utilized. Remote terminals using telephone lines, for example, can transmit data instantaneously to the computer so that information in the common data base can be updated immediately. Likewise, inquiries by management, requesting either specific reports or isolated items of information, can be transmitted directly to the computer, with responses being returned over communication lines.

4. A Large Central Processing Unit (CPU) To adequately process data in an MIS environment, a CPU of considerable size is required for the sophisticated supervisor and control system which is needed. The control system provides the computer with the capability to handle an online real-time system, incorporating the use of data communications equipment. In addition, this sophisticated supervisor usually provides the ability for the computer to operate in a multiprogramming environment. You will recall that multiprogramming enables the computer to process several inquiries from managers using different terminals at the same time.

5. Extensive Time for Development A Management Information System typically takes three to five years of systems design and
programming effort to implement. Much effort must be expended
to thoroughly interrelate all subsystems and tie them together to
produce an integrated information system.

6. High Costs for Development The cost of developing an MIS
environment is, for many companies, a serious constraint. The expense involved often runs into millions of dollars. Because of the
number of analysts and programmers required, the equipment
needed, and the time involved, an MIS project cannot be undertaken by every company.

Note, however, that MIS projects are becoming increasingly
popular. As hardware and software packages become cheaper to
operate and implement, the cost of MIS becomes correspondingly less.

In summary, we have seen that some of the basic characteristics of a Management Information System include:

Characteristics of MIS
1.   A Common Data Base
2.   Online Real-Time Capability
3.   Data Communication Equipment
4.   A Large Central Processing Unit
5.   Extensive Time for Development
6.   High Costs for Development

B. Limitations of MIS

Management Information Systems have extensive potential and
capability for the decision- and policy-makers in a large company.
Note, however, that not all MIS projects undertaken have met with
success.

Some of the reasons for failure of MIS projects to provide
management with the type of information it requires follow.

1.   The task of planning, designing, and implementing an
     information system to be used by management has been
     left to the computer specialist, a person sometimes not
     skilled in the area of management and thus poorly
     equipped to understand the requirements of such a sys-
     tem.

2.   The task of planning, designing, and implementing this
     vast and complex system has often been underestimated.
     Management often is inaccurately briefed as to the time
     and cost estimates of such a system by computer
     specialists who are very enthusiastic to undertake such a
     project.

3. It has been difficult to establish priorities so that the most critical departments' executives who are the prime users of the system obtain information first. Unfortunately, when priorities are to be established, power politics becomes a major factor. Thus it is often the most influential executive, and not the prime user, who has the priorities within the system.

II. Advanced Techniques Used in MIS and Other Systems

A. Simulation

Simulation is an operations research[1] technique that refers to some representation or model of a system which can be manipulated and studied in order to better understand the behavior of the actual system itself, and to make predictions about the future.

There are, in essence, two basic kinds of models used. There is the *physical model*, such as a model airplane which is flown in a wind tunnel to simulate actual flight conditions. The other kind of model is the one of primary interest to the businessman, the conceptual or *mathematical model*, which can be described by an analyst and then programmed by a programmer.

The technique of simulation affords managers the opportunity to ask the computer "What would happen if I were to do this?" thus allowing them to test the effectiveness of decisions without actually implementing them. In this manner, the computer can *simulate* the conditions the manager *intends* to impose on a system and can then project the corresponding results. Listed below are some typical applications to which simulation can be applied for the businessman.

1. How much should the sales force in a department store be increased in order to adequately handle customer demands at peak times?
2. By how much will the addition of a specific number of new machines in a manufacturing plant alleviate production backlogs?
3. How will a specific change in policy of the Inventory Control Department reduce inventory investment and, at the same time, maintain adequate availability of merchandise to meet consumer demands?
4. How will the company's profit picture be affected by specific proposed capital expenditures?
5. How will a change in the store's policy affect sales?
6. How will the addition of a new branch office affect the company's total profits?

---

[1] Operations research (OR) basically refers to the use of mathematics to solve business problems.

Simulation is an extremely powerful technique that is becoming more widespread for several reasons:

1. It uses the computer to *simulate* time so that the effect is the representation of time, in minutes on a computer, of events that would take an actual time span of days, months, or years. Thus, a manager can see immediately what the effects of a particular policy might be over an extended period of time.

2. It is often prohibitively costly, especially in terms of financial risk, time spent, and manpower, for management to implement a particular decision on the gamble that it *may* be successful. The use of simulation can increase the likelihood that a simulated decision which is found to be successful will, in actual practice, be a wise one.

3. In many business structures, the interrelationships among the various systems are extremely complex. As a result, it is not possible to determine simple relationships. If management varies some facet of one system, for example, the effects on all other systems may not be precisely known. Thus, by using simulation, the possible effect of a major policy decision can be more precisely defined.

4. Special high-level programming languages have been developed specifically to facilitate the programmer's task of writing a program to perform simulation experiments. These languages, to mention a few of the more common ones, include:

   a. GPSS—General Purpose Systems Simulator
   b. DYNAMO
   c. GASP—General Activity Simulation Program
   d. SIMSCRIPT

   With the use of these programming tools, the programmer or analyst need only supply a series of system specifications in order for the computer to perform a simulation. Thus, simulation, today, has become more widespread because of software assistance.

5. Simulation is used in many companies as a training tool for management, to enable managers to enhance their decision-making skills. Managers can thus participate in *management games,* a technique whereby business leaders experiment with a hypothetical company to see if they can pinpoint problem areas and to see whether the various decisions made by them to alleviate the *problems* would be effective if implemented. With the use of management games, it is hoped that these business leaders will become more effective in their decision-making role.

B. Management Games

As was mentioned above, management games as a simulation technique are used in many companies as a training aid for management. Many management games have been developed for this purpose. We will now briefly describe how one of these, the IBM Management Decision-Making Game, operates. The following illustration has been oversimplified in order to present the major concepts of the game, without dwelling on the intricate details.

Let us assume that there are three hypothetical firms in a particular marketing area that produce just one product for sale. At the beginning of the game, all firms start with the same cash, inventory, and plant facilities. The net worth of each firm, in this game, is equal to the total assets of the firm, since none of the firms is allowed to incur debts.

Management personnel are asked to make executive-level decisions for each of these hypothetical firms. In this way, the business leaders can observe the effects of any decisions and, depending on which firm produces the greatest profit, the best decision-maker for this specific type of firm can be determined.

At the beginning of each operating period, each of the firms makes its own decisions regarding:

1. Price
2. Marketing expenditures
3. Plant improvement expenditures
4. Production expenditures
5. Research and development expenditures

The decisions are punched into cards and fed into a computer. The computer then simulates the behavior of each firm and produces reports showing the results of the activity in the period. This process can be repeated as many times as desired in order for the manager to see the results of the decisions and what kind of improvement is being made.

C. Linear Programming

Linear programming, like simulation, is an operations research tool that can be used in an MIS system to find the best way of performing a particular activity. That is, linear programming determines the optimal method for performing a task. The term "programming," in this case, refers to the planning of economic activities rather than to the activity of a computer programmer. The term "linear" refers to the fact that this mathematical technique is applicable only if the economic activities being investigated are related in a straight line, or in a linear way. That is, if it costs $1.00 to produce one item, a linear relationship exists if it costs approximately $2.00 to produce two items, $4.00 to produce four items, and so on.

Fortunately, many business activities that can be analyzed using linear programming usually have a reasonably close linear relationship. The two main types of linear programming problems concern: (1) the allocation of resources, and (2) the transportation problem, as discussed below.

The *allocation of resources* involves a situation where there are numerous activities that can be performed in many ways, but since the necessary resources are limited not all activities can be carried out in the best way at the same time. The basic idea of the linear programming technique is to allocate the available resources in such a way as to optimize some objective, such as maximization of profits, or minimization of costs, depending on the nature of the problem. As an example, management might want to determine the best way of assigning work to its employees in a factory or, the best way of scheduling jobs on machines. Management might also want to determine the best way to allocate corporate financial resources. Since there are so many variables, a simple problem-solving set of equations cannot be used. Instead, the computer is employed to maximize the desired result. In this way, necessary changes to the variables are listed by the computer to effect maximization of profits, for example.

The *transportation problem* is a common type of problem solved by the linear programming technique. As an example, a company may have several warehouses located throughout the country which supply various items of merchandise to different stores. The question arises as to the best way to stock merchandise in the warehouses so as to minimize the cost of distribution. Here again, the use of linear programming can help the manager to determine the best decision to make.

Important Terms Used in this Chapter

Common Data Base	Online
Linear Programming	Operations Research (OR)
Management Games	Real Time
Management Information Systems (MIS)	Simulation

Self-Evaluating Quiz

1. MIS is an abbreviation for _____.
2. MIS is a recent advance in computer technology that _____.
3. A common data base of a Management Information System is _____.
4. Data communications must be used with MIS systems to provide _____.
5. (T or F) MIS projects are very costly.
6. Management Information Systems have sometimes failed because of _____.

7. (T or F) Management Information Systems are generally used by large companies.

8. _____ is a technique that uses a model of a system which can be manipulated and studied in order to understand the behavior of the actual system itself.

9. A computer is used with simulation studies to simulate _____.

10. (T or F) There are programming languages in use today that can facilitate simulation techniques.

11. The use of management games is a technique whereby business leaders _____.

12. Linear programming determines the _____ method for performing a task.

Solutions

1. Management Information Systems
2. provides management with an integrated, all-encompassing approach to the total company in order to facilitate the decision-making process
3. a storage medium containing data required of all subsystems
4. online real-time capability
5. T
6. (a) management's misunderstanding of the system's capability
    (b) the computer specialist's lack of understanding of management's requirements
7. T
8. Simulation
9. time
10. T
11. experiment with a hypothetical company to see if they can pinpoint problem areas and to see whether the various decisions made by them to alleviate the problems would be effective if implemented
12. optimal

Review Questions

I. True or False

1. (T or F) Most companies with computers have Management Information Systems in operation.

2. (T or F) MIS provides management with current information that is obtained from computerizing the interaction of the various departments within a company.

3. (T or F) In a company that has implemented MIS, departmental systems usually function autonomously.

4. (T or F) A common data base means that each subsystem does not have its own unique files.

5. (T or F) Data communications equipment forms an integral part of a Management Information System.

6. (T or F) A knowledge of BASIC is essential in order for a manager to access data from a common data base through a terminal.
7. (T or F) Few Management Information Systems are now functioning as originally conceived.
8. (T or F) Many MIS projects have failed because they have utilized batch-processing techniques rather than online processing.
9. (T or F) A typical Management Information System can be handled by a computer system that rents for $2000 per month.
10. (T or F) Simulation can be used to study the possible effects of a management decision before it is actually implemented.
11. (T or F) An example of a management game is a company-sponsored contest to determine which district sales manager has had the greatest increase in sales during the year.
12. (T or F) Linear programming basically refers to the planning of economic activities rather than the activity of a computer programmer.
13. (T or F) Linear programming is often used to solve the "transportation problem."

II. Fill in the Blanks

1. A Management Information System provides management with current information that is obtained from computerizing _____.
2. A _____ refers to one vast file of data that contains all information needed by the various subsystems within the company.
3. Two major advantages of a Management Information System are _____ and _____.
4. An online, real-time capability is essential for a Management Information System because _____.
5. Online, real-time capability is achieved by the use of _____.
6. A multiprogramming environment is usually an essential characteristic of a Management Information System since it allows _____.
7. Several years are often required for the development of a Management Information System because _____.
8. Two major reasons why all companies do not undertake MIS projects are _____ and _____.
9. Simulation can be very important to the businessman because it _____.
10. A(n) _____ is a training tool for businessmen which establishes a hypothetical company to test the effectiveness of various decisions.
11. Linear programming is a mathematical technique which can be used to determine _____.

Unit Five: Selected Bibliography

Role of Data Processing Organization

1. A more comprehensive breakdown of salary ranges by job, industry, and geographical location appears in *Infosystems*, June 1977, p. 58–64.

2. See also "DP Salary Survey," *Datamation*, November 1976. Both *Infosystems* and *Datamation* supply yearly salary surveys.

Systems Analysis and Design: Texts
1. *Business Data Processing Systems*, Lawrence Orilia, Nancy Stern, and Robert Stern, 2nd ed., (New York, 1977).
2. *Business Systems Analysis and Design*, Gary B. Shelly and Thomas J. Cashman, (Fullerton, Ca., 1975).

Feasibility Studies
"A Dynamic Approach to Selecting Computers," Phillip Ein-Dor, *Datamation*, June 1977.

MIS
1. "Management/Copyright Law and Your Data Base," Robert P. Bigelow, *Computer Decisions*, 5 May 1977, p. 28.
2. "Integrity in Data Base Systems," Robert M. Curtice; "Six Approaches to Distributed Data Bases," G. A. Champine, *Datamation*, May 1977.
   a. Focusses on new features of data base systems.
   b. Provides students with information written in computer vernacular that will assist them in understanding the concepts involved.

Unit 6
Computers in Society

The Impact of Computers on Society

17

17

I. Introduction: The Issues

Computers are information processing tools which have a wide variety of uses in both business and other fields. We have considered, in depth, the uses of computers in business, from simple data processing functions to complex analysis and decision-making tools. These fundamental applications of computers have, in a quarter century, revolutionized the business field. In addition, there has been widespread use of these machines in many other disciplines including linguistics, education, medicine, and artificial intelligence, just to name a few. The "computer revolution," then, as it is commonly called, extends beyond the business area and affects our day-to-day lives. Yet, the application of computers in society has only recently begun and the potential for even more far-reaching utilization is consistently being predicted. Despite all the possible advantages to be gained from computerization, the positive impact of these machines on society is not something that has been universally accepted.

Some of the criticisms of computers include the following:

Criticisms of Computers

1. Computers are dehumanizing. People become entities, numbers; they lose their uniqueness.
2. Computers replace manpower and hence contribute to unemployment.
3. Computers are alienating; that is, they serve to divorce people from the final product of their labor in which they should take pride.
4. Computers result in standardization and thereby inhibit creativity and originality.
5. Computers are becoming a dependence; people will be unable to function without their constant intervention.
6. Computers invade our privacy, often threaten our credit ratings because of errors, and are a security risk.

17

The time has come for technologists and scientists to assume some social responsibility for their inventions and discoveries.

Similarly, the time has come for critics to better understand the technologies about which they are critical.

In this chapter we will explore the advantages gained from some social uses of computers and the ways in which these uses need to be controlled to avoid dehumanization, and other negative effects feared by technological critics.

II. Electronic Funds Transfer (EFT)

Electronic Funds Transfer (EFT) is a system projected for the near future which will revolutionize banking and perhaps the economic structure of the country as well. Its effects on the economy will be somewhat analogous to the impact of credit cards. The Point-of-Sale systems, discussed in chapter 12, which have been installed in many retail establishments in an effort to eliminate paperwork associated with charged purchases are a step toward EFT.

As broadly conceived, EFT will eliminate the need for a cash exchange of funds. A cashless society, then, is its objective. The transfer of funds will be effectively accomplished by computers across communication lines. An employee's pay will automatically be deposited in the bank of his or her choice. All subsequent transactions will be made by using a bank card which will be universally accepted. The individual authorizes any electronic transfer of funds by using this card and by providing a password or number which verifies his or her right to use the card.

To a limited extent, the use of bank cards to authorize cash transactions has already been instituted by some banks. Self-service automated teller machines which eliminate much of the paperwork in the funds transfer process are a step toward EFT. This automated teller allows an individual with a special bank card to obtain money from a machine, even when the bank is closed. By inserting the card into the machine which is usually located at the outside of the bank, an individual can obtain funds without writing a check or completing a form. The amount desired is keyed in along with a special code, the money is supplied, and the transaction is recorded automatically.

The major purpose of EFT is to use data communications and computers to reduce the high cost associated with the transfer of funds from one account to another. With the use of an EFT system, for example, when a customer buys merchandise there will be an automatic transfer of funds from the customer's bank account to the merchant's account immediately.

Note that EFT is, at present, in the planning stages. Many features must be standardized before the system will be in universal operation. First, there is very little consensus as to how it will specifically operate. Such details will require a good deal of time and effort to resolve. Second, there will need to be a governmental agency to regulate such a system. Third, there has been no firm understanding of precisely what impact such a system will have on individuals as well as on financial institutions.

Recent reports have indicated that banking institutions are concerned with customer acceptance. Many individuals depend on the time delay between when a check is written and when it is cashed. This lapse allows an individual who does not currently have sufficient funds in his or her account to nevertheless issue a check, as long as the funds are deposited prior to its cashing. This can sometimes take weeks. With EFT, however, when an individual wants to purchase an item, for example, he or she will need to have adequate funds available immediately in order for the funds to be transferred automatically. In order for EFT to be accepted by individuals, they will need to be convinced that advantages of such a system will accrue to them as well as to the banking institutions. In addition, banking institutions are concerned about the equipment expense and operating cost of EFT.

Nebraska banks speed EFT plan despite Washington opposition

A consortium of Nebraska banks is moving to configure a sophisticated minicomputer-based electronic fund transfers (EFT) system in the face of opposition from the U.S. Justice Department. In a letter, which stopped short of ordering work on the project halted, the Justice Department stated its view that there would be an over-all lack of competition in the system.

The statewide switch, to be called the Nebraska Electronic Terminal System (NETS), is significant apart from the antitrust issue, because it is considered to be a prototype for inexpensive EFT networks not directly connected to banking terminals. NETS is said to have hopes of seeing its concept spread to other states.

The system's central switch will connect with the data processing centers of five banks which, in turn, will service smaller banks and bankteller terminals, automated teller machines, and point-of-sale units.

"The key thing about the NETS switch is that it's behind the banks," said Ronald G. Keiser, electronic banking coordinator at Omaha National Bank, one of the five principal banks in the system. "The NETS switch itself doesn't operate bank terminals."

Reliability. The network is being configured around minicomputer equipment supplied by Tandem Computers Inc. that offers reliability features the Nebraska designers felt were important. Before it was decided to use the Tandem equipment, several banking officials expressed doubts about the proposed configuration's reliability. An earlier hardware design gave rise to fears that any malfunction might bring down the entire system.

A three-year, $1.3-million contract to configure and operate the switch has been awarded to Micor Corp. of Phoenix, a Ramada Inns subsidiary that specializes in transaction processing. An important subcontractor involved in the Nebraska operation is Omniplan Corp. of Santa Monica, Calif. In addition to the central processing unit, the network will have video display units, printers, interfacing equipment, and tape and disk drives.

Failsafe. The Tandem equipment consists of three processors for failsafe operation, said James Cody, president of Applied Communications Inc., a Nebraska software company handling NETS communications programs and transaction software for some of the banks.

Two processors will operate on each message concurrently, with the output taken from one of them. The third processor will act as backup if either of the others goes down.

Data Communications, May 1977, p. 14. Reprinted with permission.

Nonetheless, there are some who predict the "near-universality" of EFT systems and of electronic mail, an analogous system of electronically reproducing messages over communication lines.[1] Both are projected for the next decade.[2]

Two major areas of concern regarding EFT and electronic computer technology in general, are those of security and privacy. These will be discussed in detail later in the chapter. Within the context of EFT, security is a real problem since an individual with a card and knowledge of the password can easily compromise the integrity of the system, both by theft and by accessing information that would otherwise be confidential. This latter threat specifically concerns citizens who see EFT as a serious threat to privacy. An electronic system that maintains records on an individual's spending patterns, on what is bought and sold, and on the place and time of transactions is objectionable to many people. With such a system, those with access can literally monitor an individual's entire behavioral pattern, that is, where one spends time, when one eats, shops, and so on. For some, such a system conjures up visions of "Big Brother" and for that reason alone is undesirable. For others, such a system will mean less paperwork and more expedient transactions and hence is exceedingly desirable. Whether, in fact, EFT systems are instituted is still somewhat debatable but if they are, proper controls will undoubtedly need to be instituted.

---

[1] Electronic mail is discussed in the next section.
[2] "The Future of Computer Communications," Vinton G. Cerf and Alex Curran, *Datamation*, May 1977, p. 105.

III. Electronic Mail with the Use of Facsimile Devices

Facsimile devices are a recent advance in data communications which enable users to transmit hard-copy documents over communication lines. A printed report can be duplicated at some remote location with the use of such a device in 30 seconds. Figure 17.1 illustrates a typical facsimile device. The use of these devices to transmit information has given rise to the term "electronic mail."

IV. Security and Privacy

Two of the most important social issues that have developed as a consequence of the widespread use of computers involve the security and privacy of computer data. As noted previously, it is not only conceivable, but it has become a reality, in some instances, that those without authority can gain access to a particular data bank. This unauthorized entry can easily result in the illegal monitoring of an individual's buying habits, credit status, salary history, and so forth. As the late Senator Hubert Humphrey said:

> We act differently if we believe we are being observed. If we can never be sure whether or not we are being watched and listened to, all our actions will be altered and our very character will change.[3]

Two principles of information security need to be better understood. First, there is no such thing in practice, as an "unbreakable code." There are theoretically unbreakable systems, but they must be used by people, and people make mistakes that can lead to lapses in security. The second principle derives in part from the first. One can get whatever degree of protection one wants (short of perfection) if one is willing to pay for it. The expectations of the thief, as well as the intrinsic value of the information to its owner, must guide the expenditure of security resources. Thus, the key to satisfactory information security is to determine the value of the information *to the potential unauthorized user*, as well as its intrinsic value to its legitimate owner, and then to design a security system that will make it more costly than the smaller of these two values to obtain the information without permission during the appropriate length of time.

Data Processing in 1980–1985: A Study of Potential Limitations to Progress, T. A. Dolotta et al., (New York: 1976), p. 30. Reprinted with permission.

---

[3] Foreword to Edward V. Long, The *Intruders* (New York, 1967), p. viii.

Figure 17.1
Sample facsimile device. Courtesy Graphic Sciences, Inc.

State Computers and the Right of Privacy

You drive to a confidential appointment—with a doctor, a lawyer, a business associate—and within hours an anonymous phone call is made to others telling of the meeting. Someone has copied your license number and obtained your name through a motor vehicle bureau computer.

It sounds like 1984, but this gross invasion of privacy may have taken place on Long Island in 1976. The Nassau County Police Department is looking into complaints that it happened to visitors to a Carle Place office complex. A medical clinic there provides abortions, but that's not the issue in this case. If a doctor's office isn't private, what is?

The operators of the clinic, the East Gate Medical Center, have complained to Nassau police that phone calls were made to the parents of two women within hours after they had visited the center last Saturday. They suspect that the identity of the women was established through their automobile license plates. This is disturbing because, according to police, only police officers have access to motor vehicle computer terminals on Saturdays.

The abortion issue is capable of raising deep emotions, but that's no excuse for this type of harassment. Leaders of organized anti-abortion groups have denied any involvement, and that's encouraging. But incidents of this sort raise a special challenge to the Nassau police.

Anti-abortionists have routinely picketed the center for the past four years. Peaceful picketing is one thing, but the operators have complained of bomb scares and of damage to visitors' cars. And the center's director of guidance says, "We receive little support from the police."

If the police department's investigation shows that any of its members were involved in the phone call episodes, they must be disciplined promptly. And the department must be more alert in the future to safeguard the rights of the users and owners of the center.

Newsday, October 12, 1976, p. 42. Copyright 1976, Newsday, Inc. Reprinted with permission.

Recognizing that no system is foolproof, in an absolute sense, it is nevertheless possible to incorporate various controls to minimize the probability of security violations. The following partial list of security precautions suggests some of the more common techniques that have been used to thwart unauthorized terminal access to a data bank.

1. Permit access to a file and particular records only for those with proper authorization codes, including terminal identification. These codes should not only be changed frequently but their distribution should be limited to those users who absolutely require them.

2. When authorization codes for a particular data bank are distributed to various users, designate by means of the code whether a specific user should have the capability when accessing records to "read only," "write only," or "read and write." As an example, a policeman who is checking a license plate number to determine if a car is stolen needs "read only" capability and should not be permitted to create new records. Allowing a user to change data on files can lead to computer frauds, so-called "white collar crimes."

3. Program the computer to automatically "log off" a terminal where the user does not precisely follow the correct procedures for entering authorization codes. In addition, a terminal should be logged off automatically if access is attempted for a file where the staff that controls that file is off duty. For example, if a company's payroll department does not work after 5:00 P.M., then no access to the payroll file should be allowed after that time unless a special code approved by the department head has been issued.

4. Verification lists that are produced by the computer after files are created or updated should be destroyed by a shredding machine after it is determined that the computer's records are accurate. Backup files should be created on media such as magnetic tape or disk which can be stored in fireproof vaults in case it is necessary to recreate files that have been lost, stolen, or accidentally destroyed.

The large number of computer banks of credit information in this country has given rise to the possibility of the unwarranted invasion of an individual's privacy. Recently, the Federal Trade Commission (FTC) accused a debt-collection agency of illegally tapping computer banks of credit information and using the data to harass debtors.[4] The FTC charged that the company obtained the information by telephoning computer companies that maintain credit information on consumers and claiming that they had subscribed to the service. The company had improperly obtained authorization codes from subscribers to the information service and then represented that they were, in fact, the subscribers. The credit information was used to determine where debtors lived and worked. This information was then used by the collection agency

---

[4]The Wall Street Journal, December 30, 1976, page 2, col. 3.

to intimidate the individuals into paying their debts, since the individuals received the impression that everything they did was being monitored.

It should be noted that this was the FTC's first action to force debt-collection agencies to comply with the Federal Fair Credit Reporting Act's provisions protecting the privacy of consumer credit information.

Several states have adopted similar laws. In New York, for example, the Credit Data Reporting Act provides that a credit bureau must, upon written request, supply an individual with the name and address of every person or governmental agency to whom it has furnished a credit report relating to that person. Any person who requests or obtains a credit report from a credit bureau under false pretenses is subject to a misdemeanor charge which carries a prison sentence of up to one year.

V. Computer-Assisted Instruction (CAI)

The use of computers as educational tools has become widespread in recent years. One way in which these devices can be employed is as tools in learning about computers themselves. The use of terminals on which students code and debug their own programs is ideally suited for this purpose. Another way in which computers may be used is to assist in the educational process itself, *regardless of the subject matter.* When computers serve to assist instructors in teaching students about a wide variety of topics the concept is referred to as Computer-Assisted Instruction (CAI).

CAI typically involves the use of keyboard terminals with which students interact (see Figure 17.2).

Teaching the Language of the Deaf with Interactive Computing

Over 200 students, most of whom have normal hearing but are interested in communicating with the deaf, are enrolled in Golden West's sign language courses which use computer-assisted instruction programs. The programs include 49 separate lessons which introduce 660 signs corresponding to frequently used words or phrases.

"We see interactive computing as a very powerful and integral component of coordinated instructional systems which also include the traditional classroom and other non-traditional learning activities," says Richard L. Mercer, supervisor of computer services at the college. "Using computer-based practice, simulation and other programs, students can add to their knowledge and improve their skills at their own pace and at their own time—almost as if each has a private tutor."

By typing in the English word or phrase at the terminal, the student activates a microfiche file linked to an IBM System/370

Figure 17.2
CAI illustration. At work in the English media lab at San Antonio College,
students are learning to write clear sentences with the assistance of a computer.
Using video display or typewriter terminals, they communicate directly with the
computer — reviewing and testing themselves. Courtesy IBM.

Model 155-II at the Coast Community College District's computing facility. A drawing showing how to make the appropriate
Ameslan (American Sign Language) sign for that word flashes on
the screen within seconds. The system can also be used in reverse
so that the student can test himself.

"We have found student reaction to computer-assisted instruction overwhelmingly positive," says Paul M. Culton, chairman of the impaired hearing program. "It makes learning fun. And
it also serves to correct misconceptions on the spot, instead of next
week in class."

The college has over 1,000 learning programs in 55 different
disciplines ranging from Ameslan to more traditional subjects like
history, science and mathematics. All of the programs were developed using A Programming Language (APL). According to Bob
Schaulis, director, information services for the Coast Community
College District, "We believe that personal computing—giving

many people simple access to the full power of the computer—will become increasingly important in many areas of instruction."

CAI Processing

1. The student "logs on" by indicating the specific subject or unit to be learned.
2. The computer prints, on a screen or a typewriterlike device, textual information which is usually segmented into frames.
3. After a small segment of text has been printed, the computer asks the student a series of questions about what he or she has read.
4. The student responds to the questions.
5. Depending upon the accuracy of the responses, the computer will:
   a. Go on to another, more advanced topic, if the answers are correct; or, if not,
   b. Repeat the topic, with a different text, so that the student can better understand the topic when presented in a different way.

There are many versions of each unit so that the student who cannot fully understand the material the first or second time will be given numerous opportunities.

The advantages of CAI are varied:

Advantages of CAI

1. Where teachers are in short supply, such devices are a very suitable method of assistance.
2. Students can proceed at their own rate of learning.
3. Students who have learning difficulties are given many different presentations, prepared by many different teachers, so that the likelihood of eventual success is enhanced.
4. Students who have learning difficulties or who do not relate well to specific teachers often benefit from impersonal communication with a computer.
5. Students who have learning difficulties are not affected by peer group pressures when communicating with a computer.

In short, then, the use of CAI equipment is a major educational advance. Yet it, too, must be placed in its proper perspective.

First, the term *computer-assisted instruction* is an apt one. Such a concept implies that computers are best suited to *assist* in the educational process, *not* to become the sole educators. That is, CAI is most effective when it *supplements* traditional teaching.

Second, while there are those students who respond favorably to impersonal communication, there are those who benefit from a close student-teacher relationship. A good teacher develops a rapport with the student that cannot be simulated by a machine.

Third, there are some subjects that are not, in general, readily adaptable to CAI. Subjects in which the student needs to conceptualize, for example, are difficult to teach by computer. Subjects where the student feels that his or her questions need immediate resolution require interaction with educators.

In short, CAI is best suited for drill or rote-type learning which then provides the teacher with additional time to devote to more complex learning. In addition, CAI is an effective method of *supplementing* the educational process but is an ineffective *substitute* for education. As noted previously in this chapter, computers are exceedingly useful as tools that can assist people. However, to use them *in place of* human interaction can lead to serious problems.

VI. Computers in Health

Computers have a wide variety of uses in the medical field. In addition to the normal record-keeping and administrative functions, computers are used in the following areas.

A. Diagnosing Illness

With the shortage of trained medical personnel, the use of computers as a diagnostic tool has become increasingly significant. Some hospitals have instituted programs in which patients are given a series of tests by trained personnel. The data is then fed into and analyzed by a computer which has been programmed to test for specific limits or established standards. If any test results are abnormal, the computer can print a tentative diagnosis or a prescribed course of action which would then be discussed with the physician.

Computer terminals have also been used by physicians who feed in data on patients' symptoms and can then obtain a listing of possible illnesses, of other sources to check, or of other tests to be performed.

In both these cases a computer serves as an information processing tool with a huge memory and a program capable of comparing input data with relevant information stored in the memory.

The use of these devices in the medical field has not been greeted with universal approval or acceptance. Many people regard the computer as dehumanizing, as a threat to the traditional relationship between patient and doctor.

When computers are used properly, the fears of these people are unwarranted. That is, when such devices are used to *assist* medical personnel in making a diagnosis and in treating patients, they have great value. When, however, any tool, even a computer, replaces the expert and becomes the controlling agent, in this case the sole diagnostician, then the threat of dehumanization is indeed a real one. The trained expert, the doctor, must continue to rely when necessary on his or her own instincts or intuition as well as on the computer's memory and programmed logic.

B. Computer-assisted Research

In many scientific fields, particularly those that rely on experimental data, the utilization of computers to read and process a voluminous amount of such data can often make the difference between a feasible research project and an impossible one. In the field of medicine particularly, computers are used to assist scientists in determining possible causes of various diseases, in linking specific diseases with particular traits related to personality, physical characteristics, environmental conditions, heredity, and so on. In instances such as these, computers are programmed to read in vast amounts of data and to perform statistical studies and correlation analyses.

People who criticize the use of computers for research often mean to be more critical of the research technique than the device itself. While some may justify a statistical result by saying that "figures don't lie," others may respond, and sometimes with equal justification, "but liars figure." There is always a statistical result to justify any hypothesis. It is therefore necessary for scientists and humanists alike to take the time to analyze the statistical methods used to justify scientific hypotheses.

C. Monitoring a Patient's Vital Signs

In cases of critical illness, patients can be linked to a computer which continuously monitors the vital signs and signals the appropriate medical personnel in the event of an abnormality.

Critics of such technical devices claim that machines can malfunction, a fact with which we are all familiar. The fact that machines sometimes malfunction is not, however, a meaningful criticism, since humans frequently make mistakes, too. In any case, the use of computers for monitoring, where patients would otherwise receive only periodic attention from the hospital staff, is clearly valuable.

D. Hospital Information Systems

A hospital information system, like a management information system, is designed to automate as much of the information processing as possible. The files that are typically maintained with such a system include:

┌───┐
Items Integrated in a Hospital Information File
Expected admissions file
Current patient file
Medical staff file
Nursing staff file
Laboratory file
Pharmaceuticals file
└───┘

The computer is programmed to provide billing, payroll, surgical and laboratory scheduling, inventory, and so on. All supplies, patients, and personnel are monitored.

VII. Computers in Science

The computer serves two distinct purposes in scientific research. It can be used as an experimental tool or as an instrument critical to the development of scientific theories.

When used as an experimental tool, the computer functions in much the same way as a microscope, thermometer, or barometer. That is, it enables scientists to assess the results of an experiment in a manner that could not be accomplished if they relied purely on their senses. Computers provide the scientists with high-speed computational power without which certain calculations would simply not be feasible. Maintaining data on electron patterns and providing insight into pattern recognition in chromosome analysis are just two of the ways in which computers can be used as scientific instruments.

Similarly, and perhaps even more significantly, computers are often used to assist in forming scientific theory. Hypotheses can be formulated in some systematic fashion by the machine and then tested. The results can be compared to the predictions expected on the basis of the hypothesis and adjustments can then be made accordingly.

A. Linguistics

In the social sciences, computers are being used in linguistics in an effort to provide insight into the development of natural languages. Many linguists have been researching the manner in which ordinary language has evolved by simulating the translation process from one language to another by computerized means.

Programs have been devised to test the linguistic experts' efforts to provide a logical framework for language. Theoretically, if computer-produced translations result in near-perfect interpretations, then the linguists will have succeeded in their efforts to understand natural languages. Such success, however, has not as yet been forthcoming. Idioms and irregularities in semantics have made computer translations exceedingly difficult.

The linguists have not yet solved their problems. In a practical sense, this has meant that computer-produced translations from one language to another have not, as a rule, been entirely acceptable.

B. Artificial Intelligence

Artificial Intelligence (AI) is another scientific field that has relied heavily on computers. Broadly conceived, AI is a subject that attempts to shed light on the nature of thinking by simulating the process of reasoning. Programs have been devised to solve typical mental problems in an effort to demonstrate that the reasoning process follows a systematic series of rules. The effort to program a computer to be an expert chess player is just such an attempt to understand the reasoning process and thus falls under the rubric of Artificial Intelligence. Programs have been developed which project future chess moves and on the basis of probability select one that is most desirable. Because of the number of possible moves that can be made in the course of a chess game, the computer has thus far been incapable of achieving total success. Hence, many expert chess players are still able to beat the machine. Nonetheless, the effort to perfect the logic necessary, and through this to better understand the human mind, is still a major undertaking.

Experts Argue Whether Computers Could Reason, and if They Should

By Lee Dembart

Can machines think? Should they? The computer world is in the midst of a fundamental dispute over these questions because an eminent computer scientist wrote a book arguing that machines could never be made to reason like people and, what was more, should not be.

Twenty years ago, in the infancy of the computer revolution, before problems began cropping up, the public was told that computers would be smarter than brains. Computer chess champions and machine translation, for example, were just around the corner. So far, neither has been accomplished successfully, and neither is likely to be any time soon.

Nor have computers had much success in making decisions that require judgment. They can rattle off the Manhattan telephone directory unerringly time after time, which no human can do, but they cannot begin to distinguish one face from another, as babies can.

Computer scientists have always said, "Give us more time. The problem is more complex than we thought." Then one of them, Joseph Weizenbaum, a professor of computer science at the Massachusetts Institute of Technology, wrote a book saying that the project was fundamentally unsound and dangerous to pursue, partly, he said, because the computers' and humans' ways of thought would always be alien, and because knowledge might become limited to what a computer could understand.

The elders of the artificial intelligence community reacted with outrage. Even those who agreed with his premises criticized the book as being too harsh in tone, too personal in its attacks. Computer journals have bristled over the last year with reviews, comments and replies provoked by Professor Weizenbaum's book, "Computer Power and Human Reason" (W. H. Freeman & Co., 1976). Now the controversy has spilled into the prestigious publication Science, in whose pages he was attacked several weeks ago.

In an article entitled "What Computers Mean for Man and Society," Prof. Herbert A. Simon of the Carnegie-Mellon University in Pittsburgh argued that computers were no more or less dangerous than any other machine of the industrial revolution.

Professor Simon, who is one of the leading figures in artificial intelligence research, asserted that Professor Weizenbaum's position was that man was not subject to natural laws and that knowledge about man's ability to think was dangerous.

"I have pronounced heresy and I am a heretic," the tweedy, 54-year-old Mr. Weizenbaum said in his office in Cambridge, Mass.

Professor Weizenbaum, who says he loves beautiful machinery, was not the first critic of artificial intelligence, but he was the first from inside the field.

"Weizenbaum has as much experience as almost anyone in the world with this subject," one of his opponents, Prof. Bruce G. Buchanan, acknowledged. "He is a much more informed critic than we have ever had."

While machines provide the ostensible cause of the debate, it has encompassed some of mankind's oldest and newest questions: How do we know what we know? What does it mean for a human to know something? What does it mean for a computer? What is creativity? How do we think? What are the limits of science? What are the limits of digital computers?

The New York Times, May 8, 1977, p. 1, col. 2. © 1977 by The New York Times Company. Reprinted by permission.

Other areas of artificial intelligence involve efforts to program machines to play more simplified games and to solve less complicated problems. Computers can play tic-tac-toe, checkers, and many other games as well as provide solutions to logical problems or riddles. In addition, computer programs have been devised to provide geometrical proofs. A program called ELIZA has even been written to simulate the psychoanalyst in a therapy session.[5] In this

[5]*New York Times,* May 8, 1977, p. 34, col. 4; *Computer Power and Human Reason,* Joseph Weizenbaum (San Francisco: 1976).

case, the computer has been programmed to process statements made by the user so that meaningful and leading questions result. While the author of this program claims that it was not a serious attempt at simulating the therapy session, many consider it an important development in the use of computers for understanding human communication.

There is currently quite a fundamental dispute in the computer world as to whether or not computers can ever be made to simulate human reasoning, and, if they can be, whether, in fact, they should be. One critic of artificial intelligence, has argued that there are certain aspects to human life that a computer simply cannot understand. Emotions such as love and loneliness, for example, are impossible for a computer to comprehend and take into account when simulating human reasoning. In addition, it is argued that it is dangerous to pursue sophisticated artificial intelligence, since machines will always be alien to humans. On the other hand, advocates of artificial intelligence have taken the position that computers are no more dangerous than any other machine of the industrial revolution. In addition, it is their view that the basic processes that underlie human thinking are essentially the same as those used by the computer for information processing, although the computer operates at a much faster rate than the human brain. While it is true that humans can learn by experience and instruction, it is equally possible for computers to learn through the use of programs. It is argued that since programs and data are stored in the computer's memory, it is entirely feasible for programs to modify themselves and thus learn.

Since artificial intelligence is only in the infancy stages, this controversy will undoubtedly continue for many years.

VIII. New Perspectives on Computers

Computers have been programmed to produce creative works in art, music, and poetry. Here, again, the intention is to demonstrate that the creative process can be schematized, that is, it is fundamentally logical. The extent to which one will agree that creativity is essentially logical will depend, in large part, on one's appreciation of these so-called creative products.

Even closer to one's own personal experiences is the concept of home computers, electronic devices that will eliminate shopping and will facilitate everyday chores in a number of ways. Here, too, there is reason for concern. Some sociologists claim, for example, that shopping is an activity that serves a social function for the housewife. Hence, its elimination by a computerized system may well have unforeseen social consequences. In this connection, the Universal Product Codes or bar codes discussed in chapter 12 which appear on products in supermarkets have caused quite a controversy. Food processors have been putting these codes on their products in anticipation of universal electronic check-out. A major consumer objection has been that supermarkets using electronic check-out have eliminated the stamping of prices on each item in the store. Consumer groups contend that price stamping is essential for price-consciousness. Several states have already passed legislation requiring price stamping.

The Computerized Supermarket

By Allan J. Mayer

43032 00777

It makes for an unlikely battle flag, but a 1½-square-inch array of bars and spaces known as the Universal Product Code has become the symbol of a bitter dispute between grocers and consumer groups. Food processors have been putting the U.P.C. on their bottles, cans and boxes for more than a year now — in anticipation of electronic check-out, a controversial automated system that grocers say offers them one of their few opportunities to improve store productivity and cut operating costs.

Basically, electronic check-out involves replacing the old manual cash register with a terminal connected to a computer in which is stored the current prices of all the items a store stocks. An optical scanner attached to the terminal automatically "reads" the name of the product from the U.P.C. printed on its label. Once the computer has identified the item, it scans its memory banks for the correct price and registers the sale — all in less than a second. (In case of a price war, the memory bank can be quickly programmed with the new price cuts.)

Not only does use of the U.P.C. spare check-out clerks the necessity of ringing up sales themselves, the system can also be tied in with a central warehouse computer to give supermarket managers up-to-the-second inventory control. What's more — and this is where the controversy comes in — it also does away with the necessity for stamping prices on each individual item in the store.

That prospect thrills grocers. "If individual price stamping can be replaced with another method of price identification," says president Joseph B. Danzansky of Washington, D.C.-based Giant Foods Inc., "there is a potential savings to the industry of between $250 million and $300 million annually."

But consumer groups argue that individual price stamping is of critical importance to shoppers. "It contributes to price-consciousness, which has a dampening effect on inflation," insists executive director Carol T. Foreman of the Consumer Federation of America.

The Personal Computer A recent trend in computer technology has been the acquisition and/or actual development of computers by people for their own personal use. These computers, commonly called hobby computers or personal computers, are being developed with increasing frequency. Many clubs have been established throughout the country for those who are attempting to either build their own computers or to use existing models for their own use. There are retail establishments geared to selling such equipment to the individual consumer. Many computer conferences include several sessions on personal computers, a fact that illustrates the growing interest in these devices. As microprocessors become more available and adaptable, the personal computer will become more widespread as well as more functional.

In summary, then, the computer can be used in a wide variety of scientific and social applications, in addition to the business sense which has been emphasized throughout this text. Despite the advantages and benefits inherent in such uses, the potential for negative social consequences, of one sort or another, is evident. This is an era in which developers of technology as well as users need to take responsibility for the social effects of their tools. It is therefore necessary for business people and computer specialists to maintain an awareness of the uses to which computers are put and the potential disadvantages as well as the benefits of such uses. It is also essential that responsible individuals take an active part in promoting their views on these issues so that all segments of society affected by computers will be apprised of how these devices should be used and regulated.

A major factor in continued exponential technological growth is certain to be an expansion of information processing capability. Studies of the trade-offs between resource availability and quality of life will undoubtedly stimulate research and development in many areas of data processing, and, collectively, they may well do for data processing in the next decade what the space program did in the last. Conversely, efforts to protect the ecology may depend as heavily on data processing as did the space program.

Important Terms Used in This Chapter

Artificial Intelligence (AI)
Computer-Assisted Instruction (CAI)
Electronic Check-out
Electronic Funds Transfer (EFT)
Electronic Mail
Hobby Computer
Hospital Information Systems

Linguistics
Personal Computer
Privacy
Security
Self-service Automated Tellers
White-collar Crimes

Self-Evaluating Quiz

1. (T or F) People who criticize the widespread use of computers simply do not understand how these devices work.
2. (T or F) Computer frauds can be reduced by more effective security precautions.
3. (T or F) Legislation has already been passed to protect the consumer from invasion of privacy which has sometimes resulted from the indiscriminant use of credit information.
4. Indicate several advantages of CAI.
5. Indicate several disadvantages of CAI.
6. (T or F) Computers used in the field of linguistics are useful in shedding light on the evolution of natural languages.
7. (T or F) Using computers as diagnostic tools in hospitals will soon mean that fewer doctors will be needed.
8. AI is an abbreviation for _____.

Solutions

1. F—although many pro-computer groups claim this, it is simply not true. Some concerns are valid and need legislation to protect the citizen and consumer.
2. T
3. T
4. to assist the instructor in teaching rote or drill exercises; to provide varied teaching methods for students who have particular learning problems; to reduce peer group pressure and student-teacher problems.
5. computers cannot intuitively sense a student's problem the way a good teacher can; computers cannot "establish a rapport" with students; students cannot effectively ask the computer questions to help them understand a particular point.
6. T
7. F—computers should never be used to *replace* professionals but to assist them.
8. Artificial Intelligence

1. Examine the following excerpt and discuss in your own words the major
    points:

    > The Monetary and Payments System Planning Committee of the Ameri-
    > can Bankers Association is moving toward a series of recommended
    > actions that will, in effect, make the records activity of the entire bank-
    > ing system in North America (and ultimately in the world) into a single
    > data base. The credit records assimilation activities . . . go hand in
    > hand with this bank activity. . . . All of this means a rapidly moving reor-
    > ganization of the world's financial institutions. Much of this reorganiza-
    > tion is going to be accomplished through the use of automation on a
    > massive, international scale. With some exceptions, integrity of data
    > and security of information will be the paramount consideration, rather
    > than instant response.[6]

2. Indicate major issues raised regarding the implementation of Electronic
    Funds Transfer.
3. Indicate major reasons why people have negative reactions to the use
    of computers.
4. Discuss some of the important social issues that have arisen as a result
    of the widespread use of computers.
5. Discuss major issues to which CAI gives rise.

Unit Six: Selected Bibliography

General

1. *Data Processing in 1980–1985, A Study of Potential Limita-
    tions to Progress*, T. A. Dolotta et al., (New York: 1976).
    Examines the problems that will be confronting the computer
    industry in the near future and outlines what courses of ac-
    tion should be taken to meet these problems.
2. "What Computers Mean for Man and Society," Herbert A. Si-
    mon, *Science*, vol. 195, March 18, 1977, pages 1186–91.
    Discusses computer capabilities including artificial intelli-
    gence, economic effects of computers, the effects of comput-
    ers on the nature of work, and the issues of control and pri-
    vacy.
3. "Experts Argue Whether Computers Could Reason, and if
    They Should," Lee Dembart, *New York Times*, May 8, 1977,
    p. 1.

Journals

1. *Computers and People*, a new journal formerly *Computers
    and Automation*, ed. E. C. Berkeley.

---

[6]*Data Processing in 1980–1985: A Study of Potential Limitations to Progress*, T. A. Dolotta et al., (New York: 1976), p. 27. Reprinted with permission.

"The magazine of the design applications and implications of information processing systems—and the pursuit of truth in input, output and processing for the benefit of people."

2. *Computers and Education: An International Journal*, Pergamon Press, ed. Prof. Andrew Pouring and Prof. David F. Rogers.
3. *Computers and Society*, a Publication of ACM.
   Contains many interesting articles on the impact of computers on society.

Security
1. *Computer Security Management*, Dennis Van Tassel (Englewood Cliffs, N.J.: 1972).
2. "Privacy and Security in Local Government Infosystems," Voin R. Campbell, *Infosystems*, vol. 23, December 1976, pp. 31–34.
3. "Police Department's Computer Security Kept Under Surveillance," Melvin F. Bockelman, *Infosystems*, vol. 22, May 1975, pp. 65–66.

EFT
1. "Towards an Agenda for EFT Research," Kenneth Kraemer, John Leslie King, and Kent Colton, *Computers in Society*, vol. 8, Summer 1977.
2. "The Issue of Electronic Funds Transfer: An Overview and Perspective," Elias M. Awad, *Computers and People*, June 1977, pp. 7–9.

Electronic Check-Out
1. "The Computerized Supermarket," Allan J. Mayer, *New York Times*, February 8, 1976, p. 54.
   Discusses the controversy over the use of Universal Price Codes in electronic check-out systems used by some stores.
2. "The Future of Computer Communications," Vinton G. Cerf and Alex Curran, *Datamation*, May 1977, p. 105.
   (a) Focusses on new developments in POS, EFTS, and electronic mail.
   (b) Provides the student with a realistic appraisal of this area.

Electronic Mail
"Electronic Mail Delivers," Stephen A. Caswell, *Computer Decisions*, 4 April 1977.

Computers and Health
"The Computer as Diagnostician: Medical Diagnostic tools are getting smarter with the increased use of computers," Peter N. Budzilovich, *Computer Decisions*, July 1977.

Personal Computers

1. "The Ultimate Personal Computer," Lawrence R. Zeitlin, *Datamation*, vol. 23, May 1977, p. 131.
   (a) Focusses on a "Tongue-in-cheek" account of the vast potential of home computers.
   (b) Provides the student with some substantive ideas of that potential.
2. "Personal Computing Network Coming; Hobbyist Fad is Spur," *Data Communications*, July 1977, pp. 13–14.
3. "Personal Computers: The Outlook for Home and Hobby Computers," Alan R. Kaplan, *Computer Decisions*, May 1977, pages 36–40.

Glossary

Accounting Machine. EAM device that can perform a series of arithmetic operations using punched cards as input and producing a printed report as output.

Acoustic Coupler. Device connected to a terminal which enables terminal to access a CPU, using any standard telephone.

Actual Machine Language. See Machine Language.

Alphabetic Field. A data field that can contain letters and blanks.

Alphanumeric or Alphameric Field. A data field that can contain any combination of letters, digits, or special characters.

Analysis. See Systems Analysis.

Aperture Card. A punched card record that contains a microfilm image.

Arithmetic-Logic Unit. The unit of a CPU that performs arithmetic operations and comparisons.

Artificial Intelligence (AI). A scientific field concerned with simulating the process of reasoning in order to shed light on the nature of rational thought.

Assembly (Assembler). The translation process that produces an absolute machine language equivalent of a low-level symbolic programming language; a simpler process than a compilation. The program that performs this is called an assembler.

Audio Response Unit. An output device that transmits messages in verbal form; a computer is equipped with various prerecorded key phrases or words that are extracted as required for the purpose of answering specific requests.

Auxiliary Storage. A separate storage unit which supplements the Primary Storage in the CPU.

Backup Tape. The old master tape which is maintained in addition to the new master tape, in case it becomes necessary to recreate the new master tape.

BASIC. A high-level symbolic programming language; an acronym for *B*eginner's *A*ll-Purpose *S*ymbolic *I*nstruction *C*ode; similar to FORTRAN; best suited for programming with the use of terminals.

Batch Processing. The processing of data in groups or batches, as opposed to the immediate processing of data.

605

Binary Coded Decimal (BCD). A computer code used to represent characters; most frequently used on second-generation computers and on 7-track tapes.

Binary Number. A number represented by a combination of 0's and 1's; ideally suited for use in computers where 0 represents the "off" state and 1 represents the "on" state.

Bit. A contraction for *binary digit*. The term refers to the representation of data in binary form, as a series of on-off, 1-0 digits.

Block (Blocking). Combining several logical records into one physical record to conserve space on a magnetic tape or disk.

Block Diagram. A pictorial representation of the logic to be used in a program; see Flowchart.

Burster. A device that separates a continuous form into individual sheets.

Byte. A sequence of eight bits used to represent a character in storage.

Card Punch. A device in a computer system that punches card information which has been transmitted from the CPU.

Card Read/Punch. A device in a computer system that houses a card reader and a card punch unit.

Card Reader. A device in a computer system that reads punched card data and transmits it to the CPU.

Card Verification. The use of a card verifier device to check that keypunched cards have been correctly punched. The operator takes keypunched cards and the corresponding source documents and re-keys the data. Any inconsistencies between what appears in the keypunched cards and what is re-keyed by the verifying operator causes the machine to stop.

Cathode Ray Tube (CRT). A terminal device that prints messages on a televisionlike tube; output is said to be "soft-copy" since it is not retained as a permanent record.

Central Processing Unit (CPU). The device that controls the actual operations of the computer system; these include input, data transfer, arithmetic, logic, and output operations which are part of each user program.

Centralized Data Processing. The performance of the DP function by a single computer center within a company. Contrasted with Decentralized Data Processing.

Character. A unit of data consisting of a digit, letter, or special symbol.

Character Printer. A device in a computer system that prints one character at a time.

Check Bit. See Odd Parity and Even Parity.

COBOL. High-level symbolic programming language, an acronym for *Common Business Oriented Language*; Englishlike; most suited for businesstype problems.

Coding. The recording of program instructions onto coding sheets.

Collator. EAM device that can merge, select, match, or check the sequence of a file of punched cards.

Collection of Data. That aspect of a systems analyst's job associated with acquiring information on a given system. Includes reading procedures manuals and discussing the present system with managers and operating staff.

Column. One of 80 subdivisions of a card that can store a character of data.

Common Data Base. The maintaining by a company of one single, major data file which can be accessed by individual departments. This data base is much more efficient than having each department maintain its own file, a procedure that results in frequent duplication of effort.

Communication Lines. The telephone or teletype lines used in a teleprocessing system to link the terminal to the CPU.

Compilation (Compiler). The translation process that produces an absolute machine language equivalent of a high-level symbolic programming language; more complex process than an assembly. The program that performs this is called the compiler.

Computer. A device that processes data automatically by electronic digital techniques.

Computer-Assisted Instruction (CAI). An educational tool by which the computer usually prints textual information on a terminal and then asks the student to respond to a series of questions. Depending upon the accuracy of the responses, the computer will either proceed to a more advanced topic or else repeat the material.

Computer Input Microfilm (CIM). Microfilm that can be read by special high-speed computer devices.

Computer Operator. Person responsible for feeding input into the computer, communicating with the computer via the console-typewriter, and transmitting the output produced, according to specifications supplied by the systems and programming staff.

Computer Output Microfilm (COM). Microfilm output from a computer system.

Conditional Branch. A branch, or transfer, that occurs in a program or flowchart only when a particular condition is met.

Connectors. Used in a flowchart or a program to alter the path of the program.

Console. Computer device used for communication between computer operator and supervisor.

Constant. A fixed value used in a program.

Constraints. Limitations on a system imposed by management. Includes legal, budgetary, and equipment limitations.

Continuous Form. The form generally used with the printer. Although it can be separated into individual sheets, it is fed through the printer in one continuous piece to increase speed and facilitate processing.

Control Panel. A feature of most EAM equipment which enables the equipment to perform the required operations. Control panels are wired to perform the necessary functions.

Control Unit. That part of a CPU which controls the operations of a computer.

Control Unit Staff. Group responsible for maintaining control of data as it is processed through the data processing installation. The staff maintains various control totals to ensure that data is not lost.

Controls. Method used to minimize system errors; includes, for example, batch totals, item counts, limit checks, and trial balances.

Conversion of Source Documents. The process of creating machine-readable input from incoming source documents.

Conversion Process. The process of stepping through a program run for the first time with "real" and "live" data to ensure that it is error-free; see Cut-Over.

Core Storage. A form of high-speed storage that uses magnetic cores in an on-off capacity.

CPU. See Central Processing Unit.

CRT. See Cathode Ray Tube.

Cut-Over. The process of stepping through a program run formally for the first time with real data to ensure that it is error-free; see conversion.

Cylinder. A series of vertical tracks on a magnetic disk pack which is used for storing data.

Data. A collection of raw facts which is entered as input, processed, and transformed into meaningful information. The term is sometimes equated with information.

Data Base. See Common Data Base.

Data Cell. A direct-access device with a larger storage capacity but slower access time than a disk.

Data Collection. See Collection of Data.

Data Communications. See Teleprocessing.

DATA DIVISION. That part of a COBOL program which defines and describes the data and storage areas to be used in the program. Consists of a FILE SECTION and a WORKING-STORAGE SECTION.

Data Processing (DP). The series of operations performed on data to produce meaningful information.

Data Transfer Operation. The movement of data from one area of storage to another.

Debug. To free a program from errors or "bugs."

Decentralized or Distributed Data Processing. The performance of data processing by various centers within a company. This term can refer primarily to teleprocessing applications where there are remote terminals within departments. Or, it can refer to the establishment of independent data processing facilities, each reporting to the user department.

Decollator. A device that removes carbons from a continuous form.

Density. The number of characters that can be represented in an inch of magnetic tape; usually expressed as bpi (bits per inch).

Design. See Systems Design.

Diagnostics. One form of output from a compilation; lists rule violations in source program.

Digit-Row. One of the 0-9 demarcations on a card.

Digital Computer. See Computer.

Direct Access. The method of processing independent of the location of the data. This method can be used with magnetic disk, drum, and data cell, all of which are classified as direct-access devices. Contrast with Sequential Processing.

Disk Operating System (DOS). The control system is stored on magnetic disk.

Documentation. The formal report that describes a new system in its entirety.

EAM Operator. Person responsible for preparing card input for computer processing. For example, an EAM operator sorts, merges, and reproduces cards when necessary.

EBCDIC. See Extended Binary Coded Decimal Interchange Code.

Editing of Input Data. The checking of data to ensure that it does not contain obvious omissions, inconsistencies, or errors.

Editing of Output Data. The inclusion of dollar signs, commas, blanks, and other special characters in printed output in an effort to make the document more readable.

Electrical Accounting Machines (EAM Equipment). Those electromechanical punched card machines that are currently used in data processing installations as peripheral or support equipment. These include a sorter, reproducer, collator, interpreter, and accounting machine.

Electronic Check-Out. System used in supermarkets whereby a bar code on a product is detected by an optical scanner and transmitted to the CPU. The CPU looks up the price and transmits it back to the cash register terminal.

Electronic Data Processing (EDP). In current terminology, EDP refers to the processing of data by electronic digital computers.

Electronic Funds Transfer (EFT). A system that will eliminate the need for a cash exchange of funds by automatically transferring funds from one account to another.

Electronic Mail. The use of facsimile devices to transmit information from one location to another.

End-Of-Job (EOJ) Routine. The instructions to be executed when there is no more data to be processed; may include a series of summary or total steps.

ENVIRONMENT DIVISION. That part of a COBOL program which indicates the equipment to be used in the program. This is the only machine-dependent division of a COBOL program.

Even Parity. The use of an internal check bit to ensure an even number of bits on in a given storage position.

Execution Phase. The operating cycle during which a program is actually being processed, or run.

Extended Binary Coded Decimal Interchange Code (EBCDIC). A computer code used to represent characters; most frequently used on third-generation computers and nine-track tapes.

Facilities Management. See Service Bureau.

Feasibility Study. A study used to determine the computer equipment that a company should select for its data processing department.

Feedback. Procedures used to ensure that a system is operating effectively; includes techniques to be used to make corrections if errors have occurred.

Field. A group of consecutive positions used to represent an item of data.

File. A collection of individual records that are treated as one unit. A Payroll File, for example, refers to a company's complete collection of employee records.

File Protection Ring. A plastic ring placed on a reel of magnetic tape when the tape can be written on. It is used as a method of preventing inadvertent destruction of important tapes. Without the ring, which is removed from all active tape files, the computer will not write on the tape.

FILE SECTION. Part of the DATA DIVISION of a COBOL program that defines and describes the input and output of the program.

Fixed-Length Records. Term used to describe a file in which all records are the same length.

Flowchart. A pictorial representation of the logic to be used in a program or a system.

Flowlines. Lines used to connect the symbols in a flowchart.

FORTRAN. High-level symbolic programming language, an acronym for *For*mula *Trans*lator, most suited for scientific or mathematical problems.

Graph Plotter. An output device that produces data in graphic form.

Hard Copy. A permanent record of output from a computer system. Contrast with soft copy (visual display output).

Hard-Wired Modem. Device providing a permanent connection between a terminal and a CPU.

Hardware. Physical equipment used in conjunction with CPU which constitutes a computer system. Contrast with Software.

Header Label. A tape record containing identifying information; it is created as the first record on the tape so that when the tape is read as input, at some later date, the header label can be checked to ensure that the proper tape is being processed.

Hexadecimal Numbering System. Base 16 positional numbering system

High-Level Languages. Symbolic programming languages that require compilation; they are easier to code than low-level languages but more difficult to translate since they are Englishlike and not machinelike.

High-Order Position. The leftmost or most significant position of a field.

Hobby Computer. See Personal Computer.

Hollerith Code. The system of punches used on a card to represent data; named for Herman Hollerith.

IDENTIFICATION DIVISION. The part of a COBOL program which identifies the program to the computer. This division has no effect on the compilation or execution of the program.

Implementation. Term used to describe conversion to a new program or system.

Index. A direct-access feature which provides the computer with the capability of "looking up" disk records, just as one looks up subjects in the index of a book.

Information. Processed data.

Information Management System (IMS). See Management Information System.

Information System. See Management Information System.

Input (I/P). Incoming data read into a computer system for processing.

Input/Output Control System. A control system that is part of the main control program that supervises input and output functions.

Inquiry. Use of teleprocessing equipment to access central computer files and to obtain information on them.

Intelligent Terminal. A terminal device that contains a built-in facility for editing incoming data even before the data is transmitted to the computer.

Interblock Gap (IBG). An area of a tape or disk between physical records.

Interpreter. An electronic accounting machine that can be wired to print on the face of a card the data that has been punched in it.

I/O (Input/Output) Bound. Input/output operations that are relatively slow compared to processing operations and inhibit the overall speed of the computer.

Job Control Language (JCL). The language in which the programmer communicates job requirements to the supervisor. JCL specifications include the type of translation desired, input/output equipment to be used, start of data and end of data indicators, and so on.

Key Operator (Keypunch, Key-to-Tape, Key-to-Disk). Person responsible for converting incoming or source documents to a machine-readable form such as punched cards.

Keypunch. A typewriterlike device that an operator uses to punch data into a card, usually from a source document.

Key-To-Disk Encoder. A typewriterlike device used by an operator to create a magnetic disk from a source document.

Key-To-Tape Encoder. A typewriterlike device used by an operator to create a magnetic tape from a source document.

Label. See Header Label.

Left-Justified. The placing of data in the leftmost positions of a field; alphanumeric data is normally left-justified.

Library. A collection of programs stored by the computer which is accessed as needed.

Light Pen. A feature used with CRT terminals to make changes to the data displayed on the screen.

Line Function. That aspect of a firm's operations which has direct responsibility for achieving company goals.

Line Printer. A computer output device that prints one line at a time.

Linear Programming. An operations research tool that determines the optimal method for performing a given task.

Logical Record. A tape or disk record that is to be processed as an individual unit; contrast with physical record.

Loop. A sequence of steps in a program or flowchart to be executed a fixed number of times.

Low-Level Languages. Symbolic programming languages that require assembly; they are harder to code than high-level languages but easier to translate since they are machinelike and not Englishlike.

Low-Order Position. The rightmost or least significant position of a field.

Machine Language. The machine's own code; a program written in machine language requires no translation process.

Magnetic Disk. A computer medium that can be used for high-volume, high-speed storage where data is stored as magnetized bits. A disk has the added feature of random or direct accessibility.

Magnetic Drum. A direct-access device with a smaller storage capacity but faster access time than a disk.

Magnetic Ink Character Recognition (MICR) Devices. Computer hardware capable of reading characters imprinted with magnetic ink, such as on checks.

Magnetic Tape. A high-speed input/output medium that stores data in the form of magnetized bits. It is commonly used to store high-volume files.

Mainframe. See Central Processing Unit.

Management Games. A simulation technique used to train management. Management personnel are asked to make executive-level decisions for hypothetical firms in an effort to improve their decision-making ability.

Management Information System (MIS). A systems approach that treats business departments as integrated parts of one total system rather than as separate entities. This approach aims at facilitating the flow of information and at providing management with greater decision-making power.

Mark-Sense Cards. Cards that are marked with a special pencil that can be read by a device and converted into standard punched cards.

Master File. The major file in a particular application; the file that contains all the data fields used to create required output. A master Accounts Receivable file, for example, is a collection of records that includes all customer account information.

Megabyte. One million bytes of storage.

Memory. Storage capacity of a computer system.

Microcomputer. A small version of the control system of a standard computer; usually used as part of other automatic devices.

Microfiche Card. A unit of film that contains microfilm images in the form of individual pages; one microfiche card can store, typically, 240 pages of information.

Microfilm. A photographed record or document in miniature.

Microform. Any reduced film image; includes rolled microfilm and microfiche.

Microprocessor. A small chip of silicon that provides a microcomputer with its capability.

Minicomputer. A small, desk-top computer with most of the same features as a standard-sized computer.

Monitor. See Supervisor.

Multiprogramming. Ability of a computer system to execute two or more programs simultaneously; this is a common feature of time-sharing and data communications systems.

Nanosecond. One billionth (10^{-9}) of a second.

Nonimpact Printer. A device in a computer system that uses electronic or photoelectric methods to produce reports at extremely fast rates.

Object Program. A machine language equivalent of a source program. Object programs are the only ones that can be executed without being translated first.

Octal Numbering System. Base 8 positional numbering system.

Odd Parity. The use of an internal check bit to ensure an odd number of bits in a given storage position.

Offline. Utilization of data processing equipment not directly under the control of the main CPU.

Online. The processing of data by a computer immediately; contrast to Batch Processing.

Operating System. A series of control programs that enables a computer to automatically handle tasks that would otherwise require manual intervention. These tasks include compilation, scheduling, input/output control, and so on.

Operations Research. The use of mathematics and mathematical models to solve business problems.

Optical Character Recognition (OCR) Devices. Computer hardware capable of reading typed or handwritten documents.

Organization Chart. Pictorial representation of the organizational hierarchy in a company.

Output (O/P). Data that has been processed by a computer system.

Pack. The process of combining two digits into one byte of storage.

Parallel Run. The process of running a new system or program, in parallel, with the old to ensure a smooth transition and an error-free conversion.

Parity. A system used to check that bits have not been lost or added during transmission; see Odd Parity and Even Parity.

Personal Computer. Computers acquired and developed by individuals for their own personal use.

Picosecond. One trillionth (10^{-12}) of a second.

Physical Record. A block of one or more logical records read from or written onto an input/output device at one time; contrast with Logical Record.

PL/1. High-level symbolic programming language; an acronym for *Programming Language One*; combines the features of FORTRAN and COBOL.

Point-of-Sale (POS) System. A recent teleprocessing advance that enables sales clerks to automatically update computer files at the same time as they prepare sales receipts.

Port-A-Punch Cards. Cards that are manually punched.

Preprinted Forms. Forms that can contain computer-produced output but that enter a computer system with heading and field information already imprinted.

Primary Storage. The storage capacity of a computer system that is located within the CPU; contrast with Auxiliary Storage.

Printer. A device in a computer system used to produce printed reports.

Printer Spacing Chart. A form that is used by the computer specialist to map out positions and spacing for a computer-produced report.

Problem Definition. Formal document prepared by the systems analyst which defines the current system and its basic inadequacies.

PROCEDURE DIVISION. That part of a COBOL program which indicates the processing to be performed.

Program. A series of instructions that reads input data, processes it, and converts it to output.

Program Documentation. The complete package that provides a detailed description, or documentation, of all operations, procedures, and features of the program.

Programmer. The computer professional who writes and debugs the program, or set of instructions, which operates on input and converts it to output.

Punched Card. A card punched with holes used to represent data.

Punched Paper Tape. A paper tape which is punched, like cards, with holes that represent specific characters.

Random Access. See Direct Access.

Read/Write Head. A feature of a magnetic tape or magnetic disk drive that enables the device to read magnetic data or to record magnetic data depending upon the application.

Real-Time System. A system with the capability of accessing and updating computer files quickly enough to affect decision-making.

Record. A unit of information, representing, for example, an employee's time card, payroll information, and so on. Records consist of fields of data.

Remote Data Entry. The utilization of terminals to enter data at remote locations; this data is automatically transmitted to a CPU via communication lines.

Remote Job Entry (RJE). The entering of data and programs on a terminal, having the programs processed, and receiving output on that terminal as well.

Reproducer. EAM device that can duplicate all or part of a file of punched cards.

Retention Cycle. The length of time in which a tape is maintained as an active file.

Right-Justified. The placing of data in the rightmost positions of a field; numeric data is normally right-justified.

Routine. A sequence of instructions that perform a specific operation or procedure.

Row. One of 12 demarcations on a card used to represent data.

RPG. A high-level program generator; an acronym for *Report Program Generator*; most suited for printing simple reports.

Sequential Processing. The method of processing data consecutively, as it appears on the input media. This method is most commonly used with card and tape processing. Contrast with Random or Direct Access.

Service Bureaus (Facilities Management). Outside consulting firms that provide programming, systems, training, and even operating support for companies for a fixed fee.

Simulation. Operations research technique that produces a model of a system, one that can be manipulated and studied in order to better understand the actual system itself and to make predictions about the future.

Soft Copy. Output from a computer system that is in the form of a visual display and cannot be retained unless linked to a hard-copy printer.

Software. Programming support that enables the computer system to operate effectively. These include the supervisor, user programs, utility programs, and so on.

Sorter. EAM device that is capable of sorting punched cards.

Source Document. The originating report or document which, when converted to a machine-readable form, is used as input to a computer system.

Source Program. A program written in a symbolic programming language; source programs must be translated before they can be executed.

Staff Function. That aspect of a firm's operations which has only indirect responsibility for achieving company goals. Data processing is usually considered a staff function.

Storage. See Memory.

Storage Protection. A technique that prevents a program from inadvertently destroying or modifying portions of another program.

Structured Programming. A relatively new term used to describe an efficient programming technique which can facilitate the processing of programs in all languages.

Supervisor. A feature of the operating system; a special program that resides inside the CPU for purposes of controlling the operations of the entire system.

Symbolic Program. A program written in a symbolic form which is easier for the programmer to understand than the machine's own code; requires a translation process.

System. An organized method for accomplishing a business function.

System Conversion. Procedures used to ensure a smooth transition from an old system design to a new one.

Systems Analysis. The procedure used (1) to study existing operations and costs, and (2) to prepare a formal definition of the system in its entirety and of the major problem areas that must be eliminated.

Systems Analyst. The computer specialist responsible for analyzing current procedures and designing the most efficient and economical systems or procedures that will better accomplish given tasks within a company.

Systems Design. The preparation of a new set of procedures that will perform the basic operations of a system more efficiently and effectively than current operations permit.

Systems Flowchart. A pictorial representation of a system's procedures and operations prepared by the systems analyst. It depicts the relationship between inputs, processing, and outputs, in terms of the system as a whole.

Tape Label. An external label that identifies the tape for the operator.

Tape Librarian. A computer center employee responsible for maintaining control of magnetic tapes.

Telecommunications. The communication network that provides for the transmission of data in a teleprocessing environment.

Teleprocessing. The utilization of communication lines to handle the flow of information from remote terminals to a central facility.

Terminal. The device used at remote locations in a teleprocessing environment to enter or receive data from a CPU.

Time-Sharing. Term used to describe a central processing unit that is shared by several users, usually with the use of terminals. Small companies that cannot afford to rent or buy their own computer find this particularly advantageous.

Timer. A feature of an operating system that is used to supply data on computer usage.

Translation Phase. The operating cycle in which the computer translates a program from a symbolic language to actual machine language; the two types of translations are called compilation and assembly.

Unconditional Branch. A branch or transfer in a program or flow-chart that occurs regardless of any existing condition.

Unit-Record. A record that is represented as an individual item, as with a punched card.

Update. The process of making a file of data current.

Utility Programs. Standard, prepackaged programs supplied by computer manufacturers or special software houses to perform some complicated but common routines. Examples of utility programs include card-to-tape programs, tape-to-print programs, and so on.

Variable-Length Records. Term used to describe a file in which records are different sizes.

Verification. See Card Verification.

Virtual Storage. A computer control system that maximizes the efficient use of storage by using overlay techniques.

Word Processing. A type of data processing that attempts to automate secretarial tasks performed in most offices; instead of typing documents, reports and letters using a standard typewriter, a secretary uses a terminal which can print the document, make necessary changes where appropriate, and store the information for future print-outs.

WORKING-STORAGE SECTION. Part of the DATA DIVISION of a COBOL program which defines and describes the work areas needed in the program.

Zone-Row. 0-, 11-, 12- rows on a card which are used in conjunction with a digit-row to represent an alphabetic character or special symbol.

INDEX

T

TAB Option, in BASIC 487
Tape Drive—See Magnetic Tape Drive
Tape Labels,
  external 162
  internal 163
Tape Librarian 163
Teleprocessing 425–458
Template 254
Terminal Symbol, in a Flowchart 253
Terminal Typewriter 440–441
Terminals 74, 79, 169–172, 421–458
Test Data 237
Testing for End of Data, in BASIC 481–482
Time-Sharing 9, 421–458, 514
Timer 356
Touch-Tone Telephone, in a Teleprocessing System 447
Tracks, of a disk 191
  of a tape 177–179
Transistors 21

Translating a Program 232–245
Translators 346
Trial Balance as a control 536
12-edge 36

U

Unconditional Branch 265, 267
Unemployment and Computers 581
Unit-record 30
Unit-record Devices 12
Universal Product Code 597–598
Update, immediate 429
User Programs 346–347
Utility Programs 189–190, 346, 352–353

V

Vacuum tubes 21
Value Clauses, in COBOL 387
Variable length record 185

Verifier 45
Virtual Storage (VS) 346
von Neumann, John 20

W

White-Collar Crimes 588
Wire Matrix 157
Word Processing 454
WRITE Statement,
  in COBOL 304, 383–384
  in FORTRAN 309
WORKING-STORAGE SECTION, in COBOL 387–388

Z

Zone Bits 179
Zone Row 35
Zoned Decimal Format 142–144